The 2nd Maine Cavalry
in the Civil War

ALSO BY NED SMITH

*The 22nd Maine Volunteer Infantry in the Civil War:
A History and Roster* (McFarland, 2010)

The 2nd Maine Cavalry in the Civil War

A History and Roster

Ned Smith

McFarland & Company, Inc., Publishers
Jefferson, North Carolina

LIBRARY OF CONGRESS CATALOGUING-IN-PUBLICATION DATA

Smith, Ned, 1947–
The 2nd Maine Cavalry in the Civil War : a history and roster / Ned Smith.
p. cm.
Includes bibliographical references and index.

ISBN 978-0-7864-7968-9 (softcover : acid free paper) ∞
ISBN 978-1-4766-1656-8 (ebook)

1. United States. Army. Maine Cavalry Regiment, 2nd (1863–1865)
2. Maine—History—Civil War, 1861–1865—Regimental histories.
3. United States—History—Civil War, 1861–1865—Regimental histories.
4. Maine—History—Civil War, 1861–1865—Registers.
5. United States—History—Civil War, 1861–1865—Registers.
I. Title.
E511.62nd .S65 2014   973.7'441—dc23   2014028509

BRITISH LIBRARY CATALOGUING DATA ARE AVAILABLE

© 2014 Ned Smith. All rights reserved

No part of this book may be reproduced or transmitted in any form or by any means, electronic or mechanical, including photocopying or recording, or by any information storage and retrieval system, without permission in writing from the publisher.

Front cover image: Storming of Fort Blakely, April 9, 1865
(*Harper's Weekly*, May 27, 1865)

Printed in the United States of America

*McFarland & Company, Inc., Publishers
Box 611, Jefferson, North Carolina 28640
www.mcfarlandpub.com*

As with my first book, this work is dedicated to
my wife, best friend, and fellow Civil War author,
Diane Monroe Smith, with many, many thanks.
And, to our sons, Rob and Alex,
who inherited the history gene.

Acknowledgments

First, huge thanks go to my wife, and fellow Civil War author, Diane Monroe Smith. Her assistance—reading and rereading the manuscript in its various versions, suggesting additons, critiquing, and helping with research—is immensely appreciated.

Our son Alex was a great help in digging out and copying material from the National Archives, saving me additional trips to Washington and many hours of work.

Anthony Douin of the Maine State Archives was very patient with my many requests for assistance and was exceedingly helpful, so thanks to him, along with his colleagues Art Dostie and Jeff Brown.

Bill Cook, the local history person at the Bangor Public Library, was of great assistance, especially with many of the photographs used in this book.

And special thanks to Joni Archer, whose question about her great great grandfather got this project started. Without that initial question, I wouldn't have gotten to investigate this most interesting story.

Table of Contents

Acknowledgments	vi
Preface	1
ONE—Slavery's Influence in the United States and Maine	3
TWO—Florida: Slavery, Political Power and Secession	11
THREE—Winter 1863: Forming the 2nd Maine Veteran Volunteer Regiment	23
FOUR—Spring 1864: Mustering the Regiment and Action in the Red River Campaign	37
FIVE—Summer 1864: Detachments in Action in Louisiana and First Actions in Florida	57
SIX—September 1864: General Asboth's Raid and the Battle of Marianna	78
SEVEN—Late 1864: Dissension Regarding Promotions and Raids on Pollard and Milton	93
EIGHT—Early 1865: Promotions, Further Raids, and Difficult Times for Florida's Civilians	106
NINE—March 1865: Raids on the Confederate Railroad and Action Near Spanish Fort and Fort Blakely	122
TEN—To the End: The 2nd Maine Cavalry at Montgomery and Reconstruction Duty in Florida	134
Appendices	
A. Roster of the 2nd Maine Cavalry	151
B. Causes of Death in the Different Theaters of the War	199
C. General Courts-Martial for Members of the 2nd Maine Cavalry	200
D. Men of the 2nd Maine Cavalry Held at Andersonville Prison	214
E. Officers Mustered out in Florida	216
Chapter Notes	217
Bibliography	225
Index	227

Preface

Everyone has heard of the 20th Maine and its colonel, Joshua Chamberlain. Many, when thinking of mounted units, may know of the 1st Maine Cavalry and its well-regarded actions against the Confederates. The regiment was awarded no fewer than 26 battle honors, beginning at First Bull Run in the early days of the Civil War and carrying through to Appomattox Court House.

However, when a friend asked what I knew about the 2nd Maine Cavalry, I answered, "Nothing." The friend, Joni Archer, told me she had a great-great-grandfather, George Cook, who as an 18-year-old had joined that regiment. Joni was interested to learn more about him and the 2nd Maine Cavalry. I told Joni I'd see what I could find out about those men and her ancestor. And so, having looked at the obvious sources—the Maine adjutant general's reports, the large collection of Civil War material at the Maine State Archives, and doing a library and Internet search for a regimental history—I came to two conclusions: the regiment had been involved in difficult and intriguing activities in a little-known theater of the Civil War, and there had not been a regimental history written. And then a third conclusion was reached: I found the regiment's activities quite compelling and started working on its history in order to tell its story.

Writing a history of most Civil War regiments, while requiring considerable effort and research, can be pretty straightforward. In many cases the regiment's movements are well defined, the battles in which they fought well documented, and their part in those battles reasonably well reported. The challenge is often one of finding the various reports, noting conflicting accounts, sorting out the reliable from the less so, and looking for previously undiscovered archival material in order to flesh out the known facts. And then, when all the pieces are put together, the author hopes that it all adds up to a new and important body of knowledge.

With the 2nd Maine Cavalry, one is faced with a very different set of circumstances and a challenge—a challenge well worth pursuing. The regiment was sent to the Deep South and took part in battles that are obscure compared to those fought in other theaters. However, its service provided quite substantial opportunities for the troopers to demonstrate their skill and bravery. Then too, the whole regiment very often was not stationed in one place, or in action as an entire regiment: various elements were scattered at different camps and took part in small engagements, sometimes as companies and often as groups of 20 or so troopers. This manner of operating often provided the opportunity for unusual tactics while in action away from the close watch of the usual chain of command. Keeping track of which companies, or smaller detachments, went where and just what happened presents a complex set of events to untangle.

Some parts of the 2nd Maine Cavalry's story are typical of all Civil War regiments. There was the usual jockeying for commissions as the regiment was being raised, the usual attempts to gain favor with the governor and adjutant general, and the usual jealousy among officers. For the soldiers involved, there was the usual combination of stretches of boredom interspersed with the stress, anxiety, fear, and the "thrill" of battle. And for those back at home, there were the same worries, coupled with the lack of timely news regarding their loved ones, especially trying for those regiments in the Deep South where news often took considerable time to make its way to that most northern Union state—Maine.

This regiment presents its own unique history of a part of the war that is too often overlooked. During much of its time in the South, the 2nd Maine Cavalry operated in conjunction with regiments of U.S. Colored Infantry, made up of ex-slaves and free blacks, who had a different view of the war against the slave-holding South than did the white troops from Maine. And not all of the members of the regiment were the typical "white" troops. There were several American Indians serving in the regiment, and a young black man serving as a member of this white regiment—a very unusual circumstance. The 2nd Maine Cavalry also contained a Medal of Honor recipient: a rather dashing figure who, at times, operated with a small detachment behind Confederate lines and on one occasion in Confederate uniform. Although designated a "veteran" regiment—and many of the men were indeed veterans of other, earlier, regiments—many were not, and this mix of experience and raw recruits posed its own problems. And, many of those veterans who joined the 2nd Maine Cavalry were veterans of infantry, not cavalry, regiments.

Operating in the Deep South had a severe impact on the health of these young men from Maine. The 2nd Maine Cavalry spent most of its service in Florida, with some time in Louisiana and southern Alabama. Death from various illnesses claimed 334 men of the regiment, a far larger proportion than in Maine regiments that were sent to the Army of the Potomac and fought primarily in Virginia. (For a comparison of the deaths from disease between the Maine regiments in the Deep South and those fighting or stationed in and around Virginia, see Appendix B.)

The nature of the war in Florida was tempered by the state's small population and the few engagements there that could be called battles—certainly none on the scale of those fought in the Eastern or Western Theaters of the war. The largest battle fought in Florida occurred at Olustee in February of 1864—well before the 2nd Maine Cavalry arrived in the state—and involved around 5,500 Union troops defeated by a Confederate force of around 5,000. (That battle resulted in the deaths of many black Federal soldiers, reported at the time as resulting from the murder of wounded or surrendering black troops. Those reported atrocities obviously had an impact on the attitudes of African American Union soldiers toward their Confederate foes. More on that later.) That lack of large battles, coupled with Florida's remoteness from the Union and Confederate seats of power, made it a less known and less well reported part of the conflict. Even for some of the Union men who fought there, it seemed at times that they were in a backwater of the action. On the other hand, for those who fought there, while they experienced a very different sort of war, that experience no doubt impacted their lives every bit as much as those fighting in other theaters.

Chapter One

Slavery's Influence in the United States and Maine

To gain a perspective on the men who fought for the Union and Confederacy, we'll begin with a brief look at the years leading up to the Civil War and examine the history and politics of Florida, where the 2nd Maine Cavalry spent most of its time, and the regiment's home state, Maine.

Let us be clear—the American Civil War was fought over the issue of slavery. The states' rights argument was secondary in that the particular "right" in question was the right to own slaves. After the Civil War, it seemed desirable to some in both the South and North to present the conflict in the romantic guise of a struggle to defend states' rights, while downplaying the role that slavery had in the origins of the war. During the centennial of the Civil War in the 1960s, it was difficult and uncomfortable to address the real reason for the war with the United States still engaged in its "separate but equal" approach to the rights of African Americans, and with the growing Civil Rights movement that challenged that view.

From the time that African slaves were first brought to North America in the 1600s to work in the tobacco fields of the Jamestown settlement, the conditions in many parts of the South favored large plantations which grew labor-intensive crops, with cotton gradually growing to prominence. In the North, smaller family farms tended to be the norm, and during the country's colonial period, a clear distinction developed between the South with its huge numbers of field slaves and the relatively few slave servants in the homes of well-to-do Northerners. As time went on the economy of the South became more and more dependent on slave labor.

The importance of slavery in the South and the willingness to defend this way of life were made clear in Southern newspapers, such as this from the *Atlanta Confederacy* of 1860: "We regard every man in our midst an enemy to the institutions of the South, who does not boldly declare that he believes African slavery to be a social, moral, and political blessing." As early as 1849, Henry L. Benning, Georgia politician and future Confederate general, wrote this to his fellow Georgian, Howell Cobb (then a U.S. congressman, later governor of Georgia and Confederate general): "First then, it is apparent, horribly apparent, that the slavery question rides insolently over every other everywhere—in fact that is the only question which in the least affects the results of the elections." And later in the letter: "I think then, 1st, that the only safety of the South from abolition universal is to be found in an early dissolution of the Union."[1] The importance of slavery is made clear in the Constitution of the Confederate States. Article I, Section 9, Paragraph 4 states: "No bill of attainder, ex post facto law, or law denying or impairing the right of property in negro slaves shall be passed."

And in Article IV, Section 3, Paragraph 3 we read: "The Confederate States may acquire new territory.... In all such territory, the institution of negro slavery, as it now exists in the Confederate States, shall be recognized and protected by Congress and the territorial government."[2]

Alexander Stephens, vice president of the Confederacy, stated regarding the Confederate government: "Its foundations are laid, its cornerstone rests, upon the great truth that the negro is not equal to the white man; that slavery ... is his natural and normal condition."[3] These and many more examples leave little question regarding slavery's importance.

And, if there is any doubt about slavery as the central issue leading to secession and the Civil War, it is important to read the very resolutions by which various states seceded. The declaration of secession issued in December of 1860 by South Carolina, the first state to secede, is typical. After giving a preamble and supposed legal justification for secession, the document lists as its major complaint the U.S. government's failure to adequately enforce the Fugitive Slave Act, saying that there is "an increasing hostility on the part of the non-slave holding States to the Institution of Slavery." It goes on to state that the election of the new president (Abraham Lincoln, although he is not named) will result in slavery being made illegal. There is no mention of tariffs, or other "states' rights" issues that some claim were the more important grievances.[4]

When we speak of "states' rights" as they relate to the Civil War, it should be remembered that the rights in question were those of slave owners to continue to own slaves and to expand slavery into new territories and states. That desire for the expansion of U.S. slavery, by the way, was not confined to the borders of the United States as they existed before the Civil War. Slave owners from the South—and in particular a group known as the "Filibusters"—attempted or plotted to take by force other territory to add to the existing slave states. Albert Gallatin Brown, U.S. senator from Mississippi, spoke about these filibuster expeditions to Central America in this way: "I want Cuba.... I want Tamaulipas, Potosi, and one or two other Mexican states; and I want them all for the same reason—for the planting and spreading of slavery."[5]

A plan to annex the Yucatan Peninsula of Mexico was being debated by members of Congress at the end of the Mexican-American War in 1848, and an armed attempt to take over Cuba and turn it into a new slave state failed in 1851. A further plan (the Ostend Manifesto of 1854) proposed that the United States purchase Cuba from Spain and contained a clear threat of war if Spain refused. In 1855, an expedition of Southern expansionists attempted to invade and take over Nicaragua. It too failed.

Given that general background, let's look first at Maine as those young men of the 2nd Maine Cavalry, and the thousands of others from the state who fought for the Union, were faced with the approaching conflict. Maine's history presents us with a series of conflicting and varying attitudes and events that relate to subjects of states' rights and slavery. In order to understand these aspects of the state's history, we must forget preconceptions about Maine as a firmly Republican and strongly Abolitionist state, although these characteristics gradually became more typical in the years leading up to the Civil War. For a time, Maine's history involved strong ties to slavery, the South, and the slave trade, positive attitudes toward states' rights proponents, and even, at times, saw people from Maine advocating its secession from the Union.

Let's establish early on that Maine played a role in the slave trade. Maine men and ships were making handsome profits bringing cotton from the South to the mills of England and New England. And even more directly, ships made in Maine, sometimes captained and crewed by men from Maine, had transported many captives from their African homeland to their forced labor in the New World. And a number of the impressive homes of sea captains in Maine's picturesque coastal towns and cities were built with the money from the cotton and slave trade. The brig *Kentucky,* built in Searsport, Maine, is an example of those slaving ships from Maine. Although the importing of slaves into the U.S. became illegal on January 1, 1808, many slave ships attempted successfully to avoid capture. Sold to Brazilians in 1844 and crewed by American and Brazilian sailors, the *Kentucky* was trapped in a Mozambique river by a British warship and burned by its crew.[6]

Built in Elliot, Maine, the clipper *Nightingale,* originally used in the tea trade, was converted to a slaver. The ship was captured in 1861 by the USS *Saratoga* of the United States Navy's Africa Squadron with 961 African slaves crammed on board and more preparing to be loaded. It was taken as a prize and sailed to Liberia where, although 160 of the Africans (and one member of the prize crew) had died of fever during the passage, the remaining passengers were landed ashore at Monrovia, in that refuge for freed slaves. The *Nightingale* then served in the U.S. Navy as a coal and supply ship.[7]

In 1860, Portland, Maine, native Nathaniel Gordon was arrested for attempting to illegally bring slaves from Africa—importing slaves having been illegal for over 50 years and punishable by death for over 40 years. When Gordon's ship, *Erie,* was stopped off the African coast by the U.S. Navy ship *Mohican*, 897 Africans were found on board. Tried and convicted of illegally attempting to import slaves, which in 1820 the U.S. Congress had made an "act of piracy," Gordon was sentenced, in 1861, to be hung. The execution was delayed by Abraham Lincoln, but was carried out in New York on February 21, 1862.[8]

And then there is the town (now abandoned) of Magnolia, on the coast of Wakulla

The clipper *Nightingale* (Wikipedia).

County, Florida. Four brothers from Maine—John, George, Nathanial, and Weld Hamlin—who had family connections operating a large textile mill in Maine, created the town as a base from which to ship cotton. With its impressive pier for ships to dock for loading, the town boasted a hotel and several stores, but only lasted from the late 1820s to the late 1850s, and had likely stopped being used to ship cotton by the mid 1840s. Although distantly related to Abraham Lincoln's first vice president, Hannibal Hamlin, at least one brother, Weld Hamlin, felt a strong enough association with his adopted state that he joined the Confederate military as a private in the 1st Regiment, Florida Infantry Reserves.[9]

But to take a step back in time, the issue of slavery's place in this country, the issue of states' rights versus a strong central government, and even the issue of the right of secession from the Union, had been argued—and in some ways had remained unresolved—since the U.S. became a nation. The first government of the United States was organized under the Articles of Confederation, which gave one vote to each state and established the right of a state's representatives to veto any law of which they disapproved. When that system proved unworkable, and the U.S. Constitution was introduced, the Bill of Rights was included to reassure those who feared the power of a strong central government.

Although the Federalist Party had been established by those who favored the adoption of the U.S. Constitution and a strong federal government, as early as 1802 many members of the Federalist Party in Maine (then a part of Massachusetts) had talked of secession if the federal government should grow too powerful. They were angered when President Thomas Jefferson's Embargo Act of 1807 prohibited shipping trade with foreign countries, and they opposed the addition of large areas of new land to the United States—the Louisiana Purchase. Federalists believed the purchase of this new land unconstitutional, while those in New England feared that the power and influence of the older sections of the country, and in particular theirs, would be diminished if new lands to the west were developed and entered the Union as new states. And then there was the question of slavery itself that concerned many in the Northeast as opposition to slavery grew—would these new lands provide areas for the expansion of slavery and add new slave states to the Union?

In 1814, the people of Maine were even more strongly involved in the issue of states' rights and the threat of secession. At that time Maine was still a part of Massachusetts and its coastal areas were heavily dependent on shipping, ship building, and trade. As previously stated, many in Maine and the rest of New England were very displeased with Thomas Jefferson's Embargo Act of 1807, an attempt to keep the U.S. out of the Napoleonic Wars by stopping trade with Europe. That act was repealed in 1808, but was followed by the Non-intercourse Act of 1809, which attempted to prevent U.S. trade with Britain and France. The War of 1812 ended legal trade with Great Britain and made shipping from any U.S. port very difficult due to a British blockade. Massachusetts (including Maine) and Connecticut had refused to place their state militias under U.S. government control, deciding that their militias would be used only for their own state's defense. As a result, President James Madison's government would not pay for the expenses of defending those states. In 1814 secession from the Union was once again being discussed in New England.

With the U.S. still at war with Britain, the governor of Massachusetts had sent a delegation to London in 1814 to discuss a peace settlement, hoping to establish its own peace with Great Britain regardless of Britain's relations with the U.S. That year, a convention was held in Hartford, Connecticut, to discuss New England's response to the war and the effect on trade. One of the delegates to that convention from what would become the State of Maine, and a member of the Federalist Party, was Stephen Longfellow, the father of poet

Henry Wadsworth Longfellow. During the convention, he and other Federalist members argued repeatedly for secession from the U.S. In the final report of the convention, there is no specific mention of secession, but there is a strong statement to the effect that the federal government was making unconstitutional limitations on the sovereign rights of the states. Representatives from New England eventually were sent to Washington to negotiate terms based on the report of the Hartford Convention. However, by the time they arrived in the nation's capital in February 1815, the Treaty of Ghent had been signed, the war was over, and the major reason for their discussion—noninterference with shipping—no longer appeared relevant.

Some 45 years later, the May 15, 1861, *New York Times* used a response to the Hartford Convention from the leading Southern newspaper in 1814 to make a clear editorial statement regarding secession, plainly showing how the attitudes of some in the South had shifted considerably over those years:

Virginia on Secession in 1814
In 1814, the New-England people became dissatisfied with the conduct of public affairs and in the celebrated Hartford Convention they took action which looked like asserting the right of secession. Whereupon the Richmond *Enquirer,* Nov. 1, 1814 said: "No man, no association of men, no State, nor set of States has a right to withdraw itself from this Union, of its own accord.... The same formality which forged the links of the Union is necessary to dissolve it.... Any other doctrine, such as that which has been lately held forth by the *Federalist Republican,* that any one State may withdraw itself from the Union, is an abominable heresy....
"We call, therefore, upon the Government of the Union to exert its energies when the season shall demand it, and seize the first traitor who shall spring out of the hot-bed of the Convention at Hartford.... The Union must be saved when any one shall dare to assail it."[10]

Six years after the Hartford Convention, when Maine applied to become a state in 1820, the unresolved questions regarding slavery played a major part in Congress's deliberations. The process of statehood and the part that slavery might play in that decision grew from the balancing act regarding slavery that had gone on since the U.S. declared independence from Great Britain. In Thomas Jefferson's rough draft of the Declaration of Independence, he had included a condemnation of slavery. The context was more specifically a condemnation of King George III and his government's support of slavery, but certainly applied to slavery within the American colonies. The committee of five that was created to craft the Declaration, made up of John Adams, Benjamin Franklin, Thomas Jefferson, Robert Livingston, and Roger Sherman, had chosen Jefferson to write the document. Upon reading that early draft, the committee, largely at the insistence of Franklin and Adams, deleted this antislavery section since they realized it would alienate slave owners and pro-slavery sympathizers. Those hoping to separate from Great Britain knew they needed the support of all the colonies to give their bid for independence a chance.

It is of further interest that Benjamin Franklin, who for pragmatic reasons had argued to delete the antislavery section of the Declaration, was clearly opposed to slavery itself. In 1785, Franklin was elected president of the U.S.'s first antislavery society—the Pennsylvania Society for the Abolition of Slavery.

The failure to directly address the slavery issue, while including the phrase "all men are created equal" in the Declaration of Independence, set the stage for antislavery speeches of the 1800s. Abolitionists could quote from the very document that had brought the country into existence for a statement that slavery ran contrary to the founding fathers' ideals.

Prior to 1820, the Northern states had made slavery illegal within their borders, the earliest state to free slaves being Massachusetts in 1780. Those who owned slaves in the South were very concerned that, if a majority of states became "free states," the U.S. Congress would act to further restrict slavery in the states where it existed, and would prevent new slave states from being admitted to the Union as statehood expanded westward in various territories. This desire to keep the number of slave and free states equal was a fairly recent concern, however, since the numbers had only been made equal at the end of 1819 with the admission of Alabama into the Union as a slave state. In January of 1820, when a bill was introduced to allow Maine to enter the Union as a free state, Congress passed that bill but included an amendment providing statehood for Missouri as a slave state. And so, Maine's admission to the Union was very much a part of the ongoing debate about slavery.

The pro and antislavery positions would, of course, be a factor in the admission of other states to the Union. When American colonists in Texas, for example, had fought for independence from Mexico in the 1830s, one of their complaints against Mexico was the Mexican government's refusal to allow colonists to bring their slaves into that territory. Mexico had outlawed slavery in 1820, but that restriction had been ignored by many Americans who moved there. In 1845, when Texas was admitted to the Union (the act that led to the Mexican-American War), it was as a slave state, over the objection of many in the North, and especially over the objection of those in the growing abolitionist movement.

In the 1840s and '50s there was a movement to reopen the slave trade from Africa. Some in the South, including politicians such as U.S. Senator Jefferson Davis of Mississippi, supported by many Southern newspaper editors, wanted to end the ban on importing slaves. They stated that, as new slave states were added to the Union, the number of slaves was not sufficient to fill the need, and further, the reintroduction of slaves directly from Africa would result in lowering the purchase price for slaves and so lower the labor costs of the plantation owners. A slave arriving from Africa could be purchased for less than a third of the cost of a slave born in the United States. This plan even had supporters who felt that reopening the African slave trade would so strengthen the economy of the South that it would end the movement toward secession and save the Union.[11]

And then there was the Great Compromise of 1850 (fashioned by Kentucky Senator Henry Clay and guided to passage by Illinois Senator Stephen Douglas) and its attempts to pacify the pro and anti slavery members of Congress. That compromise conceded to the slavery contingent the strict enforcement of the new Fugitive Slave Act, which insisted on the return of escaped slaves to their masters. The compromise further included the concept of "popular sovereignty" which would reverse the Missouri Compromise by letting new states vote whether to be slave or free. That perspective, of course, became a large part of Stephen Douglas's political position and a core issue of the Lincoln-Douglas debates of 1858. In 1857, the Dred Scott decision of the U.S. Supreme Court not only stated that a slave was still a slave, even if brought to a free state, but that Congress could not ban slavery in the U.S. territories. Moreover, persons of African descent in the U.S. were not citizens and were without the protection of the U.S. courts or Constitution.

We can see, therefore, that many if not most of the great political and moral controversies of the years leading up to the Civil War related to the issue of slavery.

The feelings of some in Maine toward states' rights (and the issue of slavery) were an interesting mixture of self-interest and political philosophy which could become rather complicated. Why, for example, would the brother of Maine's Civil War hero, Joshua Lawrence Chamberlain, be named John Calhoun Chamberlain, after the U.S. vice president and senator from South Carolina? Calhoun was, after all, a Southern firebrand who was a militantly outspoken defender of both states' rights and slavery, and a fiery proponent of "nullification," the right of a state to nullify a federal law with which that state disagreed. The circumstances leading to John Calhoun Chamberlain's name are stated in Diane Monroe Smith's biography of Joshua Chamberlain, *Fanny and Joshua*: "Many Maine people, feeling they had suffered from the national government's high tariffs and policies on trade and currency, saw John C. Calhoun, the mastermind behind nullification and its challenge to federal authority, as a champion."

Joshua Chamberlain's grandfather was involved in shipping, primarily as the owner of a shipbuilding yard. He had suffered from losses to the shipping industry created by President Jefferson's embargo on trade from 1807 to 1809, the effect of the War of 1812, and the Tariff of 1816. (One of Grandfather Chamberlain's ships was burned by the British when they came up the Penobscot River in 1814.) Smith's book goes on to say that when Joshua Chamberlain's father was an adult,

> there was still considerable opposition in Maine to what was viewed as the national government's interference on issues of trade and currency, which were believed to have impacted negatively on Maine's fortunes. In 1833, five years before John Chamberlain's birth, John C. Calhoun, in order to openly oppose national tariffs and defend South Carolina's nullification law, resigned as vice-president of the United States to again become senator for his state. As a champion of nullification, he was credited by many with forcing the confrontation that would result in compromise and a lowering of tariffs. In the year before John Calhoun Chamberlain's birth, many Americans also believed that the economic panic of 1837 was caused by President Jackson's policies on the nation's banks and currency. Senator Calhoun's previous denunciation of both Jackson and his policies had seemingly proved right, and Calhoun enjoyed such popularity in Maine that a movement in the state's Democratic Party advocated his candidacy for president.[12]

Of course, judging the feelings of the people of Maine specifically toward slavery is more complicated. While many apparently saw slavery as the "necessary evil" upon which Southern economic health was based, others were merely ambivalent toward slavery. On the other hand, Maine and other New England states contained a substantial number of ardent abolitionists. As the Democratic Party became more clearly associated with a pro-slavery stance, the Republican Party emerged from an odd mixture of "Know-Nothings" (a "nativist" anti-immigrant and anti–Irish Catholic movement), remnants of the Whig Party, temperance supporters, and abolitionists.[13]

The election of Maine's governor in 1856 can be seen as a clear reflection of the feelings of Maine's people on the issues of slavery and states' rights. The Republican candidate for governor, Hannibal Hamlin, was opposed to slavery, and as a U.S. senator had opposed the Kansas-Nebraska Act, which repealed the Missouri Compromise's limitations on the expansion of slavery. Hamlin had left the Democratic Party in June of 1856, when the Democrats voted to support the Kansas-Nebraska Act, and joined the newly formed Republican Party. When Hamlin won the gubernatorial election by a wide majority over the Democrat and Whig candidates, it was not only a victory for an antislavery candidate, but a boost to the national efforts of the Republican Party.[14]

The presidential election of 1856 was also, to a large extent, a referendum on slavery. The Democrat, James Buchanan, ran on a platform that included opposition to federal interference with slavery. Millard Fillmore, former president of the U.S., ran as a Know-Nothing candidate, and is therefore a representative of that party's anti-immigrant, anti–Catholic policies. The candidate of the new Republican Party, John Fremont, ran on a platform that included strong antislavery statements. The voters of Maine gave Fremont a large majority with 67,279 votes (61 percent) as compared to Buchanan's 39,140 (36 percent), and Fillmore's 3,270 (3 percent). But Buchanan won the national election, with all of the electoral college votes from the South, as well as Pennsylvania, Indiana, Illinois, California, and Missouri.

In the presidential election of 1860, Maine once again came down strongly on the Republican side and voted overwhelmingly for Abraham Lincoln and his running mate from Maine, Hannibal Hamlin. The Republicans received 62,811 votes in Maine (62 percent), while the Democrat, Stephen Douglas, received fewer than 30,000 (29 percent). The Southern Democrat and strongly pro-slavery candidate, John Breckinridge, received 6,368 votes in Maine—a relatively small number, but an indication of some sentiment that favored slavery's continuation.

When war did come, the strong support by the majority in Maine for the fight to preserve the Union was also of interest given coastal Maine's continued reliance on the shipping industry. Many ships from Maine were involved in the cotton trade, and while some cotton was still making its way to the North, including New England, much of it traveled overland rather than by ships. Moreover, the Union blockade of Southern ports severely restricted the shipping of cotton to Europe. In addition, in the 1850s and early '60s, many Maine and New England towns had economies that were tied to cotton mills, and many immigrants to Maine had come to work in those mills. Those mill workers and the mill owners would resent any cutbacks in the supply of cotton that might threaten their jobs or income. Oddly enough, a relatively small trade in cotton continued between the South and the North during the Civil War—in part, at least, to allow some cotton to be sent to those Northern mills.[15]

There was, as in other Northern states, a relatively strong minority in Maine who opposed the Civil War, feared the freeing of slaves, and wanted to negotiate a compromise settlement with the Confederacy. These "Copperheads" held meetings throughout the state and drew substantial crowds. Nevertheless, support for the Civil War was strong enough for Maine to send a higher proportion of its population to fight than any other state of the Union.[16]

Chapter Two

Florida: Slavery, Political Power and Secession

It was in Florida that the 2nd Maine Cavalry spent the majority of its time of active service, and so a look at conditions there at the start of the Civil War will give an indication of the personalities and politics that the men from Maine would encounter. A brief look at Florida's history, economics, and population is important to the story. (The 2nd Maine Cavalry also spent some time in Louisiana, and for a look at the situation in that state leading to the Civil War, I would naturally recommend my previous work: *The 22nd Maine Volunteer Infantry in the Civil War.*)

Maine had been a part of what became the United States since well before the country's founding, with the first British outpost there in the early 1620s, then later as a part of the state of Massachusetts and, from 1820, as a state in its own right. Florida, when it voted for secession, had been a state for less than 16 years and a part of the United States for less than 40 years. And its colonial history was quite different from that of New England. The first European exploration and settlement of Florida took place in the 1500s, primarily by the Spanish. Considerably earlier than the first English settlement of Jamestown in 1607 and the first English settlement of New England in 1620, the Spanish had established St. Augustine in 1565. During the 1700s, many African slaves were fleeing to Florida to escape from their masters in the British colonies just to the north. Once in Spanish Florida, those slaves were granted their freedom on the condition that they convert to Catholicism. In addition, many escaped slaves simply melted into Indian communities in the remote areas of Florida. In 1763, Florida was ceded by Spain to Great Britain in return for Havana, Cuba, which had been captured by the British in 1762 toward the end of the Seven Years' War. With that, many of the Spanish in Florida, as well as numbers of the native population, left for Cuba, and the British began a campaign to recruit settlers for their new colony, dividing Florida into "West" and "East." West Florida was the land west of the Chattahoochee River to the Mississippi, and including a part of what is now southern Alabama.

The British colonists in Florida remained, almost entirely, loyal to the British king during the American Revolution, but when the war ended with the Treaty of Paris in 1783, that treaty returned Florida to Spanish rule in order to remove a British colony from the southern border of the new United States. In the early 1800s, Seminole Indians from eastern Florida were raiding settlements in Georgia and once again Florida was providing a sanctuary for runaway slaves. The Adams-Otis Treaty of 1821 made Florida a part of the United States, and in an attempt to end the "problems" with the Seminoles, the U.S. government sent troops to remove those Seminoles who had refused to leave for lands promised to them west of the

Mississippi River. This turned into a long, bloody and costly war, with the Seminoles employing effective guerrilla tactics. Their leader, Osceola, was arrested while under a flag of truce in 1837 and died in captivity within a few years. By 1842 most of the Seminoles were forcibly moved west of the Mississippi. A small group, however, did not surrender and remained hidden in the Everglades.[1]

With the election of President Lincoln in 1860 and his commitment to limiting the spread of slavery, Florida was the third state to secede from the Union, following South Carolina and Mississippi. That decision to leave the Union, however, was far from a universally popular one in Florida, and was reached by less than fully democratic means.

The power—political and economic—in the young state of Florida was largely held by a small number of wealthy plantation and slave owners, who, as with many other large plantations, were mostly in the cotton-growing business. From its total population in 1860, of 140,424, 44 percent of those persons were slaves and were owned by 5,132 whites—less than 4 percent of the white population. That slave owning minority also owned 71 percent of the cash value of Florida farmland. These planters had many ties—family, political, and economic—to the nearby slave states of Georgia, Alabama, Mississippi, and the Carolinas. And, because of the Constitution's requirement to count three-fifths of the slave population as "people" when determining voting representation (although of course, slaves could not vote), the slave holding counties, principally 7 counties in the central part of northern Florida, were more highly represented in the state's legislature than were other counties.[2]

That concentration of power was not popular among large numbers of Florida's non-slave owning population. Many of the descendants of Florida's early European settlers resented the loss of prestige and political influence that they were compelled to gradually yield to the more recently arrived planters. In addition, there were substantial numbers of small farmers who had never enjoyed much power and were not pleased to see the conspicuous wealth of the slave and plantation owners. It must be said, however, that among this non slave-owning majority, there were certainly those who dreamed of gaining the wealth and status that a slave-based plantation could bring them.[3]

Given the above, when the Florida State Legislature voted to authorize a secession convention, that vote disproportionally represented the wishes of that slave owning minority. The pro-secession legislators not only succeeded in the vote for a secession convention, but thwarted attempts to put the matter to a popular vote. Just how many of Florida's voters would have rejected secession is not known, and the popular vote might, indeed, have favored secession. But, in the election of 1860, a substantial minority of Floridians—slightly more than a third of those who voted—had cast their votes for John Bell, whose Constitutional Union Party had committed itself to a platform of keeping the Union intact. Abraham Lincoln's name did not appear on the ballot in Florida, or in any of the states that became part of the Confederacy, except Virginia, just as antislavery Republican John Fremont's name had not appeared on the 1856 ballot in those states. (In fact, Fremont's name did not appear in three additional states: Virginia, Kentucky, and Missouri.)

We can never know just how many of the general (white male) population of Florida would have voted for secession when faced with the ultimate choice. However, an indication that the majority might well have voted for secession can be inferred from the election of John Milton, a very strong pro-slavery and pro-secessionist candidate as Florida's governor in 1861. So wedded was Governor Milton to the Confederacy that, with the Union victory in the spring of 1865, he declared that death would be preferable to reunion with the United States and committed suicide. But then again, Governor Milton's majority was rather slim—

6,994 to 5,248 over his anti-secession opponent, Edward Hopkins, and perhaps when faced with the reality of secession, some voters were having second thoughts.[4]

While accepting that a majority of Floridians may well have supported secession, we can also know, from specific actions and circumstances during the Civil War, that a considerable number supported the Union. Some of these gave active assistance to the Union forces in Florida and many a Confederate deserter found refuge in that state. And with its large sparsely populated areas, Florida was also a convenient state into which a deserter could simply disappear.

However, with the preponderance of the delegates representing the powerful slave-owning minority, and with those delegates clearly favoring secession, when the convention was held on January 3, 1861, the outcome was certain. After several days of discussion, on January 10 the vote of the delegates was 62 to 7 in favor of secession. Even as the delegates debated, however, Florida's outgoing governor, Madison Perry, ordered the state militia to seize Federal forts and arsenals within the state, and during the first week of January—before the vote for secession was taken—that order was carried out. However, the Federal installations seized in Florida were not, in general, the most substantial or important.

The Union officer who found himself in charge of some of the more important U.S. military facilities of the state—the forts near Pensacola—was 1st Lieutenant Adam Slemmer of the U.S. 1st Artillery, and he was faced with a dilemma. His commanding officer, Major John Winder, was not present when Florida's governor demanded the surrender of all federal forts and other installations to the state militia. (That circumstance—Winder's absence—no doubt served the Union cause, since Major Winder later became a general in the Confederate Army, as did Slemmer's 2nd Lt. Jeremiah Gilman.) There is a report that the first shots of the Civil War were fired by Slemmer's men on January 7, 1861, at Fort Barrancas near Pensacola when "an unidentified party of men approached the fort, apparently with the intention of taking possession." The Union sentries challenged, and when they received no answer, fired, and the approaching party quickly withdrew. It does seem, however, that warning shots fired by sentries is clearly not remotely on the same scale as the firing on Fort Sumter some 3 months later.[5]

On January 9, Lt. Slemmer received direct orders from Washington "to prevent the seizure ... of the forts in Pensacola Harbor by surprise or assault." But the lieutenant realized

Lt. Adam Slemmer (Library of Congress).

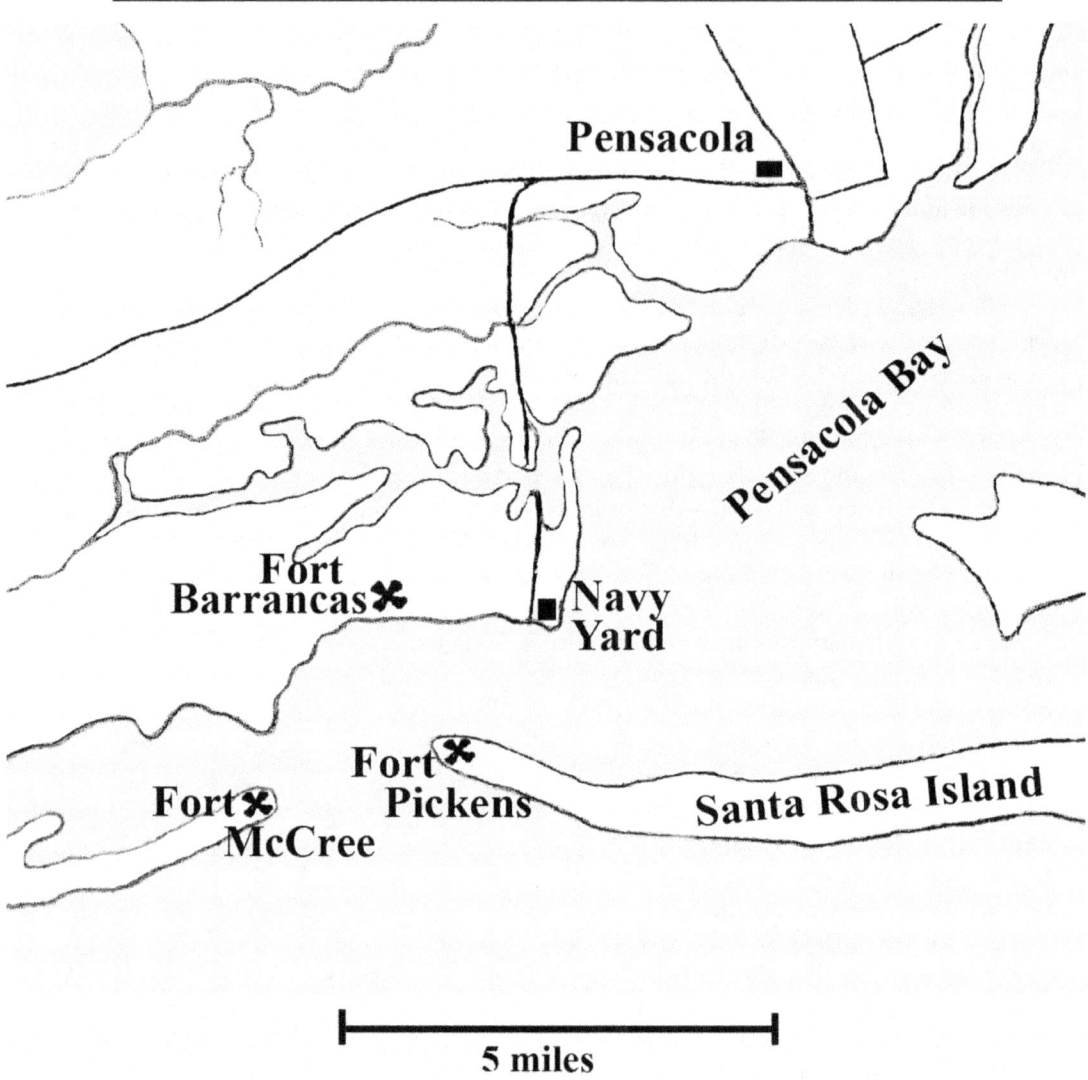

The forts guarding Pensacola Bay (adapted from plate CX; *Official Atlas*).

that his small force of 46 men and 3 ordnance sergeants could not hope to hold more than one of the three forts—Forts McRee, Barrancas, and Pickens—so he spiked as many guns of Forts McRee and Barrancas as time permitted, loaded what ammunition and supplies he could on a flatboat and ferried his men across the bay to Fort Pickens. At that point, his force was supplemented by 30 armed seamen from the *Wyandotte,* sent to aid in the defense of the fort by the ship's commander, Lieutenant Otway Berryman. Located on the western tip of Santa Rosa Island, Fort Pickens, although not in good repair and not garrisoned since the Mexican War, was in an excellent position to be defended and could dominate the passage of shipping in or out of Pensacola Bay from a single location. Lt. Slemmer successfully completed the transfer, and his small force established themselves at Fort Pickens and began making what preparations they could to defend their post. These Union troops were reinforced in April of 1861, and although attacked by Confederate forces in October of that year and subjected to an artillery bombardment in early 1862, Fort Pickens remained in Fed-

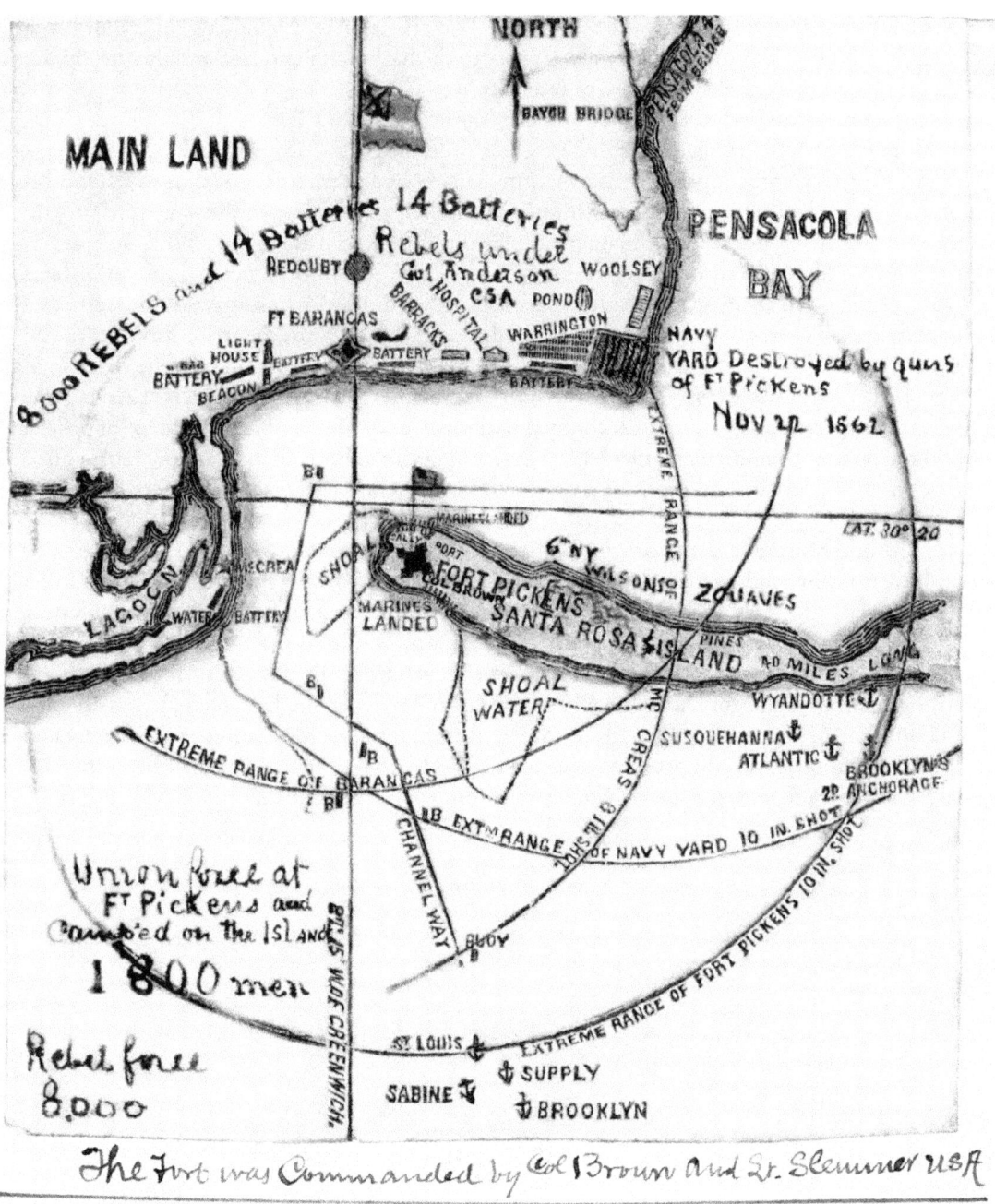

This drawing lists the numbers of Confederate and Union troops, shows the positions of the Union ships supporting Fort Pickens, and shows the range of the guns of the forts and navy yard (adapted from map vhs00202, Library of Congress).

eral hands for the duration of the Civil War. The result of Lt. Slemmer's timely and well considered action was to effectively block entry to the harbor at Pensacola and thereby render the navy yard there useless to the Confederacy.[6]

In contrast to Lt. Slemmer's actions, the commander of the Pensacola Navy Yard, Commodore James Armstrong, although he had received orders to "protect public [U.S. government] property and cooperate with the army," made little or no preparation to defend his post. When a militia force of several hundred marched to the gates of the navy yard on January 12, 1861, and demanded the installation's surrender, Armstrong wired the secretary of the navy, "I surrendered the place and struck my flag." The militia, made up of volunteers from Florida and Alabama, quickly secured the ammunition magazine, commissary, and quartermaster stores. The two major U.S. ships at the navy yard, the storeship *Supply* and the steamer *Wyandotte*, did not surrender—the *Wyandotte* later helping in the defense of Fort Pickens. For his actions and his decision to surrender his post, Commodore Armstrong was court-martialed on March 12, charged with neglect of duty and disobedience of orders, and conduct unbecoming an officer. He was found guilty of both charges and was suspended from duty for 5 years and received a reprimand in general orders from the secretary of the navy.[7]

Another figure in the drama unfolding around Pensacola was retired U.S. Army major and West Point graduate (class of 1815) William Chase. Born in Buckfield, Maine (still a part of Massachusetts at the time of his birth), Chase had married into a Southern family and became a strong advocate of Southern secession. While in the U.S. military, Captain and later Major Chase had been the superintending engineer in charge of construction and strengthening of the fortifications at Pensacola. In particular he had been responsible for the building of Fort Pickens, begun in 1829 and completed in 1834, and the expanding and upgrading in masonry of Fort Barrancas from 1839 to 1844. He had resigned from the U.S. Army in 1856 and, as war approached, he was president of the Alabama and Florida Railroad.

In this drawing, the U.S. gunboat *Wyandotte* is shown firing a salute for Washington's birthday. The view is drawn from Fort Pickens; Fort Barrancas is in the far left background (*Harper's Weekly*, April 6, 1861).

Leaving his civilian occupation, he was given a commission as colonel commanding forces of Florida. When Chase reached Pensacola with orders to take possession of the forts there for the state of Florida, he learned that Lt. Slemmer had, just hours before, moved his men to Fort Pickens and appeared ready to defend that installation. Chase, with Alabama and Florida volunteer militia, demanded and accepted the surrender of the navy yard. A few days later, when Chase asked that Lt. Slemmer surrender Fort Pickens, his request and his threats to take the fort by force were rejected. When Col. Chase told Lt. Slemmer that any loss of life that might follow would be Slemmer's responsibility, Slemmer replied that Chase and his militia would be the aggressors "and if blood is shed ... you are responsible." Further attempts to gain Slemmer's surrender also failed. Nor, in January of 1861, was Chase in any position to try to take the fort by assault with his untrained band of volunteers. As one Alabama officer stated, "Colonel Chase built it [the fort] and he was sure it was impregnable." As noted earlier, when Fort Pickens was attacked, those attacks failed.[8]

The decision to continue to hold Fort Pickens came after serious discussion and some disagreement within President Lincoln's administration. In late March 1861, General Winfield Scott, in command of the United States Army, recommended that if Fort Pickens and Fort Sumter were evacuated by Union troops and given over to the Confederacy, this might "give confidence to the eight remaining slave-holding states" and convince them to remain within the Union. Lincoln's cabinet was apparently stunned by this suggestion, and as we now know, Scott's plan was rejected. In fact, Secretary of State William H. Seward regarded the defense of Fort Pickens as more important than that of Fort Sumter.[9]

And so, for a time, Fort Pickens remained the only Union stronghold guarding the

This drawing, by "our attentive correspondent in the fort," shows the United States flag flying after Fort Pickens was secured by Lieutenant Slemmer and his men (*Harper's Weekly*, April 6, 1861).

entrance to Pensacola Harbor, with Confederate troops manning Forts McCree and Barrancas.

As secession later turned to war, Florida sent 15,000 soldiers to fight for the Confederacy, while many militia or home guard units were raised within the state—generally civilians who armed themselves, and who often operated without any official recognition or designation by the state or Confederate authorities. Perhaps Florida's greatest contribution came, not in the number of men it sent to the Confederate Army, but in the form of food and supplies that the state provided. Florida became an important source for much-needed salt,

Confederate battery near Fort McRee (State Archives of Florida; floridamemory.com).

Columbiad guns of the Confederate water battery at Fort Barrancas, February 1861 (National Archives).

used to preserve meat for shipment in those days before refrigeration. And a good part of the meat that would be salted came from Florida's large herds of beef cattle, probably the state's most important single food provided to the Confederacy. In addition to beef, while cotton remained the dominant crop on the large Florida plantations, the state did devote a considerable amount of land to food crops and so supplied the Confederacy with important produce, especially corn and citrus fruit. But, while food for much of the Confederacy became more and more scarce as the war went on, the plantation owners in Florida stubbornly continued to grow cotton as their primary crop. The value of cotton remained high and a great deal was shipped out through the Union's blockade of Florida's ports. Indeed, Florida's mile upon mile of sparsely populated coast provided opportunities for smuggling both to and from the state. This blockade-running did diminish, however, as the war went on and the ports that were most suited to the loading and unloading of cargo came under tighter Union control. Also, of course, the somewhat oddly arranged legal sale of cotton to Northern buyers continued.[10]

In addition to the use of much needed farmland for cotton, many of the planters who did grow corn to sell would not sell that corn for the highly inflated Confederate currency. When some corn crops were taken by Confederate officials in return for promises of future payment, this led to considerable anger and resentment on the part of the planters. Another problem for the supply of corn as a food came from the practice of using substantial parts of the crop for producing corn whisky, even though that was made illegal without a permit by the state's legislature in 1862. One of the largest consumers of this corn whisky was the Confederacy's own surgeon general's office, whose field hospitals often had little else to dull the pain of those wounded or undergoing surgery. Nevertheless, with all of these problems, Florida did play an important part in helping feed the Confederacy.[11]

While contributing men and supplies to the Rebel cause, Florida also provided a haven for those avoiding the Confederacy's April 1862 conscription laws and for those who deserted from the Confederate Army. Some of the deserters banded together to attack Confederate patrols as well as raiding plantations, stealing cattle, and providing intelligence to the Federal army and navy. Beyond that, while some who were loyal to the Union left the state, a substantial number of white Unionist Florida men served in Federal Army units such as the 1st and 2nd Florida Cavalry. And, over a thousand black men from Florida served in colored units such as the Corps de Afrique and a number of regiments of U.S. Colored Infantry.[12]

Well into the Civil War, in February of 1864, some felt that Unionist sentiment was strong enough in Florida to present an opportunity to bring that state back into the Union. President Lincoln's proclamation of December 8, 1863, had announced a plan for reconstruction that would allow a state back into the Union if 10 percent of the eligible voters would swear an oath of allegiance to the United States. Lincoln sent his secretary, John Hay, to Florida to assess the possibility of working with the voters there to achieve that end. Mr. Hay felt that it would be very difficult to find enough legal voters, and voters who were loyal to the Union, to make the 10 percent plan possible. Many, according to Hay, had fled: "I find scarcely anybody left in the country. Whole counties seem almost thoroughly depopulated. The few that remain seem heartily tired of the war, and willing to swear allegiance in any terms to the power that will protect them, but these are really not enough, as it seems to me, to justify a movement just at present, for rehabilitation." Further, the Union losses at the Battle of Olustee led Mr. Hay to conclude, "I cannot but think that we must wait for further developments in military operations before we can hope for a reorganization of the state under a loyal government."[13]

There was another aspect to this plan to bring Florida back into the Union, and the requests by citizens for a speedy reentry. In 1863, Secretary of State Salmon P. Chase was hoping to challenge Abraham Lincoln for the nomination to be the Republican Party's candidate in the 1864 election. Chase, as a part of that effort, was attempting to set up a pro–Chase government in Florida and had his ally, Lyman Stickney, busily arranging meetings of loyal citizens—specifically citizens loyal to Chase—to petition Washington for readmittance to the Union. These petitions also included the request that Florida be allowed to participate in the 1864 presidential election. Lincoln was warned of this plot in early 1864 and had sent John Hay to Florida to assess the facts of the situation. It was Hay's reports of conditions, coupled with the realization that Chase's man Stickney was greatly exaggerating the numbers of "loyal" citizens, that led to the unfavorable report regarding Florida's rejoining the Union.[14]

Another and perhaps somewhat bizarre plan to bring Florida back into the Union was begun in late 1862. This plan, set in motion by Eli Thayer, a member of the U.S. House of Representatives from Massachusetts, involved sending large numbers of armed "colonists" to Florida to secure it for the Union. This plan had the support of a number of people from New York, who actually held meetings to recruit volunteers to go to Florida, and had the support of such men as General Joseph Hooker, Senator Samuel Pomeroy from Kansas, powerful Republican abolitionist Cassius M Clay of Kentucky, and many others. The Kansas senator even wrote that such a plan had worked well in his state—although the results of that plan are better known to us as "Bleeding Kansas."[15]

As a final word on the conditions in Florida at the start of the Civil War, the treatment and situation of African slaves in Florida present an interesting story. Unlike Louisiana, which had a considerable population of free blacks, especially in New Orleans, Florida's population of free blacks was fewer than 1,000, about two-thirds of whom were people of mixed race, while its slave population was about 62,000. (That number of free blacks does not, of course, include the uncountable number of "free" runaway slaves living in remote areas.) The slave population was almost entirely located on the large plantations in the central counties of northern Florida.[16]

In a later chapter, we will see how one Confederate veteran of the Civil War described the kindly treatment of slaves in Florida by their masters. Another source, from a 1913 book on Florida in the Civil War, states that the Southern slave was "well-fed, well-housed, well-treated." That book also reports that "the social discipline of Southern slavery did not break down when subjected to the test of war." And in 1865, the governor of Florida said, "The world has never seen such a body of slaves, for not only in peace but in war they had been faithful to us." Comments about how peaceful and contented the slaves in Florida were are, to say the least, suspicious in their positive view of slavery.

In the 1913 work mentioned above, the author, in a continuation of his statement about the good treatment of the slaves in Florida, also states that those slaves were "well-watched and controlled." This need to watch and control, the author reports, was even more clearly in force during the Civil War. With worry about how slaves might react to the conflict, the state legislature in Florida designed a "patrol" law in 1861 due to "the apprehension in the South over the negro question." This law, intending to "restrain the too free movements of the black," created citizen patrols which were given specific beats within designated areas of the state. These patrols "moved mostly at night in parties—usually on horseback." Keeping themselves "informed on the condition and the opinion of the negroes in their districts," these patrols were authorized "to arrest and examine negroes found out at night; to apprehend thieves (black and white)," to seize those "harboring or dealing with negroes" in a disorderly manner, "to prevent or disperse any unlawful assembly of negroes—free or slave—and to take from the hands of slaves all firearms." An "unlawful assembly of negroes" was defined as "four or more negroes together in a confined or secret place." The patrolling whites were also authorized to "enter by force if necessary all negro cabins and to inflict a punishment by whipping, not to exceed twenty lashes, on all slaves found off the premises of their owners without a written permit from the master." And further, "If while arresting or whipping a slave the black should act 'insolently,' the patrol was authorized by law to inflict additional punishment, not to exceed thirty-nine lashes." The author also states, "There was nothing new in principle for Florida in this patrol act of 1861, nor was its application a departure from past practice." All of that would seem to call into serious question the contented nature of the slaves in Florida and their loyalty to their masters. Indeed, the thousand or so black men from Florida who joined the Union Army, and the many hundreds of slaves who, when given the opportunity, fled from captivity and followed columns of Union troops to freedom, would seem to cast further doubt on the contentment of Florida slaves.[17]

There are stories of slaves voluntarily joining the Confederate Army to help defend the institutions of the old South. These stories are used to demonstrate that slaves were happy and contented with the social conditions of the South before the Civil War and even willing to risk their lives to preserve those conditions. In fact, during the Civil War, there was strong resistance from white soldiers and citizens to arming slaves to fight for the Confederacy. Confederate General Patton Anderson, from Florida, gave a typical response when he said that the proposal to arm slaves was "a monstrous proposition, revolting to Southern sentiment, Southern pride, and Southern honor." Confederate General Cobb, who commanded Central Florida, stated, "I think that the proposition to make soldiers of our slaves is the most pernicious idea that has been suggested.... You cannot make soldiers of slaves or slaves of soldiers. The moment you resort to negro soldiers your white soldier will be lost to you."[18]

With these sentiments so clearly expressed and reflecting the opinions of so many, it might seem surprising that in December of 1862 the Florida Legislature authorized the governor to "impress slaves for military work." The owners of the slaves would be compensated for the loss of a part of their work force. In 1864, the Confederate Congress also passed a law authorizing 20,000 slaves for service with the Confederate military. The slaves impressed under these laws, however, were put to work in menial service and were engaged, unarmed and under white supervision, in constructing fortifications and other such tasks—not volunteers fighting for the Confederacy. It was not until March of 1865 that the Confederate Congress authorized the raising of 300,000 black soldiers. At that point in the war the situation for the Confederacy was desperate indeed, and the Confederate surrender meant that neither the plan nor the black soldiers were ever actually put in place.[19]

In spite of all that, there are well documented cases of black soldiers—armed men taking part in combat—serving in Confederate units as early as 1862. At least in some military organizations, and at times well before the law authorizing black soldiers in the Confederate Army, some state regiments did have black men serving along with whites. On one expedition carried out by members of the 2nd Maine Cavalry, several "colored" Confederates "armed and mounted" were reported as captured. As will be shown in a later chapter regarding these and other black Confederate combatants, things are not always as simple as one might think.

Florida presented a greatly varied landscape, large areas of little population, and a populace that varied greatly in politics and opinions. The number of Confederate forces in the state was not large when compared to most other parts of the Confederacy, but they were supported by many units of home guard and militia. In addition, while a state with a small population, it was a state from which the Confederacy obtained substantial foodstuffs. The 2nd Maine Cavalry would find all of these factors of importance during their service in that state.

CHAPTER THREE

Winter 1863: Forming the 2nd Maine Veteran Volunteer Regiment

In the fall and winter of 1863, new regiments were to be raised in Maine and other states under the guidelines set out in General Order 191, forwarded to the various states by the War Department in Washington in late June: "In order to increase the armies now in the field, volunteer infantry, cavalry and artillery may be enlisted at any time within ninety days from this date in the respective States, under regulations hereinafter mentioned. The volunteers so enlisted, and such of the three-years' troops now in the field as may re-enlist in accordance with the provisions of this order will constitute a force to be designated 'Veteran Volunteers.'"[1]

The order goes on to say that these veteran regiments are open to "all able bodied men between the ages of 18 and 45 years, who have heretofore been enlisted and have served for not less than nine months and can pass the examination required by the mustering regulations of the U.S." As a mark of their veteran volunteer status, men would be authorized to wear "service chevrons," issued by the War Department.[2]

There were also very practical inducements for enlistment or reenlistment. In addition to the regular pay of $13 per month for a private, the men were to be paid a Federal bounty and premium in installments, starting with $40 at the time of muster, and totaling $402 at the end of their term of service. In addition, towns within the state were offering their own bounties for recruits—often amounting to $350. The towns that could afford that sort of bounty created quite a problem for the smaller, poorer towns that could not compete with the more affluent. Towns were given quotas to fill, and a man could enlist from a town paying a higher bounty if he so wished. Also, the offer of a bounty and the first month's

Sign from the Kennebunk, Maine, recruiting office (Maine State Museum; photograph by author).

This poster, recruiting for another "Veteran" regiment, raised under General Order 191, promises a state bounty of $100 in addition to the Federal bounty (Collections of Maine Historical Society).

pay at the time of enlistment created a situation in which some young men took the money and promptly deserted. In fact, 49 men of the 2nd Maine Cavalry deserted before the regiment left Maine.

The requirements for the raising of veteran volunteer regiments were so clearly stated that it seems odd to discover how many men with no previous military experience were recruited and mustered into the 2nd Maine Cavalry. The only company that recorded the veteran status of the men who enlisted was Company A, and of the 104 enlisted men who joined that company in November and December of 1863, only 14 are listed as "veteran" in the company's roster. The numbers of veterans who enlisted in other companies is not recorded, but we may safely say that it was not a majority.

The regiment's commanding officer would later explain, "This 2nd Regiment Maine Cavalry Vet Vols was authorized to be raised under General Orders War Dept No 191 dated June 25th 1863 and failed to meet the requirements of the order but were permitted to raise the Regiment and receive into it men for Officers and Soldiers who were not Veterans. The Regiment was organized under this modification ... as a new organization including many officers and soldiers who had never served in the U.S. Army. The designation of the Regiment has not been changed."[3] The regiment kept its designation as "Veteran Volunteer" until its muster out of U.S. service.

The orders regarding the raising of these veteran regiments also provides recruiting guidelines for officers wishing to enlist volunteers: "Officers of regiments whose terms have expired will be authorized, on proper application and approval of their respective Governors, to raise companies and regiments within the period of sixty days, and if the company or regiment authorized to be raised shall be filled up and mustered into service within the said period of sixty days, the officers may be re-commissioned of the date of their original commissions, and for the time engaged in recruiting they will be entitled to receive the pay belonging to their rank."[4]

As with regiments raised earlier in the war, an officer's commission was offered as a reward for recruiting. This often resulted in companies within a regiment being raised from a well defined geographic area, and such a system was often effective in creating a group of men who knew each other before enlistment and whose behavior and performance in the service would be reported back to their town by their comrades. For the 2nd Maine Cavalry, this meant that Company A, for example, would be made up to a large degree of men from Aroostook County, Maine's most northerly county, while many from "Downeast" Maine's Washington County, enlisted in Company D. A large percentage of the men in Company G hailed from Penobscot County, with a substantial number living within a 15 mile radius of the county seat, Bangor. Other companies also reflect this regional nature to various degrees. One must also wonder if the clearly stated rewards for recruiting, coupled with the bonuses being offered, led to the situation in which officers were happy to accept any volunteer who came forward, and those volunteers saw a financial advantage to joining one of the veteran regiments. And, for those who aspired to a rank higher than private, the opportunities for promotion were much greater in a newly formed regiment. Those who enlisted in 1863 into one of the regiments raised in 1861 or 1862 would find that seniority was already well established.

In the fall of 1863, as the 2nd Maine Cavalry was being formed, the provisions of the general order resulted in dozens of letters to the governor of Maine and its adjutant general recommending, for a variety of reasons, a number of men for officers' commissions. Most letters are quite similar and quite predictable, recommending men for their honesty, integrity, energy, good morals, political party loyalty, history of military service, etc. But some stand out.

A letter to Maine Adjutant General John Hodsdon from J. S. Chadwick makes it clear that the ability to successfully recruit men is of importance to those wishing to obtain a commission: "Lieut Saml W Knowles is desirous of obtaining authority to recruit a company.... He is confident that he can start with 20 from his old Co of the 22nd Regt. Lieut Knowles returns from the Army with a first rate reputation and he is deserving of this privilege." Samuel Knowles had been 1st sergeant and then 2nd lieutenant of Company B, 22nd Maine Infantry.[5]

Lt. Knowles himself also wrote to the adjutant general: "I know that it would be very easy to raise a company ... from the old members of the 22nd and that it could be raised in a very few days." Whatever other recruiting Lt. Knowles may have done, only one man of "his old Co of the 22nd Regt" signed up to be in Captain Knowles' new company. However, the request for a commission was effective and Lt. Knowles became Captain Knowles of Company G, 2nd Maine Cavalry.[6]

And, does this following letter to Maine Governor Abner Coburn reflect the politics within the writer's home town of Appleton, Maine, or his reluctance to offer references? The writer, formerly a member of the 1st Maine Cavalry, who had been captured and had been for a time a prisoner, wrote asking for a commission and adds: "I would refer you to the selectmen of this town but Sir they are Copperheads, and I cannot stoop so low feeling indignant almost that I live in a town where there is such a class of men." Isaac B. Harris joined the 2nd Maine Cavalry as sergeant of Company H, but was reduced to the ranks as a private in 1864.[7]

The term "Copperhead" (a type of venomous snake) was a less than complimentary name given to those who actively opposed the Lincoln administration and its policies. Often associated with the Democratic Party, the Copperheads raised considerable objection from within the North to Lincoln's use of force to pursue the war to reunite the country.

In some letters from those seeking appointments, there is a certain air of entitlement, such as this to Governor Coburn from George Martin. Martin was in the 4th Maine, and while he had served as assistant surgeon, he had been put in sole charge during the regular surgeon's illness, but apparently did not feel he had been sufficiently appreciated or rewarded for that effort. "You know the history of my unfortunate connection with that Regt. For my services there is nearly $1,200 due me, which you know it is very doubtful if ever I get." He goes on, "Since my return from the field I have felt that I had strong, yes very strong claims on the Governor of Maine for an appointment as Surgeon in some regiment. I am conscious of doing my duty in 13 battles and all who know me in the field know that I would not shun my duty to save my life. The Surgeancy of the Cavalry Regt will satisfy me, and I do not hesitate in saying that I believe I am entitled to that position."[8] Whatever the merits of his complaint, Dr. Martin was appointed surgeon of the 2nd Maine Cavalry.

The fact that some men were not above accepting the bounty—and perhaps more than one town's bounty—and then disappearing is reflected in this letter, which also presents an interesting view that a town had "bought" a man's service. It was sent in early December 1863 to Adjutant General Hodsdon from the "Assessors" of the township of Haynesville, Maine, and also demonstrates the problems that poorer towns were having when trying to compete with those able to pay higher bounties:

> We thought we would drop you a few lines in regard to a man that [we] bought to fill the
> quota of our TP [township] which was one we raised a town Bounty & Bought a man & he

received a porsion [sic] of it before he left here. We learn that he has sold him self again. Mr. Twitchell enlisted him. His name was Wm Tucker.... We received a certifercate [sic] from Capt Twitchell to show that Wm Tucker hailes [sic] from Haynesville. Please answer by return mail to let us know that particulars in regard to this matter. We have raised a Bounty for one man & if we loose [sic] him we shall be obliged to stand the draft for their isn't but two or three men that are able to pay a dollar and not but two or three that are subject to a draft.[9]

In 1860, Haynesville, a small town in Northern Maine's Aroostook County, had a population of only 168, living in 27 households, and the great majority of these families were engaged in farming.[10]

In reply to the concerns of the Haynesville assessors, Captain Twitchell, explaining the requirements for filling a town's quota, wrote: "I find that and you will see by the adjutant General orders that the residence of a man does not hold him. The Quota must be filled out at the top of the Enlistment paper. William Tucker has hailed from another town. His residence was only put in Haynesville Plantation.... I will make him pay back to you what you advanced him if you will send on your bill." Captain Twitchell then explains that when it comes to town bounties, "men are going as high as $350 three hundred and fifty dollars" and that "business is very lively in Augusta [Maine's capital]. Our regiment is filling up fast."[11]

Several letters followed regarding Private Tucker, his residence, and which town could claim him as a part of their quota. After all of the interest shown in William Tucker, the 18 year old deserted in February 1864 from Augusta, Maine, before the 2nd Maine Cavalry had left the state.[12]

Others apparently also took money from more than one town, or under more than one name:

> I have the honor to inform you that one John George [Severance? Laurence?] of Patten has enlisted in the Company of JF Twitchell under the name of "John George" and received $350 town bounty. He had presumably given his written obligation to go on the quota of Patten and I think he was paid five dollars at the time the obligation was given to bind the bargain. He now has $300 deposited with Capt Twitchell. I have respectfully to inquire if such frauds are to be permitted. Please address me at Patten.[13]

In 1860, the little town of Patten, Maine, had a total population of just 659. John George was enlisted in the 2nd Maine Cavalry and served until discharged for disability in late June 1865.

This next letter provides yet another look at the stresses felt by some small towns and the ability of some towns to pay a higher bounty than others: "Have the Kindness to inform me the number of men Pembroke is credited for on her quota. Capt John M Lincoln of Perry (an adjoining town) who has been recruiting in this county for the 2nd Maine Cavalry has taken several of our men into headquarters and as 'tis Some time Since, and nothing being advised by you of any credits of men for this town, I fear under the existing state of things they have been 'gobbled up' by other towns paying larger bounties."[14]

Pembroke, in far "Downeast" Maine, had a total population of around 2,000 in 1860. The make-up of Captain Lincoln's Company D shows that a substantial number of the enlisted men came from that Downeast area—Washington County.

Some letters are refreshingly straightforward about the reasons for a request, such as one in which the writer hopes that his nephew could be made an orderly sergeant or "some such position which will raise him somewhat above the hardships of a private." The request was evidently effective, and George Field was appointed a sergeant in Company L, 2nd Maine Cavalry.[15]

And not all requests for letters of recommendation provided the glowing testimonial hoped for. For some reason, when Andrew Woodman asked his friend, James Deering, to send a letter of recommendation to Governor Coburn, the governor received the following:

> Mr Andrew J Woodman of Saco desires an appointment in the Second Maine Cavalry to some position I know not what, he has asked a letter of me, I wish I could recommend him as being endowed with all the qualities necessary to qualify him to fill (after sufficient military training) any commission which you might see fit to confer upon him—But I cannot. Still he may make a very respectable & efficient officer, I have no doubt but he will be very well recommended and perhaps by gentlemen better qualified to judge of his qualifications than I am. PS I have no personal feeling against Mr Woodman. We are personal friends.[16]

Andrew Woodman did receive his commission, however, and became 1st Lieutenant Woodman of Company L, 2nd Maine Cavalry.

Some recommendations stand out simply because of the number of letters sent. Owen O'Brian of Houlton, Maine sent his own letter requesting the position of hospital steward. That request was accompanied by eight letters sent to the governor and adjutant general from private citizens, the postmaster, selectmen of Houlton, and a doctor. The result was that O'Brian was transferred from quartermaster sergeant of Company M to hospital steward, serving under surgeon George Martin, the doctor who was among those recommending him.[17]

A few letters become notable because we know the fate of the men concerned. A long list of men from Company M recommend Isaac Adams to be lieutenant, citing his military experience (he had been a corporal and sergeant in the 8th Maine Infantry), as well as his "correct habits and fine abilities." He was indeed promoted from orderly sergeant to 2nd lieutenant, was wounded and taken prisoner in the battle of Marianna, Florida, in September 1864, and died of his wounds.[18]

In the late summer of 1864, while the 2nd Maine Cavalry was in Louisiana, the colonel, Ephraim Woodman, made the following recommendation in a letter to Adjutant General Hodsdon: "I would respectfully recommend that Ellis W Ayer of Gardiner, now Quarter Master Sergeant of Co I, in this regiment, be promoted to be Second Lieutenant in the same Company." Sgt. Ayer was promoted to lieutenant and a short time later was killed in action at Marianna.[19]

In the late fall of 1863, the regiment was in Augusta, Maine, and, starting on November 30 and ending on January 2, 1864, the various companies were mustered into United States service. One writer described the 2nd Maine Cavalry in these terms: "This regiment when organized was composed of robust and strong men, well armed, equipped and disciplined."[20]

The original field officers were Ephraim W. Woodman of Wilton, colonel, John F. Godfrey of Bangor, lieutenant colonel, Charles A. Miller of Rockland, Major, Eben Hutchinson of Athens, Major, Andrew B. Spurling of Orland, Major, and Nathan Cutler of Augusta, adjutant.

As with a substantial number of the enlisted men of the regiment, in spite of the "veteran" specifications set forth in General Order 191, some but not all of these officers had seen previous service. (The basic information concerning the following officers, unless otherwise noted, comes from the *Maine Adjutant General's Report* for 1861 through 1865. For a complete roster of the 2nd Maine Cavalry, taken primarily from the Maine adjutant general's reports, see Appendix A. That roster lists the field officers and all of the members of each company, and gives information regarding deaths, illness, transfers, promotion, demotion, desertion, etc.)

Colonel Woodman was the son of a War of 1812 veteran and the grandson of a private in the Continental Army during the Revolutionary War. He had been a captain and later lieutenant colonel in the 8th Maine Infantry. He resigned from the 8th Maine in the spring of 1862 and was appointed colonel of the 28th Maine, one of the 9 month regiments raised in the fall of 1862, and was mustered out with that regiment in August of 1863. With the 8th Maine, he had seen service for several months in South Carolina, and with the 28th Maine he had been a part of General Banks' Nineteenth Army Corps. In January 1863, Colonel Woodman and a large part of the 28th Maine (most of 6 companies) were garrisoned at Pensacola, doing picket duty during the Union Army's occupation of the town, while 4 other companies were sent to Fort Barrancas. In March 1863, the regiment was sent to Louisiana, where detachments were engaged in and around Donaldsonville, often skirmishing with elements of the Confederate infantry and cavalry. In late May, Colonel Woodman and his 6 companies of the 28th Maine were sent to Port Hudson, Louisiana, where they joined in the investment of that impressive Confederate fortification which controlled the

Col. Ephraim Woodman (courtesy Maine State Archives).

Mississippi River south of Vicksburg. There, led by Colonel Woodman, the regiment participated in various assaults, including an attack on a Confederate strongpoint on June 21 in which promised support did not arrive and the 28th Maine withdrew with the loss of 3 killed and 9 wounded. Colonel Woodman remained with a substantial portion of the regiment at Port Hudson until the surrender of the Confederate garrison on July 8. He therefore can be assumed to have knowledge of the health hazards that his new cavalry regiment would face in the Deep South. On the other hand, as with many other officers of the 2nd Maine Cavalry, Colonel Woodman had no experience in command of cavalry troopers.[21]

Lt. Colonel John F. Godfrey was a member of well known and well to do Bangor family—the son of Judge John E. Godfrey. The younger John Godfrey joined the military as 2nd lieutenant in the 1st Battalion, 1st Maine Mounted Artillery, and spent his first months of service doing recruiting duty in Maine, a duty which he found very dull. He also was not favorably impressed with the men he enlisted, for he wrote, "Those who now enlist as privates are not all such as we would wish to look upon as patriots, or care to think about as heroes."

Left: Maj. Charles Miller; *right*: Lt. Col. John Godfrey (courtesy Maine State Archives).

With a group of his recruits, he joined the battery in Massachusetts for their journey to Louisiana. While there, Lt. Godfrey applied for and was granted the opportunity to raise a company of cavalry, which he described as "my favorite arm of the service." He did raise his company, and in early August 1862 became Captain Godfrey, Company C, 1st Louisiana (Union) Cavalry. He had apparently not been particularly happy with his artillery assignment, for in a letter home he expressed his relief at being "clear of the Battery I hope for ever." With the 1st Louisiana Cavalry, Captain Godfrey saw considerable action at and near Port Hudson, Louisiana.[22]

Major Miller had been a lawyer in Rockland, Maine, and there is no record of his having any previous military service. There were, of course, others who attained high rank in other regiments without previous military service—Joshua Chamberlain became lieutenant colonel of the 20th Maine when a professor at Maine's Bowdoin College, and Simon Gerrard had been a dairy farmer before being appointed colonel of the 22nd Maine—but in this "veteran" regiment, this lack of previous service stands out. Major Miller enlisted as a private in Company B and was mustered at that rank on December 11, 1863. His promotion to major is dated (backdated?) December 14, which made him the senior major in the regiment. As we will see, Major Miller was apparently good friends with Maine's adjutant general, John Hodsdon, and that may well have been a factor in Miller's commission.

Major Hutchinson had been major and lieutenant colonel in the 24th Maine Infantry, another 9 month regiment. This regiment, as with the 28th Maine and others, had spent most of its time in the Deep South and had also seen combat at Port Hudson. The 24th Maine took part in the ill-planned and costly assaults on the Confederate fortifications at Port Hudson on May 27 and June 14 and was present throughout the siege of Port Hudson until the surrender of that Rebel stronghold in late July.

Left: Maj. Eben Hutchinson; *right*: Maj. Andrew Spurling (courtesy Maine State Archives).

Major Spurling will emerge as an important figure in the story of the 2nd Maine Cavalry. He often would be called on to lead detachments of the regiment, was frequently in command of the entire regiment, and at times led large groups of Union troops made up of elements from several regiments. Before the Civil War, Andrew Spurling had left Maine at age 18, had been a miner, a farmer, and a hunter in California, and had returned to his home state in 1855, "taking up a sailor's life as captain" at age 22. Major Spurling enlisted in 1861 and became lieutenant and then captain of Company D, 1st Maine Cavalry, a regiment whose exploits would gain them a formidable, very positive, reputation. With the 1st Maine Cavalry, Spurling saw considerable action, beginning with battles during the spring of 1862 such as Middleton and Winchester, Virginia. Later he served in General David Gregg's division of experienced and highly regarded cavalry fighting against J.E.B. Stuart's Confederate troopers in the Battle of Brandy Station on June 9, 1863, (an action for which Stuart was said to feel "humiliated" and for which he was strongly criticized in the Confederate press). Just a short time later, on June 17–19, Spurling, with Gregg's cavalry, was in action against the Confederates at Middleburg, Virginia, and on June 21 they fought again, this time at Upperville, Virginia, where the Confederate cavalry, after delaying advancing Union troops, was forced to withdraw. At Brandy Station, Spurling was shot through the thigh with a pistol ball, and during the fighting at Upperville, he was wounded "in a personal hand-to-hand fight," receiving a saber cut to his right hand and "two blows" to his right arm. He was, by far, the most experienced cavalry officer to join the 2nd Maine Cavalry.[23]

Adjutant Cutler had started his military career as a young private, not quite 18 when he left Harvard College after his sophomore year to enlist in Company E, 21st Maine Infantry. He saw no engagements with Confederate forces while in the 21st Maine, being discharged after only a bit more than 4 months for a medical disability. However, he reenlisted and became adjutant of the 28th Maine. With that regiment, Cutler was involved in the siege of Port Hudson, Louisiana, and while with the 28th Maine, he had served under Colonel Woodman.[24]

As well as those regimental officers, the regiment also contained a chaplain, adjutant, quartermaster, commissary officer, a surgeon and assistant surgeon, and because this was a cavalry regiment, there was also a veterinary surgeon.

The 12 companies (sometimes referred to as "squadrons") of the 2nd Maine Cavalry were mustered into United States service by 2nd Lieutenant J.A. Fessenden, 5th U.S. Artillery. (Readers may be surprised to see 12 companies listed, since a typical Union infantry regiment was made up of 10 companies.) Several of these men, who had previously served in other regiments, accepted a reduction in rank when they joined the 2nd Cavalry. Also, although it may seem that officers should be mature men, of an age that gave them seniority in more than just rank when compared to those under their command, we see that some of these company commanders were rather young. Indeed, we often find in today's military that a young 2nd lieutenant may find himself senior in rank to noncommissioned officers who are older and who have more military experience. Captains commanding these companies are as follows:

COMPANY A: Captain Joseph Twitchell. Captain Twitchell, age 26, of Mattawamkeag, Maine, had seen previous service in the 8th Maine Infantry as captain of Company B, and later as major. He was promoted to lieutenant colonel in that regiment after Lt. Col. Woodman resigned. As a result, he was no doubt well known to Col. Woodman, and this previous service relationship very likely influenced decisions that Col. Woodman would make regarding promotion in the 2nd Maine Cavalry.

COMPANY B: Captain Benjamin Merry. Captain Merry, age 30, from Bath, Maine, had been a major in the 21st Maine Infantry, a 9 month regiment which had seen its active duty in the Deep South, especially in the fighting at Port Hudson, Louisiana. The 21st Maine was mustered out of U.S. service in August of 1863.

COMPANY C: Captain Elijah D Johnson. Captain Johnson was from one of Maine's larger cities, Lewiston, and was 31 years old at the time of his enlistment in the 2nd Maine Cavalry. He had served as a lieutenant in Company K, 1st Maine Infantry, a 3 month regiment raised very early in the war that saw no action against the Confederates but served in the defenses of Washington, D.C. Captain Johnson later was adjutant and lieutenant in the 7th Maine, from which he resigned and was then appointed colonel of the 21st Maine. The 7th Maine was in action in Virginia, beginning with General McLellan's Peninsula Campaign, where the 7th saw its first action at Fort Lee on Warwick Creek. It was there that the regiment suffered its first loss in battle, Private Joseph Pepper, who was also said to be the first casualty of that campaign. Their engagements with the Confederate army continued up the Yorktown Peninsula and ended with McClellan's retreat. When he later joined the 21st Maine Infantry as its colonel, Captain Johnson served with that regiment in action described previously, primarily at Port Hudson. When joining the 2nd Maine Cavalry, Colonel Johnson accepted the lower rank of captain.

COMPANY D: Captain John M. Lincoln. Before joining the 2nd Maine Cavalry, Captain Lincoln had been a lieutenant in Company F, 6th Maine Infantry, where he, like Company C's Captain Johnson, saw action in the Peninsula Campaign in 1862. He resigned from the 6th in late summer 1862 and then became captain of Company E, 28th Maine Infantry. While in the 28th Maine, Captain Lincoln would have served under Colonel Woodman

Opposite: Pvt. Rufus Wilder, a member of the 2nd Maine Cavalry's regimental band who became the principal musician. He is holding the typical "bell rear" brass instrument of that era. The bell faced backward over the musician's shoulder to project the sound to troops behind the band (Special Collections, Bangor Public Library).

and taken part in the attacks and the siege at Port Hudson. From the Downeast Maine town of Pembroke, he was 31 years old when he joined the 2nd Cavalry.

COMPANY E: Captain Samuel W. Clarke. Captain Clarke, age 25, from coastal Newcastle, Maine, had been the captain of Company H, 21st Maine Infantry. As with others mentioned above, he was involved in the attacks and siege at Port Hudson.

COMPANY F: Captain Gustavus Stanley. Gustavus Stanley, age 31, from Farmington, Maine, was another veteran of the 28th Maine and had been the captain of that regiment's Company B. During the 28th Maine's early days in Louisiana, Captain Stanley and several of his men were captured by Confederate cavalry and held prisoner for a time. He, like others from the 28th Maine, was involved in the action against the Confederates in and around Port Hudson, and would have served under Colonel Woodman.

COMPANY G: Captain Samuel W. Knowles. Captain Knowles, age 29 from Bangor, Maine, had served in another of the 9 month regiments sent to the Deep South, seeing action at Indian Bend and Port Hudson. Samuel Knowles had been sergeant and then lieutenant of the 22nd Maine's Company B.

Pvt. George Moore, saddler, Company M (Special Collections, Bangor Public Library).

COMPANY H: Captain Adolphus B. Mathews. Captain Mathews, age 29 at the time he joined the 2nd Maine Cavalry, was from Belfast, Maine, on Penobscot Bay, and had been a sergeant in Company I, 26th Maine. This was yet another of the 9 month regiments from Maine sent to the Deep South, also seeing action at Irish Bend and Port Hudson.

COMPANY I: Captain Isaac W. Haskell. Before enlisting in the 2nd Maine Cavalry, Captain Haskell had served as Captain of Company D, 20th Maine, and had resigned from that regiment (along with his 1st lieutenant) in November of 1862, after the 20th Maine's grim baptism by fire at Shepherdstown Ford, Virginia, but before its December losses in the futile charges at Marye's Heights during the Battle of Fredericksburg. And, of course, he was not with the 20th during its best known action defending Little Round Top against the Confederates at Gettysburg. When he joined the 2nd Maine Cavalry, Captain Haskell was 37 years old and was from Garland, Maine.[25]

COMPANY K: Captain Moses French. Captain French, from the small town of Solon, Maine, did not have previous active military service, but had been orderly sergeant for the Maine Militia, doing recruiting duty from Solon. At age 42, he was the oldest of the 2nd Maine Cavalry's company commanders.[26]

COMPANY L: Captain Samuel H. Libby. Captain Libby, age 23, from Limerick, Maine, was the youngest of the company commanders, and had been a lieutenant in Company A of the 27th Maine Infantry. The 27th was another of Maine's 9 month regiments, but unlike the others mentioned previously, had seen no engagements with the enemy, and spent its entire time of service in the defenses of Washington, D.C.

COMPANY M: Captain John H. Roberts. Captain Roberts, age 32, from Alfred, Maine, had previously been lieutenant and then captain of Company F, 8th Maine. Like Company A's Captain Twitchell, Captain Roberts would have known Colonel Woodman from their service in the 8th Maine.

As well as a captain as company commander, each company typically had a 1st and 2nd lieutenant. And, each company, along with the 90 or so privates, would also have the usual group of sergeants and corporals, as well as a company quartermaster sergeant, commissary sergeant, and bugler. In addition, each company had its wagoner, and, because this was a cavalry regiment, there was also a company farrier and saddler.

We also know that there was a regimental band, although no separate unit is so designated in the adjutant general's roster. We do see, however, a number of men who are listed as "detailed to regimental band," or "transferred to band." In addition, on the regimental level there is a principal musician listed. It is unlikely that the band played while mounted; although there certainly were and are mounted military bands (Britain's Household Cavalry, for example), it is much more likely that the band played on foot for parades and may have provided music for any special events.

Among the private soldiers who enlisted in the 2nd Maine Cavalry was a young man from China, Maine, named Orrin Seco. Here was a 20 year old farmer who, like many other volunteers, had no military experience. What makes Orrin Seco stand out is the fact that he was of African ancestry. There was, at the start of the Civil War, a small African American community in China, Maine, and Orrin Seco, with his father, William, and

Cpl. Frank Holt stated he was 18 years old when he enlisted from New Sharon, Maine. Despite his youthful appearance he may have been 18 in December 1863; the 1850 census gives his age as 4 (courtesy Maine State Archives).

mother, Almira, is recorded in the 1860 census as members of that community. Quakers in that area had provided a safe haven for escaped slaves and others of African ancestry who might have lived in fear of being returned to the South by slave catchers sent to the North by plantation owners.[27]

In theory, and in general practice, Union regiments in the Civil War were strictly all white or all black (though black regiments typically had white officers), but it appears that Orrin Seco was not the only African American to serve in a white regiment. Given how very unusual it was to find a black soldier outside a colored regiment, in the history of the 1st Maine Heavy Artillery the writer comments that 4 of the men "were of African descent." That book also mentions that 8 members were "Maine Indians." The 1st Maine Heavy Artillery was one of several heavy artillery regiments converted to infantry to meet Ulysses S. Grant's need for more troops during the Overland Campaign in the spring of 1864. It would be tempting to think that the 1st Maine Heavy Artillery, when it had to rebuild the regiment after its devastating losses at Spotsylvania and Petersburg (about two-thirds of the regiment killed, wounded, or captured), was happy to not look too closely at the racial ancestry of new recruits and enlisted black soldiers to fill their greatly diminished ranks. Or, perhaps we might think it simply became expedient to take whoever offered their services as the war went on and the numbers of available new recruits diminished. However, a look at the muster rolls of the regiment shows that all 4 of the soldiers listed "of African descent" were mustered into the 1st Maine Heavies several months before the regiment had left the defenses of Washington to take their place in the Overland Campaign.[28]

CHAPTER FOUR

Spring 1864: Mustering the Regiment and Action in the Red River Campaign

In January 1864, when the 2nd Maine Cavalry had been mustered into U.S. service, the Civil War was entering its third year. From early in the conflict, the Union had employed the "Anaconda Plan" to defeat the Confederacy: the opening and control of the Mississippi River by Union ships, the blockade of the Southeastern and Gulf coasts, and the army's campaign into the Confederate heartland—especially the capture of Richmond, the Rebel capital.

In the summer of 1863 the Mississippi had been opened with the capture of Vicksburg and the surrender of Port Hudson, the two Confederate strongholds on that river. This cut the eastern Confederacy from the west and disrupted, but did not halt, the flow of supplies eastward through Mexico and Texas. The Union blockade was having a crippling effect on the South's economy and the ability to ship out cotton and other products, and to import food, manufactured goods, and war materiel.

In the early phases of the war—in 1861 and 1862—the Union had suffered serious setbacks and a series of crushing defeats in battles such as First Bull Run, General McClellan's Peninsular Campaign and the Seven Days' Battles, 2nd Bull Run, and Fredericksburg. And 1862's Union victories such as Antietam and Shiloh had been gained at an appalling loss of life. That high price in lives, coupled with the string of Union defeats, saw many in the North questioning the wisdom of the Union's war efforts.

In 1863, President Lincoln's Emancipation Proclamation had created a new purpose for the Civil War—not only preserving the Union, but freeing the slaves. In July of 1863, the Union victory at Gettysburg became a symbol of the Union's ability to fight and decisively defeat a Confederate army under its much admired leader, Robert E. Lee, who, up until then, had seemed invincible. In the West, Union victories at Chattanooga and the Union's successful defense of their position at Knoxville further encouraged the people and armies of the North. The result of these actions was to create a mood where the push on to Richmond and the defeat of the Confederacy was seeming quite possible. It was with this history already written that the 2nd Maine Cavalry began its period of active service.

For the men of the 2nd Maine Cavalry, December 1863 and the months of January and February 1864 were spent at Camp Coburn, Augusta, Maine. While much of the time was spent engaged in training and drill, we also see that life in that camp was not without incident. There were, for example, 16 noncommissioned officers reduced to the ranks. The reasons range from their own requests for reduction to offenses such as "inefficiency," drunkenness on duty, disobedience, bringing liquor into the camp, absence without leave, and "conduct

Camp Coburn, Augusta, Maine (photograph taken from the cupola of the Maine state capitol; original was taken in two parts) (Maine Historical Preservation Commission).

prejudicial to good order and military discipline." In addition, "field officers" courts-martial were held within the regiment for 5 men.[1]

As with any military organization, the day's schedule was set in place by orders. General Order No. 1, issued in December 1863 gives the particulars:

> The following Camp Regulations will be strictly observed on this command until further orders.
>
> Reveille will be sounded at 6:30 A.M. when the National Colors will be hoisted by the Sergeant of the Guard.
>
> 1st Sergeants will promptly form their respective Companies on their respective company parades and call the Roll under the supervision of one of the Commissioned Officers of their Company. Sentinels will cease challenging and salute all officers according to rank. Immediately after Roll Call the Company grounds will be thoroughly policed, blankets shaken and aired then neatly folded over the bunks.
>
> Breakfast Call at 7 A.M. when the Co's will be formed for breakfast
>
> Sick Call at 7:15 A.M.
>
> Watering Call at 7:30 A.M. The horses will be watered under the supervision of at least one Commissioned Officer to each Company
>
> Orders for Orderly Sergeants at 8 A.M. when the 1st Sergeants will bring their Company morning Reports to the Adjutants Quarters and receive the orders of the day.
>
> First Call for Guard Mounting at 8:15 A.M. when the 1st Sergeants will ... turn out the men previously warned for Guard Duty, form them on the Company Parades, inspect them and see that their arms and equipment are in order, that they are in proper uniform, with their boots cleaned and in every respect in readiness for Guard Duty.
>
> Assembly of the Guard at 8:30 A.M. when the 1st Sergeants will march their details to the color line.

Drill Call at 10 A.M. when the Companies will be exercised in squad drill
Recall from drill at 11:30 A.M.
Dinner Call at 12 M.
Distributions at 2 P.M. when the R.Q.M. [regimental quartermaster] will issue forage to the Co. Q.M. Segts [company quartermaster sergeants].
Watering Call at 4 P.M.
Retreat at 5:30 P.M. The colors will be lowered, 1st Sergts will form their companies for Roll Call, Sentinels will cease saluting and challenge all who approach their beats.
Orders for Orderly Sergeants at 7 P.M. when the 1st Sergeants will report to the Adjutant for Report Books and Details.
Tattoo at 9:00 P.M. Co. Roll Call
To extinguish lights at 9:30 P.M. after which time lights will not be allowed in the barracks.
Enlisted men when on Stable Duty will wear their stable frocks.
No horses will be kept out of the stables except by express order of a Com'd Officer.
The Senior Officer in Camp, the Officer of the Day and Officer of the Guard are charged with the faithful execution of this order.[2]

That schedule was modified on January 12 by General Order No 3 as follows:

The following Calls will be observed in this Command till further orders.

Reveille	6:30 a.m.	Dinner	12	M
Assembly	6:35 "	Fatigue Call	1	p.m.
Sick Call	6:40 "	Drill Call	2	"
Stable Call	6:45 "	Recall	3:15	"
Recall	7:15 "	Water Call	3:20	"
Breakfast	7:25 "	Stable Call	4:15	"
Fatigue Call	7:50 "	Recall	4:45	"
Orderly Call	8 "	Retreat	6	"
Water Call	8:10 "	Orderly's Call	7	"
Guard Mounting	8:15 "	Tattoo	8:30	"
Officers Call	9 "	Taps	9	"
Drill	10 "			
Recall	11:15 "			

Sunday Inspection 10 A.M.[3]

And there were further details of camp life to be addressed. Special Order No. 42, issued on February 22, 1864, at Camp Coburn gives us examples of the matters dealt with by the commanding officer:

I. Company Commanders will cause their commands to fall in at "Stable Call" morning and evening each day and march to the Stable under the command of a Commissioned Officer and there remain until the horses are all fed and thoroughly groomed and the Recall sounded, when they will re-form and march back to their quarters.

II. Hereafter no passes will be granted either to Commissioned Officers or Enlisted men unless at Morning Inspection the Stables are found in good condition and the horses well cleaned.

III. All halters in the hands of Company Commanders not receipted for will be returned immediately to the Quartermaster.

IV. On going to and from water no man will be allowed to take more than two horses at a time. Companies will keep well closed up and not march faster than a trot.

by order of Col E.W. Woodman comd'g[4]

The importance given to the care and condition of the regiment's horses is also reflected in orders establishing inquiries into the disabling of horses. This, from January 3, is an example: Three officers were named to "constitute a Board of Survey to judge upon the disabling of a horse in the hands of Lieut. J F Milliken, R.Q.M. [regimental quartermaster] 2nd Cav Me Vols while being led to 'watering' this day."[5]

And, there were issues regarding relations with the civilian population of Augusta. On March 22, Major A. B. Spurling, Captain J. H. Roberts, Company M, and Lieutenant William H. Moody, Company L, were named as a "Board of Survey" and instructed "to examine into and judge upon certain alleged damage to property owned by citizens of Augusta Me incident to encampment of 2nd Cav Me Vols on their lands and its use for drill ground, and watering horses etc."[6]

There was also at least one incident that apparently required a special investigation. On March 9 a board of inquiry of 3 officers was established "to investigate the circumstances attending the sickness and death of Sergeant John P Jordan, Co G, 2nd Cav Me Vols." The results of that inquiry were not found in the regiment's records.[7]

During its time at Camp Coburn the regiment was also issued weapons. From various orders found in the regimental books, we learn that the 2nd Maine Cavalry was armed (in addition to cavalry sabers) with the Burnside carbine and Remington revolvers. The Burnside carbine, as the name implies, was designed and patented by Ambrose E. Burnside and was the third most used carbine of the Union cavalry, following the Sharps and Spencer carbines. Ambrose Burnside was an 1843 West Point graduate and had been a lieutenant in the U.S. Army. He resigned his commission in 1853 to begin the design work and production of the carbine. (He rejoined the military at the outbreak of the Civil War and rose to the rank of major general in the Union Army.) The obvious difficulty of reloading a muzzle loading rifle from horseback prompted the use of these shorter barreled, breech loading weapons by the cavalry. This breech loading capability also greatly increased the rate of fire over a muzzle loader, since a spent cartridge could be quickly ejected and another put in place. The Burnside was a .54-caliber carbine and used a conical-shaped metal cartridge, unique to this weapon, which was also invented by Burnside.[8]

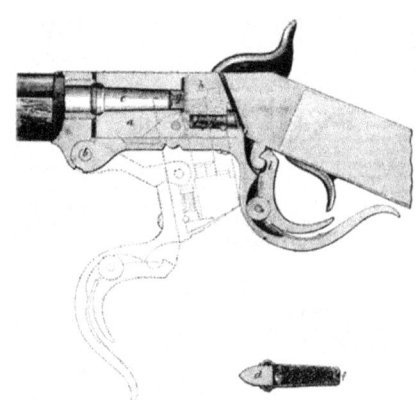

The Burnside carbine's loading mechanism and tapered cartridge (*Scientific American*, December 20, 1862).

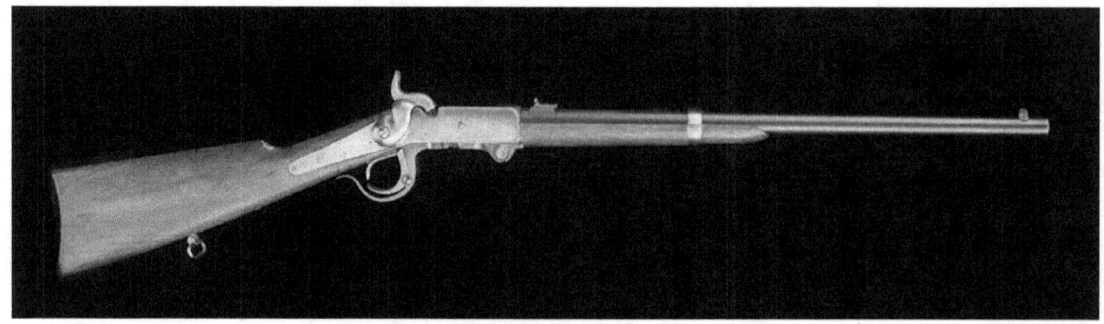

The Burnside carbine (Armed Forces History, National Museum of American History, Smithsonian Institution).

The Remington revolver, most likely the .44-caliber model 1858 or its 1861 version, was a standard issue for the Union army. The time required to load each chamber of the cylinder with powder and ball, and to attach the very small percussion cap to the nipple for each chamber, made it difficult to load quickly. It was, therefore, typically used as a secondary weapon for close fighting when its ability to fire 6 rounds quickly would be most effective. To aid in the ability to reload and fire, some soldiers would carry a second, pre-loaded cylinder, complete with percussion caps, which could be quickly inserted to replace the empty cylinder.[9]

In mid–March of that year the companies of the regiment began to leave Augusta and head for the South. Special Order No. 52 from March 18 shows the means by which one company of the regiment began its journey: "Capt S W Clarke, Comd'g Co E, 2nd Cav Me Vols will forthwith proceed with his Command by rail to Portland and there embark on Ship Tamerlane. He will take with his Command one hundred of the Government horses in his hands." There were also orders given regarding the care of the horses while on the ship.[10] From Portland, the regiment would be taken by transport ships to New Orleans. The entire regiment did not travel together; the first companies left Portland on or about March 16 and the last companies did not leave until the first week of April.[11]

The reports from the various companies make it clear that many of their voyages were not pleasant. This from Company B: "March 19—Went on the U.S. transports *Continental* and *Frank Boult* and sailed from Portland. The voyage was very stormy and 17 horses died." Other companies, although sailing from Portland at different dates, also reported a stormy trip and the loss of horses. The voyage was difficult enough that the *New York Times*, after announcing the departure of the transports *Continental* and *Frank Boult* on April 19, "each taking a portion of the Second Maine Cavalry," reported on April 1, "The Ship Frank Boult Missing, Laden with Cavalrymen and Horses." (The *Frank Boult* arrived in New Orleans on April 17.) It appears that overall, of the 1131 horses sent with the regiment, 172 died on the journey. In a letter to Adjutant General Hodsdon, Colonel Woodman gives the details of arrival of the various transports and states, "Lost on the passage two soldiers." According to the regimental roster, however, three men of the 2nd Maine Cavalry died during the voyage and never made it to the Deep South: Company A's Private Michael Stewart, an 18 year old from Hodgdon, Maine; Company D's 20 year old Private Augustus Nash from Calais, Maine; and Company F's Private John Sheldon, 38 years old, a married man from Wiscasset, Maine.[12]

New Orleans had become an important entry point for Union troops arriving by ship for duty in Southern and Central Louisiana. Before the Civil War, the city was a major shipping center for the Deep South with cotton and tobacco exported from its docks, while imports from the North as well as Europe were unloaded there. Also an important banking center with an 1860 population of 160,000, New Orleans was the largest city of the Confederacy. At the start of the Civil War, it was seen as important to take this valuable port city and naval base from the Confederacy as soon as possible. In the early spring of 1862, on April 16, a Union fleet under Captain David Farragut had begun operations against the Confederate positions on the Lower Mississippi River. The first obstacles to be encountered were Forts St. Philip and Jackson at the mouth of the Mississippi.

The difficult decisions in those days as the Union fleet began to move into the lower Mississippi are reflected in letters to and from General Robert E. Lee. Well before his appointment to lead the Army of Northern Virginia, in November 1861 Lee had been named as commander of the Confederate "Department of South Carolina, Georgia, and Florida." In that capacity he worked to develop coastal defenses. In March 1862, he was called to Richmond to serve as military adviser to President Jefferson Davis.[13]

On April 22, 1862, General Lee wrote to General Samuel Jones, the Confederate commander at Mobile: "It is represented by General Lovell [Major General Mansfield Lovell, in command of New Orleans] that he needs heavy guns for the defenses of the city of New Orleans. He states that but three of those removed from Pensacola were sent him, while fourteen 10-inch columbiads were kept at Mobile. I desire to know if you cannot spare him some of those in your command, and, if so, request that you will cause them to be forwarded to New Orleans without delay ... please send such as are not positively necessary for the defense of your department."[14]

On the same day, April 22, General Lovell wrote his own letter from New Orleans to General Jones: "Bombardment still goes on day and night; casualties few, but forts much cut up. Can you send two 10-in columbiads in haste, or spare any powder?"[15] And again on April 22, General Lovell received the following from Confederate Assistant Adjutant General W. H. Taylor. After restating General Lee's orders for heavy guns to be sent from Mobile, he goes on to say: "As regards the small-arms you desire, he [General Lee] regrets there are none on hand for issue. The demand is great from all sides and the supply inadequate. There are some afloat [in transit], however, and it is hoped they will soon arrive, when, as far as practicable, your wants in this respect will be supplied."[16]

On April 24, Farragut's fleet had fought its way up the Mississippi River past forts St. Philip and Jackson, just below New Orleans. With a force of some 15,000 Union troops under General Benjamin Butler approaching New Orleans by land, the Confederate troops at Forts St. Phillip and Jackson, who had been bombarded by Farragut's fleet, learned that General Lovell had withdrawn his 4,000 man force from New Orleans. Now on their own, and with any means of escape blocked by Butler's troops, the Confederate garrisons at those forts essentially mutinied and their commanders surrendered the forts on April 28.

Having observed the situation, General Lovell wrote to General Earl Van Dorn, in command of the Confederacy's Trans-Mississippi Department, "Just returned from New Orleans. The men at forts refused to hold out longer and Duncan [Brigadier General Johnson Kelly Duncan] had to surrender. The enemy will therefore occupy the city under his [the Union forces'] guns. All seems quiet and orderly, and I think there will be no trouble for citizens and families."[17]

With no military defenses left, Confederate President Jefferson Davis wrote to the mayor of New Orleans on April 28: "I deeply sympathize with your situation, and recognize with pride the patriotism of the citizens of New Orleans.... My prayers are with you. There is no personal sacrifice I would not willingly make for your defense."[18] The civilian authorities surrendered New Orleans on April 29, and Union forces were able to occupy the city without a fight.

In 1864, at the time of the 2nd Maine Cavalry's arrival, New Orleans was the headquarters for the Union's Department of the Gulf, commanded by Major General Nathanial Banks, who was one of the "political generals" and had been a governor of Massachusetts and speaker of the U.S. House of Representatives. General Banks had replaced the controversial General Benjamin Butler in December 1862.

Upon their arrival at New Orleans, the first elements of the 2nd Maine Cavalry were presented with the following order from General Banks:

HQ, Dept of the Gulf April 3, 1864

The Second Maine Cavalry, now arriving from the North, will be reported to the office of the chief of cavalry, to be assigned quarters and equipped for the field, without delay.

Richd. B. Irwin Assistant Adjutant-General[19]

On April 16, the commanding officer for the defense of New Orleans, Major General Joseph J. Reynolds, ordered "all the available portion" of the 2nd Maine Cavalry to proceed at once to the front. "Squadrons A and D, and about half of G, being the only part of the regiment which had arrived, under command of Major Miller, embarked immediately for Alexandria [Louisiana], on the Red River, where they arrived on the morning of the 21st [of April]." This detachment, according to later reports by Colonel Woodman, was made up of either 185 or 196 enlisted men (the number changed from one report to another) and 181 horses. Other than Major Miller, the commanders of the 3 companies involved, Captain Twitchell of Company A, Captain John Lincoln of Company D, and Captain Samuel Knowles of Company G, are mentioned in Colonel Woodman's reports as being part of the detachment.[20]

This part of the 2nd Maine Cavalry was to take part in the last engagements of General Banks' disastrous Red River Campaign in Louisiana. That campaign had begun in early March, well before the arrival of the 2nd Maine Cavalry, and was intended to engage the Confederate Army under General Richard Taylor, defeat them and capture Shreveport, Louisiana. It would also, it was hoped, stop the flow of supplies from Texas via the Red River to the Confederacy and to Confederate military forces in the East. This flow of supplies was of much less importance than in earlier years, for with the capture of Vicksburg and Port Hudson in the summer of 1863 and Union control of the Mississippi, the supplies moving eastward across the river had been considerably reduced. But, Shreveport was of symbolic importance as the Confederate capital of Louisiana, and that city was still being well supplied through Texas. In addition, it was the main base for the Confederate Navy's river fleet. Add to this its status as the headquarters for the military District of Trans-Mississippi and the fact that General Taylor's army at Shreveport had not been seriously opposed by Union forces, and those conditions alone might have been sufficient reasons for the campaign. However, the Union forces also hoped to confiscate thou-

Gen. Nathaniel Banks (National Archives).

sands of bales of cotton from the plantations in the area to supply the always eager cotton mills of the Northeastern U.S.[21]

The idea for the expedition had not come from General Banks, who in fact did not favor such an expedition, but rather from General Henry Halleck, who as early as 1862 had recommended a Union advance along that route. Halleck had been in command of the Department of Missouri and the Department of the Mississippi in 1861 and 1862, commander in chief of the Union forces from July 1862 to March 1864, and then became President Lincoln's chief of staff until the end of the war. Halleck was known for giving orders for operations that were so vague that, while he could claim the credit for any success achieved, the details of the operation, and any blame for failure, would fall on those asked to carry out the orders. Along with General Banks, Generals Grant and Sherman had also expressed some opposition to Halleck's proposed Red River expedition.[22]

On the other hand, Union Admiral David Porter had wanted to take a part of his Mississippi squadron up the Red River on his own, back in late 1863, hoping to capture large amounts of Confederate cotton and gain the prize money for doing so. It is doubtful, however, that Porter welcomed the addition of the army's participation in a campaign up that river. Reports from Confederate intelligence show that they were well aware of Porter's proposed plans in 1863 and the potential lure to the Union forces of the large quantities of cotton at Shreveport.[23]

The Confederate General Richard Taylor, whose army was to oppose Banks' expedition, was the son of U.S. President Zachary Taylor and the brother of Confederate President Jefferson Davis' first wife, Sarah Knox Taylor, who had died in 1836. Taylor was a graduate of Yale University and, at the start of the Civil War had been appointed colonel of the 9th Louisiana Infantry. Promoted to brigadier general in October of 1861, he commanded a Louisiana brigade under Stonewall Jackson during the Valley Campaign and the Seven Days' Battles. By the time of the Red River Campaign, he had been promoted to major general (July 1862) and was in command of the District of Western Louisiana.[24]

In early 1864, General Banks, with apparently some considerable reluctance, agreed to Halleck's proposed expedition and began to communicate with the Union commanders with whom he might cooperate. The plan General Banks developed for the campaign involved himself in command of about 20,000 troops, coming north from New Orleans to Alexandria, Louisiana, and then proceeding up the Red River Valley to capture Shreveport, Louisiana. Another force of some 15,000 Union troops, under

Admiral David Porter (National Archives).

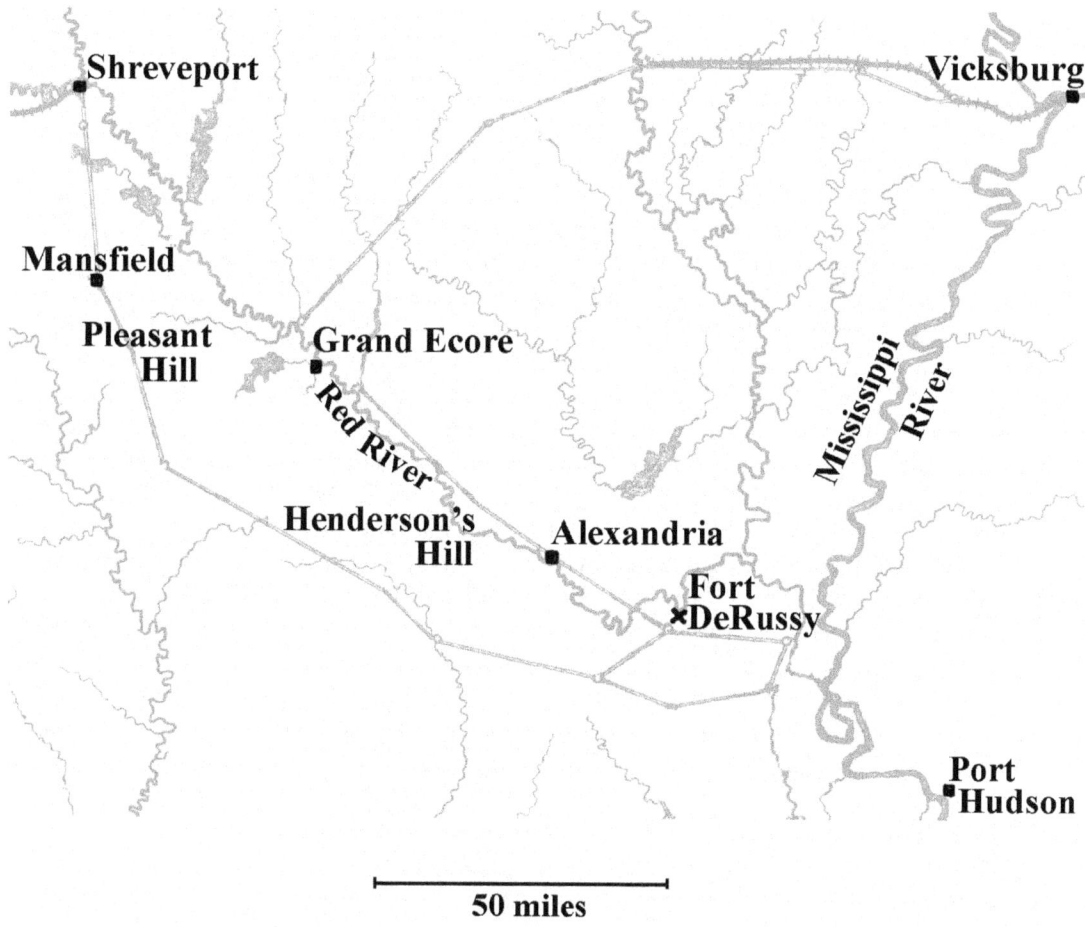

Overview of the Red River Campaign (adapted from map cw0063000, Library of Congress).

Brigadier General Andrew Jackson Smith, were sent south from Major General William T. Sherman's force at Vicksburg, Mississippi, to join Banks' expedition at Alexandria. An additional 7,000 Union troops from Arkansas, commanded by Major General Frederick Steele, were to join these forces at Shreveport. The land forces coming up the Red River Valley were to be supported by Rear Admiral David Porter's Union gunboats and supply boats on the Red River.

General Banks' force of 35,000 (including those from General Sherman's command) was opposed by General Taylor, whose Confederate force never totaled more than 18,500, and was usually considerably less. In spite of his numerical advantages, General Banks' Red River Campaign did not go well.

The earliest phases of the operation, however, seemed encouraging to the Union commanders and their troops. Fort de Russy, whose heavy guns would have posed a problem for Porter's gunboats, was easily captured by Gen. Banks' men on March 14. The Confederates, seeing that their only serious blockade on the lower Red River was gone, abandoned Alexandria, thus leaving central and southern Louisiana under tentative Union control, or at least not under Confederate control. The river fleet, now free from the potential threat of Fort de Russy, advanced up the Red River. When General Banks arrived at Alexandria on March

24, he was surprised, if not shocked, to see that the men of Porter's fleet were very busily loading cotton onto boats and barges of every description, seizing that lucrative prize of war. The soldiers of Banks' army could only look on while the navy commandeered wagons and sent parties several miles from the river to gather up as much cotton as possible from any source they could find.[25]

A few days before General Banks and the main body of his force arrived at Alexandria, the Confederates had been dealt an embarrassing defeat by an advance Union reconnaissance force under General Joseph Mower. On March 21, Mower's men, advancing upriver from Alexandria, surrounded a Rebel camp at Henderson's Hill and captured 250 of the surprised Confederates—a substantial part of General Taylor's available cavalry—as well as a battery of 4 guns.

During the last week of March and the first week of April 1864, cavalry skirmishes took place as the Union army moved out of Alexandria and continued its advance toward Shreveport. On April 8, however, the Union advance was halted. The battle of Mansfield, Louisiana, resulted in General Banks' force retreating to Pleasant Hill after sustaining approximately 2,400 casualties to the Confederates' losses of around 1,000.

The next day, April 9, Confederate General Taylor attacked the Union forces at Pleasant Hill. The result was, in theory, a Union victory, with Taylor's attacks repulsed and the Confederate forces driven from the field. The Union lost about 1,000 men killed or wounded with 375 missing or captured. Although Confederate losses at Pleasant Hill were slightly higher, two successive days of heavy losses left the Union forces in disarray and their commander confused and discouraged. The following day, General Banks abandoned his plan to capture Shreveport and ordered a retreat to Grand Ecore and from there back to Alexandria.[26]

Admiral Porter and the navy faced their own problems during the campaign. The fleet of some half dozen gunboats and two dozen supply ships had struggled to make their way upstream with a narrow and twisting river full of stumps and snags and the occasional Confederate mines hindering progress. Various ships ran aground and had to be pulled to safety, and yet the navy made further progress toward Shreveport than did Banks' land force—progress such that, with the news of Banks' defeat and retreat, the navy found itself in danger of being cut off from rejoining the Union forces.[27]

This was not the first time that a flotilla under Admiral Porter had found itself in great peril. During the attempts to take Vicksburg in early 1863, Porter brought a navy contingent up the Yazoo River where it became trapped in a narrow channel, the Confederates "having dropped trees in front of it and sunk a coal barge behind him to prevent withdrawal." General Sherman was able to bring troops to save Porter's boats and men before Porter had carried out his plan to blow the boats up so that they would not be captured by the Rebels.[28]

When the retreat of General Banks' Red River troops began and the navy needed to make its own withdrawal downstream, Porter's thoughts must have harkened back to the Yazoo. His flotilla's ships were faced with particularly low water in the Red River, and at times the Confederates on the shore peppered the fleet with musket fire and artillery shot. Union army troops on the transports assigned to help protect the fleet had mounted their own artillery on some supply ships and were able to return the Confederate fire. Some Union ships, however, were lost. When the most powerful of Admiral Porter's ironclad gunboats, the *Eastport*, became firmly lodged on rocks and logs, and with Confederate sharpshooters firing from the banks, Porter had the ship blown up to prevent its falling into Rebel hands. The greatest single tragedy occurred when Confederate artillery shot burst the boiler of the transport *Champion No. 3*. The scalding steam and water killed all but 3 of 175 men, women, and children—slaves who had been freed from plantations along the river and who were being transported by the Union navy.[29]

Confederate General Taylor's report on this disaster stated, "A shot striking the boiler of the transport exploded it.... The loss of life on the transport was fearful."[30]

With these losses, the dead and wounded among the sailors and soldiers on other boats, and serious damage to many of the vessels, the flotilla made its way to join General Banks' force at Alexandria. There, Porter was faced with another serious problem—the river was now so low that only a bit more than 3 feet of water was flowing through the shallowest part of the river, while about 7 feet would be needed to bring his 10 heaviest and most important ships safely downstream. And so, there would be a period of waiting. General Banks did not wish to leave the fleet stranded, which would mean its destruction to avoid capture, and Admiral Porter could not move his fleet down the river. At this point Lt. Colonel Joseph Bailey convinced Porter that, by building temporary dams to raise the water level, the fleet could escape. Lt. Col. Bailey had studied civil engineering and while working in the lumbering industry had seen and used such dams to help move logs down shallow rivers. Porter was initially skeptical of such a plan, and in a play on words, is reported to have said that "if damning would get the fleet off, he would have been afloat long before." But by the end of April, Porter was in no position to disregard any plausible plan for saving his fleet. Construction of the dams was begun.[31]

The portion of the 2nd Maine Cavalry that had been sent to the Red River (most of Companies A and D, and about half of G, about 190 men) were to join General Banks' force at Alexandria. The troopers arrived on April 21 and were ordered to remain there to await

Union gunboat USS *Eastport* (from the Collection of the Public Library of Cincinnati and Hamilton County).

the arrival of Banks' retreating forces, the leading elements of which arrived on April 25, with the remainder following the next day. Of their journey from New Orleans up the Red River to Alexandria, Sgt. F.W. Pearce of the 2nd Maine Cavalry's Company A, wrote in a letter to his brother:

> I must tell you now of my voiage [sic] up the Mississippi River Capt J F Twitchell and Lieut [Warren] Mansur left New Orleans last Monday with fifty five men. On the next day (Tuesday) I started after them with sixteen men. Lieut [Silas] Barker remaines [sic] at New Orleans with the rest of the Company. We should have taken the whole Company if horses could have been furnished us. While going up the Mississippi we enjoyed ourselves at looking at the beautiful plantations ... we passed through a gloomy looking country made more so by the thoughts of being fired into by the Rebels. But it so happened that we were ... fired into. A boat loaded with Cavalry came up a little behind us and were fired into by the Rebs killing three and wounding sixteen. We arrived at this place [Alexandria] at about twelve oclock last night [April 20]. In the morning we came ashore....
>
> Gen Banks has been having a big fight. gess [sic] he didn't get much the better of it. He is now falling back with his army. The water is so very low that supplies cannot be taken up. He will probably make this his headquarters, another battle is expected soon.[32]

As General Banks' retreating Union troops withdrew toward Alexandria, they left in their wake a line of burned plantations and brought with them a substantial number of slaves who had followed the blue-clad force. At Alexandria, the 2nd Maine Cavalry contingent became a part of the 19th Corps' Cavalry Division and was assigned to the Third Cavalry Brigade under Lt. Col. John Crebs (which also included the 1st Louisiana Cavalry and the 87th Illinois Mounted Infantry). In the Maine men's first action against the Confederates, the Third Brigade—a force of about 500 men—was sent south from Alexandria on May 2, and after proceeding about 10 miles, engaged a "considerable picket force of the enemy." The Confederates were driven to Wilson's Landing, where Lt. Col. Crebs reported finding an enemy force estimated at 500 to 1,500. After skirmishing with this force, "the rebels opened upon him with one piece of artillery," and Col. Crebs, "deeming that no advantage would result from an attack ... held his ground for a while, and then slowly retired." During this action, Col. Crebs learned from "both blacks and whites ... that a considerable rebel cavalry force was stationed at Cheneyville, with some artillery."[33]

While camped at Alexandria, the Federal troops still waited for Admiral Porter to extricate his gunboats from the Red River. Lt. Col. Bailey's dams were finally constructed, and on May 8, the first group of gunboats floated, on the raised water level, through a gap in the dam and on to relative safety. When, on May 13, the entire remnant of Porter's fleet had negotiated the dams, the Union troops began the next phase of their retreat along the Red River to Simmesport and the Mississippi. The orders specifying the order of march when leaving Alexandria stated that two brigades of cavalry, including the 2nd Maine in the 3rd Brigade, would constitute the advance guard.[34]

Later, in November of 1864, Admiral Porter had dinner with President Lincoln's secretary, John Hay, and Hay records the following in his diary, which may shed some light on the importance of the Confederate cotton to the mission, and the reason that the fleet had persisted in continuing farther up the Red River: "During dinner Porter talked in very indecent terms of abuse of Banks, saying that the fleet got ahead of the army & stole the cotton which the army intended to steal. He spoke of some articles which had appeared in the papers criticizing his action & said he could stand the criticism as long as he had his pockets full of prize money."[35]

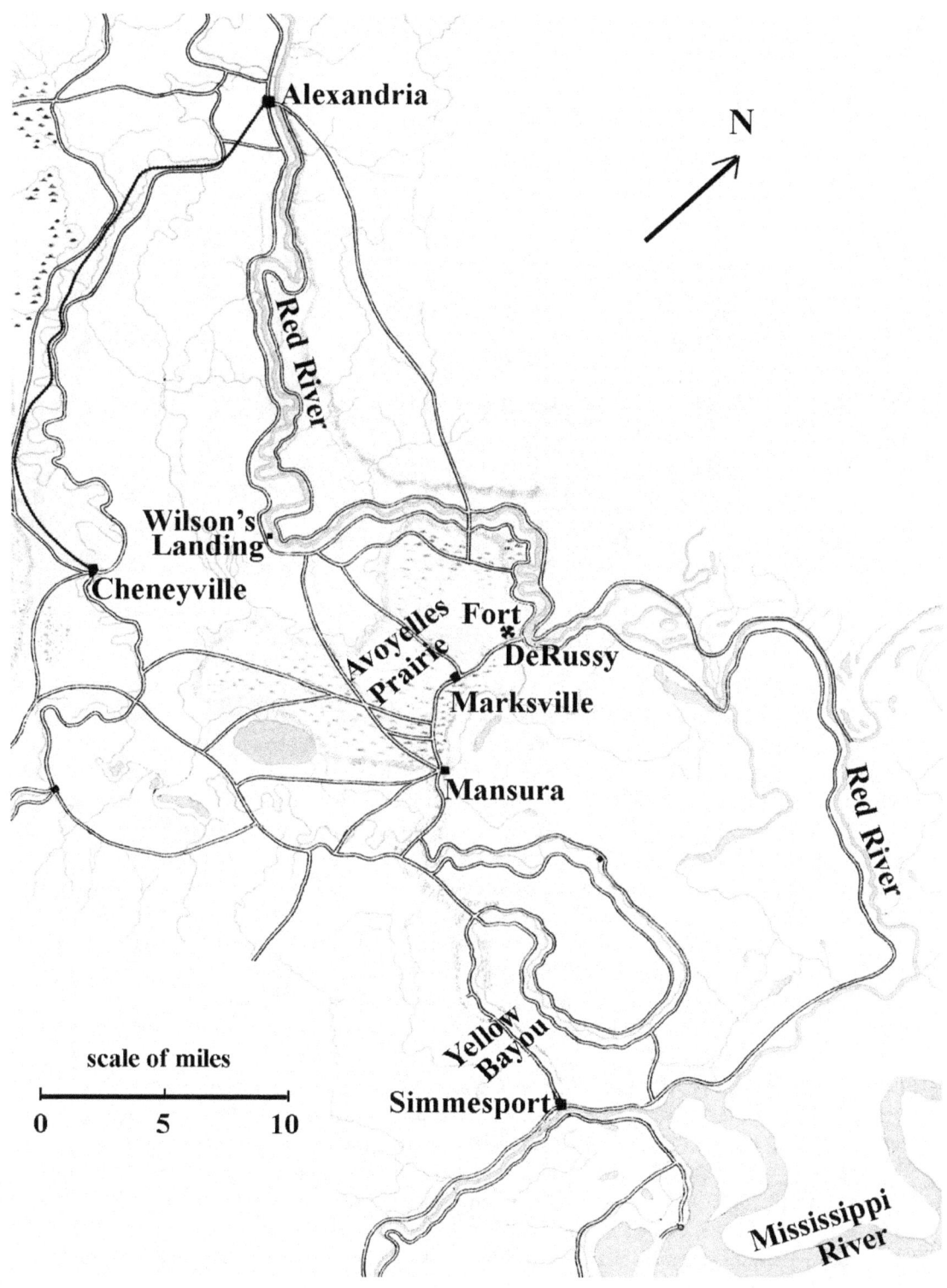

The Red River from Alexandria to Simmesport (adapted from plate LII; *Official Atlas*).

Drawing showing a part of Admiral Porter's fleet making its way through the breach in Lt. Col. Bailey's dam (U.S. Army Military History Institute).

Although they had left a note to a town official in Alexandria promising that a cavalry unit would safeguard the town, it seems clear that many of Banks' soldiers, including some of those same cavalry troopers who were meant to protect the town, did start many fires before departing. This is in spite of specific orders: "When the army commences its movements the chief of cavalry will order a sufficient number of men to patrol the town of Alexandria to prevent any building being set fire to or any other act that can advertise the movement to the enemy." The order not to start fires was not issued to prevent damage to the town, but as a measure to avoid alerting the Confederates that the Union troops were leaving. It appears that members of General Banks' staff and provost guard did attempt to fight the fires, but the blazes were many, fanned by wind, and were beyond control. Confederate General Richard Taylor's report said, "The enemy left Alexandria after midday to-day, burning the place.... Heavy fighting all day with gun-boats and troops.... We have experienced some loss, but will continue to fight them to the bank of the Mississippi, and beyond, if possible."[36]

During its time with the Red River Campaign, the 2nd Maine Cavalry was involved, according to the *Maine Adjutant General's Report,* in skirmishing and engagements at Cheneyville Crossroads, Marksville, Avoyelles Prairie, and Yellow Bayou. The latter three engagements will be described below, but the nature of the engagement at Cheneyville Crossroads is not reported. It may well refer to the May 2 action by the Third Brigade, during which Lt. Col. Crebs learned of a substantial Rebel force at Cheneyville.[37]

By the time General Banks began his move back toward Simmesport, Confederate General Taylor's superior, General Kirby Smith, ordered much of Taylor's force away toward Arkansas and left Taylor with perhaps about 6,000 men to oppose Banks' army. General Taylor had very much opposed that decision and the loss of perhaps half his force—3 infantry divisions, including Walker's division ("Walker's Greyhounds"), which had been critical to the Confederate success at Mansfield. On April 24 Taylor wrote that the trip he had made to Shreveport, where he learned of Kirby Smith's plans to remove the infantry divisions, "and the loss of Walker's division have assuredly saved Banks' army from utter destruction."[38]

The Confederate commander faced another problem—the lack of ammunition. On May 4, he wrote to Headquarters, District of West Louisiana, "The want of artillery horses presses heavily, and ammunition for Enfield rifles and artillery is running very short." On May 6, Taylor described the damage and losses his men had inflicted on the Union forces: "The enemy has been driven 75 miles and fought over every mile of the distance both on land and water. We have destroyed or captured 1 heavy iron-clad, 2 wooden gun-boats, and 7 transports, and have killed, wounded, or captured at least 2,000 of the enemy." He then repeated, "All I ask to complete the work is a supply of horses for artillery and ammunition for Enfield rifles and 3-inch and 12-pounder guns."[39]

As General Banks' army was leaving Alexandria, Taylor reported on May 14, "My troops are so disposed as to harass the enemy in rear and flank and attack the boats from both banks of the river.... I have not the pretension to attempt to fight a general battle with my little force against four times their number ... but I hope to force the enemy to destroy large amounts of property, and harass and worry him until he reaches the Mississippi." This reduced Confederate force would still present what problems it could for the retreating Union troops.[40]

Realizing he could not stop the Union retreat or engage the Federals in a formal battle, Confederate General Taylor's cavalry nevertheless skirmished with the lead elements of Banks' column and harassed its rear.[41] On May 10, Taylor wrote, "Every day the enemy is attacked and driven on some road and kept continually harassed by feints, driving in pickets, Etc. Thus he is expecting an assault at every moment, and is uncertain of the direction whence it may come.... On several occasions we have forced the enemy from strong positions by sending drummers to beat calls, lighting camp-fires, blowing bugles, and rolling empty wagons over fence rails.... From present appearance the end is drawing near.... His [Banks'] troops are disheartened, sullen, and disinclined to fight."[42] On May 7, General Taylor had reported, "Forage and subsistence of every kind have been removed beyond the enemy's reach. Rigid orders are given to destroy anything useful that can fall into his hands. We will play the game the Russians played in the retreat from Moscow."[43] And, in his report of May 10, Taylor wrote, "He [Banks] is short of provisions and almost entirely without forage. All captured horses are like scarecrows and show want of forage."[44]

On May 15, General Taylor's force halted the Union troops for a time as they crossed the Choctaw Bayou Swamp and made their way onto the Avoyelles Prairie beyond. The reports for the Union's cavalry division for this time period indicate that on May 15, "The rebels were posted at the entrance to Avoyelles Prairie with ten pieces of artillery, but were driven slowly back during the day by the 1st and 3rd Brigades [of cavalry, which included the 2nd Maine] through the village of Marksville, when they opened a heavy artillery fire on the [Union] advance, checking it."[45] General Taylor's report on this day's action states, "The fighting was well sustained. [Our forces] beat back several times the head of his column as he attempted to debouche on the high ground of the Marksville Prairie from the Choctaw Swamp. Heavy losses were inflicted on the enemy, Bagby skillfully masking his artillery and using it at short range."[46]

On the following day, May 16, "The 1st and 3rd [Cavalry] Brigades advanced cautiously, skirmishing with the enemy, who were found in line of battle near the village of Mansura."

The initial phase of this battle involved an artillery duel of about 4 hours, with few casualties on either side—about half of the Confederate's 32 artillery pieces consisting of guns captured from the Union forces at the Battle of Mansfield in early April, adding, in this case, injury to insult. As General Taylor reported, "The broad, open prairie, smooth as a billiard table, afforded an admirable field for artillery practice, and most of our guns were 3-inch rifle and 10-pounder Parrotts captured from the enemy." Then, with Union infantry massing for an attack on the Rebel flank, the Confederates were soon forced to retire. Again, from General Taylor's report, we read that as the Union infantry began to demonstrate on his left, "This rendered our position dangerous, as the enemy had probably 16,000 men on the field, and perhaps more. Our men withdrew with the steadiness of veterans on parade."[47]

On May 17, the cavalry's "1st and 3rd Brigades having arrived at Simmesport, the 4th and 5th [brigades] encamped near Yellow Bayou." The fighting had not ended, however, and on May 18 at Yellow Bayou, the last engagement of the Red River Campaign took place, an engagement in which the 2nd Maine Cavalry was involved. With General Taylor's Rebel troops continuing to make sporadic attacks at the rear of the Union column, a force of approximately 5,000 Federals under General Joseph Mower was sent to confront these Confederates. The Union force, therefore, recrossed the Yellow Bayou and attacked around 4,500 Confederates, primarily cavalry under General John Wharton. Fighting in thickets and among dead trees which caught fire, the battle saw the opposing lines pushed back in turn, but with strong support from Confederate artillery, the Union troops were unable to dislodge the Rebels. The Federal troops then withdrew back to Simmesport. The battle had cost the Confederates a reported 608 killed, wounded or missing, while Union losses were reported at 350. One of those wounded on May 18 was Sgt. Wallace DeBeque of Company A, 2nd Maine Cavalry. The Confederate's own estimate of their losses, according to General Taylor, were, "500, of which 30 were killed, 50 severely wounded, and some hundred prisoners taken.... The remaining wounds are of a trifling character."[48]

Of that action on May 18, General Taylor reported, "Yesterday a very severe action occurred near Yellow Bayou.... We drove the enemy handsomely on our right, killing all the horses and most of the gunners of a battery, and forcing the enemy to abandon it.... We held the field," and the enemy fell back. Taylor added, "The campaign will probably close to-day at Simsport [sic], its point of departure, after nearly seventy days of uninterrupted fighting."[49]

Meanwhile, General Banks was moving the rest of his force across the Atchafalaya River, and by May 20, all of the Union forces had reached the safety of the eastern bank of the river. The Red River Campaign was over.

In his report of May 18, General Taylor, although having driven the Federal Army back to the Mississippi, was again expressing his frustration and wrote, "Nothing but the withdrawal of Walker's division from me has prevented the capture of Banks' army and the destruction of Porter's fleet. I feel bitterly about this, because my army has been robbed of the just measure of its glory and the country of the most brilliant and complete success of the war."[50]

On May 20, the Union cavalry command proceeded toward Morganza, on the Mississippi River, where it arrived on the 21st. On June 2, Major Miller's troopers rejoined the rest of the 2nd Maine Cavalry, "having performed six weeks of honorable and active service with the loss of ten or twelve wounded."[51]

Not only was the Red River Campaign now over, but so was General Banks' career as a leader of troops in the field. When Banks arrived back in Simmesport, he was met by his new commanding officer, Major General Edward Canby, who on May 7 was given command of the Military Division of West Mississippi, with complete authority over General Banks and the Department of the Gulf. General Banks tried to regain his former authority, even traveling to Washington, D.C., to press his claims, but was not successful. Until the fall of 1864, Banks remained behind a desk in New Orleans, then went to Washington "on leave" until the end of the war.[52]

General Canby had graduated from West Point in 1839 (30th out of 31 in that class) and received two brevet promotions for his service during the Seminole and Mexican Wars. He remained as the Union commander for the Division of West Mississippi for the duration of the Civil War.[53]

At the end of the Red River Campaign, General Richard Taylor faced a very different future from that given to General Banks. Although he had wanted to resign in response to the ongoing friction between himself and General Kirby Smith, he was in fact promoted to lieutenant general on May 16, with the promotion to be backdated to April 8—his victory at Mansfield.[54]

Gen. Edward Canby (Library of Congress).

Upon his arrival at New Orleans, Colonel Woodman was not pleased to find part of his regiment had been ordered to join General Banks' forces. On April 23 he reported to Maine Adjutant General Hodsdon that "Maj Miller was ordered up to Red River and unwisely dismounted the soldiers of one Co to mount soldiers of another." He added, "I think the Maj was not required to go up to Red River. The order was for all 'that part of the 2 M Cavalry *fit for duty*.' There was not in my opinion a single horse *fit for duty*. No horse is fit for duty immediately on his arrival even if in good flesh. I very much regret that I did not arrive three days sooner & prevent the departure of those horses and men as I think I could on explaining to the Genl."[55]

From references to the troops under Major Miller being at the Red River, the timing of the activities of some of the rest of the 2nd Maine Cavalry can be determined. And it seems that during May of 1864 other parts of the 2nd Maine Cavalry were active indeed. Four companies, under Major Spurling, were sent to Brashear City, Louisiana. Reports disagree as to exactly which companies: the *Maine Adjutant General's Report* lists "Squadrons" (Companies) C, F, I, and M being posted to Brashear City, while another account (Roberts' *Story of General Andrew Spurling*) lists Companies C, F, L, and M. Individual reports from Companies I and L are not recorded, and so it is unclear which of those two companies was with Major Spurling. At any rate, while this detachment was at Brashear City, it was reported that Confederate Cavalry was "quite active across the river and greatly annoyed the colored

This drawing shows the method of unloading men and horses from transports. Notice the horse already unloaded is swimming behind the boat at center mid-distance (*Harper's Weekly*, May 25, 1861).

regiment stationed there." Major Spurling, apparently feeling that he could help alleviate that situation, "requested permission of Col. Harris, the commander [at Brashear City], to fight the rebels in his own way, which was given him, and he then scoured the country, ambuscading them and fighting when necessary, soon capturing a large number and ridding that locality of all guerrillas and giving his four companies a good commencement in testing their fighting qualities."[56]

Later in May, Major Spurling and some of his men had another encounter with Confederates, this time in the person of local women as well as Rebel soldiers. Apparently some "unreconstructed rebel women" had been rude to the men of the 2nd Maine Cavalry and were told by Major Spurling, "Show that you are ladies in both deportment and speech and you will always find the men of the Second Maine Cavalry gentlemen." In another situation, Major Spurling was told that a certain Mrs. Knight was often being visited by Confederate soldiers. Again getting permission from Colonel Harris, Spurling and 3 men went to Mrs. Knight's home and found that Confederates had apparently been there, but had left. Spurling and his men then "withdrew and entered a hedge near the house, and lying down there remained on watch all night. In the morning four men rode up to the house and were told by the women the direction the Yankees had taken. They rode furiously toward the hedge only to be met by the fire of the four men, three of them being wounded and captured." When the women approached and begged that the prisoners' lives be spared, Major Spurling is reported to have said, "We do not murder prisoners, as you did at Fort Pillow." The mention of Fort Pillow refers to reports that Confederate soldiers had murdered wounded and sur-

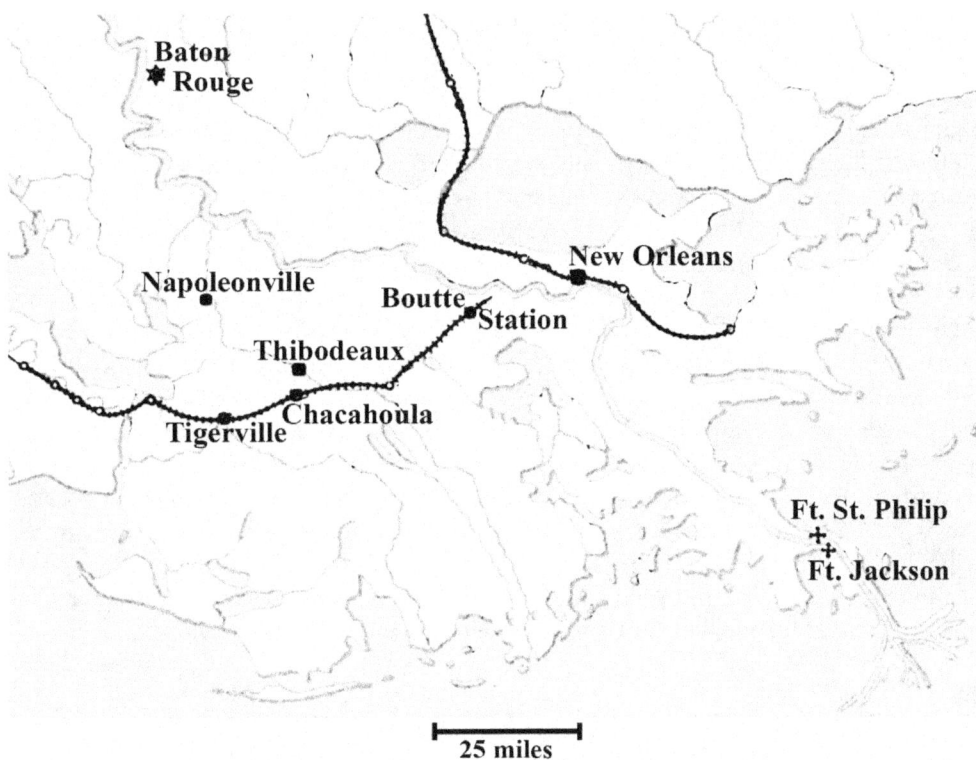

The area where elements of the 2nd Maine Cavalry operated in May, June and July 1864 (adapted from plate CXXXV-A, *Official Atlas*).

rendered Union soldiers as well as fleeing black civilians after the Confederate victory at that Tennessee fort.[57]

As we will see later, there are often varying accounts of actions taken, and even when reporting the same events, various researchers or authors may interpret actions very differently. One may respect and even admire a person for the quantity and quality of their research and yet disagree strongly with the conclusions drawn or the interpretation of the facts discovered. As an example, author Dale Cox, who has amassed a remarkable body of facts, biographical details, and background material regarding the Civil War in Florida, reports a very different version of the above confrontation. After quoting reports of Major Spurling entertaining the troops by shooting the wick from a candle on the head of his black servant, and a time when Spurling apparently fired low on purpose to splatter his servant with candle grease, Cox states: "Spurling's cruelty also took on more violent tones. In Louisiana, prior to his regiment's transfer to Pensacola, he and three of his men hid in a row of shrubbery and brutally ambushed four Confederate soldiers who were making a social call." Cox does not mention the "social call" that those Confederate soldiers were apparently riding off to pay on Spurling and his men.[58]

During the month of May, there were also internal issues within the 2nd Maine Cavalry to be dealt with. Colonel Woodman had reported in April that Lt. Col. Godfrey's health was not good, and on May 9, the colonel reported that Godfrey had resigned. Major Andrew Spurling was the colonel's recommendation for promotion to lieutenant colonel, and the adjutant, Nathan Cutler, would fill Spurling's position as major. The promotions were approved and went into effect in early June.

At the end of May 1864, the *Official Record* gives an estimate of cavalry forces in the Department of the Gulf. In that report, the 2nd Maine Cavalry is listed as having 12 companies with an estimated aggregate strength of 1,200, "a new regiment, well appointed; Nine companies at Greenville and three companies in field." Greenville, Louisiana, now a section of "Uptown," a suburb of New Orleans, was the location of the Union cavalry's school of instruction, and Col. Woodman was ordered to take command of that post.[59]

In other theaters of the war, the first 5 months of 1864 brought substantial changes to the Union military chain of command. In March, U.S. Grant was given the rank of lieutenant general and put in command of the entire Union Army. Attaching himself to the Army of the Potomac, in May Grant began his Overland Campaign. This campaign saw a series of attacks against Lee's Army of Northern Virginia as Grant attempted to get between the Confederates and Richmond and draw Lee into a battle that would end the war. (During a cavalry battle of that campaign, Confederate commander J.E.B. Stuart was killed at Yellow Tavern on May 11.) As Grant's plans unraveled and Lee thwarted Grant's attempts to outflank the Confederate army, the Army of the Potomac's troops were ordered to make a series of costly frontal assaults against Rebel defensive lines and earthworks. This resulted in more terrible losses, as will be described at the end of Chapter Five. For a detailed look at the Overland Campaign and the political maneuvering for rank and favor within the Union Army, see Diane Monroe Smith's *Command Conflicts in Grant's Overland Campaign*.

CHAPTER FIVE

Summer 1864: Detachments in Action in Louisiana and First Actions in Florida

In June 1864, various components of the 2nd Maine Cavalry were in action. In order to capture some Rebels "operating in the swamp beyond Tigerville," a detachment was put together made up of 20 men of the 2nd Maine Cavalry (dismounted), who were to join 20 men each of the 11th and 26th Indiana Infantry and 20 men of the 11th Wisconsin, under the command of Captain Benjamin Merry of the 2nd Maine Cavalry. On June 15, this detachment was ordered "to proceed through the swamp and blockade the Bayou Cheramie [northwest of Tigerville], having information that the enemy had a camp on or near the place."

Capt. Benjamin Merry (Special Collections, Bangor Public Library).

Captain Merry and his troops were to lay in ambush and wait for another force of 40 Union soldiers under Captain Lewis of the 11th Wisconsin. Lewis and his men were to advance to the east of the bayou and push the Rebels westward toward Merry's waiting detachment. The expedition was successful, capturing 6 Rebels and their weapons, including two officers, and their pirogues (small boats) and having destroyed other small boats on the bayou. The report on this action from Captain De La Paturelle (inspector of U.S. forces in the Thibodeaux, Louisiana, area), ends, "I most respectfully recommend Captain Lewis, of the Eleventh Wisconsin, for his behavior on this expedition, also Captain Merry, of the Second Maine Cavalry, and the men under both commands, for their conduct, marching 30 miles a day through the swamps."[1]

In what might seem a very short time later for that period, the news of this raid was sent north by telegraph and reported in the Washington, D.C., *Daily National Republican* on June 24—with the name of the waterway apparently garbled: "Several guerrillas have been captured at Chafalche river by the 2d Maine cavalry."

In early June, the regiment's headquarters was at Thibodeaux, Louisiana, with Colonel Woodman once again in command, having at his own request been relieved of the command of the Cavalry School of Instruction at Greenville (*Maine in War for Union*, 564–565). During that month, various parts of the regiment were assigned to a variety of posts. At the end of June 1864, the *Official Record* gives details of the troops in the Department of the Gulf at that time, and lists the locations occupied by the 2nd Maine Cavalry as follows:

> Not Brigaded at Thibodeaux, Louisiana: 2nd Maine Cavalry, Colonel Ephraim Woodman
> (This contingent at Thibodeaux which was not assigned to a brigade, we must assume, consisted of the regimental headquarters, since there are 4 companies also listed at Thibodeaux, and the other 8 companies were spread out in the surrounding area.)
> Brashear City: 2nd Maine Cavalry (4 companies), Lt. Colonel Andrew B. Spurling
> Thibodeaux: 2nd Maine Cavalry (4 companies), Major Nathan Cutler
> Napoleonville: 2nd Maine Cavalry (2 companies), Major Charles Miller
> Boutte Station: 2nd Maine Cavalry (1 company), no commander listed
> Chucahoula (assumed to be "Chacahoula"): 2nd Maine Cavalry (1 company), Captain Adolphus Mathews[2]

On July 1, Colonel Woodman was ordered to collect his regiment at Thibodeaux, Louisiana. Over the next few days the dispersed companies broke camp at their various locations and made their way to Thibodeaux, where they remained for much of July. With Colonel Woodman given command of the post there, Lt. Colonel Spurling assumed the leadership of the 2nd Maine Cavalry.

In a report to Adjutant General Hodsdon on July 6, Colonel Woodman wrote,

> For the first time since we left Maine, the reg't is encamped together. For nearly three months no communication was possible between the reg't & the detachment of three Cos at Red River. Since their return we have until the 3rd inst been divided with only four Cos in a place at most. It has therefore been difficult to get the Returns required consolidated correctly as they have to be returned frequently to company commanders for changes.
> The general health of the reg't has been very good up to within a week or ten days. But the considerable amount of Scouting and picket duty taking Detachments out at night and the unhealthy location of the various camps has increased the sick list.[3]

When the regiment assembled at Thibodeaux, they were reported to have 1,075 men present, of whom 105 were reported sick. On July 15 the *Official Record* report of the distribution of troops in the Department of the Gulf lists the 2nd Maine Cavalry at Thibodeaux with an effective force of 950 men. (The regiment, it may be remembered, was reported in May 1864, as having 12 companies and a total estimated strength of 1,200 men. That round number was, no doubt, a convenient approximation of the actual strength.)[4]

As the regiment was brought together, the politics of promotion became an issue, at least for some. Back in April, as he reported the illness of Lt. Col. Godfrey to Maine's governor, Colonel Woodman had stated that the lieutenant colonel "talks of resigning. I dread the vacancy that would occur. There are probably several officers who would be disappointed in expectation already being raised." That concern about possible jealousy and anticipation of promotion proved to be very accurate.[5]

On July 12, a disgruntled Major Charles Miller, the commander of the 2nd Maine Cavalry detachment that had served during the retreat on the Red River, wrote to Adjutant General Hodsdon in Maine. In his letter, Major Miller begins with reports of praise by other officers for his and his men's actions during the Red River Campaign. "Whatever of favorable reputation this regiment now enjoys was won by me and my battalion in the Red River Campaign.... On the battlefield of Marksville I rec'd the personal compliment of two general officers and Gen [A.J.] Smith himself wanted to know what gallant little regiment mine was." Major Miller also complains bitterly about the promotion of Major Spurling over himself to be lieutenant colonel, and blames that "foul scheme" on Colonel Woodman. "Tis too bad that a miserable partizan partiality should be allowed to control the interests of a Regt of 1200 men." In addition, Major Miller complains that Captain Twitchell "who was with me at Red River desired most rightly the position of Major," the position given to Nathan Cutler. And Miller goes on to say of Captain Twitchell, "A more gallant officer never led a company of men.... 'Tis not therefore an individual disappointment but a general distrust." He also remarks, "Thus while we were fighting the battles that we came here to fight, this most damnable scheme of wholesale robbery of men's reputations & men's honor was being carried on." Major Miller claims that "had the choice of a Lt. Col. been left to the officers of the Reg't, I should have rec'd 9 out of every 10," and that many officers have tendered their resignations in protest to Spurling's promotion. He also states, "With regard to Col. Spurling and Maj Cutler personally I've nothing to say. They've got their commissions & they are history. Men & officers will not peril their lives & seek occasions to do some gallant act when others who stand by with arms folded receive the rewards." He goes on: "I regret to say the health of the regt is poor. We have over 200 on the sick list. This afternoon our Chaplain buried 4 privates. The little squad of soldiers going out of our camp with 'arms reversed' to pay the last offices of respect to a companion gone is a sight of too frequent occurrence to excite remark." And he ends, "Are other Regts to be formed in Maine, and would my transfer be possible?"[6]

One must wonder whether Major Miller's sentiments were his own or actually reflected a general discontent among the officers and men of the regiment. It is unknown or unrecorded whether "many officers" had "tendered their resignations in protest" as Major Miller states. If so, not many actually resigned. But toward the end of July, two officers did leave the regiment: Lt. William Banton of Company G resigned on July 26 and Lt. George Seavey of Company D was discharged for disability on July 27. The previous month (June 1864), Captain Twitchell had written to Maine's adjutant general asking for a transfer to any new regiment to be raised. Twitchell stated, "The season for active campaigning is over in this Department.... I am anxious to take the field where there is some active service going on." And, perhaps quite unrealistically, Captain Twitchell states that he can have Col. Woodman's recommendation for the rank of major. Twitchell did not transfer to another regiment, nor did he resign during 1864.[7]

Major Miller had, previous to his appointment to the 2nd Maine Cavalry, been a lawyer in Rockland, Maine, and had not seen previous military service. Lt. Col. Spurling, on the other hand, had a seen considerable action as an officer in the 1st Maine Cavalry. Major Cutler had served with the 28th Maine, a 9 month regiment in the Deep South, and had served with Col. Woodman in that regiment. Captain Twitchell, who did not receive a promotion, was also well known to Col. Woodman, having not only served with Woodman in the 8th Maine Infantry, but for a time serving as a major while Colonel Woodman was the 8th Maine's lieutenant colonel. The relative merits of all of these officers (and others) was a topic that surfaced a number of times over the next months. The insubordinate attitude shown in Major Miller's letter regarding Colonel Woodman can be seen again in future correspondence with Maine's adjutant general, who, from the tone and comments within the letters, appears to have been a personal friend of Major Miller's.

It is always interesting, and sometimes even amusing, to see different reports on the same situation. In 1904, a veteran of both the 10th Maine Infantry and the 1st Maine Heavy Artillery was "requested by members of [the 2nd Maine Cavalry] ... to compile and prepare" a book recording Lt. Colonel Spurling's exploits to be presented at a regimental reunion. In that work, the author, Cassius C. Roberts, states of Spurling, "a junior major, he had been promoted to lieutenant-colonel, but both Majs. Miller and Hutchinson, excellent officers as they were, were satisfied, recognizing, as they did, his [Spurling's] superior qualifications as a commander and leader of men."[8]

Colonel Woodman had a very different view of the merits of various officers from that expressed by Major Miller. In early August he wrote to Governor Samuel Cony (who had replaced Abner Coburn in January of 1864) regarding promotions. He states, "Major Miller has applied for the Position of Provost Martial [Marshal]. He has got recommendations of Col. Rust, Col. Beal, & Gen Nickerson. Gen'l Banks ... has referred the matter to me for remarks. I oppose the detail because I believe those easy positions should be given to officers who have seen more service."

There is, in this letter, some verification of Major Miller's statement of the desire of men to transfer out of the 2nd Maine Cavalry. Col. Woodman states, "We have had 75 soldiers transferring to the Navy." Regarding the overall morale of enlisted men in the 2nd Maine Cavalry, the Maine adjutant general's reports show that there were quite a number of desertions. Most of the deserters, however, were those who simply took the bounty money and deserted before the regiment had even left Maine, and so it does not appear that they deserted because of any dissatisfaction with their officers.[9]

When considering the possible reasons for men transferring from the 2nd Maine Cavalry to the navy, one may indulge in some educated speculation. We may begin by contemplating why men would join a cavalry regiment over the infantry. The most obvious would be that cavalry troopers ride horses rather than walking. That in itself must have provided a considerable attraction. And then, there was a certain romance attached to the cavalry, and many apparently thought of that branch of the army (and some in the cavalry thought of themselves) as rather elite. When men got to Florida and found that the 2nd Maine Cavalry often did not have enough horses, would that provide an incentive to transfer to the navy? The fact that the navy's men rode on boats and ships of various sorts must have seemed quite desirable. And then there was a possible financial incentive—men on the navy's ships might take a portion of the prize money for Confederate ships' cargoes that were seized or goods that were confiscated from various river or ocean ports. The ships of the blockading squadrons would obviously have a lot to gain from that prize money, but even the gunboats of the river fleet might well intercept Confederate boats attempting to bring supplies to the South along various rivers or capture cotton being prepared for shipment. (The U.S. Supreme Court did eventually rule, in the spring of 1865, that the prize law did not apply to "inland seizures.") It would seem that any of the above might make a soldier look at the navy as an attractive alternative. In fact, this availability of prize money to sailors and not to soldiers caused General Halleck to write to Senator Milton S. Latham of California offering to help write a bill that would change the prize policy and would allow the army to participate in the same scheme. Halleck also made the dubious suggestion that, by having prize money given for captured goods, soldiers would not be inclined to plunder for their own personal gain.[10]

To return to Colonel Woodman's letter and his discussion of transfers and overall morale, the Colonel was also expressing reservations about some of the officers in his regiment. The 1st lieutenant of Company G, William Banton, resigned on July 26, 1864, and the colonel recommended the transfer of Lieutenant [Thomas] Brann from Company I to Company G "because Co G needed a better officer than could be found in it. The Captain [Samuel Knowles] is dissipated somewhat and very negligent. The 2nd Lt. [Jason Chandler] is a well disposed but thoughtless officer, needs to be well commanded. The orderly Sgt. [Alphonzo Patten] I have had in arrest several times & Court-martialed once. He now asks to be reduced to the ranks in preference to being tried by Court Martial." Second Lieutenant Brann was transferred to Company G from Company I and promoted to 1st lieutenant.[11]

Lt. Thomas Brann (courtesy Maine State Archives).

Captain Knowles himself faced a court-martial on September 1 for behaviors alleged to have occurred in June, July, and August of 1864. The charges were as follows:

> Charge I. Neglect of duty. Under this charge, it was said the Captain Knowles had abandoned a box of ammunition for which he was responsible.
> Charge II. Conduct to the prejudice of good order and military discipline. The specification for this charge stated that Captain Knowles "did abandon his command when formed for the march and remained absent therefrom without leave for about three hours."
> Charge III. Violation of the 45th Article of War. For this charge, it was alleged that Knowles "was drunk when in command of his squadron" during their move from Terrebonne to Algiers, Louisiana.
> Charge IV. Disobedience of Orders. This charge's specifications stated that Captain Knowles was absent from stable call on two successive days.

To all of these charges and specifications, Captain Knowles pleaded "not guilty." After "mature deliberation," the finding of the court was that Knowles was not guilty of all except the second charge—being absent on the march, but the amount of time of his absence was changed from "three hours" to "two hours." Captain Knowles was therefore acquitted.[12]

The testimony regarding the charge of being drunk shows, perhaps, how difficult some judgments can be, or how perceptions can vary, or how various men's definitions can vary. Witnesses Lt. Col. Spurling and Lieutenant Chandler felt that Knowles was drunk such that his ability to perform his duty was impaired. In their testimony, however, Major Hutchinson said that Captain Knowles had been drinking, but was not drunk, and Lieutenant William Gillespie of Company D and Captain George Kerswell of Company G stated that Knowles was not apparently impaired. The court could not resolve the matter such as to find Knowles guilty.

On the charge of being absent from stable call, we may see some indication of Col.

Woodman's attitudes toward compliance to orders, or perhaps some indication of favoritism. It seems clear from the testimony that Captain Knowles had been detailed as counsel for Captain Stanley, who had also been facing a court-martial and Captain Knowles was absent in consequence of that duty. The permission to be absent while representing Captain Stanley had been granted by Colonel Woodman, who had then made the charge of absence without permission against Captain Knowles.

The charge relating to the abandoned ammunition box remained unproved. Captain Knowles claimed the box had been lost while the company was on the march and he had thought it had fallen into the bayou and sunk. The box that was found had no markings on it to indicate if it was the one that Captain Knowles had lost.

If these charges were meant as an example of Captain Knowles being somewhat "dissipated" and "very negligent," as Colonel Woodman stated, and were serious enough to warrant a court-martial, the court did not agree. Was it perhaps, a case of Colonel Woodman being annoyed with Captain Knowles for acting as counsel for Captain Stanley? Captain Stanley, after his own court-martial hearing, had been reprimanded in general orders for "disrespectful conduct to his superior officer." Captain Stanley was, in this case, acting as counsel for Captain Knowles. (For a summary of the other general court-martial trials held for officers and enlisted men of the 2nd Maine Cavalry, see Appendix C.)

Regarding the other officer that Major Miller had said was deserving of promotion, Colonel Woodman stated, "Captain Twitchell does not meet my expectations." And so, while the politics within the regiment are quite apparent, the positive qualities or shortcomings of the various officers can be difficult to judge objectively at this distance of time. Colonel Woodman and Major Miller do agree on one point. The Colonel writes, "The health of the Reg't is rather bad owing to bad weather and bad location" at their camp in Thibodeaux.[13]

As some confirmation of the infighting and bad feelings regarding promotions, the 2nd Maine Cavalry's regimental quartermaster, John Milliken, wrote to Governor Cony asking for a transfer to another regiment: "For some fourteen months I was a member of the 8th Reg't [Col. Woodman's earliest regiment in which he had served as a captain and then as lieutenant colonel] in which I saw no service but very much fighting among the officers of the Reg't in which I took no part, but tried to perform my duty. I was obliged to resign because I would not side with the Col. A fight is raging now between field and line [officers] in this, one of the best Regiments that ever left the State of Maine. I can side with neither again I am not in the line of promotion.... I am fully satisfied that the period of my usefulness has

Lt. John Milliken (courtesy Maine State Archives).

passed here and that I might do more service to my Country in some other Reg't if in a subordinate position." Milliken did not resign from the 2nd Maine Cavalry, nor was he transferred to another regiment. He was, however, discharged for disability in March of 1865.[14]

In early August 1864, the 2nd Maine Cavalry was transferred from Louisiana to the Union Army's post at Barrancas, Florida. Again, the regiment did not move as a whole, but various companies were taken by steamer from New Orleans to Barrancas beginning on August 3, and all of the companies were apparently at Barrancas by August 11. The arrival of the first two battalions of the 2nd Maine at Barrancas coincided with the celebrations of Admiral Farragut's victory at Mobile Bay. By that action, the Union fleet had succeeded in opening the way to the last of the Confederacy's major ports on the Gulf of Mexico, although it would be well into 1865 before the last forts guarding Mobile, and that city itself, fell to the Union forces.[15]

When they arrived in Florida, the 2nd Maine Cavalry came under the command of Brigadier General Alexander Asboth, who was in charge of the District of West Florida, Department of the Gulf. General Asboth had been born in Hungary, where he received his training as a soldier and served in the Austrian Army as an engineer. He rose to the rank of captain, but after fighting for the losing side in the 1848 revolution in Hungary (an attempt, led by Lajos Kossuth, to gain freedom from the Austrian Empire), Asboth moved to the United States in 1851 and was a naturalized citizen at the outbreak of the Civil War. He saw early service as chief of staff to General John C. Fremont and was promoted to brigadier general in 1862.[16]

The transfer of the 2nd Maine Cavalry to Barrancas was made in response to a series of requests from General Asboth that had started from the time of his assignment to command in West Florida, about one year previously. Asboth had been concerned that he did not have enough troops to garrison the forts around Pensacola and to protect the navy yard. The 28th Connecticut Infantry and the 15th Maine Infantry had been transferred away from Barrancas in the spring of 1863, and when Asboth arrived he saw that as Federal troops had been reduced, reports indicated that Confederate forces in the area had been strengthened, and his requests for reinforcements became even more insistent. General Asboth had apparently something of a reputation as an alarmist—overreacting to perceived threats from the enemy, and having made requests for reinforcements during a previous command in Kentucky which were seen

Gen. Alexander Asboth (National Archives).

by higher officers as unnecessary. On the other hand, Barrancas was deep within Confederate territory, was rimmed by nearby outposts of Confederate soldiers, and some of those Confederate positions contained substantial numbers of troops.[17]

Before going on with the 2nd Maine Cavalry's story, a brief recap of the situation up to the time of their arrival at Barrancas may be useful. Fort Barrancas, it will be recalled, was one of the three forts (with Forts McRee and Pickens) that guarded the approach to Pensacola by sea. It had been abandoned by the small Union garrison when Florida's state militia troops were ordered to seize Federal installations as that state was about to secede from the Union in January of 1861. As related in an earlier chapter, Lt. Slemmer, the Union commander, realized quite correctly that Fort Pickens would be a better location in which to concentrate his small force. The remaining forts in Pensacola Harbor, Forts McCree and Barrancas, and Pensacola itself, with its navy yard containing supply and shipbuilding facilities, was soon occupied by at least 5,000 and perhaps as many as 7,000 Confederate troops under General Braxton Bragg. The Confederates were disappointed to discover that a substantial portion of the food stored at the navy yard was no longer fit for consumption. In addition, thanks to the Federal occupation of Fort Pickens, the Union control of the entrance to the harbor made it necessary to find an alternative route for supplies and troop movements. By early May 1861, the Confederates had completed the Alabama and Florida Railroad, linking the Pensacola area with Montgomery, Alabama.[18]

In February of 1862, General Bragg was transferred to Mobile and General Samuel

Confederate mortar battery, Pensacola, Florida (State Archives of Florida; floridamemory.com).

Confederate army camp behind Fort Barrancas, Florida, 1861 (State Archives of Florida; floridamemory.com).

Jones took over the Confederate troops in Pensacola. Jones was a West Point graduate (class of 1841) and had served there as an instructor for several years. He had resigned from the U.S. Army in April of 1861 and had been chief of artillery for Confederate General Beauregard at First Bull Run.[19]

On April 22, 1862, a letter to General Jones from General Robert E. Lee (at that time in command of coastal defenses for South Carolina, Georgia and East Florida) requested heavy guns from the Pensacola forts to help with the defense of New Orleans. Then, just after the Confederate military evacuated New Orleans, a second letter regarding Pensacola and its defenses was written to General Jones by General Lee on April 27:

> I would state that it is deemed expedient to remove at once all Government property, including guns, munitions of war, etc, not necessary for present service, to some place of security, and to make every preparation for concentrating the whole available force of your command at Mobile, should occasion require it.
> Such of the heavy guns as are not needed in your department could be sent to Montgomery or other safe point....
> Everything of value that it is possible to remove should be sent away, and what cannot be secured should be destroyed when you withdraw from the position, to prevent its falling into the hands of the enemy. As much as in your power deceive the enemy as to your real intent, keeping a bold front and doing the work of the removal with all the secrecy possible.[20]

In early May of 1862, when the Federal navy had opened the mouth of the Mississippi River and Federal troops occupied New Orleans, the Confederate forces abandoned Pensacola, destroyed as much of the navy yard as they could, and Federal troops took over the town and navy yard. The Confederate troops from Pensacola, it was felt, could be more useful helping defend other Rebel cities and strongholds. And Pensacola itself was of little value to the Confederacy since its port was blockaded and the entrance to that port was under the guns of Fort Pickens.[21]

Unlike the Confederacy's struggle throughout the Civil War to shift artillery and ammunition to the places where it was most needed, and away from capture by Union forces, General Asboth and Admiral Farragut were having no such problem. In fact, before his entry into Mobile Bay, Farragut was able to spare 16 "heavy guns" from the navy to be used by Asboth in the forts near Pensacola. It will be remembered that when the Union troops abandoned Forts Barrancas and McCree in favor of holding Fort Pickens, they had spiked as many of those forts' guns as possible. Now, with the guns from the navy, General Asboth was able to mount these additional guns, including 150-pounder rifled Parrott guns, 9-inch smooth-bore Dahlgren guns, 11-inch smooth-bore Dahlgren guns, 20-pounder rifled Parrott guns, and one 18-pounder rifled Parrott gun.[22]

When Pensacola was evacuated, the Confederates also abandoned Forts McRee and Barrancas and Union troops took possession. These forts, along with Fort Pickens, were reoccupied by Federal troops and remained in Union hands for the duration of the war. Barrancas and the nearby navy hospital grounds became a focus for Union troops stationed in that area. About 8 miles to the northeast of Barrancas, and north of Bayou Grande, the town of Pensacola itself was eventually evacuated by Union troops in March 1863, and while it saw occasional visits from both Confederate and Union scouts and pickets, it was almost entirely abandoned by its civilian population. Some of the townspeople had left with the Confederates, but many followed the Union troops to the protection of the garrison at Barrancas and the navy yard.[23]

Captain John Wilson of the 15th Maine stated that "nearly the entire population [of Pensacola] desired to accompany the [Union] troops to their new station, and for days and nights large numbers of the inhabitants, of every age, condition and sex, with all their goods and chattels, were gathered upon the public squares, awaiting transportation. Captain Wilson further stated that these "Union-loving citizens … not only claimed the protecting care of the military authorities but were also in a measure dependent upon our commissary department for supplies." Over the coming months, the influx of even more Union loyalists and refugees into the area would pose a problem for the Union commissary officers who had to provide for the subsistence of these civilians as well as the Union troops.[24]

After the Confederates abandoned Pensacola and its nearby forts and navy yard, the importance of the Alabama and Florida railroad was not diminished. Another rail line, the Mobile and Great Northern, was completed in 1862 and linked the Mobile area with the Alabama and Florida Railroad at Pollard, just north of the Florida-Alabama state line. Pollard, therefore, became a position of importance for the Confederacy, and in late 1863 a brigade of Alabama troops—two regiments of infantry, two cavalry regiments, and two batteries of artillery—under Brigadier General James A. Clanton was posted to guard the rail junction in that town. Neither was the significance of the railroad lost on the area's Union commander, General Asboth, who wrote that it "passes through the best cotton and corn lands of the state of Alabama … now almost exclusively engaged in raising corn for the Confederates." Asboth also stated that it was "the only reliable, speedy route in transporting troops from the Mississippi River east," a point driven home when Asboth reported, in November of 1863, that it had been recently used to transport 30,000 troops from General Joseph E. Johnston's command to assist the Confederate army at Chattanooga.[25]

As the Confederates built up their forces to guard the railroad, they also had made attacks on the Union picket line near Barrancas and caused concern for the garrison's commander. General Asboth complained that he had neither the steamships to transport his troops nor horses to give his newly recruited Florida cavalry (made up of Union loyalists from Florida) the mobility they needed to be effective in countering Confederate activity. Even when, in late April and early May of 1864, substantial numbers of Confederate troops from Pollard were transferred west to assist General Johnston's Army of Tennessee, General Asboth was frustrated that he was still unable to make any meaningful offensive against the various Rebel camps in his area and that the Confederates' use of the railroad continued unchallenged.[26]

In April of 1864, Asboth had written to General Banks, the commander of the Army of the Gulf, and renewed his requests for reinforcements, saying that his troop strength at Barrancas was "entirely inadequate to secure a long resistance to a tenfold superior force." Whether that ratio of Confederate to Union troops actually existed and whether that sort of Confederate force could have been brought against Barrancas is unclear from the available records. General Asboth reported that he had received information "from refugees and deserters" that Confederate troops in his area amounted to some 10,000 men at Pollard, Alabama, and another 2,000 were concentrating in Walton County 40 or so miles east of Barrancas. In addition, detachments from the 15th Confederate Cavalry under Col. Henry Maury were reported to be encamped at various locations close to Barrancas. And Confederate deserters told Asboth that these Rebel troops were expecting to be reinforced and that the large scouting parties approaching the Union lines were preparing the way for an attack. Indeed, on April 2, Company M of the 14th New York Cavalry had been engaged in a skirmish with a Confederate scouting party just a few miles from the Barrancas lines. (That one company of the 14th New York had been stationed at Barrancas since September of 1863.)[27]

In mid–April of 1864 General Asboth's request brought the 82nd Infantry Regiment, U.S. Colored Troops, from New Orleans to Barrancas, a regiment of black soldiers that had been organized as a part of the Corps de Afrique. That regiment was commanded by Colonel Ladislas Zulavsky, who, like General Asboth, was from Hungary and had previous military training—in Zulavsky's case, as an officer fighting for Italian independence in the Hungarian Legion under Giuseppe Garibaldi. By the end of June 1864, in addition to the 82nd U.S. Colored Troops (USCT) and Company M of the 14th New York Cavalry, General Asboth had under his command (at Barrancas and Fort Pickens) the 25th Infantry USCT, the 86th Infantry USCT, the 7th Vermont Infantry, and 5 companies of the 1st Florida Union Cavalry (the Florida Cavalry, however, were neither mounted nor armed as of July). These units added up to 2,847 troops present for duty. The 7th Vermont, however, had its term of service ending and those men who reenlisted were given a furlough back to Vermont starting on August 10. When they returned to duty in the Deep South, the 7th Vermont was sent to New Orleans.[28]

While worrying about his limited garrison near Pensacola, General Asboth reported in early July that the Confederate troops near his post included 5 companies of infantry and Colonel Maury's 15th Confederate Cavalry at Pollard, Alabama, 500 more cavalry and three pieces of artillery at 15 Mile Station (Gonzales) on the Pensacola to Pollard railroad line, and three companies of cavalry northeast of the Escambia River, with half companies of cavalry at 4 towns from Milton to Marianna. He amended that report in the second week of August 1864, stating that the Confederate forces in the surrounding area included "according to information received from refugees and deserters," three companies of the 15th Confed-

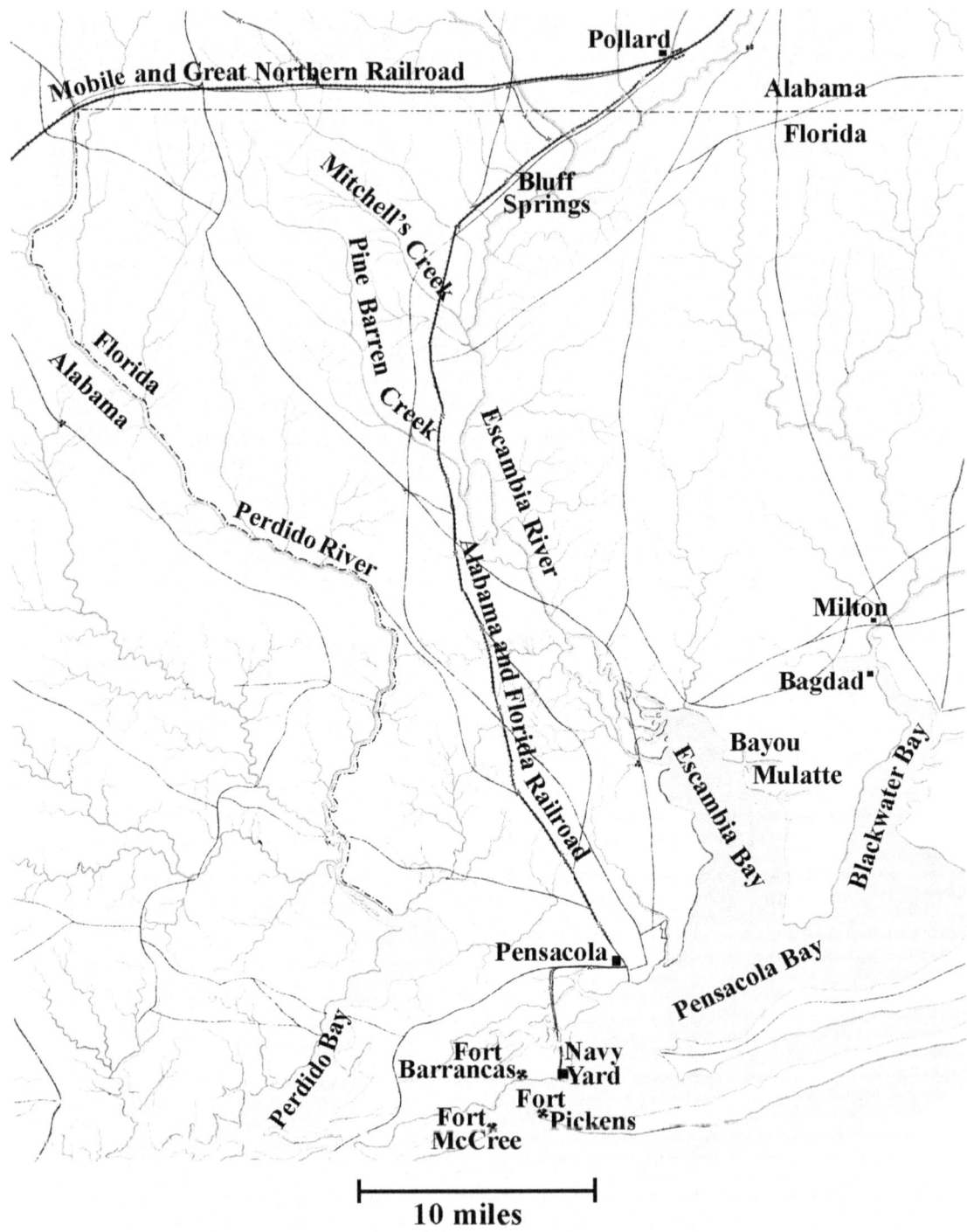

The Pensacola area and railroads through Pollard (adapted from plate CX; *Official Atlas*).

erate Cavalry at Pine Barren bridge, with four pieces of artillery, and three companies of the 7th Alabama Cavalry near Gonzales (just north of Pensacola on the railroad line). West of Barrancas, General Asboth reports that there was a picket post and five companies of Confederate soldiers. Fort Morgan was reported to hold about 600 Confederates of the 1st Alabama Artillery and Tennessee Artillery. While stating that he would prefer to arm and mount the Florida Cavalry, who were "all good horsemen, all good marksmen, and perfectly familiar with the country and people," and would "prove more efficient here than any veteran cavalry regiment," he nevertheless wrote in late July thanking his superiors "for the promised additional regiment of cavalry. They will not lie idle, the commanding general may rely upon that."[29]

And so, the men of the 2nd Maine Cavalry found themselves, in the late summer of 1864, reassigned to help General Asboth's defense of Barrancas and to assist in raids on the Confederate railroad, as they attempted to stop, or at least interfere with, the flow of Rebel troops and supplies along that important route. As the 2nd Maine Cavalry began to arrive at Barrancas, General Asboth reported on August 6:

> The chartered steam transport Merrimac ... arrived this morning with one battalion of the Second Maine Cavalry, Colonel Woodman commanding, and is disembarking at the navy-yard. The steam transport Mississippi, with the Second Battalion on board, was left behind yesterday evening, aground at the Southwest Pass of the Mississippi River. I expect her tonight, and as soon as the Second Battalion is disembarked will start to cross the Perdido and control the east shore of Mobile Bay. The horses of the Second Maine Cavalry are in poor condition and the men very sickly, but there is no time at present for recuperation; they will have to move at once.[30]

And, on August 8, General Asboth wrote, "The Second Battalion of the Second Maine Cavalry has arrived on the steam army transport Mississippi, and the disembarkment has just been completed at the navy-yard. I will endeavor to cross the Perdido to-morrow with a combined force not over 1,000 strong, to control, as far as possible, the east shore of Mobile Bay, and deprive Fort Morgan also of its land communications."

After complaining that the steam transport he had hoped to use was not available, and the steamer *Lizzie Davis* was "declared by its captain and engineer entirely unsafe," he goes on to state, "Thus I am left at the present critical moment entirely without steamers; yet I made arrangements to cross the Perdido near its mouth on a variety of boats, scows, and other small vessels."[31] It was actually not until August 13, as we will see, that the expedition to the Perdido began. In those early days, as the 2nd Maine Cavalry settled into their quarters at Barrancas, the routine for the day was set by Colonel Woodman as follows:

First call for Reveille	4:45 AM	Water Call	4:00 p.m.
Reveille	5:00 "	Stable Call	4:30 "
Sick Call	5:05 "	Recall	5:00 "
Stable Call	5:30 "	Supper	5:15 "
Recall	6:15 "	First Call for	
Breakfast	6:30 "	Dress Parade	5:30 "
Water Call	7:00 "	Dress Parade	5:45 "
First Call for		First Call for	
Guard Mounting	8:45 "	Tattoo	8:00 "
Guard Mounting	9:00 "	Tattoo	8:15 "
Orderly Call	11:30 "	Taps	8:30 "
Dinner	12 M		

Roll call at Reveille, Tattoo, & before Dress Parade[32]

There was also a general order issued at around that time regarding the exact procedure to be followed for stable call, the need for written passes to leave the camp, and the manner in which men were formed and marched to meals "in single file under the charge of a commissioned officer who will remain there till each man has received his rations to see that the food is properly cooked, that the dishes are clean, and that each man gets his proper share and in an orderly manner." As with this very detailed order about meals, one may also wonder why it was seen necessary to state, "in no instance will a man be allowed to kick his horse or strike horses over the head."[33] We also may wonder what incident may have led to this order: "Hereafter no firing of Pistols or Carbines will be allowed in or about Camp except by Permission from these Head Quarters."[34]

There were also, during the first 2 weeks or so at Barrancas, the usual promotions and demotions within the regiment. In August, 6 men were reduced to the ranks from sergeant or corporal and men promoted to fill those ranks. The reasons for the demotions range from "absence without leave and disobedience of orders" to "inefficiency as non-commissioned officers." The reshuffling of men both up and down in rank continued throughout the 2nd Maine Cavalry's time of service, and can be seen in the regimental roster (Appendix A).[35]

Other matters also needed to be looked into. On August 16, a "Board of Survey" consisting of 3 officers of the regiment was assigned "to examine Beef now in the hands of Lieut James Cleaveland," the 2nd Maine Cavalry's regimental commissary officer. And, there appears to have been some sort of separate camp area for the sick, perhaps even a quarantine area, as indicated by the order that Captain Stanley of Company F was "assigned to the command of the camp 2nd Maine Cavalry, in charge principally of ineffective men and unserviceable horses."[36]

During that August of 1864, more comments regarding the health of the men and also the horses of the regiment were recorded. The monthly report from Company M states, "The company has, during the last 2 months, suffered severely from sickness incident to acclimation, which has greatly interfered with its efficiency."[37]

The health and camp conditions of the Union regiments in Florida was apparently of concern to many. The surgeon in chief of cavalry, Department of the Gulf, Julius A. Skilton, sent the following directive to regimental surgeons in his command, including the 2nd Maine Cavalry's Surgeon George Martin: "You will make an immediate inspection of your Regiment with reference to its sanitary condition, policing of camp, cleanliness of the men, suggesting any change in cooking or dietetic nature necessary in your opinion.... You will report upon the above, and also the probable number who must be sent to the rear, in case of an immediate advance, and the degree of necessity for the rest of the men for recuperation before again undertaking a campaign."[38]

In spite of attempts to insure healthier conditions for the soldiers, a letter from Sgt. Elisha Clark, of Company L, 2nd Maine Cavalry, gives further information concerning the regiment's increasing numbers of sick. In August, Sgt. Clark wrote that when the regiment came to Florida, the health of the men "was improving and I had reason to believe that it would continue. Everything seemed to look favorable.... instead of improving every day adds to our list of sick. Every day carries some 2 & 3 of our poor boys to their long home.... Every exertion has been made by our Surgeon to furnish us with Vegetables but have not been able to get any as yet. Our men have contracted a disease called the Scurvey [sic]."[39] Scurvy, as we now know, results from a deficiency of vitamin C. But well before and during the Civil War, it was known that it could be prevented by eating fresh fruits (especially citrus fruits) and vegetables. A second letter from Sgt. Clark refers to diarrhea, and serious cases of that ailment along with scurvy would continue to be a problem over the next months.[40]

Within just a few days of their arrival at Barrancas that August, various elements of the regiment were engaged in scouting and raids against Confederate camps in the vicinity. The scouting expedition that General Asboth had mentioned in his August 6 report was now planned for August 13. Once again, on August 12, as he prepared to leave Barrancas, Asboth complained about the lack of sufficient transport vessels and explained why the expedition did not begin some days earlier, as he had intended. Asboth stated that, "having no Government steamer able to enter the Perdido, I engaged on the 9th instant Mr. Clapp's tug to take scows and other small vessels in tow for crossing the Perdido with the promise that it would be ready to start the next day. I made all arrangements accordingly, but the tug is not yet at the Barrancas wharf on account of repairs required.... It is now more than five months that I have been constantly applying for two small steamers of 4 to 5 feet draught, so urgently required."[41]

Surgeon George Martin (courtesy Maine State Archives).

When the scouting mission did start out, it seems to have been quite routine and uneventful, or at least was reported as such in some accounts. For example, the 2nd Maine Cavalry's Company H reported that, on August 13, "the company received marching orders. Marched to Perdido River, a distance of 15 miles. Not encountering the enemy in force, returned to camp the next day; distance marched 30 miles." Company M's report of that same expedition is even more direct in the writer's assessment of the event: "Was ordered out upon an expedition to the Perdido River under General Asboth, the object of which I am as yet unaware, and returned to camp Aug 14."[42]

General Asboth's report of that same raid gives an impressive rationale for the expedition. In his report, Asboth indicates that he achieved what he had intended from the expedition and returned to Barrancas just in time to avert a planned Confederate attack on that fort. On August 13 he left

> with a combined force of infantry, cavalry, and artillery, about 1,400 strong, with the view of crossing the Perdido at its mouth and operating in the peninsula between Mobile Bay and the Perdido, [to] capture the rebels' camp in the neck below Fish River, and ascertain if any Federal forces, and in what strength had landed this side of Fort Morgan.
>
> Marched 12 miles through marshy country—reached old rebel camping grounds on the narrow neck between the Gulf and Perdido, 4 miles from its mouth and camped for night.

Pvt. Charles Rand and his brother Erastus were among those who died of disease in July and August 1864 (Special Collections, Bangor Public Library).

General Asboth went on to report that the next day,

> At daybreak my pickets brought 3 deserters in, coming from the other side of the Perdido, with the report that the rebels had vacated the cavalry camps (Withers and Powell) as well as the Bonsecours Salt Works, under orders to report at Pine Barren bridge, this side of the Perdido, and asserting most positively that 5,000 Federal troops had landed on the north side of Fort Morgan, investing it upon Mobile Point.
>
> Under these circumstances there was not only no further necessity for my crossing the Perdido and continuing to force my march ... at considerable risk through the hardly passable marshy country, but there was apparently more need for my troops this side the river, and I therefore returned to Barrancas, arriving here the same day, 14th, at 4 p.m.
>
> Next day it was reported that the rebels, informed of my leaving Barrancas with the large portion of my forces, decided to risk a dash, and were actually moving down at the head of the Bayou Grand when I was returning up the beach of the Grand Lagoon. Thus it seems that my return was just in time, although I am confident that the rebels would have met, without my return, a warm reception and certain repulse on the ditch between Fort Barrancas and the redoubt.[43]

Historian Ed Bearss, writing of this raid, has quite a different interpretation and questions General Asboth's stated reasons for his command's return to Barrancas—the need to prevent an imminent Confederate attack on the Barrancas fortifications. Bearss indicates

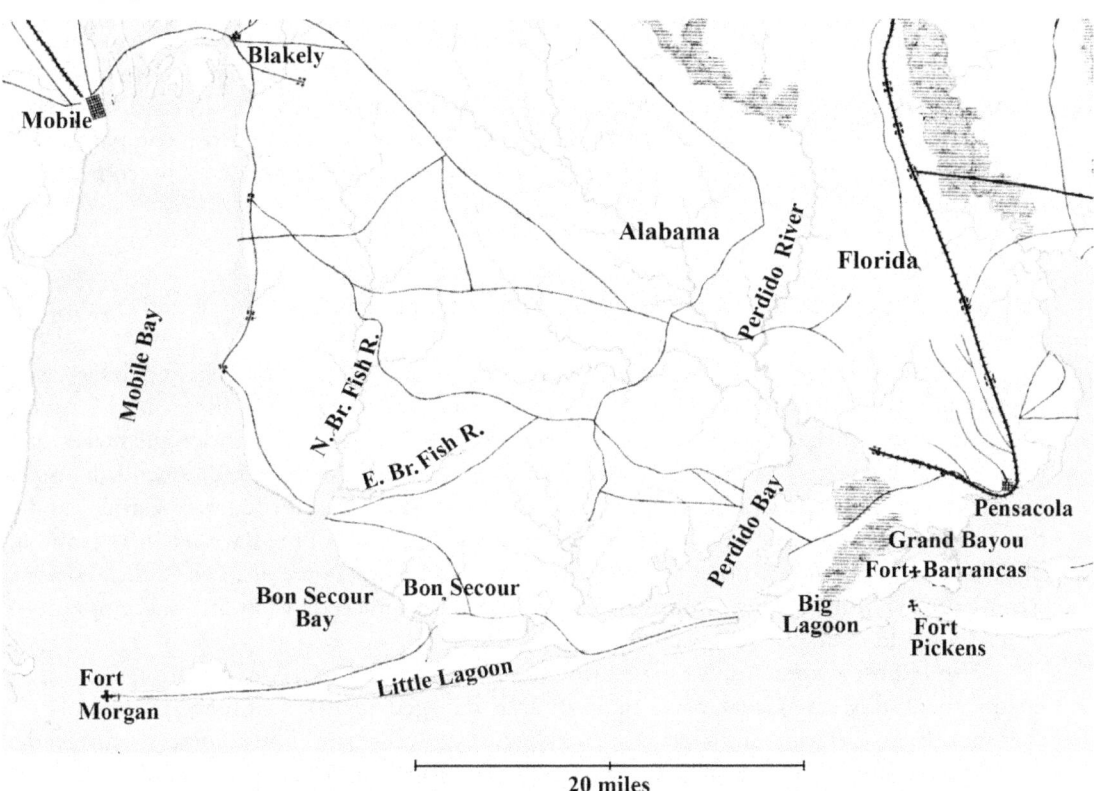

West from Fort Barrancas (adapted from plate CXLVII, *Official Atlas*).

that General Asboth, as his force proceeded toward Perdido Station, learned that the Confederate command at Mobile, "alarmed by his [Asboth's] rapid thrust up the Alabama and Florida Railroad, were rushing all their available reserves to the threatened area to intercept his task force." Asboth was told that the Confederate force consisted of Colonel Henry Maury's 15th Confederate Cavalry, numbering about 1,300 troopers and a 6 gun battery of light artillery. According to Bearss, it was at this point that Asboth decided not to proceed further and to return immediately to his base at Fort Barrancas. It seems that Asboth's spin—his timely return to bolster the Union troops at Barrancas who were under threat of attack—was quite likely an attempt to gloss over his own desire to retreat from an impending enemy attack on his own column.[44]

In General Asboth's defense, however, it should be noted that just before starting on the August 13 expedition across the Perdido toward Mobile, he had received a warning on August 10 from Assistant Adjutant General Christensen, writing for General Canby at Headquarters, Military Division of West Mississippi: "Sir: The operations in the vicinity of Mobile may determine the rebels to make some demonstration against Pensacola, and the commanding general desires that you be on your guard against any enterprise of this kind. Keep your troops so well in hand that your position will be entirely secure. At the same time he wishes such demonstrations made with your cavalry force as will deter the enemy from any attempt to re-enforce Fort Morgan from the eastward of the Mobile Bay."[45]

From various accounts, it appears that Colonel Maury's force numbered around 2,000: the 15th Confederate Cavalry, 3 companies of the 7th Alabama Cavalry, and Captain Thomas

Tobin's Tennessee Battery. With this substantial contingent, Maury may well have had high hopes of intercepting and defeating Asboth's column. When the Confederate troops reached Gonzales (also called Fifteen Mile Station), Colonel Maury and his men learned "to their disgust" that Asboth's Union force had fallen back to Barrancas. Maury left 3 companies of the 7th Alabama Cavalry to hold Gonzales and returned with the remainder of his command to Pollard.[46]

Later in August, other expeditions of Union troops sent from Barrancas had a more definite, if somewhat mundane, result. On August 24, Company C recorded: "The company went out after beef cattle, returning during the afternoon, being successful and capturing about 30 beeves."[47]

And, toward the end of August, General Asboth reported that "refugees and deserters" had again provided information regarding Confederate troop strength in his area. This time the general stated that General Maury, at Pollard, has "3,000 troops and eight pieces of artillery at his disposal" and that "along the railroad to Pollard every trestle-work is well guarded." A few days later, General Asboth stated that the 15th Confederate Cavalry and Seventh Alabama Cavalry were being withdrawn from the area of Pine Barren Bridge (south of Pollard), and that they, along with two companies at Milton, were ordered to the Tensaw River, north of Mobile. These troops were being "partially replaced by new militia companies of boys and old men."[48]

While those earlier August expeditions had not resulted in a confrontation with the enemy, the 2nd Maine Cavalry was more directly engaged against Confederate forces late that month. From Company C's report for August 29 we learn, "The company embarked on a steamer and went within 13 miles of the town of Milton, where we disembarked and marched to the town, charging through it and capturing a few Rebel prisoners, surprising their camp, taking some stores, etc. Bivouacked near the town for the night, returning to camp the next day without loss on our part." Companies D, F, and I were also involved in this action.[49]

At the time of the Civil War, Milton was the seat of Santa Rosa County. Its name may be a corruption of "Milltown," and Milton's lumbering and lumber mills were indeed very important to the town and the surrounding area, including the town of Bagdad, just south of Milton. In addition to lumber, Milton also was known for its brick kilns. Future raids to Milton would be made to procure logs, lumber, and bricks for the Union's use in everything from rebuilding the Pensacola Navy Yard and surrounding buildings to supplying logs for the shipyards that were building and repairing Union vessels.[50]

General Asboth's report on that action at Milton states that on the morning of August 29, he left Barrancas with a force consisting of "200 men of the Second Maine Cavalry, two companies of the Nineteenth Iowa Infantry, and two pieces of the First Florida Battery, on the steamers *Clinton* and *Planter*, with a view to capture three new companies of rebel cavalry reported to be at Milton, Fla."[51]

The Union force "arrived early in the forenoon at the mouth of the Bayou Mulatte, or Black Bayou, Escambia Bay, but being unable to enter it with the *Clinton* (she drawing 8 feet of water) the disembarkation of cavalry was delayed until 3 p.m. when I proceeded to Milton, a distance of 9 miles." The general reports that after rebuilding the destroyed bridge on Arcadia Creek, he and his men "came upon enemy, about 100 strong, and consisting of Captain [Thomas J.] Goldsby's (Alabama) cavalry company and a new militia infantry company, mounted."

The report by General Asboth goes on to indicate that the enemy, hearing of Union steamers at Bayou Mulatte, had sent their supply stores on wagons north toward Pollard, Alabama. He also reported that the Rebels "seemed prepared and decided to accept a fight in the camp at the upper end of the town, but fled, upon our impetuous charge, in all directions. We pursued them closely for 7 miles, and captured 4 privates of Goldsby's company and 3 colored men, mounted and armed, with 7 horses and mules and equipments, and 20 Austrian rifles." The Union force returned to Milton late in the evening to rest and at 1 a.m. started back to Mulatte Bayou, where they re-embarked at daylight and returned to Barrancas at 6 a.m. There were no losses except 1 horse "killed after total exhaustion."

General Asboth blamed the failure to capture more of the Rebel cavalry on the inability of the *Clinton* to cross the mouth of Bayou Mulatte due to its deep draft. He says that future movements of his troops will require transport by water to similar locations, "tributaries of the Pensacola Bay or Perdido River." Therefore, he requested the steamers *Planter* and *Matamoras*, which had a relatively shallow draft, and were more suited to that sort of environ, be ordered for duty in his command.[52]

Thomas J. Goldsby's Company of Alabama Cavalry was a part of Major Joseph Barbiere's cavalry battalion, which had been organized in 1864 from several independent companies, all of which appear to have been raised to support soldiers of the Confederate Army's Conscript Reserve.[53]

The report that "3 colored men, mounted and armed" were captured is not included in a recent book on Civil War actions around Pensacola (*Pensacola During the Civil War*), which only reports the capture of 4 privates. We may wonder if the 3 "colored" men were actually conscripted black men acting as servants or brought to do menial tasks, or whether they were soldiers in a more typical meaning of the word. (Also, did the term "colored" in this case refer to men of mixed race, as opposed to Negroes, or black soldiers?) But General Asboth's account is supported by other Union reports in the *Official Record* of black soldiers serving with Confederate units. The enlisting of slaves or free blacks into the Confederate Army was not authorized until very late in the war, but it does appear that African American men did serve "mounted and armed" with some elements of the Confederate Army. For example, a Union officer's report of a skirmish at Pocotaligo, South Carolina, in May 1862 states that the Confederate force included "a considerable number of colored men." And, regarding the Battle of Murfreesboro, Tennessee, in July of 1862, a Union officer reports that, among the Confederate forces he fought, "There were also quite a number of negroes attached to the Texas and Georgia troops, who were armed and equipped, and took part in the several engagements with my forces during the day." Other reports, late in the war, regarding the inclusion of black troops serving in General Nathan Bedford Forrest's cavalry are perhaps surprising given the accusations (apparently well supported) of his allowing the slaughter of black Union prisoners at Fort Pillow and his later association with the KKK, serving as its first "Grand Dragon." He's an interesting individual, however, and having been a slave owner and slave dealer before the Civil War, in his later years he gave a speech noted for its statements of reconciliation between the white and black races. As we will see later, his farewell address to his troops at the end of the war was a rather eloquent plea for harmony.[54]

Regarding the weapons captured by Asboth's command, the Austrian rifle is generally less well known than the Enfield and Springfield rifled muskets used by both Union and Confederate infantry. The rifles he refers to are the Lorenz Austrian rifled musket, a weapon purchased, as the name implies, from the Austrian government. The basic pattern of the rifle had been developed in 1854 by Josef Lorenz, a Viennese gunsmith, and had been modified in 1861. Both the Union and Confederacy bought substantial numbers of this weapon—the Confederacy apparently buying mostly the 1854 model from existing stocks, while the Union bought the 1861 model. The musket was originally made in .54-caliber, but many of those used by the Union Army were re-bored to use the standard .58-caliber ammunition. The Union's purchases were perhaps in part motivated by a desire to eliminate the supply of weapons that the Confederacy would otherwise acquire. With the U.S. government purchasing almost 227,000 and the Confederacy purchasing about 100,000, the Austrian rifle was second only to the British Enfield rifled musket in the numbers imported during the Civil War.[55]

With the reports of the military activities of the 2nd Maine Cavalry and the ongoing arguments about promotion, it is also important to remember the soldiers in the ranks and their families back home in Maine. How different and how difficult, in that time, to have a son fighting far from home and without any means of rapid communication. Letters such as this, written in late August by Samuel Sprague to Maine's adjutant general, give us a sense of what that was like. "I have a son who enlisted in the 2nd Maine Cav Col Woodman and they went out to New Orleans last spring. I rec'd a letter from him last May since then I have not heard from him & think he is a prisoner in Texas or somewhere else and now I want to write to Col Woodman. Will you be kind enough to inform me if they have been changed to an infantry Reg't and if so how should I direct a letter to have it reach the Reg't, and oblige an anxious father."[56]

His son, Pvt. Theodore S. Sprague, age 18, of Company F had been ill and died September 7 at Barrancas.

And then there was a letter, in response to a request from the wife of Company I's saddler, Jacob Emery, in which Adjutant General Hodsdon tells Lt. Colonel Spurling that Mrs. Emery received a package containing her husband's effects, but with no explanation as to what had happened to him. After several inquiries were made, it was discovered that Jacob Emery, age 32, had become quite ill and was left in a hospital in New Orleans when the 2nd Maine Cavalry was moved to Barrancas. Emery was put on the steam transport *Merrimac* for home, but died August 24 during the passage. Over a year later, at the end of October 1865, the widow had apparently still not received the medical records from the hospital that were needed to complete her requests for her pension.[57]

There are also letters that may amuse and intrigue us, such as the one Captain Samuel Clarke, of Company E, 2nd Maine Cavalry, wrote to his brother in September of 1864. One may recall that in early episodes of the TV show *MASH*, Corporal Radar O'Reilly was sending home a complete jeep, piece by piece. Was Captain Clarke engaged in the Civil War equivalent

Capt. Samuel Clarke (courtesy Maine State Archives).

of similar activities? "About the carbine. I do not think Leander ought to claim it. He had the revolver and that ought to do for him. I have sent to Hiram Metcalf a lot of cartridges. When he gets them he will give you some of them and then you can try the carbine. I also sent my best saddle which I want you to get.... I want you to oil it in neat's foot oil, and keep it where it wont be exposed to the rain. If you use it you must put a blanket under it or the saddle cloth which is just as good."[58]

And then there is an order, from late August 1864, from Colonel Woodman to his officers which starts off understandably enough, but goes on in a manner perhaps very different from our expectations: "One hour after each meal, the Company Commanders will cause all rations and broken pieces of bread and meat to be removed from the soldiers tents—that which is good will be put into the hands of the Commissary Sgt for reissue and the worthless pieces buried."[59]

In other theaters of the war, during June, July, and August of 1864, U.S. Grant's Overland Campaign had continued beginning with the Battle of the Wilderness (May 5–6) and moving on to Spotsylvania (May 8–21), the North Anna (May 23–26), the Totopotomoy (May 28–30), and Cold Harbor (June 1–June 7). These battles are best known for General Grant's continued use of costly frontal assaults, as General Lee seemed to anticipate Grant's movements and be prepared to thwart them. The Overland Campaign eventually brought the Union Army to Petersburg in mid June, where early opportunities to take the thinly defended town were missed and Confederate reinforcements soon strengthened those defenses. There, after further costly Union frontal assaults that June and an attempt to explode a mine under the Confederate lines in late July, the Federal army at Petersburg then settled into a siege that would last through the fall and winter. Total Union casualties for the entire Overland Campaign and the assaults at Petersburg that summer are hard to judge, largely because Union officers were told to underreport their losses for fear of turning Northern opinion against Grant's efforts. However, most Civil War historians would agree that in the battles of the Overland Campaign and the assaults leading up to the siege of Petersburg, the Union very likely lost between 72,000 and 75,000 killed, wounded, captured or missing, while estimates of the Confederate losses are in the area of 35,000.

Farther South, June saw the Army of General William T. Sherman making a frontal assault against the Confederate Army of Tennessee, led by General Joseph E. Johnston at the Battle of Kennesaw Mountain, near Marietta, Georgia. That battle, although a tactical Union victory, saw the Federals losing a total of approximately 3,000 casualties while the Confederate's losses were nearer 1,000.

CHAPTER SIX

September 1864: General Asboth's Raid and the Battle of Marianna

In mid September of 1864, the 2nd Maine Cavalry played a major role in a raid which took them to Marianna, Florida. General Asboth had informed General Canby on September 12 that he planned a raid northeastward from Barrancas to the area of West Florida around Marianna. Marianna, with a population of about 500, was the seat of Jackson County, and it was reported that a number of Union prisoners were being held there. In addition, General Asboth intended to capture the relatively isolated Confederate cavalry and infantry units that could be found along his route.[1]

For some in the 2nd Maine Cavalry, this operation was apparently their first encounter with Confederate forces. On September 10, Company E's Captain Samuel Clarke wrote from Barrancas, "I am considerably puzzled to tell what they intend to do with us. We have been in the service now something more than nine months, and have not seen a 'reb.' So you will see that our Regt has not a very glorious record. Still I suppose in the course of time we shall find something to do."[2]

The anticipation of another raid did not seem to overly impress other men of the 2nd Maine Cavalry if this letter from 1st Sgt. Elisha Clark of Company L is typical of the troopers' feelings. It was written the day before the regiment left Barrancas:

Dear Father,
   Again I am compelled to write to you in haste—our Regt is under marching orders ... our object is a Raid—probably just such ones as our last two ones have been—tramping along on fatiguing march—no fighting by few prisoners captured—say 8 or 9 at each raid—I am enjoying myself ...
   P.S. As soon as I get in I will write without fail.[3]

As we shall see, the upcoming raid was not at all similar to the last two, and it would be some time before Sgt. Clark could write to his father.

With Colonel Woodman commanding a brigade and remaining in camp at Barrancas, Lt. Col. Spurling was in command of the 2nd Maine Cavalry, at least for the initial phase of this expedition. Reports and accounts of that raid vary considerably, and so we'll look at official reports, accounts by eyewitnesses, and the stories that have come down over the years. In each case, an attempt will be made to put the information into context regarding the sources and possible motives of those sources. The basic information, on the other hand, is quite clear and is corroborated by various accounts. Here is the report from Major General

Gordon Granger's command, the District of West Florida and South Alabama, in the *Official Record*:

> Sept. 16: A force of 700 cavalry and infantry, mounted, left Barrancas, under command of General Asboth, on an expedition into the west part of Florida. They penetrated as far as Marianna, where they met and repulsed, after a sharp fight, a rebel force under Colonel Montgomery, capturing him and 80 of his men, 200 horses and mules, 100 stand of arms, several wagons, 400 cattle, and 600 contrabands [liberated slaves], all of which were brought safely within our lines. Asboth was severely wounded, but retained command, until the close of the expedition. Major Cutler and Lieutenant Adams, with several enlisted men of the 2nd Maine Cavalry, were badly wounded and left at Marianna. Captain Young, 7th Vermont Volunteers, and Lieutenant Ayer, 2nd Maine Cavalry, were killed. The losses are not reported on this return, as no official reports were received from the regiments in season.[4]

The expedition that led to the battle at Marianna started from Barrancas on September 16, with various elements of the Union force leaving on that day and the following day. The entire force of 700 mounted Union troops consisted of 3 battalions of the 2nd Maine Cavalry (assumed to be the entire regiment, which was made up of 3 battalions of 4 companies each), 1 battalion of the 1st Florida Cavalry, and 2 companies of mounted infantry "selected from the 86th and 82nd Regiments U.S. Colored Infantry." In this Union force, the 1st Florida Cavalry was one of the two Union cavalry regiments raised in Florida and comprised of Union supporters from that state. They were organized in the late months of 1863. The 82nd U.S. Colored Infantry had been organized in April 1864 from the 11th Corps de Afrique Infantry, while the 86th U.S. Colored Infantry was organized that same month from the 14th Corps de Afrique Infantry. The Corps de Afrique had its origins in regiments made up of free black men, largely in Louisiana, but gradually included many liberated slaves, often recruited from "contraband" camps.[5]

The various units crossed from Barrancas to Deer Point near Navy Cove and, when

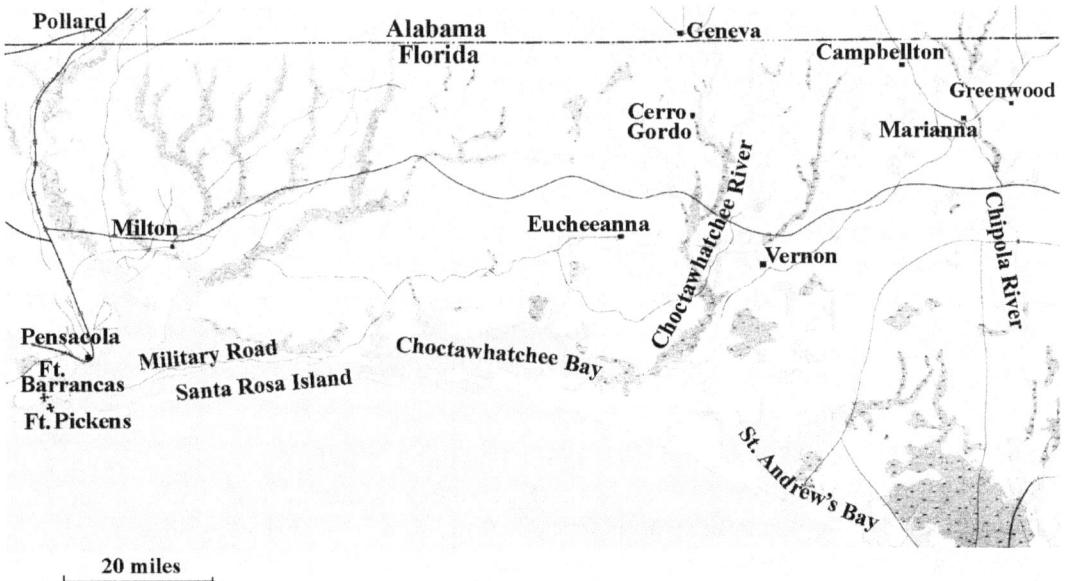

From Fort Barracas to Marianna (adapted from plate CXLVII, *Official Atlas*, and 1859 map of the State of Florida; Library of Congress).

assembled there, drew supplies from the U.S. steamer *Lizzie Davis*. On September 19, the Union force began to move eastward on the Military Road (built in 1824 shortly after the 1st Seminole War, and now largely incorporated into the Gulf Breeze Highway, Rt. 98). The *Lizzie Davis* also moved eastward along the coast and was to provide a supply base for the expedition.

Moving from the Military Road northeastward across what was known as Pine Ridges, the expedition proceeded up the Ridge Road. On September 23, General Asboth reported that the expedition "surprised this morning at daybreak Euchee Anna Court-House, with the following result, viz: Nine prisoners of war and 6 political prisoners, 46 horses with equipment, 8 mules, and 28 stand of arms. With the prisoners are W. H. Terrance, militia colonel, 1st Lieutenant Francis M. Gordan, 15th Confederate Cavalry; William Cawthorn, an influential rebel leader, and Allen Hart, a wealthy rebel beef contractor."[6]

As with other aspects of this expedition, the details of the Eucheeanna fight often vary considerably, including the number of captured Confederates and the makeup of that group. In the report from the 2nd Maine Cavalry's Company A, we read that out of "some 20 or 30 Rebel cavalry ... 5 were captured." Company D's report gives the number captured as 15, and a letter to the Bangor, Maine, *Whig and Courier* says that 25 were captured and 11 escaped. A report written to Maine Adjutant General Hodsdon states that at Eucheeanna, the 2nd Maine under Col. Spurling "surpressed and captured 25 Rebel Cav who were there enforcing the conscription." According to a recent book on the expedition to Marianna, General Asboth's report of 9 "prisoners of war" was accurate and the "political" prisoners were questioned and released. Another source states that, from the captured Confederates, 15 were selected to remain as prisoners, including the two civilians listed in General Asboth's report.[7]

The story of this engagement in the *Northern Monthly* states that the town was "Euchelia," where Lt. Col. Spurling and the 2nd Maine cavalry charged, "yelling like demons," frightened the inhabitants and took the Confederate camp by surprise, capturing a lieutenant and some 25 men. (This account gives the destination of the expedition as "Marietta." Further, "Euchelia" is the name for Eucheeanna that is in the report sent to Adjutant General Hodsdon.)[8]

In his blog of September 1, 2010, Dale Cox reports that the November 1864 edition of *The Northern Journal* includes "a new eyewitness account" which "adds much to what is known of the encounter." Reporting the Rebel cavalry at "Euchelia" as "a detachment of Chisam's famous rebel cavalry," Cox writes,

> The fighting over, the Union troops spread out through the community, taking what they wanted and doing as much damage as possible to the local farms and plantations. One member of the Second Maine described it as something of a picnic: "We got our horses some corn and dug some sweet potatoes and shot some pigs, cows, ducks, geese, hens and anything that we wanted and as many sweet potatoes as we wanted and that was some considerable many. I tell you we got all we wanted to eat while we stayed there and when we went away we took all we wanted with us and had a good time. Stayed their [sic] 2 days."[9]

This latter quote does not appear in the November *Northern Monthly*, however, and no citation is given as to the source of the letter by the unidentified 2nd Maine trooper. The content of the letter regarding parties sent to gather food is somewhat consistent with the report in the *Florida Historical Quarterly*, which states that the main body of the expedition stayed overnight at Eucheeanna and sent out raiding parties which "destroyed Douglas Ferry and small boats on the Choctawhatchee River, while another was sent to round up beef cattle on the Shoal River."[10]

Another perspective on the nature of the events in Eucheeanna comes from the Walton County web site: "The Civil War came to Eucheeanna on September 23, 1864, when the federal troops, under General Asboth, came to raze and plunder on their way to Marianna and Tallahassee."[11] And, in *History of Walton County*, written by a Confederate veteran, we read, "While at Euchee Anna he [General Asboth] sent out squads of men into the country gathering up the old men and boys and putting them in the little old two-story hewn log jail. He sent out some of his negro troops that acted disgracefully." It seems that one of the houses entered by Union troops near Eucheeanna was that of the author's parents. Given that, and the veteran's previous Confederate allegiance, coupled with his almost stream of consciousness style and clear biases, it seems quite reasonable to rely very little on that author's work when examining the action at Eucheeanna, and it would seem that a reader must look upon his account with a fair amount of caution. As an example, he describes the overnight detention of some civilians under the heading "Euchee Anna Prison."[12]

The Confederate veteran author spends considerable time decrying the behavior of the Negro troops under Asboth's command. His attitude toward African slaves is made clear in his chapter "The Negro in Walton": "I will say without fear of contradiction that the negroes of Walton, as a whole, were the happiest and best contented people in our country; and why not? They all had good masters." He goes on to state, "They were looked after and punished by their masters for their wrong doings as they corrected their own children and it was seldom they had to receive corporal punishment." This paternalistic attitude toward blacks was not unusual, of course, and is often a part of the view that these people were "in need" of being cared for like children—and that that treatment showed, in fact, a kindly attitude by the slave owners. In a later chapter, the Confederate veteran author is extremely critical of the period of Reconstruction and entitles that section "The Carpet Bag Negro Rule of Reconstruction."[13]

To return to the expedition to Marianna, from General Asboth, we learn that the Confederate prisoners taken at Eucheeanna were escorted by 2 companies of the 1st Florida Cavalry to LaGrange on the north shore of Choctawhatchee Bay, there to be taken on board the *Lizzie Davis*. In addition, "16 colored recruits, enlisted this day" were sent with the prisoners and escort. We may assume that these colored recruits were slaves freed by the expedition.[14]

At this point, General Asboth was concerned that the Rebels who had escaped from Eucheeanna would alert the countryside and perhaps direct a Confederate force to intercept his expedition. He ordered Lt. Col. Spurling, with a small detachment totaling 19 men, including Company D's Lt. Benjamin Jones and Company B's Sgt. Frank Butler, to scout the surrounding area and, if possible, capture the Rebels who had escaped from Eucheeanna. This left Major Miller in command of the 2nd Maine Cavalry.[15]

The exploits of Lt. Col. Spurling's detachment involved the Union troopers disguising themselves in Confederate uniforms—very likely taken from the Eucheeanna prisoners—and presenting themselves as Confederate soldiers. The detachment proceeded north from Eucheeanna and, without finding the Rebels who had escaped them, the disguised Federals arrived in Geneva, Alabama. Lt. Col. Spurling, introducing himself as Lieutenant Clark of the 15th Confederate Cavalry, was welcomed by the citizens of that town. Then, while returning to Florida, "Lt. Clark" and his men were warned by the residents along their way of a substantial Union force moving through the area. When one of Spurling's Union troopers became ill while on this mission, he was placed in a stolen wagon and was said to be a captured Yankee. Learning that a Union soldier had indeed been captured and was being kept at a nearby home, Lt. Col. Spurling stopped there and claimed the Union soldier as a prisoner of war, whom he would take with him. The soldier himself was apparently amazed to see his own lieutenant colonel dressed in a Confederate uniform, and nearly gave the game away in his confusion before being taken away by the disguised Yankees.[16]

Proceeding toward Campbellton, Florida, Col. Spurling's detachment captured a train of 3 Confederate wagons with the 3 drivers. Once again, while looking at the facts as reported, we can see how widely the interpretation of those facts can vary. In his book on the Battle of Marianna, Dale Cox records the capture of the three wagon drivers as follows: "Three prisoners, militiamen from Dale County, Alabama, were taken prisoner." Cox continues: "What became of them is a mystery to this day. They never showed up on Union prisoner of war lists nor did they ever return home to their families. The only logical assumption, as unsettling as it may be, is that Spurling had them executed. He and his men knew they would face execution themselves if their true identities were revealed and they may have decided not to take chances."[17]

Cox's statement is one that we may take exception to, or which, at the very least requires examination. The assumption that Spurling would order the execution of 3 men one day and then take prisoners and keep them with his detachment the next day would seem to argue against Spurling having decided "not to take chances" by keeping Confederate prisoners with his troops. Not knowing what happened to 3 specific men does not logically mean that those men were murdered. The only source cited by Cox for the fate of the 3 captured wagon drivers is a letter to the Bangor, Maine, *Whig and Courier* dated October 8, 1864. In that letter, the writer states that Lt. Col. Spurling and his men "overtook a train of three rebel army wagons, laden with salt. This he captured, with three prisoners, and turning off, proceeded toward Marianna." The letter goes on to report the capture of other Confederates on the following day. That newspaper source cited by Cox contains no information about the identities or fate of the 3 wagon drivers, other than the fact that they were captured.[18]

Moving in a generally southerly direction, and after passing Marianna, where, as we will see, the rest of General Asboth's force had been involved in a battle, Spurling and his men were able to avoid capture by various Confederate cavalry detachments, and indeed captured several more Rebels. Col. Spurling and his men continued their move to rejoin the main Union force.[19]

From Eucheeanna General Asboth's expedition had turned north to Cerro Gordo, and from there it crossed the Choctawhatchee River on September 25 and moved, according to Gen. Asboth's report, "speedily via Campbellton to Marianna." For some reason, General Asboth does not mention an engagement with Rebel troops that apparently took place on September 26 at Campbellton. A Confederate cavalry force of 30 to 50 men under Captain Alexander Godwin began skirmishing with the Union force in an attempt to delay their advance. This Confederate force consisted primarily of partisans, local men with farms in that area, not in uniform, and fighting with their own weapons which included shotguns and hunting rifles. Their tactics involved waiting for the head of Gen. Asboth's column to come within range, firing a few shots, and then withdrawing. At least two members of this partisan unit were captured by Gen. Asboth's men, but it appears that no record of the exact number of Confederate casualties, if there were others, has survived. At this point, a rider from Captain Godwin's force was sent to alert the Confederates in Marianna of this approaching Union expedition. Meanwhile, General Asboth and his command, tired from their march over muddy roads in the rain, camped at Campbellton for the night of September 26, with the intention of getting an early start the next day.[20]

It is said that this news of the Union force a mere 18 miles away came as a considerable shock to the Confederate commander at Marianna, Colonel Alexander Montgomery, a former U.S. Army artillery officer, and a Confederate veteran who had been wounded at 2nd Bull Run. While the Federal units had been advancing in a generally eastward or northeastward direction, their possible route and their intentions were unclear. Col. Montgomery had apparently sent one company of his cavalry to the west from Marianna to investigate the reports of fighting at Eucheeanna. Other Confederate cavalry companies had been ordered to the southwest to intercept a rumored Federal incursion from St. Andrew's Bay.[21]

Colonel Montgomery had at hand two companies of cavalry and newly recruited conscripts from the area's training camp. Riders were quickly sent to gather as many as possible of the cavalry units that were within recall distance. One writer has questioned why Colonel Montgomery did not request reinforcements from Tallahassee or Quincy, Florida, to aid in his defense of Marianna. The distance from Marianna to Quincy is almost 40 miles as the crow flies, with Tallahassee another 20 miles or so beyond. It may have been that Colonel Montgomery simply didn't feel that he had the time to summon help from that distance. It also seems that Colonel Montgomery could still not be sure of the goals or routes to be taken by the Union force, perhaps did not know the numbers of Union troops to be faced, and so could not be sure where and in what force he might confront the Federals.[22]

It was, in fact, General Asboth's intention to head for Marianna. Marianna was (and is) the seat of Jackson County, was the home of Florida Governor John Milton, and in 1864, although its population was only about 500, it was the largest Northwest Florida town still firmly held by the Confederates. At the time of General Asboth's raid, Marianna had become noticed by Union informants for its Confederate military base which, along with a store of quartermaster supplies and pens for Confederate government livestock, was a mustering and recruiting center for the Florida militia and the site of a large camp for men conscripted into the Confederate army.[23]

To alert the Confederate forces in Marianna if the Federal advance continued in that direction, Col. Montgomery ordered the available conscripts to picket duty on the Campbellton and St. Andrew's Bay roads. Of this group, at least a dozen took the opportunity to quickly desert and disappear into the woods.[24]

On the morning of September 27, when Asboth's column passed the last significant crossroads before Marianna, there was no doubt in Colonel Montgomery's mind as to the route the Federals would take. A letter from an inhabitant of Marianna, quoted in Dale Cox's book, *The Battle of Marianna, Florida*, states, "At 8 o'clock the citizens were called to arms and formed into a company ready for service. Women heard the dreadful tidings with blanched faces and hastened with trembling hands and hearts that almost ceased to beat with very heaviness to gather up some things that might be saved from the pillaging band that would soon be upon us. Can anyone realize the feelings of mothers and wives and fathers and husbands as they gave the parting kiss to dear ones that morning, knowing not the fate that might be theirs."[25]

With the ringing of the church bells as an alarm call, the citizens of Marianna met in the courthouse to organize their defense. There had been a company of Jackson County Home Guards formed in Marianna in 1861, but with no military operations taking place in or near the town, that company had gradually become inactive. And so, as a result of this mass meeting, a new company—a "cradle and grave" company of young boys and old men—was formed.[26]

This local militia force, commanded by Captain Jesse Norwood, was joined by a few

Confederate soldiers who happened to be home on leave. In addition, Captain Henry Robinson's cavalry from nearby Greenwood also arrived in Marianna to oppose the approaching Union troops. Robinson's cavalry was largely made up of school boys who were drilled by Henry Robinson, their teacher and captain. The total number of this militia force of Confederate defenders of the town has been estimated at around 150 men.[27]

As Gen. Asboth's expedition approached Marianna, it is reported that his men looted some of the plantations along the route, including that of the pro-Union mayor of Marianna, Thomas White. By the time the Federals reached Marianna, they were carrying a substantial amount of supplies taken from various plantations, and were accompanied by several hundred slaves who had attached themselves to the protection of the Union column.[28]

A few miles west of Marianna, Colonel Montgomery decided to take up a defensive line to delay the advancing Federals. His two cavalry regiments, joined by Captain Godwin's partisan horsemen, who had previously skirmished with Asboth's force, now numbered around 160 and took their position on the east bank of Hopkins' Branch, a wide, slow-running stream. The Union troops not only had a strong numerical advantage over the Confederate defenders here and later in Marianna, but were armed with breech-loading carbines, while the Confederates were generally armed with muzzle loaders. Thus the Union force could fire and reload much more rapidly than the Rebels. Outnumbered and outgunned, the Confederates were compelled to withdraw, but they kept up a harassing fire on the advancing Federals.[29]

As author Dale Cox explains, "These accounts of a sharp fight just northwest of town have long been ignored or written off by those researching the Battle of Marianna. Possibly this is because evidence that the engagement began three miles outside of town does not match well with the traditional story of a small home guard fighting without support from Colonel Montgomery or his cavalry."[30]

When Colonel Montgomery's forces withdrew to Marianna, his cavalry was drawn up in a wide line to confront the advancing Federals. This gave the Confederates the opportunity to deliver a volley at the Union troops who would, as they entered the town, be coming around a tight corner, were still compacted into their marching formation, and would be surprised by the new Confederate line. Behind the Rebel cavalry, the local militia erected a barricade of wagons and carts across the street which would prove to be a substantial barrier to the Union cavalry. Meanwhile the militiamen took up their positions, hidden behind fences and in buildings along the street. As the Federal troops advanced, however, this plan for the initial volley by the Rebel cavalry almost did not take place. Fearing that his men might be outflanked by the Federals, Colonel Montgomery ordered his cavalry force to withdraw, and he ordered a general retreat to another defensive line on the Chipola River, just east of Marianna. This order was not well received by either the cavalry or the home guard militia, and neither group immediately withdrew. While Colonel Montgomery was attempting to explain his reasoning, the first units of General Asboth's force rounded the corner, and the battle commenced.[31]

Various reports of this part of the battle are in general agreement as to the facts, but as we will see, there are differences in emphasis, explanation and interpretation. Private Edgar Davis, who was a 25 year old clerk from Belfast, Maine, at the time he enlisted in the 2nd Maine Cavalry, wrote the report of the battle that was sent to Maine Adjutant General John Hodsdon. Pvt. Davis gave this account of General Asboth's engagement at Marianna:

[We] encountered a strong Rebel force at Marianna, the county seat of Jackson County. The 2nd Maine Cav. was in the advance, Maj. Cutler's Battalion ahead, and as they advanced they received a volley from the Rebel Cav, which dismounted quite a number and killed Lt. Ayer outright. The 1st Battalion wavered and fell back, Maj. Cutler gallantly striving to rally them, but without success. Maj. Hutchinson was ordered to charge his battalion, which he did, he and Maj. Cutler leading the charge, the Rebs fleeing like a flock of sheep before them.

Charging down a street they [the 2nd Maine Cavalry] met a barricade of wagons which they cleared in gallant style, when they received a volley from a body of militia concealed in the stores, houses and churches, which literally mowed down the head of the column. Maj. Cutler fell badly wounded, his leg broken, wrist fractured and other wounds. Maj. Hutchinson, wounded in leg & foot, Lieut. Adams mortally, shot through the chest—Lieut. Moody, Co. L in the thigh. Sergeant [Elisha] Clarke ["Clark," according to the regiment's roster], Co. L, mortally wounded, Corp. [Thomas] Davis Co. L killed, and many other wounded whose names I have not yet obtained. I am informed our casualties will reach 30.

Our force remained at Marianna about 5 hours. They left Maj. Cutler, and Lt. Adams, Serg't Clark and several others at that place. The occupants of the house where they are promised they should have the best of care.

The other commands took no part in the fight. It was all done and well done by the 2nd Maine, and the large number of casualties among our officers is a proof that they do not ask their men to go where they dare not lead.[32]

(In fact, Sergeant Clark was not mortally wounded but was left at Marianna and taken prisoner. Although he survived his wounds and was later paroled, it would be some time before he could write to his father as he had promised in the letter quoted at the start of this chapter.)

General Asboth's report is much different, and he was very critical of the 2nd Maine Cavalry's first advance into Marianna. The general begins by stating that the Rebels had skirmished with his troops since he had crossed the Choctawhatchee, but "gave us battle only at Marianna, which resulted in a brilliant victory for my command."

Lt. Isaac Adams
(courtesy Maine State Archives).

Pvt. Edgar Davis
(courtesy Maine State Archives).

Lt. William Moody (courtesy Maine State Archives).

Essentially ignoring the initial volley fired by the Confederate cavalry as the Union troops rounded the blind bend in the road, the nature of the barricade and ambush laid within the town, and the number of casualties suffered by the 2nd Maine troopers as a result, General Asboth's report goes on to state: "The first charge upon the town, with the rebel cavalry in front formed in line of battle and the militia sharpshooters concentrated in the grave-yard, church, and other buildings on the left flank of the narrow path through which we had to pass, was repulsed. The second, however, led by myself, was a brilliant and successful one, and all my troops except the repulsed battalion of the 2nd Maine Cavalry behaved with the utmost gallantry and secured for our raid a most decided success."[33]

Another report quotes General Asboth as being even more clearly critical of the 2nd Maine Cavalry's initial advance or "charge" into Marianna: "Presently General Asboth gave orders to charge and two companies of cavalry advanced about two thirds of the way to the barricade, when the rebels opened fire and drove the charging Federals back in disorder. General Asboth was greatly disappointed and cried, 'For Shame! For Shame!' as the cavalry rushed past. The men, however, soon re-formed and another charge was ordered."[34]

Again, it would seem, despite General Asboth's disparaging comments, that the casualties suffered by the 2nd Maine Cavalry in their initial advance into Marianna, the volley fired by the Rebel cavalry, the barricade they encountered, and the fire of an unknown number of Confederate militia from behind cover would justify the cavalry's withdrawal and its need to reform for a second, and successful charge. It is difficult, at least to this reader, to see General Asboth's remarks as anything other than self-congratulatory. On the other hand, Pvt. Davis' report recorded above—that only the 2nd Maine was engaged and that "other commands took no part in the fight"—is a considerable exaggeration, unless he is referring only to the opening phase of the battle. If Private Davis was referring to that initial advance and the charges into the town, his statement is quite likely accurate. However, the fact that other parts of General Asboth's command also suffered casualties and that there are clear reports of other elements of the Union force taking part in the battle certainly indicate that the whole Union force was engaged in various phases of the fighting at Marianna.

During the opening engagements of the battle—the Federal troops advancing into the town on the main road—it seems that after the first charge was repulsed, General Asboth sent a contingent by an unguarded road to outflank the defenders of Marianna. This group was apparently in place at the rear of the Confederate force, and when Asboth led his charge and the Rebel cavalry had withdrawn, that group—Montgomery's troopers—was confronted by the Union flanking force. Some of this Confederate cavalry managed to cross the Chipola River just east of Marianna and burn the bridge, but Colonel Montgomery and a number of his men were captured. The exact count of those captured at that time varies quite considerably, but it seems reasonable that about 30 of Colonel Montgomery's men shared their commander's fate and became prisoners.[35]

After the Confederate cavalry had fired their volley at the 2nd Maine troopers and had withdrawn from their position to move toward the Chipola River, the local militia–home guard remained in place. Reports of this next phase of the battle vary considerably regarding many points. Some supposed actions have apparently taken on the status of legend, while other actions are based on one's presumptions and attitudes. As an example, consider the way in which the actions of members of the Colored Infantry are reported. An apparently straightforward report taken from the muster rolls of the 82nd U.S. Colored Infantry states that members of that regiment attacked home guard members behind the Episcopal Church. The black troops "dismounted under a galling fire of buck ball at a range of thirty yards and, fixing their bayonets, charged over the church yard fence compelling the enemy's company to surrender, killing and wounding some eighteen."[36]

Another account of the actions by the black Federal soldiers is found in *The West Florida News*, October 3, 1864, which reported, "Most of our killed were butchered and beaten to death after they had surrendered, by the infernal Negro troops who finding them in their power took the advantage of it."[37]

Of course various reports can be interpreted differently. It is interesting, and perhaps a bit puzzling, that Dale Cox in his *The Battle of Marianna, Florida*, when speaking of the reports of brutality by black soldiers states that,

> Charles Wilson, a member of the 2nd Maine Cavalry, confirmed these allegations when he wrote: "To those at home who are doubtful as to the fighting qualities of the Negro, let me say that the Negro will fight. No one who witnessed the conduct of the colored troops on this expedition will ever doubt their being brave and able soldiers. They are stimulated by a love of freedom and a spirit of revenge, and woe to the unfortunate grayback who falls into their hands."[38]

It would seem that the above quote from Sgt. Wilson could easily be interpreted simply as a statement of the positive fighting qualities held by the black soldiers that he had observed, and not an affirmation of their brutal behavior. Cox gives the names of two other Union soldiers who reported atrocities committed by black troops in the churchyard—the 2nd Maine Cavalry's Privates Alvarez Austin and Edward Marson, and cites Noah Trudeau's work, *Like Men of War*, as the source. The roster of the regiment shows no men of those names, although there is a Private William A. (possibly Alvarez?) Austin in Company G, and a Corporal Edward Manson in Company L.[39]

But, in fairness, Cox does say, "Despite the claims of the *West Florida News*, however, there is no reason to believe that extensive atrocities were carried out by the Union troops." And, as he gives statistics of the number of killed and captured in St. Luke's Churchyard, Cox states that the evidence "precludes any post-surrender massacre of Southern troops."[40]

Captain George Maynard, one of the white officers of the 82nd Colored Infantry, reports a reason why feelings among his troops may have run high: "after an engagement of three-quarters of an hour they [the Confederates in the Churchyard] made overtures to surrender. No sooner had the Union troops ceased firing than they [the Confederates] immediately reopened fire, killing one of our boys, which infuriated us." This officer states that his men were so outraged that they did, indeed, begin "an indiscriminate attack upon the Confederates as they were being captured." Captain Maynard goes on to state that he regained control of his men by threatening to shoot any who harmed a prisoner, and that "this course prevented a massacre of our captured foes." Other Union troops, including Louis E. Norris, an assistant surgeon of the 2nd Maine Cavalry, described the aftermath of the engagement at the churchyard in similar terms. Captain Maynard was later a recipient of the Congressional Medal of Honor, and a part of the citation lists his actions protecting the surrendered Confederates in Marianna.[41]

A few of the Confederate home guard did not surrender in the churchyard, but took cover inside St. Luke's Church and continued to fire at the Union troops. At that point, the order was given by General Asboth's second in command, Colonel Lasislas Zulavsky, to set fire to the church, and soldiers of the U.S. Colored Infantry complied, using kerosene and artillery swabs to start the fire. As the church burned, eyewitness accounts say that some Rebels who ran from the building were shot. Four others apparently burned to death in the building.[42]

And so, it seems likely there was considerable anger and fear by the local people upon seeing black soldiers in their town and a tendency to report the behavior of black soldiers in as unfavorable a way as possible. It also appears that some of those black soldiers may have, indeed, seen a chance to take revenge on white Southerners for the conditions suffered by slaves. They may also have been reacting to the reported atrocities committed by Confederates at Fort Pillow in April of 1864, reports of similar murders after the battle of Olustee,

This banner, from the 22nd U.S. Colored Troops, gives a clear indication of the attitudes of at least some black soldiers toward their Confederate enemy (National Archives).

Florida, in February 1864, and the killing of wounded and helpless black soldiers at Port Hudson back in the summer of 1863.[43]

The losses for the Confederates who defended Marianna are given as 10 dead and 16 wounded. Union losses are listed as 8 dead or died of wounds and 19 wounded. There were also a number on both sides who were captured, as we will see.[44]

To return more specifically to the 2nd Maine Cavalry, once the fighting at Marianna had ceased, their total casualties were 6 killed outright or died of wounds, 12 wounded, and 8 taken prisoner. The 2nd Maine's high proportion of the total Federal casualties would seem to support the contention that they bore the brunt of the fighting. Of the 12 listed as wounded, 5 were seen as too badly wounded to travel and were left in the care of the towns-people. At least one of these, Major Cutler, had his wounds attended at the home of the town's mayor before being sent to Andersonville Prison. Of the other wounded members of the 2nd Maine Cavalry later sent to Andersonville, one—Daniel Ellis of Company H—died in the prison. We also have an unusual opportunity to see how anticipation turns to a more grim reality: recall how 1st Sgt. Clark of Company L, whose letter is quoted at the start of this chapter, had written the rather upbeat letter about going on another apparently routine raid. Sgt. Clark was also wounded and left as a prisoner at Marianna and he, too, was sent to Andersonville, but survived. (For a list of the men from the 2nd Maine Cavalry taken prisoner at Marianna and held at Andersonville, see Appendix D.)[45]

To give one last bit of the lore that grew up around the Battle of Marianna, there are conflicting reports as to how Major Cutler was wounded, the most commonly recorded story saying that he confronted two very young Rebels and, because of their youth, hesitated to attack them with his saber, at which point he was shot from his horse by one of them. Another report, by the 2nd Maine Cavalry's surgeon, Dr. George Martin, says that he "saw Major Cutler wounded at Marianna. He was charging at the head of his command down the main street when a volley was fired by the Rebs from the churchyard, making 8 wounds in the left leg, thigh and forearm. His horse fell dead, riddled with bullets. I had him taken to the mayor's house and dressed his wounds." And Major Cutler's own account agrees with that of Dr. Martin. The mayor was the same Thomas White whose plantation, northwest of Marianna, was said to have been looted by the Union troops in their approach to the town.[46]

That account of Major Cutler's wounds also would seem to call into substantial question another bit of local lore—that when St. Luke's Church was set on fire to drive out the last of the Confederates, the major ran into the burning building and rescued the Bible, and it was after he came out of the church that he was confronted by the two youths and received his wounds. Somebody did, indeed, save the Bible, and it is now displayed in a glass case in the sanctuary of the current church. It bears a note stating that it was rescued by Major Nathan Cutler. We may never know how it was actually saved.[47]

After the Battle of Marianna, General Asboth, who was himself badly wounded, abandoned any thoughts of proceeding farther and began a withdrawal toward Washington Point on the head of Choctawhatchee Bay. Their route took the Union forces through Vernon, and although no mention is found in General Asboth's account, or those of the 2nd Maine Cavalry, it is reported that a final engagement of the Marianna expedition took place at Vernon. A force of 50 or so Confederate militia, commanded by Captain William Jones, came upon the head of the Union column and were ordered by the Federals to surrender. Reports of just what happened next are conflicting, but in the end, the majority of the Confederates were captured and the rest fled.[48]

General Asboth's report states that his troops "reached in safety the steamer Lizzie Davis with provisions for my command." He goes on: "We captured 81 prisoners of war, 95 stand of arms, quantities of commissary and quartermaster's stores, over 200 fine horses and excellent mules, 17 wagons, and over 400 head of cattle, already brought within our lines, besides over 600 contrabands who followed us with greatest enthusiasm. The most prominent among the rebel officers taken and already brought within our lines are Brig. Gen. William E. Anderson, of the militia, and Col. A. B. Montgomery, a West Pointer, of the regular Confederate Army, commanding the District of West Florida."[49]

We cannot know if General Asboth's report concerning Colonel Montgomery's history and importance was exaggerated by the general to make Montgomery's capture seem more important, or whether Colonel Montgomery exaggerated his own story, but this Alexander Montgomery was not actually the Confederate Commander of the District of West Florida and was not a West Point graduate. The only Alexander Montgomery to graduate from West Point before the Civil War was in the class of 1834, was from Pennsylvania, and served on quartermaster duty for the Union Army during the Civil War. The Colonel Alexander Montgomery captured at Marianna had been educated as a physician and was from Georgia. He had, however, been in the Union Army before the Civil War as a 2nd lieutenant of artillery, and had resigned to join the Confederate Army in 1861. He had been wounded at 2nd Bull Run as lieutenant colonel of the 3rd Georgia Infantry, and was then promoted to colonel and given the command of the Confederate post at Marianna. This post, although sometimes referred to as the headquarters of the Confederate's "district" or "military organization" of West Florida, was in fact just the small Confederate force in and near Marianna.[50]

General Asboth's report continues, "Although in consideration of the character of the fight our loss is not large, yet it is deeply felt by the whole command." And, when writing this second report on the expedition, had General Asboth reconsidered his rather harsh criticism of the 2nd Maine Cavalry? In his list of officers killed or wounded he included among the wounded "the dashing young Majors Hutchinson and Cutler, Second Maine Cavalry." He continues: "I myself was honored by the rebels with two balls, the first in the face, breaking the cheek bone, the other fracturing my left arm in two places. In consequence of those serious wounds received," General Asboth embarked with the wounded and prisoners on the *Lizzie Davis* for Barrancas and command of the Union force was given to Colonel Zulavsky, 82nd Colored Infantry, with "directions to move down the peninsula and Santa Rosa Island to Fort Pickens, where they are expected to arrive" on October 4, after a march of over 400 miles from their starting point at Barrancas.[51]

Lt. Col. Spurling and his 19 men, still in Confederate uniforms, rejoined the main body of the Union force on its return from Marianna. When they were sighted by the rest of General Asboth's expedition, they were, at first, assumed to be one of the Rebel cavalry squads that were pursuing the Yankees. But, according to C.C. Robert's account, "displaying a dirty pair of drawers, by way of a flag of truce," Col. Spurling and his men were safely able to rejoin their comrades who, not having heard from him for several days, had thought he and his men had been killed or captured. Lt. Col. Spurling "and his command came in with fifteen prisoners, fifty horses, several teams, and a large train of cattle, mules and contrabands, having been absent five days and accomplished all this without the loss of a man. During this jaunt he traveled one hundred and twenty-five miles and experienced several adventures."[52]

Some of those "adventures" have been mentioned earlier, but as Lt. Col. Spurling and his men, still disguised as Confederates, made their way to rejoin Gen. Asboth's force, they were apparently encouraged along their way by Confederate sympathizers who had heard of the fighting at Marianna. The impostors were fed by these locals, and were even given arms and ammunition at at least one house.[53]

The Federal troops of the expedition to Marianna marched to Washington Point at the east end of Choctawhatchee Bay, then proceeded westward along the south shore of the bay and were taken by boat to Santa Rosa Island. Marching the length of Santa Rosa Island to Fort Pickens, the men were then ferried back to Fort Barrancas, where they arrived on October 5.[54]

When the regiment had returned to its quarters at Barrancas, Lt. Col. Spurling singled out two men for special mention. Corporal Daniel H. Wheaton of Company D was promoted to sergeant "for good conduct in the engagement at Marianna Sept 27th," and Corporal Edward A. Cushman of Company M was also promoted to the rank of sergeant "for meritorious conduct at Marianna Fla."[55]

Chapter Seven

Late 1864: Dissension Regarding Promotions and Raids on Pollard and Milton

Within just days of the 2nd Maine Cavalry's return to Fort Barrancas, the issues concerning favoritism and dissension were raised once again. A letter to Maine's Governor Cony on October 9, from Captain Twitchell of Company A states,

> A number of our Officers have requested me ... to drop you a line in regard to certain officers in our Regiment. A number of the Officers feeling themselves wronged by Col. Woodman saw fit to tender their resignations. He Endorsed up ["upon?"] them, Recommending that they be dismissed the service with loss of all pay. They were returned by the General Commanding the Department, disapproved. The envy that heretofore existed against us has now of course turned into hatred and we know of now [no] means of redress only by applying to your excellency.[1]

Twitchell was an officer who had previously voiced his discontent with conditions in the regiment and had unsuccessfully requested a transfer back in June of 1864. He was also mentioned in Major Miller's complaining letter of July 1864 as one who should have (but did not) receive a promotion at that time. Themes of that nature were interspersed throughout the time of the 2nd Maine Cavalry's service, and we'll hear more concerning Captain Twitchell later.

In October of 1864, the 2nd Maine was at Barrancas and various groups were sent out into the nearby area on missions involving scouting and collecting supplies, including bricks and logs. On October 18, a detachment of 200 men and one section of the 1st Florida Battery, all under Lt. Col. Spurling, were sent up Escambia Bay on the steamer *Planter* to collect logs. While there, the Union troops were attacked by the Rebels, "about 300 strong, who were repulsed after one hour's heavy skirmishing."[2]

For some reason, the men under Lt. Col. Spurling's command on this mission were not from the 2nd Maine Cavalry. In Col. Spurling's report of this action, he states,

> I left the wharf at this place [Barrancas] on the morning of the 18th instant at 10 o'clock, on the steamer Planter, with a detachment of 200 men from the 19th Iowa Volunteers and one section of the 1st Florida Battery, and proceeded up the Blackwater within 9 miles of Milton, where I landed, and, after establishing a strong picket-line, commenced to secure logs in that vicinity. While thus engaged the enemy attacked me with a force, I should judge, of 300 men. After a skirmish of two hours the battery opened upon them, when they fell back out of range. I then succeeded in securing 140 logs, and returned with a loss of 1 man killed and 1 wounded of the 19th Iowa Volunteers, and 1 man wounded of the 1st Florida Battery. I could not ascertain what damage we did to the enemy.[3]

It seems a bit odd that reports from officers, although not engaged in this action, nevertheless gave their own estimates of the Confederate losses. Gen. Joseph Bailey, in command of the Union's District of West Florida, reported that "the rebels must have suffered severely," while a summary of the action in West Florida in the *Official Record* states that the "rebels lost 4 killed or mortally wounded."[4]

On October 19, "about the same number [200 men] under Lt. Col. Spurling were sent up Escambia Bay to collect bricks. Returned the same day with 10,000 without having been molested." General Bailey's report of this expedition to collect bricks includes the information that Spurling and his men also brought back "a lot of doors and window sash."[5]

On October 25, a larger expedition was sent to Milton. General Bailey reported:

> An expedition of 700 men ... under Lt. Col. Spurling, 2nd Maine Cavalry, to Blackwater Bay, which left here on the 25th instant, returning today [Oct. 28].
>
> The rebels were driven through Milton by the cavalry, and 8 captured, besides 5 or 6 known to have been killed or wounded. My plans were to catch the whole gang of Confederates, about 100 strong, but failed, through the misconception of orders on the part of one of the detachment commanders. Eight cribs of Confederate lumber, containing over 85,000 feet, seasoned (1 inch or 1¼ inches thick, and 5 or 6 inches wide), 15,000 feet besides of seasoned lumber, and 130 logs were the proceeds of the expedition. No casualties in my force.[6]

Colonel Spurling's report of the same action gives the details of the makeup of the expedition and the reasons why the plan did not fully work as intended. Spurling states that he embarked on October 25 from Barrancas in charge of a force consisting of a 100 man detachment of the 2nd Maine Cavalry, 100 dismounted men of 1st Florida Cavalry, a detachment of 19th Iowa Infantry, 25th, 82nd, and 86th U.S. Colored Infantry, and Captain Roberts' Company M, 2nd Maine Cavalry, dismounted for battery purposes, and in charge of two howitzers, the whole force amounting to over 700 men.

Captain Stearns of the 82nd Colored Infantry with 200 infantry on the transport *Lizzie Davis* had orders to land 8 miles below Pierce's Mill to "raft logs, which are numerous along the shore, and by other and all his actions endeavor to draw the enemy upon the narrow point of land or peninsula formed by Escambia Bay on the west and East Bay and Blackwater River on the east." (See map of Pensacola area in Chapter Five.)

Lt. Col. Spurling then proceeded with another transport, the *Planter,* to Pensacola, remaining there till late in the afternoon, and from there went up Escambia Bay, and late in the night landed 300 infantry, under Major Mudgett, of the 86th Colored Infantry, at

> a point on the east side of Escambia Bay, opposite Pierce's Mill, with orders that he should march to the head of the bayou and remain there till he should hear cannonading on the other side of the narrow point of land, when he would deploy his force across to Pierce's Mill, thus cutting off the retreat of the enemy, whom I expected, and had good reason to believe, Captain Stearns would succeed in drawing into the trap which I had prepared for them, inasmuch as they had in considerable force on former occasions attacked me while I was engaged in procuring logs at points 7 or 8 miles below the mill. After landing Major Mudgett, I proceeded back with the *Planter,* and on the following morning, having rounded the point of the peninsula, was on my way up East Bay or Blackwater River.

Colonel Spurling did not find the *Lizzie Davis* or Captain Stearns and his command where they were supposed to be; "Instead of landing where he was directed, he had gone 6 or 7 miles too far" and had anchored in a small cove a mile or two from the mill. "Thus the enemy was not induced to come far down upon the point of land as I designed, and as would have been the case had my orders been fully carried out."

On coming up with the *Lizzie Davis,* I directed Captain Lincoln, of the 2nd Maine Cavalry, to relieve Captain Stearns of his command, to land with all possible dispatch the 200 men on board, and march direct to Milton. By 11 a.m. Captain Lincoln had landed the troops from the *Lizzie Davis.* I proceeded with the *Planter* to Pierce's Mill and landed the cavalry and battery, which I had been holding in reserve, and immediately moved toward Milton, soon coming upon Captain Lincoln, whom I found engaged with a force of the enemy's cavalry. It seems that Captain Lincoln, after landing, before he had hardly taken up the march, was met by a considerable force of cavalry, with which he became engaged. He drove the enemy to the mill, and beyond it on the Milton road, where they made a stand under cover of some old buildings. On my arrival at this point, the firing was quite rapid, and a brisk skirmish was going on. I immediately charged with the detachment of cavalry which I had brought up, and drove the rebels from the old buildings. They fled in wild confusion on the Milton road. At a bridge they attempted to make a stand, but all to no purpose. I pursued them through Milton and out on the Pollard road, a distance of over 8 miles, capturing 9 prisoners and wounding quite a number. Their rout was complete. Their arms and equipment, and everything that could impede flight, were thrown away.

Capt. John Lincoln (courtesy Maine State Archives).

There were no casualties in my own force. The enemy's forces consisted of a detachment of between 70 and 80 of the 8th Mississippi Cavalry and a small force of Militia.

After keeping up the pursuit of the Rebels

as long as it was prudent, my horses becoming exhausted, and it growing late in the day, I returned to Milton, and leaving the cavalry to hold the place, went back to the *Planter,* which I ordered to be moved up to a place called Bagdad, less than 2 miles from Milton, where I secured quite a large amount of lumber....

On the following morning [October 27th] the pickets were taken in, and the *Planter* moved up the river to Milton, thus exploding, if not the torpedoes, the idea and belief that they are planted in the river to obstruct its passage by boats. Here several flat-boats were secured, and the ferry across the river completely demolished. Quite an amount of commissary and quartermaster's property were found, among which was about 290 bushels of corn and meal and considerable ham and beef, and since there was no means of transportation by which it could be got to the boat, it was destroyed. Considerable surplus ordnance, accouterments, and horse equipments were also destroyed. Several horses and mules were captured. Having brought off or destroyed everything that could be of use to the enemy, and having accomplished all that circumstances could admit of, I returned to Barrancas with my whole force, where I arrived on the morning of the 28th.[7]

Of this action, General Bailey, the commander of the District of West Florida, wrote, "Lieutenant-Colonel Spurling is deserving a very great deal of credit for his management of this and other expeditions. I find him a most invaluable officer."[8]

At the end of October 1864, the "Organization of Troops ... District of West Florida" lists Bvt. Brig. General Joseph Bailey in command of the district with Colonel Ephraim Woodman in command of the 2nd Brigade of cavalry. That brigade was made up of the 1st Florida Cavalry (6 companies), under the command of Major Albert Ruttkay, and the 2nd Maine Cavalry, commanded by Lt. Col. Andrew Spurling. As with General Asboth and Colonel Zulavsky (82nd U.S. Colored Troops), Major Ruttkay was yet another Hungarian. And, like Colonel Zulavsky, Major Ruttkay was a nephew of the Hungarian freedom fighter Kossuth and had fled Hungary after Kossuth's failed attempt to win Hungarian freedom from the Austrian Empire.[9]

Even with the various earlier discussions of deaths due to disease and the letters expressing concerns about the health of the regiment, it may still be all too easy to overlook those many soldiers who died of sickness rather than from battle wounds. As seen in the reports of action against enemy troops above, these accounts include the losses of dead and wounded, but meanwhile, men were dying back in camp and in hospitals in far greater numbers. Many more men died of disease than died in battle during the Civil War and this was particularly true of the Union soldiers sent to the Deep South. In mid October of 1864, Orrin Seco's name was added to the long list of men who died from sickness. The young African American soldier serving in the "white" regiment was one of the 334 men of the 2nd Maine Cavalry who died in that way.

In early November of 1864, a small detachment of "50 picked men" was sent under Captain Elijah D. Johnson of Company C and Lieutenant Marcus Vose of Company H "for special duty" to Mobile Bay. And, as the regiment's records for November indicate, "The regiment, with the above exception, lay quietly in camp [at Barrancas] until November 16, furnishing quite large details for fatigue upon an abatis, lately constructed across the neck of the peninsula."[10]

On the morning of November 16, an order was received directing Col. Woodman, commanding the brigade, to have all the men that could be mounted in his command to report to Lt. Col. Spurling with 3 days' rations. The force that was assembled consisted of 450 men of the 2nd Maine Cavalry and 1st Florida Cavalry. That number would seem to indicate a lack of available horses, since the actual number of men available for duty was much higher. Lt. Colonel Spurling was to command the entire detachment of Union troops, while Major Hutchinson

Capt. Elijah Johnson (courtesy Maine State Archives).

Pvt. Charles Kimball (left) and Pvt. Daniel W. Barker. Both died of disease in 1864 (courtesy Maine State Archives).

would command the 2nd Maine Cavalry and Major Ruttkay would command the 1st Florida. Leaving Barrancas at about noon on the 16th, the expedition moved northward and bivouacked about 11 miles north of Pensacola. Starting early the next morning along the road that runs parallel to the Alabama and Florida Railroad, at around 6 a.m., Col. Spurling reported that "at sunrise, the advance guard, commanded by Lieutenant Sanders, Company F, 1st Florida, came upon a rebel picket of three men" and captured them. A mile beyond, "another picket of four was surprised and captured; and a mile farther on six men, constituting the reserve, were made prisoner." From these prisoners, Lt. Col. Spurling learned that the Confederate picket was to be relieved at 10 a.m. and the advance guard of the Union force was sent forward "to intercept and capture the men who were anticipated as relief." That was, indeed, what happened, and the men who were to relieve those on picket duty were added to those already captured.[11]

Moving on, the Union column reached the bridge

Lt. Marcus Vose (courtesy Maine State Archives).

at Pine Barren Creek and Spurling reports, "I succeeded without difficulty in capturing the rebel picket on the bridge, not a single shot being exchanged, and without alarming their camp, although it was close by, within 20 rods" (a bit over 100 yards). The bridge was in "a very bad condition," but Col. Spurling was able to cross his advance guard, mounted, and "several squadrons dismounted" without being detected by the Rebels. At that point,

> a sudden dash was made upon the camp; nearly every man was captured, all their equipments, arms, horses, etc. The whole number of prisoners taken was 38; 47 horses, 3 mules, and 75 stand of arms, were captured. Nearly every effective man, including the lieutenant commanding, of Captain Leed's [Leigh's] company, Colonel Maury's 15th Confederate Cavalry, was made a prisoner. Two companies had been ordered away the day before to some point on the railroad in the direction of Pollard, or undoubtedly they would have shared the same fate. All the barracks, stables, shelters, etc, sufficiently extensive for a regiment, were burned, together with what commissary and quartermaster's stores were found.

At that point, "Having accomplished all that was intended," Col. Spurling and his detachment destroyed what remained of the bridge at Pine Barren Creek and started back for Barrancas, arriving shortly after midnight, "bringing with me all the prisoners, captured mules, horses, etc." Col. Spurling reports that there were no casualties among his troops, "not a man was injured," and "the conduct of both officers and men was at all times good and all that could be desired." He then makes special mention of specific men's actions:

> It would hardly be doing justice did I not make special mention of Lieut. Joseph G Sanders, Company F, 1st Florida Cavalry. He is a worthy officer, and deserves high praise for his meritorious conduct. He was at all times in command of the advance guard, and much of the success is due to the prompt and faithful manner in which all orders were executed. Among those under his command who did excellent service may be mentioned Sergeants Hollinger, Co E, Woodham, Co F, and Morgan, Co C, 1st Florida; Sergeants Butler, Co B and Baker, Co F, 2nd Maine. These sergeants were at all times brave, active, and zealous in performing their duties. Major Hutchinson, commanding the 2nd Maine, and Major Ruttkay, commanding the 1st Florida Cavalry, were prompt and energetic.[12]

With the conclusion of that expedition, the 2nd Maine Cavalry returned to its duties in camp at Barrancas for the remainder of November. This relatively inactive time spent in camp was not appreciated by at least some members of the regiment. On December 4, 1864, Major Charles Miller, who was the 29 year old lawyer from Rockland, Maine, and who had complained of conditions and his lack of promotion back in July of 1864, wrote again to his friend, Maine Adjutant General John Hodsdon. Major Miller started with a statement that he and the men were bored by "the tedious hours of uninterrupted camp life." Major Miller stated that he had commanded the regiment for most of its time at Barrancas, and that "Colonel Woodman commands the Brigade, not a very onerous task. Colonel Spurling is temporarily attached to the General Staff and spends most of his time rafting logs & bringing them in with a little steamer." It is not a very flattering, let alone accurate, report of Col. Spurling's activities during October and November.

Major Miller then complained of the lack of horses available to the 2nd Maine: "We have not probably 250 serviceable horses in the Reg't." He further complained at being left out of the cavalry's actions that were taking place or were about to take place: "You may imagine our disappointment at being left here while Gen Lee our chief of Cav, is organizing an immense Cavalry expedition to go in search of Hood. He takes all the Cav of New Orleans, Baton Rouge, Port Hudson & Vicksburg with him. I don't know when he will strike, but if Hood attempts to turn back after Sherman, he must fight Lee all the way."[13]

The General Lee referred to in this letter is Union General Albert Lindley Lee, who was in command of the Cavalry Division, Department of the Gulf. During General William T. Sherman's "March to the Sea," Confederate General John Bell Hood had been threatening Sherman's communications. General A.L. Lee did not, in fact, lead this large cavalry division to assist General Sherman. The cavalry division that accompanied Sherman's forces was the 3rd Division of the Cavalry Corps, Army of the Cumberland, led by General Hugh Judson Kilpatrick. Sherman left Union forces under Generals George Thomas and John Schofield to deal with Hood (which they did very effectively) while Sherman and his men continued on their march.

To return to Major Miller and his letter of December 4, the major complained, "Colonel Woodman is making no effort for us & unless some one else interests himself in us, we shall lie here till we fertilize the Land of Pensacola." Miller reported, "At present the health of the Rgt is good & when the chaplain comes today with the good things from Maine I know we shall be as healthy as any Regt in the service. We are drilling daily, & if I had the Regt on the parade grounds of Camp Coburn [in Augusta, Maine] I think I could astonish you at their proficiency of drill."

Pvt. William Rogers (15th Confederate Cavalry). William and his brother were captured at Pine Barren by the 2nd Maine Cavalry and sent to Ship Island where William died of dysentery in March 1865 (State Archives of Florida; floridamemory.com).

Once again, it is clear that Major Miller was a personal friend of Adjutant General Hodsdon, and the major sent his regards to two of the clerks in the adjutant general's office as well as "assurances of my remembrance to Mrs H [Hodsdon] and Lizzie." Lizzie Hodsdon, the adjutant general's daughter, sometimes worked in her father's office and was apparently noticed and admired by a number of young officers. Major Miller clearly did not want this letter to be retained or made public, because he ends with, "I need not intimate that, of course, your good sense will suggest to you the propriety of committing this leaf to the flame."[14]

Less than 10 days after writing that letter, the bored Major Miller would find himself in action. On December 13, the 2nd Maine Cavalry took part in an expedition to Pollard, Alabama. This time the regiment was a part of a Union force of about 1,800 men, under the command of Colonel George Robinson, 97th U.S. Colored Infantry. The contingent of the cavalry detachment for this expedition was under Col. Spurling's command, and his order to join the expedition reads, "Lieutenant Colonel Spurling, 2nd Maine Cavalry, has been instructed to report to you [Col. Robinson] with all the available cavalry at this post for duty." The cavalry that took part in this raid included the 2nd Maine, commanded by Major Miller, the 1st Florida Cavalry, under Captain Francis Lyons, one company of the 14th New York Cavalry, and a detachment of the 2nd Maine serving as light artillery, commanded by Captain Roberts. The other units taking part were the 82nd, 86th, and 97th Regiments of U.S. Colored Infantry. The cavalry numbered approximately 500, and the entire force numbered around 1,800. The object of the raid was to "destroy the large quantity of military stores and supplies supposed to be at Pollard, Alabama, also to burn or destroy the extension trestle bridge across the Escambia River, of the Mobile and Charleston Railroad, and do what other damage to the enemy that could be done conveniently."[15]

Lt. Col. Spurling, with the 2nd Maine, advanced from the main column and reached Pine Barren Creek, where, as before, he hoped to capture the Rebel pickets. Lt. Glidden was sent with a small dismounted force to cross the creek and attempt to get behind the pickets to capture them if they retreated. The poor condition of the bridge and the high, deep water of the creek made this plan impossible, and Spurling's detachment camped there for the night. The next morning (December 14), two Confederates pickets who were scouting the area of the bridge were captured while one escaped. Spurling and his men then repaired the bridge and waited for the infantry column, which arrived that evening and bivouacked for the night.

At 3 a.m. on December 15, the Union troops set out once again toward Pollard. At Bluff Springs a "small force of Rebels" was encountered which was "routed and pursued to Escambia River." The Confederates had destroyed the bridge over the Escambia and "appeared in considerable force on the other side." The cavalry then dismounted to wait for the main column, and engaged the Rebels with "the sharp crack of the carbine as the Second Maine opened with repeating rifles."[16]

At the same time, 100 men from the 2nd Maine were sent "to take possession of another bridge about four miles up the Escambia." Nearing Pollard, this contingent "came suddenly upon a station of the Mobile and Great Northern Railroad." The men of the 2nd Maine captured the station master and 50 black laborers who were working on the railroad. The Union troops then burned the railroad bridge over the Escambia River, destroyed a large quantity of corn, tore up the tracks "for a long distance," and demolished the trestle works supporting the bridge. "After doing all further damage possible they returned to the main column."[17]

The reports by the 2nd Maine Cavalry do not mention Lt. Colonel Spurling's injuries during this phase of the expedition, but the regiment's surgeon later stated that Spurling fell 20 feet or more from the railroad bridge over the Escambia River, landing on rocks and logs below, suffering injuries to his right shoulder, left side, right tibia, and head.[18]

Meanwhile the main force of the Union troops had driven the Rebels from the bridge over the Escambia, repaired the damage done to the bridge by the Confederates, and at between 3 and 4 p.m. on December 15, the expedition crossed the river. A "sharp skirmish" took place at the Little Escambia River as the Federals approached Pollard and Captain Roberts of Company M, 2nd Maine Cavalry, brought his artillery into use in this engagement. With the cavalry having dismounted and deployed, they soon drove the Rebels from the river, crossed the remnant of the bridge "on the stringers" and drove the Rebels out of range. With the end of that fighting, the Union column went into camp for the night. "The next morning (December 16) the advance guard entered Pollard without opposition. The

Union troops "remained in town during the day and destroyed all the government property," and "everything that was of any value to the enemy."[19]

At that point, "having accomplished all that was intended in the commencement, late in the afternoon the column took up the line of march back to Barrancas." Concerned that the Confederates might have gathered reinforcements to block the route, Lt. Col. Spurling and the 2nd Maine Cavalry were sent ahead to secure the bridge over the Escambia River. Col. Spurling found that the Rebels had torn up the planks of the bridge and posted a picket on the other side. When the rest of the Union column came up early the next morning, the artillery was unlimbered and "opened fire with grape and shell on the building which sheltered the rebels." The infantry then charged and Col. Robinson, who was in command of the expedition, was "severely wounded in the thigh." And so, "command now devolved upon Lieut Col. Spurling."[20]

He then put the infantry into line of battle and advanced, and the enemy retreated. However,

> But a short distance had been marched when the enemy appeared in our front and gave evidence of preparation for battle. The engagement became general. The column was moved forward, the infantry opening with telling effect, causing the rebels to fall back, which they did for five miles, trying all the while to gain an advantageous position and give battle, but to no purpose. They did not even take off their dead and wounded. Thus four distinct battles were fought. They [the Confederates] made many charges upon our train with a view to capturing it, but as many times they were fearfully repulsed and sent back badly punished. The last engagement took place at Pine Barren Creek, which the expedition was obliged to ford.[21]

Of that last engagement, the report in the *Supplement to the Official Records* states, "At Pine Barren Creek they again attacked us in our rear as we commenced crossing, but our forces were soon brought into position and this time the enemy was severely punished, strewing the ground with their killed and wounded.... The force proceeded without further molestation, arriving in camp [at Barrancas] at noon on December 19."[22]

At that crossing of Pine Barren Creek, Col. Spurling found it was not possible to cross with all the wagons, and so those that could not be taken were destroyed. During the expedition the 2nd Maine Cavalry lost one man killed and five wounded. The report in *Maine in the War for the Union* goes on to praise Col. Spurling and to state that the colonel was able to bring the Union column and the train of 50 wagons through 60 miles of enemy territory while it was "attacked almost every hour in front, rear and flanks by a force superior to his own in numbers.... Five times at different places the rebels chose their ground and position, and attacked us with an equal force, and were not only handsomely repulsed but terribly punished. The expedition having been a complete success the whole command returned to Barrancas, arriving on the nineteenth [December 19] in camp."[23] The entire returning Union column brought some 30 prisoners and suffered the loss of "1 officer and 16 men killed and 3 officers and 61 men wounded."[24]

The expedition's commander, Colonel Robinson, states, "We lost no prisoners, buried all our dead [and] brought off the wounded." Colonel Robinson also refers to Lt. Col. Spurling, saying, "Whatever success has attended the expedition is due in a great measure to his exertions. After being wounded at the Big Escambia I placed him in command of the whole force and he had the disposition and arrangement of the troops throughout the following actions, and his signal success in each of these goes to prove what is already known of his accomplishments as an officer and as a soldier."[25]

Again, one's perspective on this expedition can vary. A report on this affair by Confederate General P.G.T. Beauregard, who at that time commanded the Confederate Division of the West, states that a Federal force of 800 occupied Pollard and, "after burning Government and railroad buildings, retreated in the direction they came. They were pursued thirty miles, losing a portion of their transportation, baggage, and supplies, leaving many dead negro troops on the road. Our forces, commanded by General Liddell, acted with spirit and gallantry."[26]

The General Liddell who had commanded the Confederate troops that attacked the Union column on the return from Pollard was St. John Richardson Liddell, who had entered West Point in 1833, but stayed there only one year, withdrawing, it is assumed, due to his low grades. Starting the Civil War as an aide de camp and then a confidential courier for Confederate commanders, he was promoted to brigadier general in 1862.[27]

In a record of this expedition written by historian Rowland Dunbar in 1908, he states: "In December, on receiving news of a Federal expedition from Pensacola to Pollard, Ala., Colonel [Charles G.] Armistead moved his brigade to Bluff Springs, a march of 150 miles in fifty-four hours, and pursued the expedition on its return, December 16–17.... Colonel Robinson, commanding the expedition, was severely wounded, and in his troops 17 killed and 64 wounded."[28]

Federal General T.J. McKean, who was then in command of the Union's Division of West Florida, reported on this expedition as follows:

> An expedition sent out from here [Barrancas] under Colonel Robinson, Ninety-seventh U.S. Colored Infantry, reached Pollard on the 16th; destroyed the depot and other public buildings, and a large amount of public property, consisting of forage, clothing, camp and garrison equipage, &c.; also, the railroad for miles, including several bridges, one very important one over the Little Escambia River. On their return our troops encountered a force of the enemy from Mobile, and considerable severe fighting took place at all the streams from the Little Escambia to Pine Barren Creek, when the enemy was finally handsomely repulsed, and did not show himself again. The expedition returned here to-day, bringing some 30 prisoners.
>
> Our loss is 1 officer and 16 men killed and 3 officers and 61 men wounded. Colonel Robinson, commanding the expedition, severely, though not dangerously, wounded.[29]

A recent report on this expedition by Chris Lyons, who has apparently done considerable research on some of the Confederate cavalry involved, offers a very different view of the affair. For some reason he omits the 2nd Maine Cavalry, the 1st Florida Cavalry, and the 86th U.S. Colored Infantry from the Union troops attacking Pollard, listing only the 82nd and 97th U.S. Colored Infantry. He then describes the gathering of Confederate cavalry troops led by General Liddell, who moved from Fort Blakely on Mobile Bay to engage the Union column. Lyons agrees with other reports that the Rebels burned bridges over the streams connecting to the Escambia River and engaged the Union troops at those bridges, but says, "The rebels routed the 82nd at Mitchell's Creek and on the night of December 17 the rebels attacked the negro troops at Pine Barren Creek. The Federals lost eighty killed or wounded and ten wagons were now in Confederate hands. The remainder escaped back to Barrancas only because the Confederates gave up pursuit because their horses were giving out."[30]

The 2nd Maine Cavalry's report of the action at Mitchell's Creek states, on the other hand, "At Mitchell's Creek the enemy made a desperate assault upon our rear, while the advance was engaged in repairing a bridge which had been burned, but they were repulsed with small loss on our side, and our train was all crossed in safety."[31]

A "small loss" depends greatly on one's perspective. In this case, the small loss in the

A force of about 2,000 men, including the 2d Maine cavalry, the 1st Alabama cavalry, the 14th New York cavalry, three regiments of colored infantry, with two pieces of artillery, under Col. G. D. Robinson, of the 97th colored infantry, left for a raid into Alabama, to sever communication by telegraph and railroad at Pollard, and to destroy such property and stores as might be found there.

Reaching Pollard on the 16th, the place was found evacuated. The railroad depot, including a train of eight cars, mostly filled with grain; the railroad storehouse, filled with grain and government property, quartermaster and commissary stores; houses filled with stores, the ordnance building, and 2,000 stand of arms, the trestle work, and a number of miles of the railroad were destroyed by our troops, which being accomplished, the expedition set out on their return, but were met at Little Escambia by the enemy, under Col. Armstead, who opposed the crossing of the bridge. The colored infantry made a successful charge, led by Col. Robinson, who fell shot through the thigh when half way across the bridge. After Robinson had been wounded, the command devolved upon Lieut. Col. A. B. Speerling, 2d Maine. A second attack was made by the enemy, which was repulsed. The rebels scattered through the woods with heavy loss including Col. Armstead, their leader, killed. Seven of the enemy's flags were captured. The expedition was not again molested during its return.

Our total loss during the raid is estimated at seventy-five killed and wounded.

In this report, Lt. Col. Spurling's name is spelled incorrectly, the 1st Florida Cavalry is misnamed 1st Alabama Cavalry, and Confederate Col. Armistead is erroneously said to have been killed (*Evening Star*, Washington, D.C., Jan. 3, 1865).

2nd Maine Cavalry included the death of Private James Lake, a 22 year old trooper in Company G—no doubt a significant loss to his family and friends back in the small town of Atkinson, Maine.[32]

As we have seen, one's perspective and sources of information can result in very different reports on the same action. Accurate history can therefore be tricky to nail down, but the apparent facts of this expedition would suggest that the Union force was successful in destroying the Confederate railroad and supplies at Pollard, did bring back 30 prisoners, did suffer a total of 80 or 81 killed, wounded, and missing, and did fight against a substantial force of Confederate cavalry, who put up strong resistance at several points along the return to Barrancas. However, the suggestion that the Federals were "routed" at Mitchell's Creek and only "escaped back to Barrancas" because the Confederates' horses were worn out would seem to be very hard to justify.

Later in the month, the 2nd Maine Cavalry was once again in action. At 1 a.m. on December 24, 1864, a 50 man mounted detachment from the 2nd Maine Cavalry's Company L, along with 150 dismounted men from the 1st Florida Cavalry and the 82nd and 86th U.S. Colored Infantry, under the command of Lt. Col. Spurling, headed out on an expedition toward Milton, Florida. According to Lt. Col. Spurling's report, the raid's purpose was "gathering logs, and also the capture of a small body of rebels reported to be doing picket and patrol duty in the vicinity."[33]

The Union troops were transported by the steamer *Matamoras* and disembarked at a point about 5 miles below Milton on Blackwater Bay. Here Col. Spurling gave orders for the dismounted men to collect and raft logs, while he, with the 50 mounted men of the 2nd Maine Cavalry, proceeded toward Milton. At sunrise this detachment reached Milton, and finding no Confederate troops, moved along the road toward Pollard, where 2 Rebel scouts were found and captured. After a march of a further 3 miles, "A rebel picket post was found and three prisoners were taken." Another 3 miles brought the Union troopers to the picket reserve post, where another 3 prisoners were captured, while 2 or 3 made their escape on horseback.

When Spurling and his men reached a point within 16 or 18 miles of Pollard, they were told that a force of 300 Confederate cavalry was at Pollard and that Armistead's Cavalry (some of the Confederate cavalry that had fought against the Union troops on the Pollard expedition of December 13–19) was operating in the vicinity of Pine Barren Creek. "Having captured the enemy's pickets and patrol between Milton and Pollard and having accomplished my object, I returned to Milton." From there, Spurling and his men proceeded on about 2 miles to Bagdad, at the head of Blackwater Bay, where he had ordered the *Matamoras* to meet them. The cavalry was embarked and then collected the dismounted contingent with the raft of some 200 logs they had collected and returned to Barrancas at daylight on December 25. Spurling had brought in "eight prisoners of war, with their arms, horses and equipments." There were no casualties in Spurling's command.[34]

At the end of December 1864, the Organization of Troops, District of West Florida, lists Colonel Woodman in command of the 2nd Brigade of Cavalry, which consisted of the 1st Florida Cavalry (6 companies), under Lt. Col. Eugene Von Kielmansegge, and the 2nd Maine Cavalry, commanded by Lt. Col. Andrew B. Spurling.[35]

In other theaters of the war, late 1864 saw General John Schofield's Union Army of the Ohio, under General George Thomas's overall command, decisively defeat the Confederate Army of Tennessee under General John Bell Hood at Franklin, Tennessee. Hood's repeated attacks against well fortified Union positions failed to break the Federal line and resulted in heavy casualties for the Confederate troops—over 6,000 killed, wounded, captured or missing. Those assaults have been called the "Pickett's Charge of the West." In December, the same Confederate Army of Tennessee suffered another devastating defeat by General Thomas's Union forces at the Battle of Nashville. This time, the outnumbered Confederates again suffered over 6,000 casualties, the great majority being captured or missing. The Union forces lost approximately 387 killed and 2,500 wounded. This overwhelming Union victory, coupled with the costly Confederate defeat at Franklin, essentially ended the effective fighting capability of the Army of Tennessee.[36]

Farther east, General W. T. Sherman had begun his March to the Sea. With a force of over 60,000, Sherman left Atlanta on November 15, and by December 21 had taken Savannah, Georgia. In the process, Sherman's forces had lived off the Confederate resources along their route and had destroyed most of the Confederacy's war-related capability and infrastructure in Georgia.

In Virginia, after General U.S. Grant's Overland Campaign had cost the Union Army of the Potomac many thousands of lives in its attempts to outmaneuver Robert E. Lee's Army of Northern Virginia, the Union force had come to a halt at Petersburg, where, after further costly assaults, it settled into a siege.

CHAPTER EIGHT

Early 1865: Promotions, Further Raids, and Difficult Times for Florida's Civilians

As far as engagements with the enemy went, January 1865 was a quiet month for the 2nd Maine Cavalry. Reports from the various companies indicate that on January 3, Company G went to Pensacola for lumber and returned the same day. Company B's report for January states that on the 8th, "Capt. Merry and 37 men ... went to Milton on a scout and returned the next day," while also on the 8th, Company C was sent on a one day scouting mission to Perdido Creek. And on January 23, Company A was ordered out on a similar mission, returning on the same day. During that month, a report was recorded from the detachment of 50 men, commanded by Captain Johnson and Lt. Marcus Vose, which had been sent for duty to Mobile Bay back in November and was now based at Pascagoula, Mississippi, about 15 miles west of Mobile Bay. While in Mississippi, "These fifty men were constantly on the outposts, doing excellent service during the demonstration made upon the defenses of Mobile by the U.S. Forces under Maj. Gen. Granger.... Several of them were wounded, whilst others in unequal contact with the enemy were made prisoner." The detachment remained there until February 6.[1]

With this lull in military action for the regiment as a whole, other matters were being considered. On January 10, one of several letters recommending the promotion of Lt. Col. Spurling to the rank of brigadier general was sent. This letter was sent to Parker Burleigh, a member of the Maine State Senate from Northern Maine's Aroostook County, by Dr. George Martin, the 2nd Maine Cavalry's surgeon. In it, Dr. Martin enclosed a petition from the members of the regiment from that county and urged the state senator to gather support from others in Maine and to then request Maine's U.S. senators and representatives "to bring Col. Spurling's recommendations before the President and urge the promotion."[2]

On January 12, the 2nd Maine Cavalry's chaplain, Charles Nason, sent a letter to Leonard Andrews, who had been a delegate to the Republican National Convention, asking for Mr. Andrews to use his influence in favor of Col. Spurling's promotion. There was also included a "circular" to E. H. Banks, a state senator from Southern Maine's York County, and similar circulars to representatives of each of Maine's other counties, signed by the members of the 2nd Maine Cavalry from the corresponding county, urging their help in obtaining the promotion to general for Col. Spurling. Also enclosed was a request to be sent to President Lincoln, signed by 110 officers at Barrancas—which included "every one present and on duty, with but an individual exception." That exception was Colonel Woodman. We must wonder if Col. Woodman was concerned that his subordinate would jump past him from lieutenant colonel to general.³

Chaplain Nason's letter details many of Col. Spurling's qualities: "He has confidence in himself, knows his ability and is never afraid to assume whatever responsibility devolves upon him. He possesses a courage and bravery which wins for him the reputation of a hero among our own forces and of dread and fear among our enemies. He has the rare gift of inspiring others with perfect confidence in his leadership." Later in his letter, the chaplain states, "I have also considered him remarkable for his presence of mind, never appearing calmer than when the storm of battle rages around him." And, as an interesting addition to the colonel's other attributes, the chaplain states, "He is strictly a temperance man, not allowing himself, like too many military men, to drink even occasionally the social glass."⁴

There is also a letter, sent on January 9, by Major Charles Miller to A.P. Emerson, a member of Maine's House of Representatives, urging support for Col. Spurling's promotion. This is the same Major Miller whose July 1864 letter to Maine's governor was so critical of then Major Spurling's promotion to lieutenant colonel. Major Miller had also written to Maine Adjutant General John Hodsdon belittling Col. Spurling's activities "rafting logs and bringing them in with a little steamer." But, in his January letter, Major Miller had apparently had a complete change of heart, for he wrote, "Since the colonel has been with us.... He has planned and executed frequent expeditions into the enemy's country and has not, in a single instance, failed. He has exhibited those traits which characterize our most distinguished generals, and has obtained the complete confidence of the officers of this department." Major Miller urged Emerson to use his "intimate personal acquaintance with Mr. Hamlin" (outgoing Vice President Hannibal Hamlin of Maine) to aid in Col. Spurling's promotion. Major Miller's letter ends, "I write this in perfect good faith. I have 'no friends to reward nor enemies to punish.' I believe simply that Col. Spurling would sustain the high renown which attaches to the office of a brigadier, and would add new luster to the military record of Maine." One must wonder whether this new attitude toward Lt. Col. Spurling was prompted solely by a change of heart, or whether Major Miller was contemplating his own possible promotion to lieutenant colonel as a result of Spurling's promotion to brigadier general.⁵

A final letter of recommendation for Col. Spurling's promotion was sent

Chaplain Charles Nason (courtesy Maine State Archives).

to President Lincoln by Brigadier General Thomas McKean, the commander of the District of West Florida. Lt. Col. Spurling is described as "a very efficient officer, being energetic, daring, and sagacious. He also has had a long experience in the field." In that letter, General McKean, in a manner similar to Chaplain Nason, mentions that Col. Spurling "has the high recommendation of being strictly temperate." The last sentence of McKean's letter, however, seems less than an enthusiastic endorsement of Col. Spurling: "less worthy appointments have been made."[6]

Later, Major General Canby added his voice to those recommending Lt. Col. Spurling for promotion, and wrote to General Halleck, the chief of staff in Washington, D.C. In that letter, General Canby stated that Spurling had "been in the exercise of commands" above his rank and had "manifested a capacity and fitness for still higher command."[7]

With all of the letters of recommendation, Lt. Col. Spurling was not, in fact, promoted to brigadier general during the regiment's time of active service. When the regiment was mustered out of U.S. service in early December 1865, he had been awarded a brevet promotion to full colonel of volunteers to date from March 26, 1865. Col. Spurling was later awarded the brevet rank of brigadier general of volunteers, also to date from March 26.[8]

There were other matters of concern to be addressed during January of 1865. Captain John Roberts of Company M was requesting a discharge from the service and Col. Woodman did not approve, stating in response to this request on January 19, "The company has but one officer on duty with it. The 1st Lieutenant being on detached service [Lt. Ivory Allen was then attached to the 4th Cavalry Brigade], and the 2nd Lieut a prisoner of war [Lt. Isaac Adams, wounded and left at Marianna]."

Further, Colonel Woodman stated that the order under which Captain Roberts was claiming a right to resign only applied to the veteran regiments raised under General Order 191. Woodman explained that the 2nd Maine Cavalry was not, in fact, a veteran regiment, but had been allowed to keep its "Veteran Volunteer" title by special permission.[9]

However, on January 20, Brigadier General Thomas McKean recommended that "the Captain's resignation be immediately accepted for the good of the service." Regarding this attempt by Captain Roberts to resign his commission, the 2nd Maine Cavalry's surgeon later stated for the record, "Captain John H Roberts Co M 2nd Me Cav came to my quarters in January, before forwarding his resignation, and strongly solicited a certificate of Disability, but as he had constantly been on duty since with the regiment and as I knew of no cause for giving such certificate, I declined to do so."[10]

In spite of General McKean's recommendation, Captain Roberts' resignation was not accepted in January. We should remember, of course, that only officers had the opportunity of resigning from the service—an option not open to enlisted men. There is an interesting comparison to the reaction to Captain Roberts' request to resign and his attempt to do so as a result of disability. Later in 1865 Corporal Otis Jenkins of Company B attempted to obtain a discharge by reason of disability. This resulted in his being reduced to the ranks, "having become useless as a Non. com'd Officer for applying to the Surgeon for discharge when in perfect health." We'll hear more about Captain Roberts' requests to resign a bit later.[11]

In a letter to Maine's Adjutant General that January, Colonel Woodman reported that the health of the regiment was good and that the regiment's "persevering chaplain has arrived with a large supply of vegetables in good condition." The regiment had collected "over $600" which was "invested" in foodstuffs amounting to about 1,000 barrels of vegetables. The colonel stated, "We will not fear the scurvy very soon if we remain here and can have the benefit of them." He said, however, that the regiment "cannot remain idle much longer and has been told that they may join a Union force moving east from Baton Rouge, La.[12]

In addition to the efforts of the chaplain and the regiment's own collection of money for food, it appears that folks back in Maine also contributed significantly toward the health of the regiment. Their efforts, during the previous month, December 1864, to provide food and supplies to the regiment resulted in special orders stating,

> Our relatives and friends in Maine have recently furnished us an example of benevolence which demands on the part of the Regiment some testimonial more significant than the ordinary expressions of gratitude. Disease had been making fearful inroads upon our ranks and we sought, in vain, from the Government that relief, which we have found through the generosity of the people of our Native State.
>
> In commemoration of a time honored custom of New England and in full sympathy with the Spirit which suggested its origin, by consent of the General Commanding, I have designated Thursday, December 22nd to be observed by the 2nd Regiment Me Cavalry Vet Vols as a day of Thanksgiving and Praise.
>
> Capt F. Twitchell, Capt B G Merry & Capt J H Roberts will constitute a board to determine the order of exercises for the day and will appoint such committees as they may deem [illegible]. The Regt is relieved from all details upon that day.
>
> by Order of Maj. C A Miller comd'g[13]

Capt. John Roberts (Special Collections, Bangor Public Library).

In his January letter to the Adjutant General, Colonel Woodman also stated, perhaps somewhat optimistically, that "harmony prevails in the Reg't. Lt. Col. Spurling gives satisfaction. Major M [Miller] does very well but he is afflicted with an appetite that occasionally gets the better of him. [another reference to intemperance?] I think he wants to do his duty. Maj. Hutchinson is a good officer, a reliable man. Captain Johnson [Company D's Elijah Johnson] has fully met my expectations. Captain Twitchell [Company A's Joseph Twitchell] holds out about as his friends expected him to. He is very changeable. Hope we shall have more work to do & health & spirit to do it well."

Referring to the men either captured or left wounded at Marianna, Col. Woodman stated, "We get nothing new from Maj. Cutler. At last acc't he was doing well. I hope our prisoners left [at] Marianna will not be sent to those large prisons depots of the South. We may be permitted to release them by and bye." (We now know, of course, that the men of the 2nd Maine Cavalry who were either left wounded or otherwise taken prisoner at Marianna were sent to Andersonville.) And, once again on the topic of strong drink, Col. Woodman reports that he hopes "to secure a temperance pledge from 1st Lieut Mansur [Warren Mansur of Company A]. The Captain's [Captain Twitchell's] influence in that respect has been no benefit to him. I have tried the pledge in two instances when it did much good. I do not like to recommend a man for promotion who cannot command himself especially until his back has been strengthened with a pledge."[14]

Maine had been a leading state in the temperance movement and in 1851 had passed a temperance law, known as the Maine Law, prohibiting the sale of all alcoholic beverages except for medicinal purposes. The law was extremely unpopular with large numbers of people in the state and was repealed in 1856. A leading figure in the temperance movement, known as the "Napoleon of Temperance" and the "Father of Prohibition," was Maine citizen Neal Dow, who became a brigadier general in the Union Army and was in command of Pensacola for a time, just after that city's occupation by Federal troops. General Dow was twice wounded in an assault at Port Hudson, Louisiana, was captured by the Confederates, and was later exchanged for Robert E. Lee's son, "Rooney" Lee.[15]

Returning to the 2nd Maine Cavalry and January of 1865, Colonel Woodman wrote again to Adjutant General Hodsdon and reported that he had heard "camp talk" that a large Union force will be moving against Mobile, Alabama. He added, "I am glad to be able to say that I am once more in command of my Reg't & hope to be permitted to remain in it. It has been my misfortune to have 8 different commands since I came to this dept.

Lt. Warren Mansur (Special Collections, Bangor Public Library).

My rank is such that I am subject to sudden transfers being one of the junior Colonels in the Dept." He ended by saying, "Health of the Reg't excellent. Are short of horses but expect some in a few days. We are impatient to share in the great work being so well done."[16]

On the last day of January, Company A's report states that they "left camp with the regiment, dismounted, under command of Lt. Col. Spurling and embarked on the steamer *Matamoras* at midnight." They arrived at Milton, Florida, at 7 a.m., "disembarked and had a slight skirmish with the enemy. Reembarked, bringing off several families of refugees, and returned to camp same night." The exact makeup of the force sent on this expedition to Milton is not known. The only other company that makes mention of the action is Company G's report for February 1, which states, "Capt Knowles and 32 men [from Company G] detailed to go to Milton. Had an encounter with the enemy's pickets with no important result." Perhaps other companies simply didn't find the event worth mentioning.[17]

At the end of January 1865, the organization of the troops for the District of West Florida lists the makeup of the Third Brigade, of Major General Granger's First Division, as the 82nd, 97th, 25th, and 86th U.S. Colored Infantry, 2nd Maine Cavalry, and 1st Florida Cavalry.[18]

In first weeks of February 1865, the regiment had another lull in action against the Confederates. The only activity involved Company C, which reported that on February 12, "the company was ordered on a scout in pursuit of deserters and ... returned the same day." Company B reported that on that same day, parts of the company were sent out "in pursuit of a Rebel who escaped through our lines ... marched thirty-six miles and returned the next day." Since no mention is made of recapturing the Rebel or of finding the deserters, we may assume these scouting parties were not successful.[19]

However, during that month there were internal matters to be dealt with once again. Early in that February, in a letter to Adjutant General Hodsdon, Col. Woodman reported that they were still short of healthy horses, but he had heard "there's some prospect of a movement being made from here.... Rumor says that Mobile is being evacuated. I get nothing new from Maj Cutler. The last acc'ts by way of Refugees were favorable. Gov't is feeding about 700 poor whites of the South at this Post. They are a 'God forsaken looking lot.'"[20]

By that point in the Civil War, food shortages were having a devastating effect on many parts of the South. In Florida, the Union blockade along the coast, the destruction of many plantations, the Union occupation of many commercial centers, the raids on farms by Confederate deserters as well as Union units, and the continued insistence of many plantation owners to grow cotton all contributed to this problem. The refugee population of Florida also provided a source of men to fill "irregular" Union military units such as the Florida Rangers, and were often employed in raids against Confederate militia and irregulars.[21]

A letter to Maine Governor Cony from Colonel Woodman, sent on February 8, starts with the news that "I rec'd a letter from Major N Cutler yesterday dated at Marianna Fla Dec 29th and shall send it direct to his father by this mail. The major is a cripple has but little use of his left hand and ankle. He informs me that Lt. Adams [who had also been wounded and left at Marianna] died on the 13th of Oct & that two of our soldiers died—the rest were sent to Ga.... I have formally recommended the app't of Emilius N D Small ... to fill the vacancy caused by the death of Lt. Adams. Emilius N D Small is our Sergeant Major and a very worthy young man."[22] But then, in another reference to the request by Captain Roberts to resign his commission, the colonel stated,

> Captain Roberts, Co M is very anxious that his brother is app't 2nd Lt. in place of Adams. the brother is now orderly of the co. The Captain is a great worker in his own interest & may try to influence you in the matter, therefore it may not be amiss for me to inform you that Sgt Roberts is a resident of Mass & in my opinion would soon resign after getting his commission. The Captain wants to leave the service and engage in business in Boston and has tendered his resignation.... I am always anxious that you should have no reason to think I would recommend any but the best men available for the place. In this case you will find ... that I recommend a good man.

And another name that has cropped up in past letters is once more mentioned:

> Captain Twitchell has tendered his resignation but being under charges filed by Lt Col Spurling he cannot get out of the service unless Lt Col S will withdraw them.

Sgt. Byron Roberts (courtesy Maine State Archives).

He was charged with being drunk on duty & when near the enemy. I know nothing about the truth of the matter. The Captain could do well if he may be steady minded and leave strong drink alone.

On the business of fighting the enemy, Col. Woodman laments, "We do not seem to have our share of work. This is truly a dull place. Recently we have looked & hoped for a movement on Mobile or further inland."[23]

Predictably enough, Captain Roberts did send his own letter to Governor Cony just a few days later. After informing the governor of the death of Lt. Adams, Captain Roberts goes on, "I take the liberty of recommending or expressing my wishes in regard to the filling of the vacancy and most earnestly desire that my Orderly Sergeant, Byron Roberts of Alfred be commissioned 2nd Lieutenant. My brother is well qualified both in point of [illegible] and education and is strictly temperate and his moral character is without blemish. Lest you may think that I am unduly biased in favor of my brother (which might be pardonable) I take pleasure in presenting the accompanying testimonials of his character, standing, and abilities." With this letter, Captain Roberts sent recommendations for the promotion of Byron Adams signed by Lt. Col. Spurling, Major Hutchinson, and Major Miller.[24]

However, one day after that letter was sent, both Majors Miller and Hutchinson wrote to the governor to say that they now understand the Col. Woodman has recommended Sergeant Major Small and both are modifying their recommendations for Sgt. Roberts. Major Miller wrote, "What I said with regard to the Sergt R I can most truly say with regard to the Sergt Major. In fact the Sergt Major has many qualities not possessed by Sergt Roberts." And Major Hutchinson states, "I do not want to interfere in the matter. The Sergt Major is a good soldier and well worthy of a commission."[25] And, once again Captain Roberts wrote to the governor:

> Since mailing my communication to you of yesterday it has been currently reported that Col Woodman had recommended Sgt Major Small for the position of 2nd Lieut in my company. I am aware that it is unbecoming of me to oppose the Col of my Reg't in any recommendation he may make and should not if Col W was, or had been, in command of the Regiment. But as he has not been in immediate command of my Co or in a position to observe the merits of my non Com officers for four weeks since we left Maine, it may be pardonable in me especially when the case effects and concerns me for more than it possibly can him and he certainly cannot consult the best interests of the service in making such a recommendation for he has repeatedly said that the Sergt Maj was not fit for the position he now holds.

He goes on in that vein for some time, praising the actions of his brother in "every fight and skirmish in which the Regt has been engaged" while complaining that his brother's promotion is being "held back by one [Col Woodman] who is entirely unused to command, who has never been in a fight or even a skirmish."[26]

These comments regarding Col. Woodman ignore his previous command, cited earlier, as a company commander and then lieutenant colonel of the 8th Maine and colonel of the 28th Maine. And the comment that the colonel had "never been in a fight of even a skirmish," while true of Woodman's time with the 2nd Maine Cavalry, was certainly not true about the attacks in which he participated at Port Hudson with the 28th Maine.

In response to all of this, Col. Woodman wrote again to the governor: "I learn that Captain Roberts has sent you a recommendation in favor of his brother for the same position and that he secured the names of several officers." He goes on:

> I have always made the recommendations in accordance with your instructions & in good faith but it seems that other officers are assuming some of the responsibility. Therefore I con-

clude to say that if you are willing to release me from the whole responsibility of recommendations & rely wholly in petitions it will be agreeable to me.

I would only ask to be informed of your wish that I might notify the Officers that I have nothing to do with the matter and those who desire promotion could act accordingly. I certainly never will enter into a contest with Officers for the purpose of securing a particular promotion.

I seldom tell the persons that I think of recommending them & when I do it is to secure a pledge from them in regard drinking strong drink. I can never be accused of acting upon selfish motives. I may err, tho I intend it shall be an error of judgement.

In the case of Sergeant Major Small I will only add that he is a brother of Major [Abner] Small of the 16 Regt and it will be easy for you to decide whether he is worthy…. If petitions will settle the matter the [Sgt] Major could get even these same officers to sign for him, but I will not approve that course until I hear from you.[27]

It seems a rather odd tone for a commanding officer to take—a willingness to abdicate authority regarding promotions as a result of his apparent disgust at the infighting and politics in his command. But perhaps the colonel was also engaged in more direct action within the regiment. The day after the above letter was sent, Major Miller, commanding the regiment wrote:

Roberts J H Co M 2nd Me Cavalry tenders his resignation unconditional & immediate. (endorsement on Same)
    Hdqrs 2nd Me Cavalry
    Barrancas Fla Feb. 13, 1865
Respectfully forwarded through commanding officer 3rd Brigade 1st Div, Approved for the good of the Service.[28]

And Colonel Woodman adds, regarding this, Captain Roberts' second resignation request:

Respectfully forwarded through the Commanding Officer Dist West Fla
Approved with the information that this officer tendered his resignation on the 18th day of January 1865 which was returned on the 11th day of Feb Disapproved. I disapproved the resignation before, but finding that he is determined to get out of the service and believing that he has lost his interest in his duties as an officer, I very earnestly and respectfully recommend that he be discharged for the good of the Service.[29]

After all of these exchanges, Captain Roberts was discharged from the service; the captain's brother, Sgt. Roberts, remained a sergeant, and Sgt. Major Emilius Small was promoted to 2nd Lieutenant of Company M.

In late February the regiment was back in action against the Rebels. On February 22, a force of 50 mounted and 250 dismounted men from the 2nd Maine Cavalry set out on another expedition to Milton. The prelude to this expedition had started back in January, when Lt. Col. Spurling had gone, disguised as a Confederate officer, to the Rebel outpost at Milton and had a conference with the commander, Captain Keyser. In the course of that discussion, it appears that Col. Spurling had convinced Captain Keyser that, with the end of the war clearly approaching, it would be wise for him to surrender his command. On February 19, Col. Spurling went again to visit the Rebel outpost at Milton "in order to make myself certain that nothing had occurred to interfere with the arrangements previously made between us for the surrender of his command." However, Col. Spurling "learned from Captain Keyser that, contrary to his expectations, instead of receiving seventy additional men, [he] had been ordered to Pollard, Ala, with the larger part of his force, leaving only thirty, under command of a lieutenant, to do patrol and picket duty at Milton." The detachment

Lt. Emilius Small (courtesy Maine State Archives).

Gen. Frederick Steele (Library of Congress).

of Confederates left for Pollard that day, and Col. Spurling concluded, "I think that a part or the whole of the remaining force at Milton can easily be captured." Col. Spurling also learned that Confederate troops were being concentrated for the defense of Mobile, Alabama, and indicates that he hears "the [Confederate] soldiers of this division are much demoralized."[30]

When the detachment of the 2nd Maine Cavalry set out for Milton, they had a fairly clear idea of what force they would face. Leaving on the steamer *Matamoras* at 3 p.m. on February 22, the steamer stopped a few miles below Milton and landed the dismounted force under Company B's Captain Benjamin Merry. This force, according to Lt. Col. Spurling's report, advanced so secretly and quietly that the enemy's picket posted there knew nothing of the approach. The enemy's camp was found six miles farther on, in the direction of Pollard, and our troops succeeded in gaining the rear without in any way giving alarm. A little after daylight [on February 23] they marched upon the enemy, completely surprising his camp, making quite a number of men prisoners, and capturing nearly all their horses, killing one man and seriously wounding another, a few only escaping into the swamps close by the camp, from which it was impossible to bring them out. All of their arms, ammunitions, equipments, and camp equipage was also captured, which was destroyed.

At 3:30 that morning of February 23, Col. Spurling had the *Matamoras* move up to Bagdad where he and the 50 mounted men were put ashore. "I then proceeded with these men on the road where the enemy's picket of four men was posted.... I reached the picket about daylight, capturing 2 men, wounding 1, and the other made his escape unharmed. Soon afterward I reached their camp, where I found the dismounted cavalry under command of Captain Merry, who had succeeded in surprising it, as has been stated." Since the *Matamoras* was not large enough to carry the whole of Col. Spurling's force along with the captured men and horses, the prisoners were sent to Barrancas that afternoon under guard. "The boat returned the next day in the afternoon, and on the following morning, February 25, I embarked my whole force and returned to Barrancas.... The results of the expedition are 19 prisoners, 1 being left behind too severely wounded to be brought off, 29 horses, and 5 mules.... Fifty stand of arms, with full accouterments, together with all the enemy's camp equipage, were destroyed. There were no casualties among my own men."[31]

On February 27 Col. Woodman wrote to Governor Cony,

> Health of the troop excellent & none more so than 2nd M Cavalry.
> Within a few weeks about 9000 ... troops have been landed here & more coming.
> All the preparations indicate an advance soon from this point. Major Genl Steele is said to be the Officer who will command the expedition. [When a column of troops from Pensacola was put together to move toward Mobile, Major General Frederick Steele led that force.]
> I presume it will cooperate with Gen Granger's advance by the way of Mobile.
> It is time that this Dept made an effort to strike a blow that will be felt by the Rebels. It seems to me that this spring campaign will prepare the minds of Jeff Davis & co for peace. It is evident they will hold out so long as there is hope and they will have hopes so long as they have Lees Army.[32]

General Steele, a West Point graduate in 1843, had been awarded two brevet promotions during the Mexican War. General Gordon Granger was also a West Point graduate, class of 1845, and was also awarded two brevet promotions during the Mexican War.

And although Col. Woodman had reported that the health of the regiment was "excellent" at this time, the report on the strength of various regiments during February of 1865 shows the effects of deaths, desertion, discharges and transfers that had reduced the ranks of the 2nd Maine Cavalry. On February 20, the regiment is listed as having 795 men fit for duty out of an aggregate of 983. We may recall that when the regiment reached the South, it was reported to contain 1,200 men (an estimate based on its 12 companies), while in July of 1864 the regiment reported 950 effective fit for duty out of a total of 1,075.[33]

In January, these diminished numbers had led Lt. Col. Spurling, then in command, to write to Maine's governor requesting new men to be sent to the regiment. In that letter Spurling makes reference to the various reasons why the ranks had been so reduced.

> I have the honor respectfully to request that some effort be made to fill up our regiment under the present call. When we first came into this Department, we were encamped in the Swamps of Louisiana and many of our men contracted malarious diseases on account of which we have suffered much loss, besides some seventy five have been transferred to the navy and Veteran Reserve Corps leaving us considerably below the minimum for a cavalry regiment. Three hundred recruits are now required to fill it to the maximum. Although a large number of our men have died since coming to Florida yet the general health of the regiment has been gradually improving and now we are one of the healthiest bodies of men in the field and the uniform good report of the Act Asst Inspector Genl of this District has given us a standing among the very first cavalry regiments in the Department. We are pleasantly situated and have very comfortable winter quarters in the Dist of West Florida which has a dry soil and very healthy climate especialy during the winter and spring, and if we could have recruits come out here early enough to become partially acclimated before the heat of the summer they would escape much of the sickness from which our men suffered last season.
> Send us three years men if possible, for one man the second year is worth half dozen men the first six months especially when they are constantly counting on going home.... Hoping

that this may meet with your approval and that recruits sufficient to fill our regiment to the maximum may soon be sent us,

    I remain
        Very Respectfully
            Your Obt Servt.
        A.B. Spurling   Lt. Col. Comdg Regiment[34]

In response to the need expressed in that letter, during that spring of 1865 the ranks of the 2nd Maine Cavalry were strengthened by the arrival of at least some of the desired new recruits. Actually, beginning in December 1864, men were arriving from Maine, and in the next few months, although not reaching close to the 300 men requested, a total of 135 new troopers had been added to the regiment's roster.[35]

Early March 1865 was a relatively quiet time for the 2nd Maine Cavalry. Company M's report indicates, "March 1–7: In camp at Barrancas, Florida. Engaged in picket and fatigue duty on wharf." A few scouting expeditions were sent out from Barrancas, and the orders recorded in the *Official Record* sound quite impressive.

> Special Orders, No. 52   Hdqrs. District of West Florida
> Lieut. Col. A.B. Spurling, with 200 dismounted and 30 mounted men from the Second Maine Cavalry, well armed and with one day's cooked rations, will embark on an expedition to-morrow morning at 6 o'clock on the steamer Matamoras."[36]

And this:

> Special Orders, No. 55   Hdqrs. District of West Florida
> Lieutenant-Colonel Spurling, with 100 dismounted men of the Second Maine Cavalry, will be in readiness to embark on the steamer Matamoras on a secret expedition at 3 o'clock to-morrow afternoon ... well armed, with one day's rations.[37]

The following reports from the 2nd Maine Cavalry give a more down to earth look at the actual nature and results of those raids. This from Company H:

> March 6: Captain Mathews, with 12 men, together with the same number from each of the other companies in the regiment, embarked on board steamer *Matamoras* and proceeded to Milton expecting to find the enemy at that place. On arriving at Milton and not finding any enemy there, returned next day to camp.
> March 9–10: 15 men from Company H, together with a like number from each company, the whole commanded by Captain E D Johnson, started on a raid to Milton. On arriving at that place and finding everything quiet, returned next day to camp.[38]

(We can see from that report, by the way, that Captain Johnson had returned from his detached service west of Mobile.)

Company M's report of one of these raids is even more direct, "A portion of the company embarked on steamer on an expedition to Milton, Florida. Returned March 8 without accomplishing anything of note."[39]

It is clear that the Confederates' intelligence system was well aware of movements by the Federal troops. Regarding the expeditions of early March, General Liddell wrote from Blakely, Alabama, to General James Clanton, the Confederate commander at Pollard: "Part of the Second Maine started up the river on the 7th in direction of Milton. Be on the lookout for them."[40]

And, from a March 9 letter to General Richard Taylor from General P.G.T. Beauregard, we learn that the Union military's plans for upcoming campaigns were not, apparently, well kept secrets: "P.S.—I enclose you herewith a slip from the Richmond Whig of the 4th instant containing some Northern news, which, doubtless, give the future plans of campaign of the enemy in your district." In a letter to General Robert E. Lee, General Beauregard calls Lee's attention to that same newspaper article.

From Gen. Beauregard's letter we also learn about the status and morale of the Confederate army: "My opinion is that (as in the days of the Revolution of '76) desertion from the army is now an epidemic. They deserted by the hundreds from the cars on the way here [Charlotte, NC]. The same complaint reaches us from Lee's army. Only an active campaign and some brilliant success can put a stop to that disorder."[41]

During the early days of March 1865, Col. Woodman's bit of pique over his authority to make recommendations for promotions seems to have passed, for on March 2 he wrote to Governor Cony:

> I have the honor to inform you that Captain John H Roberts Co M this Regt is discharged U.S. service. To fill that & other vacancies in consequence I very respectfully recommend the following named persons.
> Ivory R Allen 1st Lieut Co M to that of Captain same Company
> Marcus A Vose 2nd Lieut Co H to that of 1st Lieut Company M
> 1st Sergeant Ronello A Barrows Company H to that of 2nd Lieut same Co
> All these men have shown themselves worthy of promotion.
> Sergeant Barrows was Lieut in the 28th Reg't Maine Vols [Colonel Woodman's previous command]
> Hoping these recommendations will meet the Governor's approval.[42]

Capt. Adolphus Mathews (courtesy Maine State Archives).

(From this and other letters, it appears that 2nd Lt. Vose had also returned from detached service west of Mobile Bay with, most likely, the rest of the detachment.)

And Col. Woodman now seems to be working in conjunction with Lt. Col. Spurling regarding recommendations for promotion, for on the same day as the above, Col. Spurling wrote to the governor:

> Sir,
> I have the honor to inform you that a vacancy exists in the Captaincy of Co M 2d Me Cavl'y occasioned by the resignation of Capt John H Roberts.
> Ivory R Allen 1st Lieut of Co M I very respectfully recommend for the position of Captain, and Marcus A Vose 2nd Lieut of Co H for 1st Lieut of Co M.
> Lieut Vose was a member of the 1st Me Cavl'y [Spurling's previous regiment] as Brvt 2nd Lieut, and is in every respect worthy and well qualified for the promotion.[43]

Lt. Ivory Allen (courtesy Maine State Archives).

Lengthy letters from Col. Woodman and from Major Miller (in command of the 2nd Maine Cavalry at this time) attempt to explain the circumstance of the initial rejection of Captain Roberts' resignation and the final acceptance of that resignation. Both officers again indicated that Captain Roberts had attempted to obtain a discharge for reasons of health, but that the surgeon refused. Major Miller then makes clear that Captain Roberts' desire to go into business was the actual reason for the resignation. The major also stated that Captain Roberts' second resignation, following so closely to the rejection of the first, should have resulted in a dishonorable discharge instead of one that read "discharged for the good of the service." Col. Woodman writes, "In a few days [after his first request to resign] the Captain sent forward another without assigning a cause for doing so. Thus violating Army rules. He did this knowing that it would bring either a dismissal or discharge "for good of the service. He expressed himself as well pleased when his discharge reached him." Both Col. Woodman and Major Miller say that Captain Roberts was already attempting to have this discharge upgraded to an honorable discharge. Neither officer had any sympathy for this attempt. Major Miller states: "On some accounts I regret that his own foolishness has brought upon himself a dismissal.... Capt R was always a competent, energetic officer," but goes on to say, "As often as his posterity shall look upon this legacy transmitted by Capt Roberts, so often will they be reminded of his criminal folly."

On the practical business of the regiment, Major Miller states, "The health of the Regt at present is nearly perfect." But he adds, "We are about wholly without horses." And goes on to say that he hopes the governor will "soon hear of the capture of Mobile, Selma, & Montgomery and the advance of the army of the Gulf to participate in the great battle of the rebellion outside the gates of Richmond."

And, again referring to practical military matters, Col. Woodman states, "We are evidently on the eve of an active campaign & that alone should cause officers to be content." And he adds, "Maj Gen Steele is here with about 15000 men & more on the way."[44]

Assistant Surgeon John Eaton (courtesy Maine State Archives).

With the various concerns expressed regarding the health of the regiment, it is of interest that a sampling of the records of the 2nd Maine Cavalry's assistant surgeon, John Eaton, has survived. We learn, for example, of the articles supplied to the hospital at Barrancas and find no surprise in such items as blankets, syringes, bed pans, tongue depressors and even a coffee mill. We must wonder, however, why a cavalry regiment's supplies included a vaginal speculum and a case of obstetrical instruments. We find that the reading material supplied to the regiment included a copy of *Gray's Anatomy* (which had been first published in 1858), and a book on hygiene. In addition, while many images are common in popular literature and films of men being held down while surgery for battle wounds was performed without anesthetic, we also see that the regiment was supplied with both chloroform and ether.[45]

While other records giving the specifics of the sick and injured men of the 2nd Maine Cavalry have apparently been lost, John Eaton's papers do include the reports of sick and wounded for April and May 1865. We can see, for example, that various types of fever, acute dysentery, and problems with the "Digestive Organs" make up the majority of the cases recorded. In April we also see 2 men treated for syphilis and 5 treated for gonorrhea. During April, 242 men were recorded as "Taken sick or wounded." Of those, most were treated and returned to duty, while 10 were sent to the general hospital. May's numbers were somewhat lower, with 110 men listed as taken sick or wounded. On that form, a section is given to execution by hanging or shooting. There were none of either reported.[46]

From the surgeon's records we are also able to see what the men in the regimental hospital were eating. For example, for March 1865, we find that the 2nd Maine Cavalry's hospital at Barrancas was issued or purchased "at contract prices," 490 rations, which included such foodstuffs as 105 pounds of pork, 124.5 pounds of ham, 100 pounds of fresh beef, 549 pounds of flour, 495 pounds of potatoes, 53 pounds of dried apples, as well as beans, pickles, butter, coffee, tea, and sugar.[47]

It is interesting to compare the invalid's diet above with the normal ration for soldiers in Union regiments as described in general orders:

> Section 2nd of the Act approved June 20th 1864 published in General Orders No 216 current series, having modified the Army ration, the following regulations on that subject will be observed:
>
> I. The ration is twelve ounces of pork or bacon, or one pound, four ounces of salt or fresh beef; eighteen ounces of soft bread or flour, or twelve ounces of hard bread or one pound and four ounces of corn meal; and, to every one hundred rations, fifteen pounds of beans or peas or ten pounds of rice or hominy, ten pounds of green coffee or eight pounds of roasted (or roasted and ground) coffee or one pound and eight ounces of tea, fifteen pounds of sugar; four quarts of vinegar; one pound and four ounces of adamantine or star candles; four ounces of pepper. The Subsistence Department as may be most convenient or least expensive to it, and according to the condition and amount of its supplies shall determine whether soft bread or flour and what other component parts of the ration, as equivalents, shall be issued.
>
> II. On a campaign, on marches, or on board of transports, the ration of hard bread is one pound
>
> III. desicated compressed potatoes or desicated compressed mixed vegetables at the rate of one ounce and a half of the former and one ounce of the latter to this ration may be substituted for beans, peas, rice, or hominy.
>
> IIII. Beans, peas, salt and potatoes (fresh) shall be purchased, issued, and sold by weight, and the bushel of each shall be estimated at sixty pounds.
>
> V. When deemed necessary fresh vegetables, dried fruit, molasses, pickles or any other proper food may be purchased and issued in lieu of any component part of the ration of equal money value. The Commissary General of Subsistence is alone authorized to order such purchases.
>
> By order of the Secretary of War
>
>   E.D. Townsend   Asst Adjt Genl[48]

Commissary Sgt. George Allen (Special Collections, Bangor Public Library).

It is clear from regimental records and soldiers' anecdotes that the full ration was not always available and those in charge of the regiments' commissary sometimes had to improvise. And, we may assume that, although special permission was needed to substitute alternative kinds of food, regiments did augment their rations with local products. Or, as we saw earlier, the folks at home might ship additional supplies to the men in the field.

In March 1865, Lieutenant Colonel Spurling, in command of the 2nd Maine Cavalry, felt the need to make a special request of the acting assistant adjutant general, District of West Florida, for flour: "Sir, I have the honor respectfully to request that my Commissary may draw flour instead of bread for the following reasons. Each company has an oven which was built when there was no bakery at this Post, and by drawing flour the men not only get

PROCLAMATION BY THE PRESIDENT, APPOINTING A DAY OF FASTING, HUMILIATION AND PRAYER, WITH THANKSGIVING.—The Congress of the Confederate States have, by a joint resolution, invited me to appoint a day of public fasting, humiliation and prayer, with thanksgiving to Almighty God.

It is our solemn duty, at all times, and more especially in a season of public trial and adversity, to acknowledge our dependence on His mercy, and to bow in humble submission before His footstool confessing our manifold sins, supplicating His gracious pardon, imploring His Divine help, and devoutly rendering thanks for the many and great blessings which He has vouchsafed to us.

Let the hearts of our people turn contritely and trustfully unto God; let us recognize in His chastening hand the correction of a Father, and submissively pray that the trials and sufferings which have so long borne heavily upon us may be turned away by His merciful love; that His sustaining grace be given to our people, and His divine wisdom imparted to our rulers; that the Lord of Hosts will be with our armies, and fight for us against our enemies; and that He will graciously take our cause into His own hand and mercifully establish for us a lasting, just and honorable peace and independence.

And let us not forget to render unto His holy name the thanks and praise which are so justly due for His great goodness, and for the many mercies which He has extended to us amid the trials and sufferings of protracted and bloody war.

Now, therefore, I, JEFFERSON DAVIS, President of the Confederate States of America, do issue this my proclamation, appointing FRIDAY, the 10th day of March next, as a day of public fasting, humiliation and prayer, (with thanksgiving,) for "invoking the favor and guidance of Almighty God;" and I do earnestly invite all soldiers and citizens to observe the same in a spirit of reverence, penitence and prayer.

Friday next, the 10th day of March, is the day appointed for Fasting, Humiliation and Prayer. The Congress of the Confederate States call upon the People, on that day, to humble themselves before Almighty God, and to beseech Him, through our Lord Jesus Christ, for the forgiveness of our sins, and for deliverance from our enemies. The President, in his Proclamation, has invoked the People everywhere to observe that day, and the Press and the Pulpit have sustained, with unanimity and fervor, the official recommendations.

The Richmond *Whig* says:

In view of the fact that our position as a people is critical, it is respectfully suggested that all persons in the Confederacy observe Friday, the 10th day of March, appointed a day of fasting and prayer, with more earnestness and solemnity than has yet been manifested, and to that end it is proposed—

1. That all churches shall have at least three public services. The first early in the morning; the second at 11 o'clock, and the third in the afternoon or at night.
2. That such churches as can, will keep their doors open and the services in operation, without intermision, during the whole day, the ministers relieving one another, and the people going and coming, as they may need.
3. That country churches protract their services through four or five hours.
4. That the people really humble themselves, and, as a means thereto, eat no more food than may be necessary to keep up their strength.
5. That all light conversation and unbecoming amusements be discarded, and the day be truly observed as a day of *humiliation*.

If there be any virtue in a day of fasting and prayer, it should be observed as the Bible directs. Heretofore many have kept it as a mere holiday. This cannot be expected to elicit God's blessing — Our condition is now such that trifling is madness —

If we give all our time and hearts to it for *that one day*, we may look for a great blessing.

Left: Jefferson Davis's proclamation was carried in the *Richmond Daily Dispatch* of March 6, 1865; *right*: The same issue also called for a day of fasting and prayer.

better bread, but their ration would also be increased which is now really too small for rugged hearty men—and since the arrival of so many troops at this Post it would be a relief to the Com'y to issue flour instead of bread to these regiments which can do their baking."[49]

In the Confederacy, March brought a realization that the end might be in sight. Confederate President Jefferson Davis, at the invitation of the Confederate Congress, had issued a proclamation calling for "A Day of Fasting, Humiliation, and Prayer, with Thanksgiving" which appeared in the Richmond, Virginia, *Daily Dispatch* of March 6. The proclamation stated that "in a season of public trial and adversity" it was the people's solemn duty "to acknowledge our dependence on His mercy, and to bow in humble submission before His footsteps, confessing our manifold sins, supplicating His gracious pardon, imploring His Divine help, and devoutly rendering thanks for the many and great blessings which He has vouchsafed to us." Friday, March 10, was named as the day for this—"invoking the favor and guidance of Almighty God."

The same newspaper also printed a call for that day of fasting and prayer, and gave the specifics of the type of observances to be held. It was made clear, in stressing the seriousness of the day that this was to be no "mere hiliday. This cannot be expected to elicit God's blessing.—Our condition is such that trifling is madness. If we give all our time and hearts to it for *that one day,* we may look for a great blessing."

The article concludes by giving the Biblical justification for such a day of fasting, and states, "And, surely, never was there an hour in the history of man, or in the life of any man now living in this country, when there was more need to invoke the forgiveness and the favor of Almighty God."

> Much might be added from the same and other authorities showing that fasting is but an instrument to an end, and that it is the individual repentance of every man seeking pardon through our Lord Jesus Christ for his own sins, to which the people are called. And, surely, never was there an hour in the history of man, or in the life of any man now living in this country, when there was more need to invoke the forgiveness and the favor of Almighty God.

The March 6 newspaper also noted a biblical justification for fasting.

Chapter Nine

March 1865: Raids on the Confederate Railroad and Action Near Spanish Fort and Fort Blakely

That spring of 1865 saw the 2nd Maine Cavalry taking part in some of the last military engagements of the Civil War. The *Maine Adjutant General's Report* states, "Early in the Spring, the army under Maj. Gen. Steele began to concentrate at Pensacola, preparatory to the movement on Mobile, which was to result in the capture of that city and the opening of the State of Alabama to the advance of Federal troops."

On March 8, General Christopher C. Andrews, in command of the 2nd Division, 13th Corps, at Barrancas wrote to President Lincoln:

> We are still here. But I would suppose we would be ready to move in five days. The cavalry is now arriving. There are the greater portion of two infantry divisions here, including Hawkins's colored division.
>
> We have had a good deal of stormy weather. The latest reports from the enemy and which are deemed reliable are that reinforcements are constantly coming down the railroad to Mobile; that 2000 men with some artillery are at Pollard, and that the rail road stations are being stockaded.
>
> Gen. Steele is here quite active, and will I understand have command of the column moving from here.[1]

Once again, from Confederate correspondence from this period, we can see how General Liddell was keeping General Maury, the Confederate commander at Mobile, informed of the Union troops' strength and movement. We also see that General Liddell's intelligence came from spies within the Union lines who were speaking with Federal troops or officers, as indicated by this letter from General Liddell to General Maury on March 9: "'D' reports that the enemy are still receiving re-enforcements; [they] will make a move about the 15th [of March]. Enemy say it is not their intention to go to Montgomery. Enemy's lines advanced."[2]

The role of the 2nd Maine Cavalry in the early phases of the advance toward Mobile was to cut the railroad which would be used to bring Confederate supplies and reinforcements through Alabama to Mobile, to scout the area to the northeast of Mobile, and to attack Confederate cavalry operating in that area.

In mid March, "by authority of Gen. Steele, Lieut. Col. Spurling was assigned to the command of a special cavalry expedition composed of about 1,000 men, the 2nd [Maine] Cavalry forming the most important part." General Steele stated:

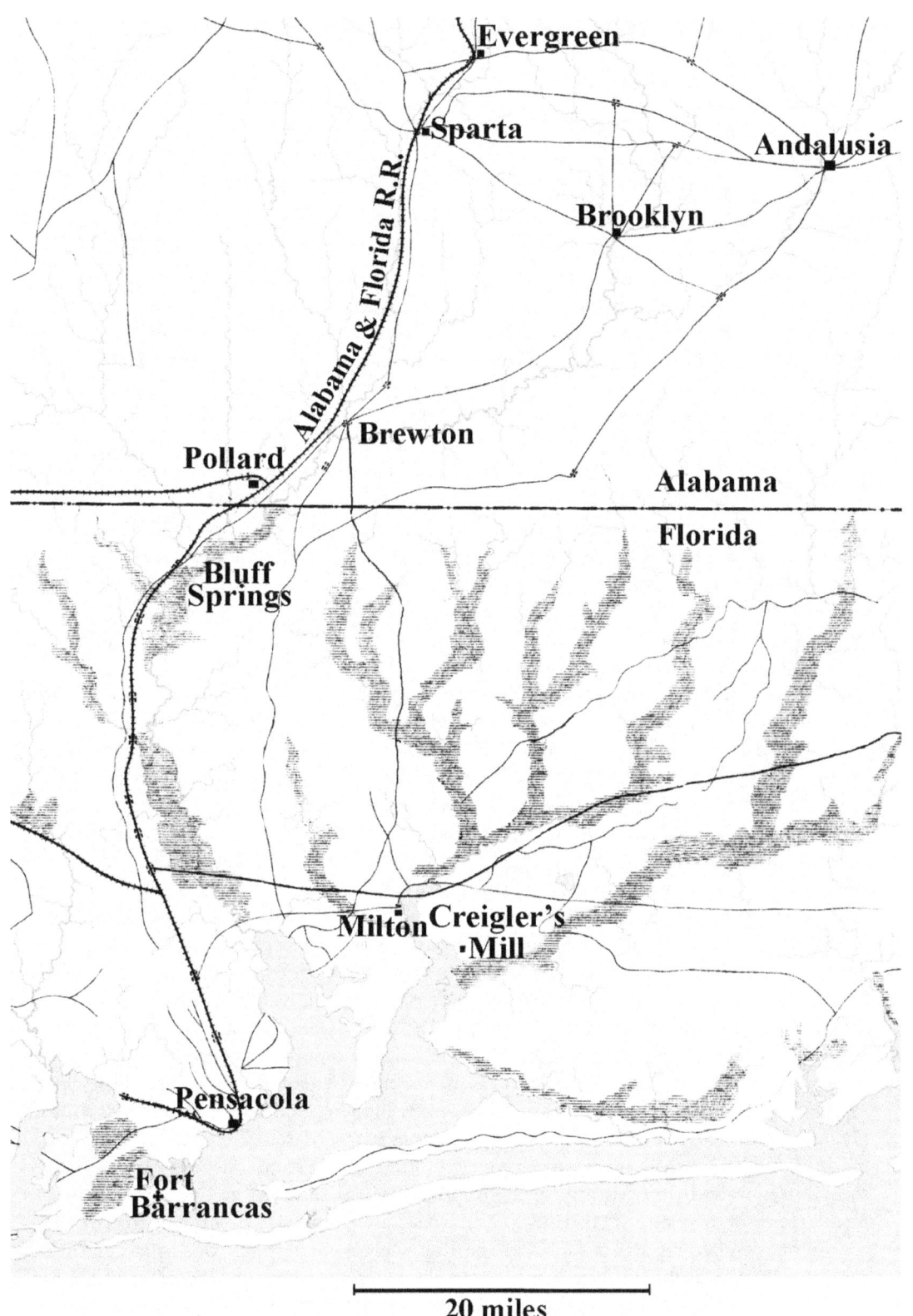

From Barrancas to Evergreen (adapted from map CXLVII; *Official Atlas*).

I have ordered Colonel Spurling with about 800 cavalry to break the railroad between Greenville and Pollard, and I am confident he will succeed.... Having captured trains and destroyed the roads sufficiently between those points, they will ... proceed toward Pollard, doing such damage to the road as may be necessary to render it useless to the rebels.... Spurling will have excellent guides, and he is well acquainted with the country himself."[3]

It seems that General Asboth was to have led this expedition, but a report from General Steele, reflecting on Asboth's recovery from the wounds of the Marianna expedition, makes it clear why the command was given to Lt. Col. Spurling: "In regard to General Asboth's physical ability to endure the fatigue of a campaign. He is full of valor and energy and seems very desirous of going into the field, but it appears to me that he is too feeble ... his weight is 140 pounds, and I observe that he requires assistance to mount and dismount his horse.... General [C.C.] Andrews informs me that Lieutenant-Colonel Spurling, of the cavalry, is thoroughly acquainted with the country, and well qualified in every respect to command cavalry on an expedition like that in contemplation."[4]

With the mounted portion of the 2nd Maine Cavalry sent on this mission by General Steele, and with other troops being sent toward Mobile, General Asboth was concerned with the strength of his garrison at Barrancas: "I have turned over to Major-General Steele's command the Eighty-second and Eighty-sixth U.S. Colored Infantry Regiments and all the mounted men of the Second Maine and First Florida Cavalry. My command is thus reduced to the Twenty-fifth U.S. Colored Infantry garrisoning the forts, and to the dismounted men of the Second Maine and First Florida Cavalry, by far not sufficient to provide properly for my long-extended picket line and the daily details for fatigue duty."[5]

The overall action during Lt. Col. Spurling's expedition to "break the railroad" is quite straightforward. His detachment from the 2nd Maine Cavalry left Barrancas on March 19 and was taken by steamer to Creigler's Mills on the Blackwater River, where they were joined by men from the 1st Florida Cavalry and the 2nd Illinois Cavalry. Spurling's combined force then proceeded "by a circuitous and rapid route" northward to Andalusia, Alabama, where they took several prisoners. Upon entering Evergreen, the next day, the troopers "tore up track of the Mobile and Montgomery Railroad and captured and destroyed 2 engines and trains of cars loaded with supplies, capturing also several prisoners. On March 27, a "slight skirmish at Murder Creek" left two men of the 2nd Maine Cavalry wounded, and on March 28 the expedition "crossed the Escambia River and joined General Frederick Steele's Army." The cavalry regiments under Lt. Col. Spurling's command for this expedition made up the 2nd Cavalry Brigade of General Thomas Lucas' Cavalry Division of General Frederick Steele's column of forces that moved toward Mobile Bay from Pensacola.[6]

The plan for this expedition was largely based on a report from Lt. Col. Spurling with information obtained from his former raids and reconnaissance: "Lieutenant-Colonel Spurling, Second Maine Cavalry, reports a picket of fifteen men [Confederate troops] at Milton, Fla., as the only force on that side of the Escambia River, March 6. He reports only 2,000 men at Pollard with three pieces of artillery.... Colonel S. gives a practicable route to Pollard to land two miles below Milton on the opposite side of the river at Creigler's Mills, and march from there by way of Andalusia, Ala. Roads are good, with no bridges to cross."[7]

More detailed reports by Lt. Col. Spurling and others flesh out this broad picture of the expedition. Spurling reports that the steamer *Matamoras* brought the last of the troops for his detachment to Creigler's Mills on the evening of March 21. His report of the makeup of the expedition, consisting of mounted troops from the 2nd Cavalry Brigade, is somewhat at odds with the Maine adjutant general's report which stated that the 2nd Maine Cavalry was "the most important part" of the force of 1,000. However, Lt. Col. Spurling states that the largest part of the detachment consisted of 443 men and officers from the 2nd Illinois Cavalry commanded by Major Franklin Moore. The 2nd Maine Cavalry, under Major Charles Miller, brought 222 men and officers, and the 1st Florida Cavalry contributed 182 men and officers, for a total of 847. As Lt. Col. Spurling's expedition proceeded northward from Creigler's Mills, Captain E. D. Johnson of the 2nd Maine Cavalry had been sent to Milton with two companies of the 1st Florida. There that contingent had "driven the enemy's pickets toward Pollard, and was holding the place [Milton] for the purpose of concealing the real movement on the opposite side of the river." Captain Johnson and his men did not move north with Lt. Col. Spurling's column, but remained at Milton until the main force had begun its march toward Pollard, when they were to overtake the force "as soon as practicable."

Col. Spurling says that the force advanced by the direct route to Andalusia, Alabama, and nothing occurred during the first day, although rain made the march uncomfortable. That evening the force encamped about 25 miles north of Milton. Starting early the next morning, "Several rebels were made prisoners and quite a number of horses and mules captured." That night the Union troopers encamped about 6 miles from Andalusia and during that night the pickets brought in two Confederate couriers. These couriers were carrying dispatches to the Rebel commander at Andalusia warning of a Union force of 2,000 heading in his direction (an overstatement, since that number was more than twice the actual size of Spurling's force). The dispatch also directed that "all the people capable of bearing arms be in readiness to make resistance." It was anticipated in these dispatches that the Union force would reach Andalusia on the evening of March 23. Spurling's expedition, in fact, arrived at Andalusia at about 5 a.m. on the 23rd and "no resistance was made whatever. I caused all the arms and ammunition that could be found in the place to be destroyed.... What little property belonged to the rebel Government, and could be found, was destroyed."[8]

The Union expedition left Andalusia at around 8 a.m. and moved toward Evergreen. No opposition was met during the day, but that evening, when Col. Spurling was riding alone in advance of his column, he later reported, "At night a little after dark, and when six miles from Evergreen, I came suddenly upon three rebels. They attempted to escape and two of them were wounded and all were made prisoners. One of them (wounded) proved to be a Lieutenant [John W.] Watts, of General Clanton's staff, and a son of Governor Watts," Alabama's Governor Thomas Watts, who had also been the attorney general of the Confederacy. For his single-handed capture of these Rebel soldiers, which also, and importantly, had the result of preventing their escape to warn other Confederate troops of the direction in which the Union column was headed, Col. Spurling was later awarded the Medal of Honor. Lt. Watts was quite seriously wounded, and Lt. Col. Spurling is reported to have sent for the 2nd Maine Cavalry's surgeon, Dr. Martin, and held Watts in his arms while the doctor probed for the bullet and dressed the wound. Then, feeling that the lieutenant should not be moved, Spurling accepted Watts' parole—a promise that he would take no part in the military until he might be officially exchanged for a Union prisoner—and released him. Some months later, after the surrender and Union occupation of Montgomery, Alabama, Col. Spurling was riding down a street of that city and Lieutenant Watts "hailed him and held up the bullet, saying 'Here is your ball.'"[9]

To continue with Lt. Col. Spurling's report of the expedition, he states that a little before midnight on the night of March 23, the Union force "reached the Alabama and Florida Railroad at a point five miles above Evergreen. I immediately caused the telegraph wires to be cut and the railroad track to be torn up. At 4.30 a.m. March 24 the train of cars from Pollard came up the road. It was thrown from the track, set on fire, and destroyed." This train of one locomotive and 7 cars was followed by a more dramatic prize a short time later. "At 7 o'clock the train arrived from Montgomery and was captured and destroyed; 100 soldiers, including 7 commissioned officers were captured on this train." There were also a number of civilians and paroled Confederate prisoners on that train, who were released. Major Franklin Moore, who commanded the 2nd Illinois Cavalry on that expedition, reported that this train, which was headed for Mobile, was also carrying "clothing, grain, horses, mail, tobacco, etc." The horses were taken off and kept, and all of the supplies were destroyed.[10]

Lt. Col. Spurling's force then proceeded to Evergreen, where they arrived at 11 a.m. on the 24th. "Here I obtained an abundance of forage and rations and destroyed some stores. What little rolling stock was found at the station was burned." After that, the force moved to Sparta and arrived there at 4 p.m. At the railroad station there, "All the rolling stock—six box-cars—was destroyed. Some quite important trestle-work on the road was burned," as was "the depot, filled with stores and warlike material." The Union troopers spent that night encamped at Sparta.[11]

General Clanton, the Confederate commander at Pollard, reported, "I believe the enemy have broken the road above Evergreen. I have 100 Reserves and 30 cavalry here. Will do the best I can, being governed by circumstances."[12]

Confederate General Richard Taylor's report to Alabama Governor Watts regarding this action was more optimistic: "The [Union] force about Evergreen can be only cavalry, and troops enough are on the march to whip it, as well as any force coming from the north." As we will see, his optimism for the outcome of the action above Pollard was not to prove true: Lt. Col. Spurling's expedition was not whipped. And, in action against General Lucas' Union cavalry brigade at Bluff Springs, just below Pollard, General Clanton's force was badly beaten and Clanton was seriously wounded. As with Lt. Watts, mentioned above, General Clanton signed a parole and was left to have his wounds tended.[13]

On March 25, the following message was sent by Brigadier General Liddell to Colonel C. G. Armistead, whose cavalry command was now at Canoe Station: "As Clanton has been captured and your force so inadequate, you will look to the safety of all public property, keeping in the enemy's front and forming a junction with General [Daniel W.] Adams [the Confederate commander at Selma]."[14]

For Lt. Col. Spurling's command, on March 25, "The column moved at 5 a.m. on the road leading to Brooklyn, which place was reached at 11.30 o'clock." Continuing until sundown, the column halted and camped about 12 miles from Brewton Station. At around 11 a.m. on March 26, the column arrived at Brewton Station and found the bridge across Muddy Creek had been heavily damaged. When Lt. Col. Spurling realized that the bridge would need substantial repair before the column could advance, he sent across to the other side "an advance guard (dismounted) to see if they could find any enemy. The rebels soon opened fire from behind a small breast-work and then ran away." During that brief engagement, Lt. Vose and two enlisted men of the 2nd Maine Cavalry were "slightly wounded."

After repairing the bridge, the Union force continued and reached Pollard late in the afternoon of March 26. In addition to the Rebel railroad track, trains, and supplies destroyed, "The results of the expedition in the way of prisoners, captured property, etc, which I have with me, are 120 prisoners, 200 negroes, 250 horses and mules." This all was accomplished without the loss or serious wounding of a single Union soldier.[15]

At Pollard, Lt. Col. Spurling's force joined with other Union troops under General C.C. Andrews, who had been sent ahead of General Steele's column to rendezvous with Spurling's command. Reunited with the remainder of General Steele's column, the Union troops began their move westward farther into Alabama toward Stockton. From there, it was hoped, they would join the other Union forces near Blakely on the eastern shore of Mobile Bay for the assaults on the remaining Confederate defenses near Mobile.[16]

On March 24, General Steele sent a request to General Asboth at Barrancas expressing an urgent need for supplies for his column. The men of General Steele's command had discovered that the Confederate food supplies which had been stored at Pollard were removed by local Confederate troops and civilians. As a result, General Steele's column was running

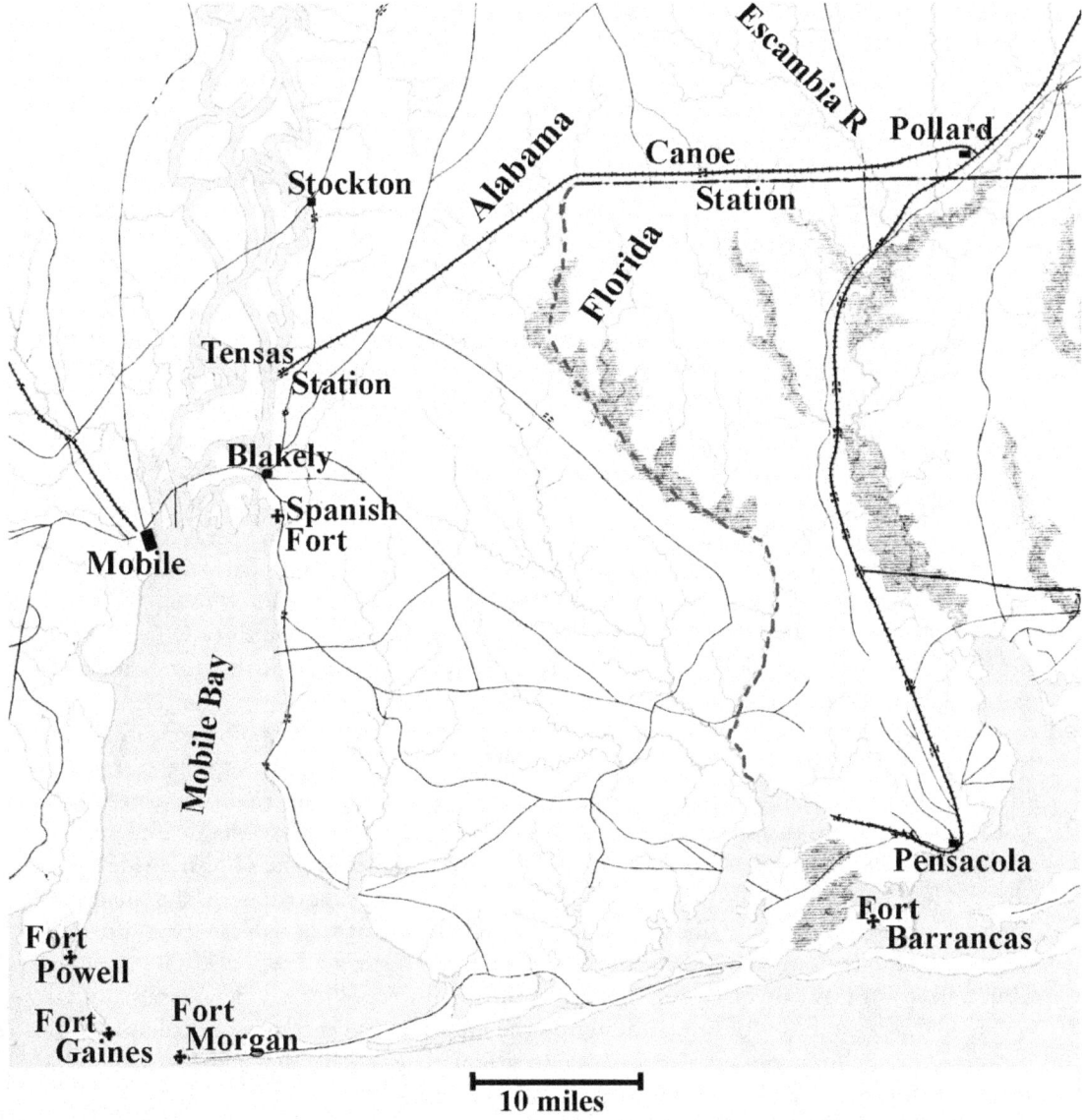

Pollard to Blakely (adapted from map CXLVII, *Official Atlas*).

very short on food. One hundred of the dismounted men of the 2nd Maine Cavalry were sent from Barrancas as guards for the supply ship *Matamoras,* which was to proceed up the Escambia River to resupply General Steele's forces operating toward Pollard, including the mounted portion of the 2nd Maine.[17]

When the *Matamoras* did leave from Barrancas, on March 25, it proceeded up toward the Escambia River, but was unable to pass the bar at the entrance to the river. The *Matamoras* needed 4½ feet of clearance and there was only 3 feet of water over the bar, and so the ship returned to Barrancas. On March 26, General Steele's command was put on one-quarter rations. When the head of Steele's column reached Canoe Station on March 27, they discovered some corn, but once again, the bulk of the foodstuffs had been carried off. At Canoe Station, some ox teams had been sent to retrieve supplies for the Union troops and some of these were butchered and "used as beef for our troops." Finally, on March 31, at Stockton, General Steele's command found sufficient supplies of corn and beef to feed his troops for several days.[18]

During this time, Confederate scouts and intelligence were aware of the intentions of General Steele's main column. On March 25, General Taylor informed Alabama Governor Watts, "Enemy's main force evidently intend attacking Mobile from the eastern side." And on March 26, Brigadier General D.W. Adams at Selma, Alabama, was told: "Enemy's main force with Canby, Steele, Granger, and A.J. Smith moving toward eastern shore [of Mobile Bay] near Mobile." The progress of the campaign can be seen in a March 27 report sent by General Taylor to General Robert E. Lee: "Enemy has thrown his large force to eastern side of Mobile Bay, leaving nothing on west side. I am ready to receive any attack he may make at Mobile. His cavalry from Florida coast has struck Montgomery railroad at Evergreen."[19]

At the end of March 1865, the organization of the mounted troops under Major General Steele (the column "operating from Pensacola") lists Lt. Col. Spurling as commanding the 2nd Brigade, still made up of the 2nd Maine Cavalry, 2nd Illinois Cavalry, and 1st Florida Cavalry.[20]

In early April, the 2nd Maine Cavalry continued to be involved in operations that were a part of the Mobile Campaign, and more specifically, the Union's plans to take Spanish Fort and Fort Blakely on the eastern shore of Mobile Bay. The *Maine Adjutant General's Report* states: "The mounted portion of the regiment continued on duty with the army before Blakely and Spanish Fort, and did valuable service in protecting the rear, being often engaged with the enemy's cavalry."[21]

During the previous summer, on August 5, 1864, the Union's attempt to capture Mobile had begun when Admiral David Farragut had attacked the forts guarding the entrance to Mobile Bay, while a Union infantry force was put ashore to lay siege to those forts by land. Fort Morgan, on the eastern side of the channel leading to Mobile Bay, was defended by 46 pieces of artillery and a garrison of around 600. Fort Gaines on the opposite side of the channel had 26 guns and also around 600 Confederate troops. Fort Powell, the smallest of the three, held 18 guns and about 140 men. A small fleet of Confederate war ships also defended Mobile, with the most impressive being the ironclad *Tennessee.* The attacking Union fleet was made up of 18 warships, most of which were older wooden vessels, but also included 4 new ironclads of similar design to the *Monitor.* The entrance to the bay was also protected by anchored mines—"torpedoes" in the language of that day. The first Union loss of the battle came when the captain of the monitor *Tecumseh,* instead of avoiding the minefield, which was clearly marked by buoys, steered directly through it. The explosion of a mine sank the *Tecumseh* in only 2 or 3 minutes with the loss of all but 21 men of its 114 man crew, including its captain, Commander Tunis Craven. It was upon learning of the *Tecumseh*'s fate that Farragut was reported to utter his famous "Damn the torpedoes, full speed ahead," and the rest of the Union fleet passed through the mined area unharmed. In a little more than three hours the Union fleet had passed the forts and defeated the Confederate naval forces. The Rebels warships, including the ironclad *Tennessee,* were destroyed, or had surrendered, except for one sidewheel gunboat, which retreated to Mobile.

Meanwhile, the Union Army, under General Gordon Granger, had landed 1,500 soldiers to make the initial attacks on Forts Powell and Gaines. Fort Powell was abandoned by its small Confederate garrison on the night of August 5, 1864, and Fort Gaines surrendered on August 8. The Union troops, now with additional men and totaling a force of some 5,500, then concentrated on Fort Morgan with its 618 Confederate defenders. The Union forces brought up artillery, which was augmented by guns of the Union fleet, and began a siege which ended with the surrender of the fort on August 23. And so, while Mobile itself remained in Confederate hands, along with 2 forts in its immediate vicinity, the Confederates were no longer able to use the harbor.[22]

And now we return to about 8 months later, the spring of 1865, as Union forces were moving toward Mobile and those nearby forts—Spanish Fort and Fort Blakely. On April 1, Lt. Col. Spurling was again in action with the Second Cavalry Brigade. The Union troopers left from Stockton, Alabama, early that morning "for the purpose of opening communication with and joining the U.S. forces operating against Spanish Fort below Blakely." About 7 miles from Blakely, Spurling reported, "My advance guard came in contact with the enemy's pickets; four were captured and one received a saber cut on the head. A short distance farther on other pickets were captured and one mortally wounded." Soon after that encounter, a more substantial number of Confederate soldiers was discovered by the Union troopers. From Lt. Col. Spurling's report, we learn, "Five miles from Blakely I came upon the enemy in force." After considering an alternative route by which to proceed to join with General Canby's forces near Spanish Fort, and finding that the only alternatives would require a detour of many miles, Lt. Col. Spurling stated,

> I concluded to fight. The Second Maine Cavalry was dismounted and deployed on each side of the road to fight on foot. This regiment was moved forward under a brisk fire, which was as briskly returned. The enemy slowly retired before this advance, taking shelter behind fences and everything that could afford protection. They retired in this way for over a mile, contesting every inch of ground. I had moved the Second Illinois up the road, and kept its advance on a line with the Second Maine, and judging that the favorable opportunity had arrived I charged the enemy with that regiment. It was a complete success. His whole force was routed and a portion of it captured.

The 2nd Illinois pursued the retreating Confederates toward Blakely until, "within half a mile of the enemy's works ... a sharp fire was opened with artillery." The results of this action were 74 Rebel prisoners, including 3 commissioned officers. "Nearly all of them were members of the Forty-sixth Mississippi Infantry. The colors of that regiment were also captured; 8 horses and mules were taken; 70 stand of arms captured and destroyed." During this fight, one man of the Second Illinois was mortally wounded, but "he was so near to the enemy's works that he could not be brought off by his comrades." Lt. Col. Spurling goes on to report, "After I had whipped the enemy and driven him into the fortifications at Blakely I got my force into a good position to halt, feed, etc." After Col. Spurling's cavalry pushed the Confederate defenders of Fort Blakely back toward their main lines of defense on April 1, General Steele began a siege of Blakely.[23]

On April 6, Col. Spurling "sent a scout of fifty men toward Stockton." The makeup of this detachment is not indicated, but, "they went within two miles of that place.... Nothing whatever of the enemy was seen, but they ascertained that a squad of twenty-five rebels was lurking about in that vicinity. Everything is quiet along the picket-line, and there are no signs of an enemy this morning."[24]

The next day, April 7, Lt. Col. Spurling and a detachment of about 30 men left from the area of Blakely and headed northward to make "a scout ... in the direction of Stockton." About 8 miles from their starting point, Col. Spurling "received information that a small squad of rebel cavalry was in the immediate vicinity." Proceeding on,

> I soon discovered them drawn up at a cross-road. They were routed, 1 of their number killed and 2 severely wounded. I pursued the fugitives for a long distance. Nine rebels in all were made prisoner; all their arms, equipments, &c, were captured, and the arms destroyed. Eight horses were also captured. Among the prisoners were two commissioned officers, a captain and a lieutenant. They belonged to Armistead's command [Col. C.G. Armistead], and were lurking about in the rear of our army to capture stragglers and small foraging parties that might be sent into the country. There were no casualties in my own force.

Col. Spurling then reported that he returned to camp at 4 p.m. bringing with him the prisoners and horses. Of the whole squad of 14 Confederates, only 4 had escaped capture.[25]

The following response to Col. Spurling's raid was sent to Major General Steele from Major General Edward R. Canby, commanding the Union's Division of West Mississippi. It is most interesting by both its praise and its understatement: "The major-general commanding has received with much gratification your report of Colonel Spurling's gallant little exploit. He [Gen. Canby] would like to see him [Col. Spurling] at headquarters early tomorrow morning." No record was found of the substance of that meeting.[26]

And, on April 8, Col. Spurling requested that Captain Lyons, of the 1st Florida Cavalry, send him 6 men from that regiment "who are best acquainted with the country between the Alabama River and the Choctawhatchee, and as far north as Montgomery." As described earlier, the Union soldiers from Florida, such as those in both the 1st and 2nd Florida Cavalry, provided an extremely valuable resource for information and scouting.[27]

General Steele's force, moving from Pensacola, brought around 13,000 Union troops to join with General Canby's 32,000 men to take part in the Mobile Campaign. To defend the two Confederate Forts on the eastern side of Mobile Bay, Spanish Fort and Fort Blakely, Confederate General Maury had approximately 4,000 men at Spanish Fort and a similar number at Fort Blakely. The siege of Spanish Fort was begun by General Canby's force on March 27, before the arrival of General Steele's column at Fort Blakely. On March 28, a message from General R.L Gibson, in command at Spanish Fort stated, fairly optimistically, "Enemy attempted to advance his lines as sunset, but was wholly unsuccessful. He is persistent in his attempts to gain all the ground he can, and fails at every point.... I lost 5 men killed and wounded today. I attribute the loss to the want of tools to throw up skirmish pits and traverses. I have an immense deal of digging to do, as the enemy are erecting heavy batteries on the right and left, which enfllade the lines."

General Gibson also reports that his aggregate present for duty is 3,400 men. And later that day, Gibson reported, "There are strong indications that the enemy will assault my lines in the morning. Allow me to keep the reserve regiment until tomorrow night."[28]

General Gibson continued giving regular reports of the Union's attacks and his defense, including his casualties and the status of his garrison. On March 30, he reported, "We are doing very well. Can you send us some tools?" His concerns over his men's urgent need to dig further defenses clearly continued.[29]

On the same day, General Gibson gave the following message to his troops:

> I. The brigadier-general commanding desires to express to the troops the admiration of their valor and endurance, and his entire confidence in their ability to defend this position.
> II. Thousands of anxious hearts turn toward you.
> III. Let every officer and man resolve to do his whole duty, to stand firm at his post, and to make the enemy pay dearly in blood for every inch he may advance, and by the blessing of Heaven we shall continue those successes which so far with scarcely any loss crowned your efforts.[30]

On March 31, with Union siege artillery in place and his own ammunition running low, General Gibson told his troops, "You must dig, dig, dig. Nothing can save us here but the spade."[31]

On April 4, the situation at Spanish Fort had become desperate. General Gibson was offering 36 hour leaves to any man who would collect 25 pounds of lead from the shot and shell fired by the Union guns. The general further threatened severe punishment to any of his soldiers who were destroying serviceable cartridges. (One must wonder whether, in an attempt to force the fort's surrender, some Confederate soldiers were purposely depleting their ammunition supply.) And, in an attempt to stop any of his soldiers from crossing to the Union lines and surrendering, General Gibson ordered that no soldier of his command was allowed "on any pretext or at any time, night or day, to go beyond the main line of works." And, "Officers and men are hereby ordered to fire on and arrest any one of these men attempting to pass beyond the main works." A furlough of 30 days was offered as a reward for any soldier who arrested "any man attempting to desert to the enemy." And, in a final and clear message of desperation, General Gibson stated, "A secret police should be organized in each company to watch them [those planning to desert], detect them, and kill them at once."[32]

In a message sent to General Maury and General Liddell on April 4, General Gibson reports slight damage done to some of his artillery by the Union bombardment and states, "The firing was so rapid we could not estimate accurately the number of guns." He goes on, "Can't you send another 64-pounder and some 10-inch mortars? I would like to have two more 64-pounders and fight the fight out in earnest." And, in contrast to his message to his troops of that same date, recorded above, he ends with, "All's well."[33]

On April 5 General Gibson reported twice to General Maury that "All's well." But, on April 8, General Liddell told General Gibson that he would send "all the boats I can get, to be used in the event of your being compelled to evacuate." And later that day, General Gibson reported, "I am beginning to retire.... Hope to lose nothing but artillery. Will have a guard at the landing, so as to hold fast to the last moment."[34]

Spanish Fort fell to the Union forces on April 8, with Confederate losses listed as 93 killed, 395 wounded, and 250 missing. On April 9, General Canby sent a message to General Steele outside Fort Blakely reporting the capture of Spanish Fort and saying he had captured 15 to 20 guns and 1,600 to 2,000 prisoners. One more recent account of the capture of Spanish Fort gives the number of captured at 500 and states that the majority of General Gibson's force at Spanish Fort was able to escape to join General Maury at Mobile. Another recent account of the capture of Spanish Fort states that during the siege of that position, 73 Confederate soldiers were killed, 350 wounded, 6 missing, and 350 captured. Whatever the details, with Spanish Fort in Union hands, General Canby told General Steele, "We leave a brigade in the fort for the present; with the balance we are coming up to join you. Thus, the concentration of forces at Blakely brought the total of Union troops there to some 45,000." On the same day that General Canby brought his men to Blakely (April 9), a general assault was ordered and within 20 minutes the fort was captured. Union losses were reported as 113 men killed and 516 wounded, while the Confederate garrison of 3,423 was made prisoner. Among those prisoners were the Brigadier Generals Liddell, Frances Cockrell, and Bryan Thomas.[35]

On April 10, the day after General Robert E. Lee surrendered the Army of Northern Virginia to General Grant at Appomattox, General Maury, of course unaware of the fate of Lee's army, concluded that he should evacuate Mobile. Maury ordered remaining Confederate batteries near Spanish Fort to fire on the Union positions to cover the evacuation and, with his approximately 4,500 remaining troops, began to move north toward Montgomery. With the evacuation completed, Confederate Major R. H. Slough surrendered the city of Mobile at noon on April 12.[36]

For many people, the surrender of General Lee's forces is synonymous with the end of the Civil War. That was, of course, not the case. Many Confederate armies in the field and various other units continued to fight. That was the situation that the 2nd Maine Cavalry encountered in Alabama. On April 10, joyous headlines and lead articles announcing the surrender of the Army of Northern Virginia appeared in the Northern newspaper.

However, in the case of the Washington, D.C., *Evening Standard,* another announcement, on the same page, reported the Union army's advances on Blakely and Spanish Fort and showed that fighting was continuing in other theaters of war. And, in that article, the part that the 2nd Maine Cavalry played in the raid that began back on March 19 is also reported. How accurate was this information? Well, the name of the regiment, "the 22d Maine," and its Colonel "Sparling" are both given incorrectly, and the "General Clawsen" who was reported captured was actually General Clanton, who was unlikely to have had 2 rebel cavalry regiments available to him. And the raid took the cavalry to Evergreen (toward Greenville) and Pollard, not "Greenwood" as reported. So, as we saw before, one must not rely overly on period newspaper reports for historical accuracy.

The exact intention of the Confed-

The Washington, D.C., *Evening Star* of April 10, 1865, announced the surrender of the Army of Northern Virginia.

erates upon leaving Mobile was apparently not clear. On April 13, Lt. Col. Spurling wrote to Assistant Adjutant General Christensen from Montgomery Hill Landing stating that he had been collecting all the flatboats that could be found within 40 miles and was collecting cattle to help provision the Union forces. He goes on, "Two men who were brought in this morning inform me that Mobile was being evacuated on Monday; that a large number of steamers and several gun-boats have gone up the Mobile River." The east branch of that river would take the Confederate forces toward Selma and Montgomery, Alabama.[37]

> Steele's column left Pensacola on the 19th. He captured two trains of cars at Greenwood and Pollard, Alabama. Two rebel cavalry regiments were met, charged, and routed, and Brigadier General Clawsen, twenty-two officers, four hundred men, and four hundred and fifty horses were captured. On the 27th, Colonel Sparling, with a detachment of the 22d Maine, and the 1st Florida cavalry, cut the Mobile and Montgomery railroad, and captured two wagon train and one hundred prisoners.

The same issue of the *Evening Star* also carried news of continued fighting.

As General Maury evacuated Mobile and headed north, any hope of using Montgomery as a base ended when he found that Union cavalry commander James Wilson and his troopers had captured that city on April 12 and occupied it for the next two days. Although Montgomery was of no great military significance, Wilson's men did destroy the city's arsenal, foundries, train depot, and other installations which might be useful to the Confederate military. Beyond that, Montgomery was of symbolic importance, having been the Confederacy's first capital and the city where Jefferson Davis had been inaugurated as the president. With Montgomery and the nearby town of Selma having been taken by Union forces, General Maury and his men moved westward toward Meridian, Mississippi.[38]

In the Eastern Theater of the war, March and the first weeks of April had seen events move to a crisis for General Robert E. Lee's forces in Petersburg. The siege was continuing and his greatly outnumbered army was being further depleted by desertion, while short supplies and disease within the Rebel lines were sapping the strength of those remaining Confederate soldiers. On March 25, General Lee ordered General John Gordon to attempt a breakout from Petersburg by attacking at and near the Union's Fort Stedman on the northeast section of the encircling Federal forts and trenches. The initial attacks seemed promising, but Federal reinforcements and artillery soon drove the Confederate troops back within their own lines. On March 31, the Confederate Cavalry of General Rooney Lee and infantry under General George Pickett attempted again to break the siege of Petersburg with an attack at Dinwiddie Court House, just southwest of that city. These attacks, particularly that at Fort Stedman, weakened Lee's own defenses, however, and set the stage for the victory of the Union army's Fifth Corps at the Battle of Five Forks on April 1 and the breakthrough of the Confederate lines on April 2. These actions led General Lee to remove his forces from Petersburg and Richmond and begin his movement westward that ended with the surrender of the Army of Northern Virginia on April 9.

CHAPTER TEN

To the End: The 2nd Maine Cavalry at Montgomery and Reconstruction Duty in Florida

In mid April, Lt. Col. Spurling and the 2nd Maine Cavalry saw a change in the organization of the Union cavalry forces. "After the fall of Mobile, the mounted detachment of the [2nd Maine Cavalry] regiment was assigned duty with the 16th army corps, being the only cavalry in that body of 30,000 men. The detachment was placed at the front and gave effectual aid in keeping Gen. Smith [Major General A.J. Smith, commander of the 16th Corps] fully informed of the strength and movements of the enemy during the long march of nearly 200 miles to the city of Montgomery, and in slight skirmishing almost daily, the cavalry continuously driving before them the broken and demoralized fragments of the rebel army."[1]

The statement in the *Maine Adjutant General's Report* quoted in the previous paragraph, that the 2nd Maine was the "only cavalry" with the 16th Corps, is evidently not accurate and this is confirmed in subsequent orders and reports. General Orders issued on April 14 state that both the 2nd Maine Cavalry and the 1st Florida Cavalry were assigned to duty with General Smith's corps.[2]

On April 20, as they moved toward Montgomery, Lt. Col. Spurling and a column of 80 troopers entered Greenville, Alabama. The few Confederate soldiers in the town were quickly scattered, with 9 officers and 115 enlisted men being captured. A party of officers from Spurling's command took over the offices of the Greenville *Observer* and put out a hastily prepared (and quite self-congratulatory) special edition:

> Amid the confusion, many beautiful ladies came into the streets, imploring protection, and in a short time the gallant and dashing Spurling was surrounded by a bevy of beauties handsome enough to soften the sternest heart. As the cavalry were dashing down one of the streets the Stars and Stripes were unfurled from a neat little cottage, where the troops halted and gave three time three [cheers] for that glorious old flag for which we have fought so long. We have heard of three American flags displayed from houses in this town, and are informed that several more would be flung to the southern breezes if they could be obtained. Since the occupation of Greenville by the Federal troops, we have not heard of any depredations being committed by the soldiers, and many [citizens] have expressed their surprise at "the good conduct of the enemy," as they expected that their houses would be pillaged and burned, and all manner of depredations committed, but to their agreeable astonishment not a single house has been destroyed, and the town quiet and orderly. The citizens have treated us cordially and kindly, and we shall long remember our army in Greenville as an oasis in the soldier's rough life.[3]

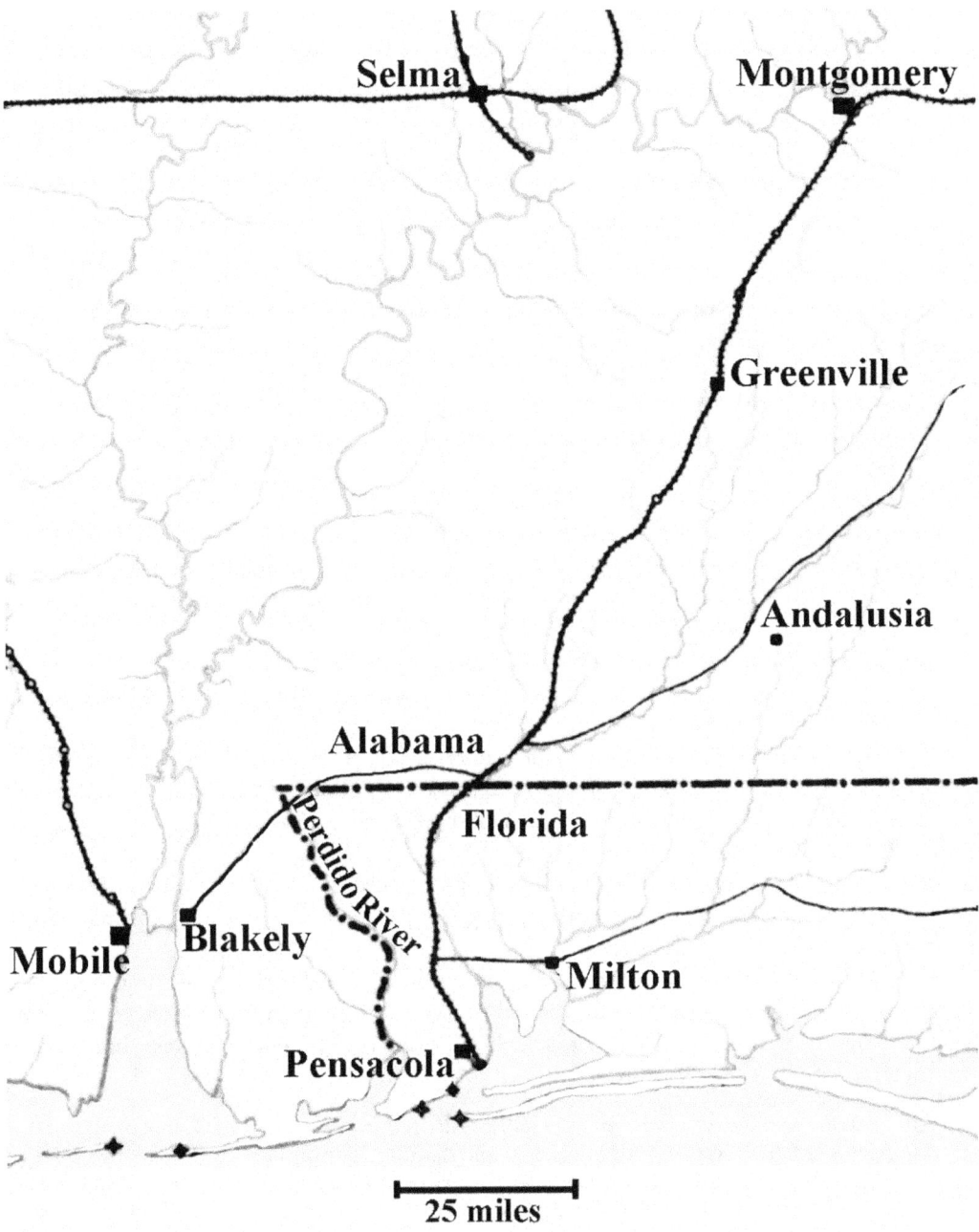

From the Mobile area to Selma and Montgomery (adapted from plate CXXXV-A, *Official Atlas*).

The fears of the citizens had been well founded. After taking the city of Selma, Alabama, in the first days of April, Union General James Wilson's forces had destroyed the Confederate arsenal, gun shops, factories, storehouses, and naval foundry, but had also looted the city and burned many private homes and businesses. And although current historians typically agree that Wilson's men were engaged in the looting and destruction, Wilson, in his memoirs, stated that "the negroes broke loose and began to plunder the shops and stores. Pandemonium followed, and before our provost guard could get control fires were raging at several places." After saying that his staff did "all they could to restore order and prevent the fires from spreading, it was nearly midnight before they got the situation completely under control." Wilson does not claim that his men were entirely blameless, and admits, "Some of the marauders and desperadoes who always find place in modern armies doubtless took part in plundering the stores and occasionally in breaking into private houses, but all such work was ruthlessly and promptly stopped as soon as it became known." And he concludes his recollections regarding the destruction of Confederate Government property by stating that during the burning of those buildings, "Every point in the neighborhood was watched with vigilance to see that not a dollar's worth of private property was injured in the conflagration." General Wilson, both during and after the war, became known for his self-aggrandizing statements and his willingness to blame others for any failures he and his men experienced. For a look at further examples of Wilson's actions and accounts, see Diane Monroe Smith's *Command Conflicts in Grant's Overland Campaign*.[4]

From Greenville, on April 22, Lt. Col. Spurling was ordered by General A.J. Smith "to proceed with your command at 6:30 a.m. to-morrow on the direct road to Montgomery, forming the advance guard."[5]

On April 24, the 2nd Maine Cavalry entered Montgomery, and the following is reported in the city's *Daily Mail*: "His honor, the mayor, has just returned from a conference with Col. Spurling, commanding the advance of the United States forces in front of the city. Col. Spurling authorized the mayor to assure the citizens that there was no cause for uneasiness, and that, upon occupation, he intended to preserve as good order as was customary in the city.... The troops under Col. Spurling may go into camp below the city. The main army is some fifteen or twenty miles below."[6]

A correspondent for the New York *Herald*, who was apparently traveling with Col. Spurling's cavalry, witnessed their entry into Montgomery. He wrote that Montgomery had suffered from the actions of Wilson's raid earlier in April (although much less than Selma) and then reported:

> After a weary and dusty march from the gulf, we arrived in the vicinity of Dixie's first capital. The Second Maine Cavalry, with the gallant and dashing Spurling at their head, constituted the advance of this corps, and entered Montgomery on the morning of April 24. The citizens crowded the doorways and street corners and observed the novel cavalcade with interest and curiosity. One of the local papers announcing the event, remarks that: "The forces of the United States have already entered the proud little city of Montgomery.... To some this may appear an unhappy event. Such persons must look upon the fact, however, as one of the fortunes of war, and make up their minds to bear it as good citizens and as gentlemen, and to afford such assistance and give such attention as may facilitate the establishment of good order and good government."
>
> The main body of Gen. Smith's army ... entered the city about noon on the 25th, and passed through the streets with color's flying and bands playing alternately "Dixie," and "Yankee Doodle." The white citizens crowded the sidewalks to get a glimpse of the "seried ranks of blue," while vast numbers of delighted little negroes followed closely after the bands. To many

they came as deliverers, and frequent demonstrations of welcome greeted the sturdy column. To others, no doubt, they appeared "dreadful as an army with banners," and this class, though silent, gave unmistakable evidence of disaffection in their looks.[7]

One must wonder whether information was not reaching Confederate commanders in the Deep South, or whether some commanders simply did not want their troops to know of events taking place elsewhere. On April 25, 2 weeks after General Lee's surrender at Appomattox, General Nathan Bedford Forrest sent a message to his troops:

> The enemy have originated and sent through our lines various and conflicting dispatches indicating the surrender of General Robert E. Lee and the Army of Northern Virginia. A morbid appetite for news and sensation rumors has magnified a simple flag of truce from Lieutenant General Taylor to General Canby at Mobile into a mission for negotiating the terms of surrender of the troops of his department. Your commanding general desires to say to you that no credence should be given to such reports; nor should they for a moment control the actions or influence the feelings, sentiments, or conduct of the troops of this command. On the contrary, from Southern sources and now published in our papers, it is reported that General Lee has not surrendered.... Also since the death of Abraham Lincoln, Grant has lost in battle and by desertion 100,000 men.... Duty to your country, to yourselves, and the gallant dead who have fallen in this great struggle for liberty and independence, demand that every man should continue to do his whole duty.[8]

Gen. James H. Wilson (Library of Congress).

Apparently other Confederate commanders were feeling the need to repeat and underscore this message, for a similar directive was issued the next day by General William H. Jackson, who led the Tennessee cavalry under General Forrest.[9]

As an indication of how some accurate news did travel in those days, on April 20 the news of the death of President Lincoln on the morning of April 15 reached the Union troops around Pensacola. As a mark of respect, flags were flown at half mast, cannons were fired at half hour intervals all day long, and minute guns were fired from noon until 1 p.m.

And so, for a time, a state of war went on for the men of the 2nd Maine Cavalry and those others of both armies serving in parts of the Deep South. The portion of the 2nd Maine Cavalry that was not mounted and operating with General Smith around Montgomery during the month of April remained doing garrison duty at Fort Barrancas.

North of Florida, Confederate General Joseph Johnston began to negotiate for the surrender of the Army of Tennessee to Union General Sherman. This surrender, finalized on

April 26, included the remaining Confederate forces in North Carolina, South Carolina, Georgia, and Florida. Once again, although most people might equate the end of the Civil War with the surrender of General Lee's Army of Northern Virginia, the surrender by General Johnston was in fact the surrender of the largest number of Confederates, some 89,000 troops. Confederate President Jefferson Davis was reported to have been extremely angry with the surrender of so many of the South's soldiers, and Johnston's surrendering these men without actually being defeated in battle. Davis went so far as to accuse General Johnston of an act of treachery. And the terms of the surrender also caused General Sherman to incur the anger of many in Washington, including Henry Halleck, chief of staff. It was felt that Sherman had exceeded his authority by defining the terms of surrender he offered to Johnston, which apparently included terms for the surrender of not just Johnston's army, but the surrender of the Confederate states and their government. Sherman had felt that the terms were consistent with President Lincoln's views, but Lincoln was dead, and General Grant, President Andrew Johnson, and his cabinet did not agree that Sherman had the authority to act as he did. Edwin Stanton, the secretary of war, publicly criticized Sherman. Eventually, terms were agreed upon between Sherman and Johnston that only involved the surrender of the Confederate forces in the Carolinas, Georgia, and Florida.[10]

In late April, a series of messages were exchanged between Union General Canby and Confederate General Taylor, and on April 30, the following message was sent by General Taylor's adjutant telling General Nathan B. Forrest that "General Taylor has arranged for cessation of hostilities until resumed on forty eight hours notice by either party. No new movement or changes from present disposition of troops to be made until such notice. Notify immediately all subordinate commanders that scouting outside our lines will cease. Detail of armistice will be published in orders."[11]

On May 4, Confederate General Richard Taylor agreed to terms for the surrender of the Rebel forces in his Department of Alabama, Mississippi and East Louisiana. These surrendered Confederates totaled around 10,000 soldiers, including the column under General Maury which had left Mobile, and all Confederate troops east of the Mississippi. On May 6, General Taylor sent general orders to all of his command giving them the terms and conditions of the surrender to which he had agreed.

And then, on May 8 the Confederate troops officially surrendered to General Canby. Under the terms of that surrender, officers retained their sidearms and mounted men their horses. All military property and equipment was to be turned over to Federal forces. The men under Taylor's com-

> **FORD'S NEW THEATER.**
> TENTH STREET, above Pennsylvania Avenue.
>
> BENEFIT and Last Appearance of
> MISS LAURA KEENE.
> THIS (Friday) EVENING, April 14 1865,
> When she will appear as FLORENCE TRENCHARD, in the celebrated comedy of
> THE AMERICAN COUSIN,
> from the original manuscript by Tom Taylor, as played at Laura Keene's Theater, New York, for upwards of three hundred nights.
> She will be supported by J. C. McCOLLUM, JOHN DYOTT, HARRY HAWK, &c.
> To morrow, Benefit of MISS JEANIE GOURLAY, when will be presented the great drama, illustrative of Southern Life, Southern Scenes, and Southern Homes, entitled THE OCTOROON.
> The talented young tragedian,
> EDWIN ADAMS,
> Is engaged for twelve nights only, and will appear on MONDAY, April 17.

Given our knowledge of President Lincoln's murder at Ford's Theater, this notice from the Washington, D.C., *Evening Star* of April 14, 1865, has special meaning.

mand were paroled and allowed to go home. Taylor retained control of the railways and river steamers to transport his troops as near as possible to their homes. He stayed with several staff officers at Meridian until the last soldier was gone, then traveled to Mobile and joined General Canby, who took Taylor by boat to Taylor's home in New Orleans.[12]

On May 9, Confederate President Jefferson Davis officially declared an end to the war. Davis, who, with his cabinet, had fled Richmond, Virginia, on April 3, when the fall of that city was imminent, was captured on May 10 by General Wilson's cavalry in Irwinville, Georgia. In his memoirs, Wilson perpetuates the story that Davis was disguised as a woman when captured, stating that his men had come upon a tent in which women were apparently dressing. When the women left the tent, they were ordered to halt, and, "In the fright and confusion that followed it became evident that one of the party was Mr. Davis in disguise, and that the others were Mrs. Davis and her sister, Miss Howell." As of the date of this book, that story is still reported in sources such as Wikipedia's "Conclusion of the American Civil War," but has been dismissed as pure fiction by current historians, and was on some occasions retracted by Wilson himself.[13]

In his message to his troops announcing the surrender, General N.B. Forrest was as eloquent as he had been in his attempts to keep up the morale of his men just 2 weeks earlier.

> Soldiers: By an agreement made between Lieutenant-General Taylor ... and Major General Canby ... the troops of this department have been surrendered.... That we are beaten is a self-evident fact, and any further resistance on our part would be justly regarded as the very height of folly and rashness. The armies of Generals Lee and Johnston having surrendered, you are the last of all the troops of the C.S. Army east of the Mississippi River to lay down your arms.... Reason dictates and humanity demands that no more blood be shed.... The terms upon which you were surrendered are favorable, and should be satisfactory and acceptable to all. They manifest a spirit of magnanimity and liberality on the part of the Federal authorities which should be met on our part by a faithful compliance with all the stipulations and conditions therein expressed.... Civil war, such as you have just passed through, naturally engenders feelings of animosity, hatred, and revenge. It is our duty to divest ourselves of all such feelings, and so far as in our power to do so to cultivate friendly feelings toward those with whom we have so long contested and heretofore so widely but honestly differed.... You have been good soldiers, now you can be good citizens.[14]

The announcements of the surrender of the Confederate troops and the end of the war was either not received or not recognized by all, however, nor did some men on both sides of the conflict exhibit the kind of attitude that Generals Taylor and Forrest had requested. On May 4, 200 men from the dismounted force of the 2nd Maine Cavalry at Barrancas were ordered to Milton. It was reported that, while the citizens of that town were to meet to consider President Andrew Johnson's amnesty proclamation, "some desperadoes threaten to disturb the meeting." Col. Woodman and this Federal contingent were ordered to "prevent any disturbances and to arrest all offenders."[15]

General Asboth, commanding at Barrancas, in May made several requests for the mounted portion of the 2nd Maine and 1st Florida Cavalry to return to Barrancas. He reported that, although the Confederate forces in the area were supposed to have been included in Gen. Taylor's surrender, "several mounted bands of rebel desperadoes ... continue in arms against the United States Government." The mounted cavalry's return would allow Gen. Asboth to "compel these rebels to lay down their arms." In addition, Asboth stated that there were "lawless bands of deserters from our army, robbing indiscriminately the people of both parties." And so, Gen. Asboth stated that he needed mounted cavalry "for the purpose of pacifying fully this portion of country." At the same time, General C.C.

Andrews was requesting that the mounted portion of the 2nd Maine be sent to aid his forces in Selma: "I have no cavalry at all. Colonel Spurling with his force could be of great benefit here."[16]

On May 21, the "detachments of the First Florida and Second Maine Cavalry on duty with the Sixteenth Army Corps are hereby relieved from such duty, and will return to their former stations in the District of West Florida [Barrancas] as soon as transportation can be furnished." On May 26, the 1st Florida Cavalry was reported to have left the 16th Corps and headed by river to Mobile en route for Barrancas. However, in the same report, General Smith, the 16th Corps' commander, stated that "the services of the Second Maine are very much needed." On May 28, in response to this request, "the Second Maine Cavalry has been ordered for the present to remain in the command of Maj. Gen. A.J. Smith, where its services are very much needed."[17]

Back in Barrancas with the dismounted portion of the regiment, Col. Woodman was quite clearly not pleased with the continued absence of a large portion of his command—the mounted men under Lt. Col. Spurling. He had written to Assistant Adjutant General Christensen on May 22:

> I have the honor to call your attention to the fact that 210 men of this Regiment and from all the companies have been detached since March 13th 1865 and all were stationed at Montgomery Ala. The detachment was made in a hurry and when the Regiment was expected to be mounted and move to the front. Consequently the mounted men of each company were sent. Having been informed that Brig Gen. Asboth Comd'g Dist W Fla. had applied for the return of the detachment I delayed making any request but the great inconvenience of having the companies broken up has urged me to respectfully ask that, if that number of men must be detached, the detachment be made by companies, and the squads be returned to their respective companies.[18]

But even with the end of the Civil War, the mounted portion of the 2nd Maine Cavalry was continuing to be involved in keeping order in and around Montgomery, and "small detachments were sent into the most turbulent localities to preserve harmony between freedmen and their former masters, and to suppress any insurrectionary movements which might take place." On June 20, a contingent of 30 men from the 2nd Maine Cavalry, under Company C's Captain Elisha Johnson, left Montgomery and went to Elba, Alabama, "to ascertain the truth of the report of robberies and depredations in that vicinity, and to remedy the evil as far as possible." Capt. Johnson reported, "It appears that deserters from both armies have been committing depredations upon the property of both loyal and disloyal men. Many citizens, among them ... the most influential, have been robbed of almost everything. From the best information I could gather, more than fifty men, mostly deserters from the First Florida Cavalry, U.S. Army, are engaged in robbing, plundering, and committing acts of violence." Captain Johnson then stated that he was unable to arrest the offenders, given the large area over which they operated, and his own small force and lack of supplies. He recommended that if a small Union force could be stationed in the area "where the troubles exist," that force would be effective "in keeping everything quiet."[19]

General A.J. Smith reported that the deserters from the 1st Florida Cavalry mentioned above had deserted from near Pensacola "about a year ago [the summer of 1864], and have billeted themselves upon the country ever since, taking whatever they need without any regard to the status of the party from whom it is taken.... [This band] has been augmented by occasional deserters from the same regiment."[20]

Orders issued by General Asboth in June of 1865 made it clear that "all bushwhackers and guerrillas infesting the country you will consider and treat as outlaws and robbers, and if arrested forward them under guard to district headquarters, with full statements of their offense. Citizens who shelter, cherish, and support guerrillas you will hold responsible with their persons and property for the acts of these outlaws." In addition, General Asboth ordered that, whenever railroads, steamboats, or U.S. transports on rivers were attacked, "the families living in closest proximity to the scene of the outrages will be held accountable for the delivery of the real perpetrators. The generous provisions of the General Government extended to those returning to their allegiance shall never shield from their doom those who continue as traitors."[21]

Pvt. Lewis Whitehouse (Special Collections, Bangor Public Library).

While the mounted and dismounted portions of the 2nd Maine Cavalry continued in their efforts around Montgomery and at Barrancas, a few troopers from the regiment took advantage of another option that was presented. Several men were discharged from this regiment during the summer of 1865 in order to accept appointments to colored regiments. The attraction of such a transfer was the offering of commissions in the regular U.S. Army, with greater pay, and the option to resign their commission. This opportunity, in some cases, resulted in a man going from private to captain. As examples, Sgt. Fred Fuller of the 2nd Maine Cavalry's Company G became 2nd Lt. Fuller in the 86th United States Colored Troops (USCT); Private Byron Lowell of Company B became 1st Lt. Lowell of the 3rd USCT Cavalry; and Private Lewis Whitehouse of Company C was promoted to Captain, 108th USCT.[22]

Of course, the end of the war did not mean an end to the worry and concern felt by the families back in Maine and the difficulties faced by some soldiers. This letter, sent to Maine's Adjutant General Hodsdon in May of 1865 by the father of Sgt. Edward Cushman, Company M, gives an indication of the problems faced by some of the young men who returned:

> Dear Sir, My son Edward A—a Sergt in Co M 2nd Maine Cavalry, wounded at Marianna, Fla, last Sept—receiving 4 wounds—a ball through the thick of each thigh, the one through the left injuring the muscles severely, from which he receives constant pain, & much inconvenience, as it is much diminished in size & strength, & quite stiff. He made preparations to return to the field early in the Spring, but, Dr Owen told him he could not do duty & since he has tried to work on his farm, he is satisfied he cannot for a long time, if at all.
>
> He says he is ashamed to receive pay of the government for which he can render no service & wished to be discharged. Please inform him or me, what will be done by return of mail.[23]

Cushman, as previously reported, had been wounded at Marianna, and was later promoted to sergeant for his "meritorious conduct" during that battle. He was discharged for disability on July 25 and had been 21 years old at the time of his enlistment in December of 1863.

For some family members, there was the issue that we today call "closure," a symbolic coming to terms with the death of a loved one. Pvt. George Wentworth, Company H, had died in the hospital in January of 1864, and his father wrote to Adjutant General Hodsdon in August of 1865:

> Dear Sir, My son died in the Soldier's Home USA ... New York City the 14th of January last. The Chaplain of the hospital wrote me and wanted to know if I wanted the Clothes & I wrote him that I did and wanted them sent through to Camden Maine and the Steward of the Hospital sent me a paper to go before a Justice of the Peace and sign but the Clothes haven't come through. He was a member of the 2nd Maine Cavalry Co H his name George A Wentworth. I would like for you to write me if you have got them.   Very Truly Yours   Arnold Wentworth Searsmont, Maine[24]

And this letter, sent to Maine's Governor Cony in September of 1865 reminds us once again of the slow and sometimes nonexistent communication with families back in Maine (spelling has been left as in the original):

> Dear Sir I am goin to write to you and wish you will be so kind as to answer. I have a husband in the 2 Maine Cavalry Co A by the name John C Whitny and the last letter I had was riten the 24 day of June and then he was in Montgomery AL and I have not heard from him sins and last Satday I got a box with some cloths in it that he [?] to was I gess and no letter with them and I afred that he is dead as something has hapden to him and I have bin told to write to you and you could find out what [?] and I wish that you would just write and let me no if you no or has the regiment is and all about it—and I will be very much obliged to you
> Yours truly Matilda J Whitny[25]

Her husband, John C. Whitney, age 28 at the time of his enlistment, had died in hospital on July 24. John's cousin Charles Whitney, by the way, had also enlisted in the same company (Company A) of the 2nd Maine Cavalry. Charles deserted in early 1864 before the regiment ever left Maine. He stayed in Maine, and in 1880 was living with his wife, Susan, and their 5 kids in Island Falls, Maine, and is listed as a farmer.[26]

The way in which the regiments were raised led to men from the same part of the state, or in many cases the same town, serving in the same company. We also can find examples of men from the same family serving together. In a situation similar to that of the Whitneys, the brothers Darius and Joseph Brooks had enlisted in Company B. Darius died of wounds in June of 1864, while Joseph, like Charles Whitney, deserted in February of that year while the regiment was still in Augusta, Maine.[27]

In Company F, a father and son, George and Augustus Soule, had enlisted together. While the father survived the war, the 18 year old son died of disease in May 1864. In Company G later that year, it was the father, Greenleaf Smart, who died in September 1864, while his son Richard survived the war.[28]

While the death of one son or family member is a tragedy for those involved, we can also find examples of even greater loss. The two Hutchinson brothers, Daniel, age 19, and John, age 18, both of Company C, died within a month of each other in July and August 1864. Company D's Crommet brothers, Leander, age 24, and Lewis, age 21, also died in the summer of 1864.[29]

In Company A we find three brothers, Alexander, Archibald, and Ebenezer Bigger. These 3 young men had enlisted to fill the quota of the town of South Thomaston, on Maine's coast, and gave their residence as Patten, in the northern part of Maine's Penobscot County. They were, however, actually from Fredericton, New Brunswick, Canada, and are listed in the census records as "Native," in other words, Native American Indians. The situation suggests that they, as with a number of Canadian men, enlisted as substitutes—men who were paid by a "principal" to take their place in the army. In this case, two of the three young men did not return home after the war. Alexander and Ebenezer died of disease in August of 1864.[30]

There are many stories of young men who lied about their age to enlist in the army, but here is a case, apparently, of a father lying about the age of his son. In Company I, we see three brothers listed: John, Eugene and Nelson Millett, all of whom enlisted in December of 1863. At that time, John gave his age as 20, while Nelson and Eugene's ages are listed as 18. Their father had stated on Eugene's enlistment papers that he is "near Eighteen," and that Nelson is 18. A look at the census records, however, shows that while Eugene could indeed be 18, or nearly so, at that time, his younger brother Nelson, who was listed as only 2 years old in 1850, would have been 15 or 16 when he enlisted. If one were to take a somewhat cynical view of the situation, one might look at the total of $950 that was paid as a town bounty for the 3 young men (and there was the Federal bounty as well). Since the 3 brothers were all under 21, the money might well have been paid to the father—an inducement to see his sons in the army? Merely speculation, of course. Eugene died of disease in August of 1864 at Barrancas, while Nelson is simply listed as discharged in September of that year. We must wonder whether, with the death of his brother, Nelson told of his real age, or whether the folks back home sent that information after hearing about Eugene's death. The older brother, John Millett, was eventually promoted to 1st sergeant, Company I, and survived the war.[31]

To return to the 2nd Maine Cavalry in the spring of 1865, the end of the war in May had still not meant the end of their term of service. The *Maine Adjutant General's Report* states that, in August, the mounted detachment, still in and around Montgomery, "was ordered to return to Florida and rejoin the regiment at Barrancas." While there, and during the months of August, September, October, and into November, "the regiment was broken up, and small detachments stationed at various points throughout Western Florida, severally under the command of Lt. Col. Spurling, Majors Miller, Hutchinson and Cutler, and Captains Merry and Allen."[32]

The Major Cutler referred to here was indeed the Major Nathan Cutler who had been badly wounded and left at Marianna back in September of 1864. He had recuperated in Marianna and had then spent 3 months at Andersonville Prison. On April 29, Major Cutler took command of the last group of prisoners held there after the camp was liberated (20 officers and 3,500 enlisted men) and was soon free to return to his comrades of the 2nd Maine Cavalry. During the early phases of the Reconstruction period at the end of the war, Major Cutler was once again in Marianna and Jackson County, this time as the commander of Federal troops stationed there.[33]

Late that summer of 1865, Colonel Woodman was given the command of the Districts of Western and Central Florida. Just as he was assigned to that command, however, he was still dealing with familiar themes in the 2nd Maine Cavalry, such as is indicated in this letter to Governor Cony from September 1865:

> I notified the Adjt Genl of the discharge of Captain Twitchell in due season but did not make a recommendation for the vacancy for the reason that the Company was too small to admit of a Captain being needed, and also because Lt Mansur had on certain occasions become intoxicated. I know Captain Twitchells influence in respect to drinking was decidedly bad on a young man but hope Lt Mansur will refrain if under different influence. I am now fully convinced that he will not disgrace a Commission as Captain and although he cannot be [mustered?] I want to respectfully ask you to honor him with the Commission.

I understand that he belongs to a good family who live at Houlton, Aroostook Co.

I have not talked with him at all on the subject altho I wrote during his absence giving my reason why I hesitated to recommend him. He does not know that I think of recommending him to you for a Commission.

And so, for Captain Twitchell, after all of his complaints and Major Miller's recommendation for Twitchell's promotion back in the summer of 1864, Captain Twitchell's rather checkered career ended with his resignation to avoid court-martial. There is no record that Lieutenant Mansur received the promotion to captain.

And, regarding the business of the regiment and the district during this period of Reconstruction, Colonel Woodman goes on to say:

> The regt is now occupying 6 posts or stations. We are engaged now in starting seven (7) Com[missioned] Officers with guard of 15 men for each officer to prepare by oath for the people of this district for the Election of delegates to the State Convention. This district is 200 miles long. I now Command the District, the Genl [General Asboth] having been discharged, I entered upon the duties yesterday. Have a colored Regt & white troops in the three Forts but the 2 M[aine] Cav have to maintain order—cannot trust colored troops to keep peace between colored and white. Too much prejudice in the minds of each.
>
> Brig Gen Asboth who com'ded here is a Hungarrian [sic], Old & full of European Notions. I can run the affairs of the dist. at ½ the expense.[34]

The small units of 15 men and an officer to prepare the way for a state convention were working as a part of the Reconstruction plan that would lead to the readmission of Confederate States back into the United States with representation in Congress. Various plans for Reconstruction were put forward, starting with President Lincoln's very lenient proposal based on his assertion that, since secession was not legal, the Confederate States had never really left the Union, and should regain the rights of states within the Union as quickly as possible. His thoughts were summed up in his second inaugural address: "With malice toward none, with charity for all ... let us strive to finish the work we are in, to bind up the nation's wounds, to care for him who shall have borne the battle and for his widow and his orphan, to do all which may achieve and cherish a just and lasting peace." With Lincoln's assassination in April of 1865, his plans were never realized, and Andrew Johnson then put forth his own Reconstruction Plan, which, on the surface, took a harder line with the Confederate States and with the military and political leaders of the rebellion. A part of Johnson's plan involved obtaining oaths of allegiance to the U.S. by a significant portion of the population who would then hold a convention to develop a new state constitution and establish a new state government.

During the summer of 1865, with the 2nd Maine Cavalry and other Union troops working to keep order and help prepare the way for the reuniting of the Union, several general orders reflect the rules under which these Union forces would operate. General Field Order 30 stated "that the laurels the Federal Army has won in the field will not be tarnished by any acts of outrage, oppression, or insult. A speedy reconstruction of the Union is at hand, and our soldiers should do nothing that would tend to keep alive a spirit of hostility."

The nature of the former officials and government of the Confederacy was summed up when Union troops were told, "You will not recognize any legality in any act done under secession auspices. Any executive, legislative, or judicial officers under the reign of the so-called Confederacy are positions unknown to the laws governing loyal citizens of the United States, and not a shadow of authority lies in the hands of governors, legislators, judges, or any other civil officers who obtained and accepted it in defiance of the Constitution of our Republic."

And General Orders No. 52 made clear that "private meetings of citizens, having for their avowed and real objective the return of the rebellious States to the Union, are permitted, but all meetings within insurrectionary States for legislative purposes are forbidden, and all parties attempting to assemble for such purposes will be arrested and imprisoned."

Regarding the rights of the newly freed slaves, General Field Orders No. 28 stated,

> All persons formerly held as slaves will be treated in every respect as entitled to the rights of freedmen, and such as desire their services will be required to pay for them. Care will be taken not to disturb abruptly the connections now existing, and all colored persons having places of employment are advised to remain whenever the persons by whom they are employed recognize their rights and agree to compensate them for their services. At present the military will have to preserve order and reconcile differences between freedmen and their former masters, Freedmen will have to work for their support, but may select their own employers. Persons forcibly retaining or ill treating their former slaves will subject themselves to arrest and trial by military commission.[35]

With all of the talk of taking a harder line with former Confederates, President Johnson was soon pardoning high officials and military leaders of the Confederacy and allowing the Southern states to quickly send new representatives to Congress. It also became clear that Johnson's ideas would not include full participation of ex-slaves within government, or as fully equal citizens of the U.S. Further, abandoned and confiscated land that had been promised to freedmen was not to be distributed to ex-slaves, but would be returned to pardoned white owners. In late 1865, Congress, led by the so-called "Radical Republicans," blocked the quick readmission of states under Johnson's plan, and after Johnson had vetoed the Civil Rights Act of 1866, which would grant equal citizenship rights to black Americans, Congress took further action. Johnson's veto of that act was overridden, along with other presidential vetoes, and those ex–Confederates elected to Congress under Johnson's plan were barred from being seated. In 1867, Congress passed its own Reconstruction plan which insisted that former Confederate states ratify the 13th Amendment, which abolished slavery, and the 14th Amendment, which was essentially the Civil Rights Act of 1866 rewritten as a Constitutional Amendment. Congress also established 5 military districts within the former Confederacy, each under the command of a military governor, with Florida becoming a part of the Third Military District governed by Major General John Pope. (Pope was removed by President Johnson and replaced by General George Meade in late 1867.) When Congress passed its Reconstruction Act in July of 1867, President Johnson vetoed it, but once again his veto was overridden. The time it took for readmission under Congress's plan varied, but in the case of Florida, the state rejoined the Union on July 25, 1868, the third Confederate state to rejoin the Union, after Tennessee and Arkansas. (The last Confederate state to be readmitted was Georgia in July 1870.)

For the 2nd Maine Cavalry, the autumn of 1865 saw them still in Florida. And for those at home, there were still unresolved problems. In October, Matilda Whitney, the widow of Company A's Private John Whitney, wrote again to Governor Cony (and again, spelling has been left as it was written, with minimal correction):

> Dear Sir, I feel it is my best way to write to you as I have heard that you was the best man to get to atend to my business I got a letter yestday from the doctor of the hospital whas my husband stating that my husband was dead that he dide [died] the 24 of Jul last and he dide a few days before he took charge of the hosptal and I dont no what the doctors name was that took care of him and I want to find out and thout I would write and ask you my husband was in the 2 Maine Caverly, Co A, and this letter I got said that I could have my husband brought home

and I want you to write to me and tell me how to have him brought here and if you think that you can have him bough here straighter and better than I can I want to employ yu and I'll come and see you or write and tell me what yo think it will cost I supose it [illegible] it under taking and I want you to write and tell me what the offers [officers] names was over Mr Whitney and tell me what you think is best and I want you to write and tell me how I shall get my papers maid out for my Penchion and back pay and all about it and if you will get it for me I will write to you again and want you to be shure and write to me as soon as you get this for I want to here from you soon for I shall haft write to the man that boured [buried] him I supose ... and dont fail in writing soon and tell me what you think and what you will doe & all.[36]

During the Civil War, families typically had to pay to have the bodies of soldiers returned home for burial. For many, this was not possible, and many tombstones of Civil War soldiers in Maine and other Northern States in fact mark empty graves—memorials rather than actual places of burial.

And there were others who were seeking information about their sons. This is to Adjutant General Hodsdon from the mother of Private James Turpin: "General, You will confer a great favour on me by letting me know if the 2nd Maine Regiment of Cavalry come home or when are they expected. There is or was a son of mine in Company H of that regiment. His name is James Turpin. I have not heard from him since last June. I expect he must be dead. If you have received a late roll of that regiment you will have the thanks of a widow by sending me whatever information you may have concerning him. I was informed some time since they were under orders for home."[37] Whatever the reasons for the lack of communication from her son, Mrs. Turpin would learn that James, who had been 18 when he enlisted, had survived the war and was to be mustered out with the regiment.[38]

There were also matters within the regiment to be resolved concerning the future of some of the troopers. One example is in this letter, sent in October of 1865 to the acting assistant adjutant general from Major Eben Hutchinson, who was in command of the 2nd Maine Cavalry at the time:

I have the honor to submit the following statement and accompanying affidavits and papers having reference to the case of Sergt Augustus Thomas Co A 2nd Maine Cavalry now in confinement at Fort Pickens.

Charges were preferred against Sergt Thomas by Capt Csermlyi 82nd U.S.C. Inftry [James Csermelyi, Captain, Company I, 82nd U.S. Colored Infantry] for an attack made upon him by a party of soldiers on the evening of the 25th of Sept (as explained in the copy of Capt Csermlyi's statement). The only ground which Capt Csermlyi had for preferring charges was upon the affidavit of Michael Cain Private Co A of this Regiment. The Captain never confronted the accused, never recognized him, neither did he ever call on the commanding officer of the 2nd Maine Cavalry for permission or assistance to do so.

The charges are based solely upon the statement of Cain, a man of disreputable character, a disorderly and quarrelsome soldier and an enemy of Thomas. There is abundance of evidence that Cain made this statement (false as it is proved to be) to clear himself, that he in fact wearing a Sergeant's jacket and disguised as a sergeant was the man who committed the assault upon Capt Csermlyi.

I have known Ser't Thomas as a reliable soldier, and have often marked his prompt and faithful attention to duty. During the whole time this regiment has been in existence, I know of no instance wherein for improper conduct he deserved a reprimand. An examination of the evidence set forth in the accompanying papers, I am led to believe, will not fail to convince any one of the innocence of Thomas and the great injustice that would be done should he be detained in Fort Pickens upon charges of so serious a character without trial after the regiment shall have been mustered out of service and disbanded.

I respectfully and earnestly request that this case may receive that careful investigation which I am thoroughly convinced it should have and that Sergt Thomas may be released from the charges preferred against him, or if that should be found impracticable that a court may be convened at as early a day as possible in order that he may receive the benefit of a speedy trial. I trust that the Comd'g General will appreciate the motive that prompts me in my effort for the relief of a conscientious and worthy Soldier of my regiment, who I well know does not deserve the fate which grave and serious charges, preferred without any real foundation may bring upon him.

I am Lieutenant, Very Respectfully Your Obt Servt

Eben Hutchinson Maj Comd' Regt[39]

Sergeant Thomas was released, and a few weeks later Private Cain was tried by general court-martial for striking Captain Csermelyi. Another member of Cain's company, Sergeant David Carpenter, testified that Cain was not the one who struck the captain, and nobody could swear to the identity of the person who did do so. Cain was therefore acquitted. (Carpenter's own record was apparently a bit colorful—he was a sergeant, was reduced to the ranks, and was later appointed to be corporal and then once again to be sergeant.)[40]

Two other trials by general court-martial took place in November of 1865 which perhaps merit special mention. Corporal Frank Butler and Private Peter Breen, both of Company B, were arrested and both were charged with "Assault and Battery with the intent to Kill." The specification listed under this charge was the same for both men: that at Barrancas on the 9th day of November 1865 each "did attempt to shoot and kill with a spencer carbine, his superior Officer Capt B G Merry, Comp B 2d Maine Cavalry, firing at him ... seven shots, some of which passed through the tent of the said Officer, one shot lodging at his feet, while other shots passed over the said Officer's tent and entering the Barracks occupied by the men of Company E 2nd Maine Cavalry, thereby endangering the lives of many men of Company E."

In his testimony, Captain Merry reported being fired at, calling out the guard, finding Butler in his tent, fully clothed, and perspiring. Merry had gone to Butler's tent because "I recognized him, or thought I did, from the flash of the carbine." The carbine was found buried in some sand and was identified as Butler's Spencer carbine, one of only 3 in that company. Captain Merry admitted he could not see clearly the two men running from the scene of the firing.

Captain Merry, in his testimony during the trial of Private Breen, stated he saw Butler fire the carbine with Breen fairly close by. He chased both to Butler's tent with a member of the guard. Another witness, 1st Lt. William Gillespie, Company D, stated he heard Breen say to somebody, "For god's sake hide the cartridges or you will be found out." Breen appeared very much intoxicated.

Both men were found not guilty of the specification and charge. Unfortunately, we don't have any record of the court's deliberations. There was no apparent evidence that either Butler or Breen fired at Captain Merry intentionally. Did the court feel that they were simply being irresponsible and not making an attack specifically against Captain Merry? And there was no evidence that Breen had fired any shots.[41]

Both Breen and Butler apparently had somewhat checkered careers. Butler was promoted from private to corporal on August 16, 1864, and to sergeant on August 18, 1864. He was reduced to the rank of corporal on April 15, 1865, and then reduced to the rank of private for "refusing to do duty as a Corporal." Private Breen was promoted to corporal on August 12, 1864, but the order was revoked on August 16.[42]

Regarding the day to day business of the regiment as their time of service was approaching its end, the question of the veteran status of the 2nd Maine Cavalry was once again raised, this time by Maine's paymaster, J. Dewey, in this letter to Adjutant General Hodsdon: "General, Will you please send me a certified copy of the order of the Secretary of War authorizing the raising of the 2d Regt Maine Cavalry? The question I have now for decision is whether or not that was considered an old or a new Regt."[43] That decision was needed in order to establish the amount due to members of the regiment as their final pay.

In October and November, as the regiment anticipated the end of its service, there were various details to be tidied up. There was, for example, a flurry of activity in the quartermaster's department. Government property—including horses, mules, "camp equipage," hospital equipment and supplies, commissary equipment, and weapons—had to be accounted for and turned in to proper authorities. The record keeping had to be in proper order before the quartermaster could be relieved of his responsiblity.[44]

The seemingly petty nature of the accounting is indicated by this letter, dated November 6, 1865, signed by the 2nd Maine Cavalry's Assistant Surgeon, John Eaton: "I certify on honor that four of the penis Syringes, while in use of the sick men were lost or destroyed." The letter has a further signature of Hospital Steward O'Brian, who supports Eaton's declaration, and is also signed by Captain Knowles.[45]

And the need for a proper accounting of government equipment did not even end with the muster-out of the regiment. In January 1866, a lengthy letter, sworn before a justice of the peace, testifies that a wall tent was lost while in transit and that "there was no fault on the part of Asst. Surg. Eaton" (the 2nd Maine Cavalry's Assistant Surgeon, John Eaton). Eaton's letter on the same subject follows, and was attested to by 1st Lt. William Gillespie. In May of 1866,

Sylvanus Small (pictured here as quartermaster sergeant before his promotion to lieutenant and regimental quartermaster) (Special Collections, Bangor Public Library).

Assistant Surgeon Eaton had an acknowledgment of his payment of $36 for two field cases of instruments that had apparently been lost.[46]

In late November 1865, Col. Woodman received orders for the muster-out of the regiment and gave orders for the various detachments to gather once again at Barrancas. "By the 1st of December, the entire regiment was gathered together, and on the 6th mustered out of service by Lieut. E.M. Schryver.... Twenty-five officers and about 116 enlisted men were discharged in Florida, to become residents of the South, making oath of their intention to remain there, and receiving of the U.S. Government, mileage in lieu of transportation [back to Maine]."[47]

Among those officers who remained in Florida were Colonel Woodman, Lt. Col. Spurling, Major Miller, Surgeon George Martin, and Adjutant Adoniram J. Pickard. For a list of the officers who chose to be discharged in Florida, see Appendix E. The names of the enlisted men who remained in Florida are not recorded in the Adjutant General's Report. And then, "On the evening of the 8th of December, the remainder of the regiment, comprising 14 officers and 500 enlisted men, under command of Major Hutchinson, sailed per steamer General Barnes from Pensacola Harbor for New York City, where it arrived on the morning of the 15th. The final payment and discharge of the regiment was completed at Augusta on Thursday, December 21st."[48]

For the men of the regiment, although this part of their life's story was ended, they returned, changed to some greater or lesser extent, by their war time experiences. Most settled back into their prewar occupations with their families. The stories of a few of the other men frequently mentioned in the regiment's history provide examples of quite varied postwar experiences.

Nathan Cutler came back to Maine and is listed in the 1890 special census of Union veterans as living in Farmington. The reason for his disability discharge from the 21st Maine is stated to be rheumatism. In 1867 he was appointed commandant of the U.S. Military Asylum (veterans' hospital) at Togus, Maine. He resigned from that post after 2 years to practice law. In the 1900 census, he is living in New York City with his wife, Louise, and his occupation is given as lawyer. He died in 1916 and is buried in Farmington, Maine.

Major Charles Miller, the frequent complainer and friend of Adjutant General John Hodsdon, stayed in Florida for a time after the war, and from 1868 to 1870 was the Reconstruction era secretary of state of Alabama. During that time, his wife, Saphrina, and two children were living in Skowhegan, Maine. Major Miller returned to Maine and died in Skowhegan in 1877.[49]

For perhaps the most colorful member of the regiment, a rather tumultuous career

Pvt. George Cook's grave, Kennebunk, Maine (**photograph by Steve Dow**).

followed. At the end of the 2nd Maine Cavalry's service, Lt. Col. Spurling, having elected to be mustered out in Florida, returned for a time to his prewar occupation as sea captain. It is reported that his vessel was wrecked and for some 22 days he was adrift before being rescued. He returned to Maine and was elected sheriff of Hancock County for two two-year terms. He was then appointed post office inspector, with his headquarters in Chicago, Illinois. In 1878, while in Illinois, Spurling invested in the Chicago Rawhide Manufacturing Company and was elected its president. In the 1890s, he invested in the building of the Spurling Block, the first steel frame building in Elgin, Illinois. However, the financial panic of 1893 saw Spurling lose substantial money, and he spent his final days living on his $50 per month government pension. He died in 1906 in Chicago—a rather mundane end for such a soldier.[50]

And what of Private George Cook, whose great-granddaughter started the investigation that led to this book? George survived the war and came back to Maine. In 1868 he married Lizzie Boston and in 1870 was living with her at his parents' home in Kennebunk, Maine. His occupation, as was his father's, is listed as house painter. By 1880, he and Lizzie had their own home in Kennebunk and were raising a family. George Cook died September 10, 1924, and is buried at Mount Pleasant Cemetery, Kennebunk, Maine.

Appendices

A. Roster of the 2nd Maine Cavalry

The following is compiled from the 1863, 1864 and 1865 *Maine Adjutant General's Reports*, which cover the period of the 2nd Maine Cavalry's service. Age and marital status (MS) are given as they were as of the time of the muster date (MD).

The regiment was established in 1863, and the AG's report for their early months of service begins at the time of their mustering into federal service and ends with condition of the various companies on the morning of January 25, 1864. In the 1863 report, the companies' Buglers are listed as "Musicians." Also, in the 1863 report, the men's residence is listed, as is the town whose quota they were used to fill. In many cases, especially with some companies, the subsequent AG's reports list the town that claimed them for the quota as their residence. When possible, the town of residence listed in the 1863 report is also given.

In the 1864 AG's report, the changes from the end of the 1863 report are given and this record ends with the condition of the company on the morning of November 1, 1864.

The 1865 company reports reflect changes that have occurred from November 1, 1864, up to the time of the regiment's muster out in December 1865.

The regiment also had its own band, although no separate unit within the regiment is listed in the AG's rosters. We know, however, of the band's existence because a number of men are listed as either detailed to the regimental band, or transferred to it.

The date under the "remarks" section of the roster indicates the AG's report from which those remarks are taken. Some words have been abbreviated for space constraints. Examples: abs. (absent); disab. (disability); disch. (discharged—hon. and dishon.); hosp. (hospital); qrtrs. (quarters); resig. (resigned); trans. (transferred).

In the Maine Adjutant General's Reports, and other sources from which information for this roster was taken, the names of regimental field and staff, as well as the commissioned officers, sergeants, and corporals for each company, are listed in order of rank, or by date of rank. For example, the company's commissioned officers would begin with the captain, then 1st lieutenant, and then second lieutenant. That convention is used in the following regimental roster. Other individuals are listed in alphabetical order by last name.

Field and Staff

Names	Rank	Residence	Date of rank	Remarks
Woodman, Ephraim W.	Col.	Wilton	Dec. 18, '63	'64: assigned to com. 4th Brigade, cav. div.

Names	Rank	Residence	Date of rank	Remarks
Godfrey, John F.	Lt. Col.	Bangor	Dec. 18, '63	'64: resig. and hon. disch., May 4
Miller, Charles A.	Maj.	Rockland	Dec. 11, '63	
Hutchinson, Eben	Maj.	Athens	Jan. 4, '64	
Spurling, Andrew B.	Maj.	Orland	Jan. 4, '64	'64: promoted Lt. Col.; '65: promoted Bvt. Col.
Cutler, Nathan	Adj.	Augusta	Nov. 16, '63	'64: promoted Maj.
Pickard, Adoniram J.	Adj.	Rockland	July 6, '64	
Milliken, John F.	Q.M.	Belfast	Nov. 13. '63	'65: disch. for disab., Mar. 13
Cleaveland, James	Com'sary	Skowhegan	Nov. 16, '63	'65: resig. and disch., Oct. 11
Martin, George W.	Sur.	Houlton	Nov. 16, '63	
Norris, Louis E.	Asst. Sur.	Hampden	Jan. 4, '64	'65: resig. June 16
Eaton, John R.	"	Wilton	Feb. 3, '64	
Nason, Charles	Chaplain	Kennebunk	Dec. 11, '63	'65: resig. Mar. 1, Co. M
Small, Emilus N.D.	Sgt. Maj.	Farmingdale	July 6, '64	'65: promoted 2nd Lt.,
Wilson, Charles E.	Sgt. Maj.	Bradford	May 1, '65	'65: from Co. G
Tyler, George F.	Q.M. Sgt.	Bowdoinham	May 20, '65	'65: from Co. B
Allen, George E.	Com. Sgt.	Augusta	May 20, '65	
Smith, Andrew R.G.	Hsp. Stew'd.	Wiscasset	May 20, '65	
O'Brien, Owen St. C.	Hsp. Stew'd.	Houlton	Mar. 19, 64	
Bean, Charles T.	Hsp. Stew'd.	Warren	Dec. 11, '63	'64: reduced to ranks at own request; assigned to Co. F
Thompson, Actor F.	Pr. Mus'n.	Canton	Dec. 11, '63	'64: reduced to ranks; assigned to Co. D
Wilder, Rufus L.	Pr. Mus'n.	Machias	Apr. 24, '64	
Mitchell, Albert A.	Saddler Sgt.	Canton	Dec. 11, '63	
Whittier, True	Vet'y Sur.	Augusta	May 23, '64	
Small, Sylvanus C.	Q.M. Sgt.	Richmond	Dec. 11, '63	'65: promoted Q.M., Mar. 20

Company A

Name	Age	Residence	MS	MD	Remarks
Commissioned Officers					
Twitchell, Joseph F.	26	Mattwmk'g	M	Nov. 30, '63	'65: resig. and disch.
Mansur, Warren	25	Houlton	S	Nov. 30, '63	'64: Det. as acting ordnance officer, 4th Brigade
Barker, Silas C.	31	Augusta	M	Nov. 30, '63	
First Sergeant					
Pearce, Frank W.	22	Houlton	S	Nov. 30, '63	'64: veteran
Q.M. Sergeant					
De Beque, Wallace A. E.	22	Houlton	S	Nov. 30, '63	'64: Wd. May 18; in hosp., reduced to ranks at own request
Brennan, Stephen B.	22	Orient	M	Nov. 30, '63	'65: disch. for disab., Mar. 1
Com'y Sergeant					
Taylor, William W.	21	Weston	S	Nov. 30, '63	'64: Under arrest since Oct. 26; '65: disch. by order, Apr. 13

A. Roster

Name	Age	Residence	MS	MD	Remarks
Sergeants					
Brennan,* Stephen B.	22	Orient	M	Nov. 30, '63	'64: veteran; prom. Q.M. Sgt.

* also given as "Brannan"

Small, David W.*	25	Belf'st AcGt	M	Nov. 30, '63	'64: veteran; wounded May 10

* Regimental Books, National Archives, list Sergeant Small as com'y sergeant promoted to quartermaster sergeant on June 13, 1865.

Blackwell, Joshua E.	22	Patten	S	Nov. 30, '63	'64: veteran
Carpenter, David	20	Linneus	S	Nov. 30, '63	'64: reduced to ranks; re-app't Corp and Sgt.
Jones, Edward F.	21	Houlton	S	Nov. 30, '63	'65: disch. by order, Apr. 13
Thomas, Augustus G.	22	Maysville	S	Dec. 22, '63	
Lucy, Timothy*	37	Littleton	M	Nov. 30, '63	'65: reduced to ranks

* Regimental Books, National Archives, lists Sgt. Lucy as reduced to the ranks for "absence without leave and drunkenness."

Corporals

Name	Age	Residence	MS	MD	Remarks
Lucy, Timothy*	37	Littleton	M	Nov. 30, '63	

* Regimental Books, National Archives, lists Corporal T. Lucy promoted to sergeant, March 25, 1865.

Lyons, Henry W.	45	Hodgdon	M	Nov. 30, '63	'64: veteran; '65: reduced to ranks; abs. sick
Chute, Samuel	20	Orient	M	Nov. 30, '63	'64: veteran; reduced to ranks
Ruggles, Joseph	19	Weston	S	Nov. 30, '63	'64: veteran; abs. sick; reduced to ranks at own request
Jackson, Jarvis P.	35	Presque Isle	M	Nov. 30, '63	'64: abs. sick; reduced to ranks at own request
Webber, Andrew P.	26	Littelton	S	Nov. 30, '63	'65: promoted Sgt.
Gerow, Abraham	21	Hodgdon	S	Nov. 30, '63	'64: died Aug. 23, Barrancas
Lane, Cornelius	37	Island Falls	M	Nov. 30, '63	'65: promoted Sgt.
Greeley, George	21	Monticello	S	Nov. 30, '63	
Woodbury, William W.	20	Shermann	S	Nov. 30, '63	
Libby, Nelson G.	28	Maysville	M	Nov. 30, '63	
Lilley, Moses	26	Richm'd NB	S	Nov. 30, '63	
Buglers					
Bishop, Cyrus	18	Presque Isle	S	Nov. 30, '63	'65: died in hosp., Nov. 24, '64
Getchell, Darling H.	19	Presque Isle	S	Nov. 30, '63	
Latta, Samuel R.	20	Houlton	S	Nov. 30, '63	'64: reduced to ranks at own request; trans. to navy Oct. 1
Farriers					
Applebee, Charles F.	27	Hodgdon	M	Nov. 30, '63	'64: reduced to ranks at own request
Libby, Lorenzo D.	33	New Sharon	M	Dec. 24, '63	
Morrill, Ira	32	Patten	M	Dec. 23, '63	'64: died July 28 N. Orleans
Savage Cyrus	40	Patten	M	Dec. 22, '63	'65: disch. for disab., May 19
Saddler					
Braman, Samuel G.	28	Orient	M	Nov. 30, '63	
Wagoner					
Moor, Thomas B.	44	Hodgdon	M	Nov. 30, '63	

Name	Age	Residence	MS	MD	Remarks
Privates					
Allen, John L.	20	Littleton	M	Nov. 30, '63	'64: died Mar. 2, Augusta, Me
Allen, John O.	21	Stetson	S	Sept. 17, '64	
Arbo, George	20	Houlton	M	Nov. 30, '63	
Bagley, George H.	25	Liberty	M	Nov. 30, '63	'64: trans. to Co. D
Barnes, Reuben B.	18	Winn	S	Nov. 30, '63	
Bell, John	20	Linneus	S	Nov. 30, '63	
Betts, David	19	Houlton	S	Nov. 30, '63	
Bigger, Alexander	21	Patten	M	Nov. 30, '63	'64: died Aug. 28, Ft. Schuyler, NY
Bigger, Archibald	18	Patten	S	Nov. 30, '63	
Bigger, Ebenezer	22	Patten	S	Nov. 30, '63	'64: died Aug. 1, N. Orleans
Bishop, Cyrus	18	Presque Isle	S	Nov. 30, '63	'64: appointed bugler
Bishop, Ransom	27	Presque Isle	M	Nov. 30, '63	
Buzzell, Edward	22	Littelton	S	Nov. 30, '63	
Bradbury, Samuel J.	20	N Limerick*	S	Nov. 30, '63	'64: died Sept. 25, Ft. Gaines, Ala

* in '63 listed from Houlton

Name	Age	Residence	MS	MD	Remarks
Brown, George	40	Orient	M	Nov. 30, '63	'63: deserted Dec. 1, Augusta
Brown, John A.	25	Woodstock, NB	S	Dec. 22, '63	'64: deserted Mar. 18, Portland
Cables, Robert B.*	32	Portland	S	Oct. 17 '64	

* Regimental Books, National Archives, lists R.B. Cables as promoted to corporal, March 25, 1865, but reduced back to the ranks on April 12.

Name	Age	Residence	MS	MD	Remarks
Cain, Michael	20	Houlton	S	Nov. 30, '63	
Carr, Darius	20	Belfast	S	Nov. 30, '63	
Chute, Samuel	20	Orient	M	Nov. 30, '63	'65: disch. by order, Gen. Dix, June 10
Clark, Charles W.	19	Weston	S	Nov. 30, '63	
Day, Albert F.	24	Houlton	M	Nov. 30, '63	'64: sick in hosp., Ft. Gaines, Al; '65: died in hosp., Nov. 3, '64
DeBeque, Wallace A.E.	22	Houlton	S	Nov. 30, '63	'65: sick in hosp.
Deering, Addison G.	21	Orient	S	Nov. 30, '63	'64: died June 2, N. Orleans
Edwards, Thomas W.	26	Houlton	S	Nov. 30, '63	'64: died June 16, Thibodeaux, La
Fernald, Mark	27	Newport	M	Sept. 2, '64	'65: disch. by order, Aug. 29
Flannigan, Andrew	19	Houlton	S	Nov. 30, '63	
Flannigan, Thomas	20	Houlton	S	Nov. 30, '63	'65: promoted Cpl.
Fox, Daniel	19	Houlton	S	Nov. 30, '63	'64: veteran
Farewell, Hannibal	18	Mt. Chase	S	Nov. 30, '63	
Farewell, Jeremiah	21	Patten	S	Nov. 30, '63	'64: veteran; died Sept. 12 at Barrancas, Fla
Flemming, Andrew J.	19	Lincoln	S	Nov. 30, '63	'65: died in hosp., Feb. 1
George, John	32	Patten	S	Nov. 30, '63	'65: disch. for disab., June 27
Gilaspee, Edward	19	Houlton	S	Nov. 30, '63	
Greeley, George	21	Monticello	S	Nov. 30, '63	'64: promoted Cpl.
Hartin, William	18	Houlton	S	Jan. 26, '64	
Harvey, Willis P.	23	Lowell	S	Oct. 10, '64	'65: disch. Oct. 9, term expired
Jackson, Jarvis P.	35	Presque Isle	M	Nov. 30, '63	'65: died in hosp., Jan. 31
Joy, Stephen D.	31	Cherryfield	M	Nov. 30, '63	'64 trans. from Co. D
Kimbell, Charles W.	19	Mt. Chase	S	Nov. 30, '63	'64: died Sept. 14 at Barrancas
Kearney, James	20	Houlton	S	Nov. 30, '63	'64: died Mar. 4, Augusta Maine

Name	Age	Residence	MS	MD	Remarks
Lambert, Reuel	18	Orient	S	Nov. 30, '63	
Lambert, Luther R.	18	Orient	S	Nov. 30, '63	'64: trans. to Vet. Reserve Corps June 17
Latta, Samuel R.	20	Houlton	S	Nov. 30, '63	'65: trans. to navy, Oct. 1, '64
Leslie, Melvin, F.	19	Patten	S	Nov. 30, '63	'64: veteran
Libby, Lorenzo D.	33	New Sharon	M	Dec. 24, '63	'64: trans. from Co. L
Libby, Nelson G.	28	Maysville	M	Nov. 30	'64: promoted Cpl.
Lilly, Aaron	24	Richmond, NB	M	Nov. 30, '63	
Lilly, Moses	26	"	S	Nov. 30, '63	'64: promoted Cpl.
Littlefield, Wardman	39	Freemont Pltn	M	Nov. 30, '63	
Lowell, William H.	27	Augusta	M	Jan. 2, '64	'64: trans. from Co. M; '65: died in hosp., Feb. 19
Mahoney, James H.	20	Bangor	S	Sept. 20, '64	'65: disch. by order, Aug. 29
Mann, Henry A.	35	Clifton	S	Nov. 30, '63	'64: veteran; died Aug. 26 at Barrancas
Marston, John C.	21	Littleton	S	Nov. 30, '63	'65: disch. by order, Oct. 21
McDonald, Fred L.	25	Littleton	S	Nov. 30, '63	'65: promoted Cpl.
McGrury, Frank	18	Houlton	S	Dec. 18, '63	'64: trans. from Co. H
Mullen, John A.	19	Houlton	S	Nov. 30, '63	'64: died Sept. 17 at Barrancas
Moody, Hiram C.	27	Weston*	M	Nov. 30, '63	'65: abs. sick; sent to northern hosp.

* in '63 listed from Houlton

Name	Age	Residence	MS	MD	Remarks
Moody, Thomas	24	Weston	S	Nov. 30, '63	
Morgridge, William	18	Island Falls	S	Nov. 30, '63	'64: died Aug. 14 at St. Louis, Mo
Morse, Josiah M.	20	Woodland Plnt	S	Nov. 30, '63	'64: died Sept. 10 at N. Orleans
Murray, Alexander	45	Mayville*	S	Nov. 30, '63	'64: veteran

* in '63 listed from Haynesville

Name	Age	Residence	MS	MD	Remarks
Nichols, John W.	18	Presque Isle	S	Nov. 30, '63	
Noyes, Fred A.	18	Mt. Chase	S	Nov. 30, '63	
Orr, Samuel	18	Patten	S	Dec. 18, '63	'64: trans. from Co. H; '65: promoted Cpl.
Powers, Abraham R.	41	Ft. Fairfield	M	Nov. 30, '63	'65: disch. by order, Aug. 26
Rackliffe, Benjamin	26	Presque Isle	M	Nov. 30, '63	'64: trans. to Vet. Reserve Corps June 17
Reading, Samuel	20	Bangor	S	Sept. 21, '64	'65: disch. by order, Aug. 29
Reed, William	18	Houlton	S	Nov. 30, '63	
Rice, Luther F.	22	Stetson	S	Sept. 17, '64	
Rideout, Hugh G.	29	Springfield	M	Nov. 30, '63	'64: veteran; sick in hosp.; '65: died in hosp., Aug. 11
Rugles, Joseph	19	Weston	S	Nov. 30, '63	
Sargent, Edward P.	18	Patten	S	Mar. 10, '64	'64: died June 25, Thibodeaux, La
Sargent, Lewis, Jr.	18	Mt. Chase	S	Nov. 30, '63	'64: died June 21 at N. Orleans
Savage, Cyrus	40	Patten	M	Dec. 22, '63	'64: appointed farrier
Shaw, Eugene	28	Hodgdon	S	Nov. 30, '63	'64: disch. for disab., Aug. 10
Shaw, Martin V.	27	Patten	S	Nov. 30, '63	'64: abs. sick
Short, John F.	32	Bridgewater	S	Nov. 30, '63	'64: died May 28 at N. Orleans
Siegers, Thomas C.	30	No 5, R. 2	M	Nov. 30, '63	'64: died June 30 at N. Orleans

Name	Age	Residence	MS	MD	Remarks
Sinclair, Robert H.	30	Sherman	S	Nov. 30, '63	'64: trans. to navy, Aug. 1
Smith, Cyrus	45	Weston	S	Nov. 30, '63	'64: died June 20, Thibodeaux, La
Smith, Sylvanus	26	Weston	M	Nov. 30, '63	
Spaulding, Charles T.	22	Springfield	S	Nov. 30, '63	'64: veteran; '65: disch. by order Gen. Dix, June 1
Stewart, Michael	18	Hodgdon	S	Nov. 30, '63	'64: died Mar. 25, on board steamer *Continental*
Stickney, Sylvanus G.	18	Newport	S	Sept. 2, '64	'65: abs. sick; sent to northern hosp.
Taylor, Richard C.	18	Limerick	S	Nov. 30, '63	
Thomas, Augustus G.	22	Maysville	S	Dec. 22, '63	'64: veteran; promoted Sgt.
Trueworthy, Henry E.	23	Newport	S	Sept. 2, '64	'65: disch. by order, Aug. 29
Tucker, William	18	Haynesville	S	Nov. 30, '63	'64: deserted Feb. 16, Augusta
Wade, Caleb F.	20	Maysville	S	Nov. 30, '63	'64: trans. to Vet. Reserve Corps June 17
Wade, William F.	42	Maysville	M	Nov. 30, '63	'64: disch. for disab., July 15
Wadlin, Ira F.	21	Patten*	S	Nov. 30, '63	'64: disch. for disab., Aug. 20
* in '63 listed from Crystal Pl.					
Whitmore, Joseph L.	21	Ft. Fairfield	S	Nov. 30, '63	'64: died June 3, Thibodeaux, La
Whitney, Charles W.	21	Hodgdon	M	Nov. 30, '63	'64: deserted Feb. 20, Augusta; '65: gives date of desertion as Mar. 12, '64
Whitney, John C.	28	Lincoln	M	Nov. 30, '63	'65: died in hosp., July 24
Wills, John	30	Houlton	M	Nov. 30, '63	
Withee, William A. R.	20	Lyndon	M	Nov. 30, '63	'64: trans. to Co. M
Woodbury, William W.	20	Sherman	S	Nov. 30, '63	'64: promoted Cpl.
Woods, John	18	Linneus	S	Nov. 30, '63	
Worth, Edward E.	18	Vassalbora	S	Jan. 2, '64	'64: trans. from Co. M

Company B

Name	Age	Residence	MS	MD	Remarks
Commissioned Officers					
Merry, Benjamin G.	30	Bath	M	Nov. 30, '63	'64: abs. in Maine
Nichols, Andrew J.	26	Augusta	S	Nov. 30, '63	'64: disch. for disab, Sept. 10
Jewett, Noah	27	Readfield	M	Nov. 30, '63	'65: disch. by order, Sept. 9
First Sergeant					
Merry, Samuel B.	37	Woolwich	M	Nov. 30, '63	'65: promoted 2nd Lt.
Q.M. Sergeant					
Mayers, John L.	18	Bath	S	Nov. 30, '63	'65: promoted 1st Sgt.
Com'y Sergeant					
Colson, Eben, Jr.	20	Bath	M	Nov. 30, '63	'64: returned as Sgt.
Scott, Albert M.	27	Augusta	M	Nov. 30, '63	'65: listed as Com'y Sgt.
Sergeants					
Rice, Thomas G.	19	Winslow	S	Nov. 30, '63	'65: disch. for promotion
Stratton, Homer R.	22	Hancock	M	Nov. 30, '63	'64: reduced to ranks

Name	Age	Residence	MS	MD	Remarks
Scott, Albert M.	27	Augusta	M	Nov. 30, '63	'64: returned as Com'y Sgt.
Twombly, Albion K.P.	29	Augusta	M	Nov. 30, '63	'64: reduced to ranks; abs. sick
Miner, Edward	18	Augusta	S	Nov. 30, '63	'64: reduced to ranks; died Aug. 24
Colson, Eben, Jr.	20	Bath	M	Nov. 30, '63	'65: died of disease, Aug. 1
Mears, James F.	26	Manchester	M	Nov. 30, '63	'65: promoted Q.M. Sgt.
Perkins, Hiram	37	Bath	M	Nov. 30, '63	'65: disch. by order, Nov. 10
Butler, Frank H.*	19	Hallowell	S	Dec. 3, '63	

* Regimental Books, National Archives, lists Sergeant Butler as reduced to rank of corporal on April 15, 1865, and further reduced to the ranks on that same date for "refusing to do duty as a corporal."

Corporals

Name	Age	Residence	MS	MD	Remarks
Barrows, Edwin C.	21	Vassalboro	S	Nov. 30, '63	'64: promoted Sgt.; reduced to ranks
Doe, Samuel K.	38	Vassalboro	M	Dec. 22, '63	'64: trans. to navy, Aug. 3
Hanson, Ambrose B.	21	China	S	Nov. 30, '63	'63: reduced to ranks
Perkins, Hiram	37	Bath	M	Nov. 30, '63	'64: promoted Sgt.
Nash, Horace M.*	19	Bath	M	Nov. 30, '63	'64: reduced to ranks

* Regimental Books, National Archives lists Corporal Nash as promoted to sergeant, April 15, 1865. He was promoted back to corporal and sergeant; see listing as private, below.

Name	Age	Residence	MS	MD	Remarks
Grant, Mark C.*	18	Augusta	S	Nov. 30, '63	

* Regimental Books, National Archives lists Mark C. Grant as promoted to sergeant on August 12, 1864, but on August 18, that order was revoked.

Name	Age	Residence	MS	MD	Remarks
Arey, Josiah S.	20	Vassalboro	S	Nov. 30, '63	'64: died Aug. 29, Barrancas
Hussey, Merrill	18	Augusta	S	Nov. 30, '63	'64: reduced to ranks, abs. sick
Mears, James F.*	26	Manchester	M	Nov. 30, '63	'64: promoted Sgt.

* also listed as "Means"

Name	Age	Residence	MS	MD	Remarks
Reeves, Sewall R.	21	Augusta	S	Nov. 30, '63	'63: reduced to ranks
Chapman, Galen A.*	28	Newcastle	S	Feb. 11, '64	'65: promoted Sgt.

* Regimental Books, National Archives, list Sergeant Chapman as appointed to color sergeant on May 7, 1865.

Name	Age	Residence	MS	MD	Remarks
Jenkins, Otis F.*	41	Gardiner	M	Dec. 22, '63	

* Regimental Books, National Archives, lists Corporal Jenkins as reduced to the ranks on June 12, 1865, "having become useless as a non com'd officer for applying to the surgeon for discharge when in perfect health."

Name	Age	Residence	MS	MD	Remarks
Jordan, William	—	Gardiner	S	Feb. 25, '64	'65: died of disease, Nov. 21, '64
Plummer, John K.	22	Weld	S	Nov. 30, '63	
Lyon, William H.	23	Manchester	S	Nov. 30, '63	
Barrows, Allen F.	20	Litchfield	S	Dec. 31, '63	
Daley, Henry C.	18	Lewiston	S	Dec. 30, '63	'65: disch. by order, June 13

Buglers (listed in '63 as "Musicians")

Name	Age	Residence	MS	MD	Remarks
Brick, William M.	18	Augusta	S	Dec. 3, '63	'64: reduced to ranks; detailed in band
Drake, John E.	19	Dexter	S	Dec. 31, '63	
Masterman, John R.	26	Weld	M	Nov. 30, '63	'64: disch. Apr. 10
Thompson, Actor P.	35	Augusta	M	Nov. 30, '63	'63: promoted chief bugler

Farriers

Name	Age	Residence	MS	MD	Remarks
Curtis, Vandorus	28	Bath	M	Nov. 30, '63	
Dunham, Edmund M.	21	Augusta	M	Nov. 30, '63	'64: sick in hosp.

Saddler

Name	Age	Residence	MS	MD	Remarks
Maloon, George E.	22	Augusta	S	Nov. 30, '63	

Name	Age	Residence	MS	MD	Remarks
Wagoner					
Wyman, Increase	40	Fairfield	S	Nov. 30, '63	
Privates					
Allen, Charles W.	21	China	S	Nov. 30, '63	'64: died Oct. 13, N. Orleans
Allen, George	44	Augusta	M	Nov. 30, '63	'65: disch. for disab., Mar. 11
Atwood, George B.	23	Flagstaff Pltn	S	Nov. 30, '63	'64: died Oct. 6, Barrancas
Babbitt, Frank	19	Augusta	S	Nov. 30, '63	
Babcock, John H.	27	Augusta	M	Nov. 30, '63	'64: trans. to navy, Aug. 3
Barrows, Allen F.	20	Litchfield	S	Dec. 31, '63	'64: promoted Cpl.
Barrows, Edwin C.	21	Vassalbora	S	Nov. 30, '63	'65: disch. by order, July 1
Beals, Benjamin A.	21	Bath	M	Dec. 22, '63	'65: appointed bugler
Bennett, Winthrop T.	44	Bath	M	Nov. 30, '63	'65: disch. by order, Aug. 25
Berry, Mellen C.	21	New Sharon	S	Sept. 29, '64	'65: disch. by order, Sept. 15
Bowing, Horace C.	28	Bath	M	Nov. 30, '63	'64: trans. to navy, Aug. 3
Brackett, Oliver	41	Chesterville	M	Nov. 30, '63	
Brackley, Eben R.	24	Bath	M	Dec. 22, '63	
Bragdon, Levi	34	Windham	M	Sept. 30, '64	'65: disch. by order, June 13
Breen, Peter R.*	18	Augusta	S	Nov. 30, '63	'64: sick in hosp.

* Regimental Books, National Archives lists Peter Breen promoted to corporal on Aug. 12, but the order was revoked on August 16.

Name	Age	Residence	MS	MD	Remarks
Brookings, Benjamin	20	Woolwich	S	Nov. 30, '63	'64: trans. to navy, Aug. 3
Brooks, Darius	18	Augusta	S	Nov. 30, '63	'64: died of wounds June 18
Brooks, Joseph	22	Augusta	M	Nov. 30, '63	'64: deserted Feb. 28 at Augusta
Bullock, Daniel S.	18	Biddeford	S	Sept. 29, '64	'65: disch. Sept. 29, term exp.
Bullock, William R.T.	21	Biddeford	S	Sept. 29, '64	'65: disch. by order, Sept. 15
Burke, Abel	33	Portland	S	Nov. 30, '63	'63: deserted Dec. 3, '63
Butler, Frank H.*	19	Hallowel	S	Dec. 3, '63	'64: trans. from Co. C; promoted Cpl. and Sgt.

* Regimental Books, National Archives lists Frank H. Butler promoted to corporal on August 16, 1864, and to sergeant on August 18, 1864.

Name	Age	Residence	MS	MD	Remarks
Carr, Gilman W.*	18	Mt. Vernon	S	Nov. 30, '63	'64: abs. sick; '65: disch. by order, May 25

* also listed as "Gilman N."

Name	Age	Residence	MS	MD	Remarks
Carson, George A.	19	Mt. Vernon	S	Nov. 30, '63	'64: abs. sick; '65: died of disease, Nov. 21, '64
Caswell, Lendall S.	17	Leeds	S	Nov. 30, '63	
Chamberlain, Geo W.	24	Lawrence, MS	S	Jan. 13, '64	'64: promoted Cpl.; trans. to navy, Aug. 3
Chapman, Galen A.	28	Augusta	S	Feb. 11, '64	'64: promoted Cpl.
Cloudman, Edwin H.	20	Gorham	S	Sept. 30, '64	'65: disch. by order, Sept. 15
Colson, Parker	18	Bath	S	Nov. 30, '63	
Cox, Charles H.	19	New Sharon	S	Sept. 29, '64	'65: disch. Sept. 29, term exp.
Cox, William E.	27	Vassalboro	M	Dec. 22, '63	'63: sick in hosp.; '64: disch.
Curtis, John	23	Portland	S	Nov. 30, '63	'63: deserted Dec. 3, '63
Daley, Henry C.	18	Lewiston	S	Nov. 30, '63	'64: promoted Cpl.
Davis, Stephen J.	43	New Sharon	S	Sept. 29, '64	'65: disch. by order, Sept. 15
Dearborn, Thomas	20	Fairfield	S	Nov. 30, '63	'64: left in hosp., Augusta (listed and apparently present in '65 report)
Dexter, Heman N.	24	Mt. Vernon	S	Nov. 30, '63	'64: trans. to navy, Aug. 3

Name	Age	Residence	MS	MD	Remarks
Dimock, Alonzo K.	39	Limington	S	Nov. 30, '63	'63: deserted Dec. 3, '63
Dingley, Benjamin R.	18	Augusta	S	Nov. 30, '63	'65: promoted Cpl.
Doe, Samuel K.	38	Vassalboro	M	Dec. 22, '63	'63: promoted Cpl.
Drake, John E.	19	Dexter	S	Dec. 31, '63	'63: promoted bugler
Dyer, Henry J.	19	Sidney	S	Nov. 30, '63	'64: abs. sick; '65: died on transport, Oct. 12, '64
Eldridge, Shubael H.	44	West Bath	M	Nov. 30, '63	'64: trans. to navy, Aug. 3
Elwell, Winfield S.	23	Westbrook	S	Nov. 30, '63	'64: died Sept. 29, Barrancas
Farrington, Gustavus*	19	Augusta	S	Nov. 30, '63	'64: abs. sick; '65: died of disease, Oct. 30, '64
* also listed as "Farmington"					
Fowler, Augustine	21	Augusta	S	Nov. 30, '63	'64: deserted May 6 at N. Orleans
Freeman, James E.	23	Gorham	S	Sept. 30, '64	'65: disch. by order, Sept. 15
Goodwin, Alonzo	20	Biddeford	S	Jan. 13, '64	'65: promoted Cpl.
Hall, William H.	45	Portland	M	Nov. 30, '63	'63: sick in hosp.; '64: sick in hosp.; '65: disch. by order, June 13
Hanks, Edward A.	18	Augusta	S	Sept. 27, '64	'65: disch. Sept. 29, term exp.
Hanna, George W.	19	Mt. Vernon	S	Nov. 30, '63	'65: died of disease, Dec. 14, '64
Hanson, Ambrose B.	21	China	S	Nov. 30, '63	
Hopkins, Leroy E.*	27	Mt. Vernon	M	Nov. 30, '63	'64: abs. sick; '65: died of disease, Dec. 26, '64
* also listed as "Leroy D."					
Hoyt, Edwin F.	39	Benton	M	Dec. 22, '63	'64: died Mar. 1 at Vassalboro, Me
Hoyt, George C.	18	Benton	S	Dec. 22, '63	'64: abs. sick; '65: abs. sick
Hussey, Merrill	18	Augusta	S	Nov. 30, '63	'65: disch. by order, June 13
Jellerson, Charles	22	Palermo	S	Nov. 30, '63	'64: trans. to navy, Aug. 3
Jenkins, Otis F.	41	Gardiner	M	Dec. 22, '63	'64: promoted Cpl.
Jordan, Joseph A.	—	Gardiner	S	Feb. 25, '64	
Jordan, Michael	35	Bath	S	Dec. 24, '63	'64: trans. from Co. L '65: disch. by order, Aug. 28
Jordan, William	—	Gardiner	S	Feb. 25, '64	'64: promoted Cpl.; sick in hosp.
Ladd, Junior R.*	19	Biddeford	S	Jan. 13, '64	
* also listed as "Julius R."					
Littlefield, Daniel S.	18	Biddeford	S	Sept. 26, '64	'65: disch. Sept. 26, term exp.
Lord, John A.	21	Gorham	S	Sept. 30, '64	'65: disch. by order, Aug. 28
Lowell, Byron	24	Readfield	S	Nov. 30, '63	'65: disch. for promotion, Feb. 28, '64
Lowell, Converse*	40	Augusta	M	Nov. 30, '63	
* also listed as "Convis"					
Lowell, Emery E.	19	Phipsburg	S	Nov. 30, '63	'64: trans. to navy, Aug. 3
Luce, Lucian A.	18	Burnham	S	Nov. 30, '63	'64: abs. sick
Lyon, David S.	22	Manchester	S	Nov. 30, '63	
Lyon, William H.	23	Manchester	S	Nov. 30, '63	'64: promoted Cpl.
Masterman, John R.	26	Weld	M	Nov. 30, '63	'63: promoted bugler
McIntire, William H.	28	Bath	M	Dec. 22, '63	'64: trans. to navy, Aug. 3
McIntosh, George E.	19	Bath	S	Nov. 30, '63	'65: promoted Cpl.
Miller, Charles A.	29	Rockland	S	Dec. 14, '63	'63: promoted Maj.
Miller, Stephen	21	Augusta	S	Dec. 22, '63	

Name	Age	Residence	MS	MD	Remarks
Moore, Nathan C.	20	Bath	S	Dec. 22, '63	'64: trans. to navy, Aug. 3
Murphy, John	18	Augusta	S	Nov. 30, '63	
Nash, Horace M.*	19	Bath	S	Nov. 30, '63	'63: promoted Cpl.; '65: promoted Cpl. and Sgt.

* Regimental Books, National Archives lists Corporal Nash as promoted to corporal on December 29, 1864, and to sergeant on April 15, 1865.

Name	Age	Residence	MS	MD	Remarks
Nockton, Thomas H.	18	Bath	S	Nov. 30, '63	'64: died Oct. 10, N. Orleans
Nutting, John B.	27	Augusta	S	Nov. 30, '63	
Oliver, Timothy B.	29	New Sharon	M	Oct. 10, '64	'65: disch. Oct. 9, term exp.
Oliver, William H.	37	Phipsburg	M	Nov. 30, '63	'64: trans. to navy, Aug. 3
Packard, Samuel A.	22	Bath	S	Nov. 30, '63	'64: disch. for promotion, July 26
Parker, Alfred	26	Bath	M	Dec. 22, '63	'64: trans. to navy, Aug. 3
Parker, James H.	19	Bath	S	Dec. 22, '63	'65: disch. Dec. 2
Peaslee, Frank W.	18	Augusta	S	Nov. 30, '63	'65: died of disease, Mar. 6
Philbrick, Milton F.	22	Mt. Vernon	S	Nov. 30, '63	'64: died Sept. 12, Barrancas
Plummer, John	22	Weld	S	Nov. 30, '63	'64: promoted Cpl.
Plummer, Russell C.	22	Gorham	S	Sept. 30, '64	'65: abs. sick
Preble, Solomon H.	32	Chelsea	—	Dec. 3, '64	'65: disch. Aug. 23, term exp.
Proctor, Charles	18	Windsor	S	Nov. 30, '63	'64: abs. sick; '65: disch. by order, Aug. 25
Reeves, Sewall R.	21	Augusta	S	Nov. 30, '63	'65: promoted Cpl.
Roberts, Albert F.	18	Vassalboro	S	Nov. 30, '63	'65: disch. by order, June 13
Sabine, Charles A.	26	Palermo	M	Nov. 30, '63	'64: trans. to navy, Aug. 3
Sanborn, Nahum Q.	31	Readfield	M	Nov. 30, '63	
Sawyer, Jones W.	18	Portland	S	Nov. 30, '63	
Small, Sylvanus C.	23	Richmond	S	Nov. 30, '63	'63: promoted Reg't Q.M. Sgt.
Snow, James F.	20	Augusta	S	Dec. 22, '63	'65: disch. for disab., Mar. 11
Stevens, George W.	23	Gardiner	S	Dec. 22, '63	
Stevens, John C.	21	(none listed)	M	Sept. 30, '64	'65: disch. Sept. 29, term exp.
Storer, Charles L.	18	New Sharon	S	Aug. 31, '64	'65: disch. Aug. 23, term exp.
Storer, George W.	21	New Sharon	S	Aug. 31, '64	'65: disch. by order, Aug. 26
Stratton, Homer R.	22	Hancock	M	Nov. 30, '63	'65: disch. by order, July 1
Thomas, John P.H.	18	Waterville	S	Nov. 30, '63	'64: sick in hosp.
Towle, Jairus	24	W Gardiner	S	Nov. 30, '63	'64: deserted Augusta, Me, Feb. 28
Twombly, Albion K.P.	29	Augusta	M	Nov. 30, '63	'65: abs. sick
Turner, Joseph A.	19	Augusta	S	Nov. 30, '63	
Tyler, George F.	20	Bowdoinham	S	Nov. 30, '63	'65: promoted Q.M. Sgt.
Wallace, Jethro S.	18	Phipsburg	S	Jan. 12, '64	'64: died July 4, Thibodeaux
Warner, Frank	24	Portland	M	Nov. 30, '63	'64: deserted at Augusta, Me, Dec. 3, '63
Webber, Albert R.	37	Woolwich	M	Nov. 30, '63	'64: deserted at N. Orleans, Apr. 26; '65: arrested and sentenced; disch. Sept. 18
White, Charles H.	18	Augusta	S	Nov. 30, '63	'64: trans. to navy Aug. 3
White, Martin V.	19	Bath	M	Dec. 22, '63	
Whitney, Joseph	18	Fairfield	S	Nov. 30, '63	
Williamson, Eli E.	19	New Sharon	S	Sept. 29, '64	'65: disch. Sept. 29, term exp.

Company C

Name	Age	Residence	MS	MD	Remarks
Commissioned Officers					
Johnson, Elisha D.	31	Lewiston	M	Dec. 3, '63	'64: on detached service
Hutchinson, Melvin S.	29	Gardiner	M	Dec. 3, '63	'64: disch. by order War Dept Feb. 18; Special Order 80: "1st Lt. Melvin S. Hutchinson, 2d Maine Cavalry, is hereby mustered out of service, to date December 3d, 1863, the date of muster in, there being no evidence of service rendered the Government."
Dodge, Rodolph L.	22	Portland	M	Dec. 3, '63	'64: detached on signal corps; '65: disch. by order
First Sergeant					
Pierce, Warren H.	24	Windsor	S	Dec. 3, '63	'64: promoted 1st Lt. (to replace Hutchinson)
Q.M. Sergeant					
Prince, Frederic C.	21	Cumberland	S	Dec. 3, '63	'64: promoted 1st Sgt.
Com'y Sergeant					
Tilton, William H.	36	Norridgew'k	S	Dec. 3, '63	
Sergeants					
Edgecomb, John	36	W Gardiner	M	Dec. 3, '63	'64: trans. to navy, Aug. 1
Paine, Simeon C.	24	Hallowell	M	Dec. 3, '63	'65: abs. sick
Holmes, George	27	Gardiner	S	Dec. 3, '63	
Butler, Frank H.	19	Portland	S	Dec. 3, '63	'63: reduced to Cpl., Jan. 1; to ranks, Jan. 10
Hunt, John B.	23	Windsor	S	Dec. 3, '63	'65: dish by order, Nov. 16
Linscott, George	21	Jefferson	S	Dec. 3, '63	'64: promoted Q.M. Sgt.
Corporals					
Linscott, George	21	Jefferson	S	Dec. 3, '63	'63: promoted Sgt.
Knox, Charles O.	25	W Gardiner	S	Dec. 3, '63	'64: promoted Sgt.
Hardy, Sidney D.	20	Naples	S	Dec. 3, '63	'64: died July 21, Thibodeaux
Mills, George G.	21	Augusta	S	Dec. 3, '63	'65: died in hosp., Nov. 28, '64
Keene, Reuel W.	33	Chelsea	M	Dec. 3, '63	
Gustin, Samuel	33	Scarboro	S	Dec. 3, '63	'65: died at home, Oct. 2, '64
McCormick, William	26	Augusta	M	Dec. 3, '63	'65: disch. by order, Nov. 16
Morrill, George O.	26	Hallowell	M	Dec. 3, '63	'64: reduced to ranks
Watson, Charles O.	20	Windsor	S	Dec. 3, '63	'64: died Oct. 1, Barrancas
Aiken, Peter	19	Vassalboro	S	Dec. 3, '63	'65: died in hosp., Nov. 13
Buglers					
Fuller, Joseph M.	24	Gardiner	S	Dec. 3, '63	
Gilbert, Frank	20	Gardiner	S	Dec. 3, '63	
Farriers					
Allen, George E.	21	Augusta	M	Dec. 3, '63	'63: promoted Reg't Com'y Sgt.
Andrews, Edward C.	24	Thomaston	M	Dec. 21, '63	'65: promoted Cpl.
Booker, William H.	24	Hallowell	M	Dec. 3, '63	'63: reduced to ranks
Mills, Hyram A.	25	Belgrade	S	Dec. 21, '63	'64: died Oct. 4, N. Orleans
Saddler					
Irving, James W.	22	Vassalboro	S	Dec. 3, '63	

Name	Age	Residence	MS	MD	Remarks
Wagoner					
Dill, George W.	41	Augusta	M	Mar. 1, '64	'65: died in hosp., Feb. 4
Privates					
Aiken, Peter	19	Vassalboro	S	Mar. 1, '64	'64: promoted Cpl.
Andrews, Arthur B.	19	W Gardiner	S	Mar. 1, '64	'64: promoted Cpl.
Andrews, Edward C.*	24	Thomaston	M	Dec. 21, '63	'63: promoted farrier
* also listed as "Edward O."					
Bennett, George F.	20	Naples*	S	Dec. 21, '63	'64: died July 12, Thibodeaux
					in '63 listed from Chelsea
Black, Daniel	38	Gardiner	S	Dec. 3, '63	'64: trans. to navy, Aug. 1
Blake, Charles A.	21	Naples*	S	Dec. 21, '63	'64: died June 17, Brashear City, La
* in '63 listed from Augusta					
Bond, James G.	18	Jefferson	S	Mar. 1, '64	'64: died July 17, N. Orleans
Booker, William H.	24	Hallowell	M	Dec. 3, '63	'64: abs. sick; '65: sick, Augusta, Me
Bowley, Gideon, Jr.	18	Gardiner	S	Dec. 3, '63	
Brann, Calvin N.*	25	Gardiner	M	Dec. 3, '63	'64: died Sept. 5, Barrancas
* also listed as "Brawn"					
Bridge, Frederick	18	Augusta	S	Dec. 3, '63	
Brown, Charles A.	18	Hallowell	S	Dec. 3, '63	
Buckley, James	21	S. Berwick	S	Sept. 29, '64	
Butler, Frank H.	19	Portland	S	Dec. 3, '63	'64: trans. to Co. B
Chase, Forest L.	18	E. Livermore	S	Sept. 16, '64	'65: disch. by order, Sept. 16
Chase, Silvester	30	Concord	M	Jan. 2, '64	'64: trans. from Co. M
Cooper, Frank	18	Chelsea	S	Dec. 3, '63	'64: abs. sick
					'65: sick in hosp.
Dalton, John	25	St John, NB	S	Dec. 3, '63	'64: deserted at Augusta, Feb. 27
Davis, Arthur N.*	19	Somerville	S	Dec. 3, '63	'64: disch. for disab, Aug. 11
* also listed as "Arthur H."					
Dill, Charles H.	39	W Gardiner	M	Dec. 3, '63	'65: disch. by order, Sept. 18
Dill, George W.	41	Augusta	M	Mar. 1, '64	(wagoner in '65 report)
Douglass, Thomas	20	Gardiner	S	Dec. 3, '63	'64: died Mar. 3, Gardiner, Me
Doyle, Howard	21	Gardiner	S	Dec. 21, '63	
Duchesne, Frank	19	Ottawa, CW	S	Dec. 21, '63	'64: deserted at Augusta, Feb. 24
Dunlap, Reuel W.	18	Gardiner	S	Dec. 3, '63	
Dushesne, Joseph N.	27	Ottawa, CW	S	Dec. 3, '63	'64: deserted at Augusta, Mar. 5
Edgecomb, John	36	W Gardiner	M	Dec. 3, '63	'65: trans. to navy
Edson, John C.	19	Hallowell	M	Dec. 3, '63	'65: disch. for disab., May 14
Emery, Gilmore	42	Newfield	M	Sept. 28, '64	'65: disch. by order, Sept. 15
Farrington, Lorenzo*	39	Vassalboro	M	Dec. 3, '63	'64: deserted at Augusta, Mar. 16
* also listed as "Farmington"					
French, George H.	19	Somerville	S	Dec. 3, '63	'64: deserted at Augusta, Mar. 16
French, Kruetzer C.	22	Norridgew'k	M	Dec. 3, '63	'64: trans. to Co. M
Fuller, Gardiner H.	18	W Gardiner	S	Dec. 3, '63	'64: died Sept. 27, Barrancas
Garland, George M.	18	W Gardiner	S	Dec. 3, '63	'64: died Sept. 6, Barrancas
Gerry, Rufus C.	27	Gardiner	S	Dec. 3, '63	'64: trans. to navy, Aug. 1
Goodwin, Joseph H.	25	Pittston	M	Dec. 3, '63	'64: trans. to navy, Aug. 1

Name	Age	Residence	MS	MD	Remarks
Gould, John W. S.	22	Windsor	S	Dec. 3, '63	'63: abs. w/o leave since Jan. 21; '64: deserted at Augusta, Jan. 21
Gowell, Frederic E.	19	Gardiner	S	Dec. 3, '63	'64: died Sept. 15, Barrancas
Haines, Albert A.	27	Dexter	S	Sept. 29, '64	'65: disch. by order, Sept. 15
Haines, David H.	19	W Gardiner	S	Dec. 3, '63	
Hall, George A.	18	Jefferson	S	Dec. 3, '63	'64: died June 4, N. Orleans
Hamlin, Michael J.	21	St John, NB	S	Dec. 3, '63	'64: deserted at Augusta, Feb. 27
Holman, Asa	41	N Gloucester	M	Dec. 3, '63	'64: died Aug. 2, N. Orleans
Holmes, John	43	Farmingdale	S	Dec. 3, '63	'64: deserted at Portland, Mar. 21
Hutchinson, Charles F.	18	Gardiner	S	Dec. 3, '63	'64: sick in hosp.
Hutchinson, Daniel W.* * also listed as "Danville W."	19	New Sharon	S	Dec. 3, '63	'64: died Aug. 4, N. Orleans
Hutchinson, John	18	New Sharon	S	Dec. 3, '63	'64: died July 2, Thibodeaux
Jackson, George F.	21	Augusta	S	Nov. 22, '64	'65: disch. by order, Nov. 21
James, Willis J.	18	China	S	Dec. 3, '63	'64: died Sept. 11, Barrancas
Jellison, Joseph W.	19	Biddeford	S	Oct. 19, '64	'65: disch. by order, Oct. 13
Johnson, Charles E.	24	Shapleigh	S	Oct. 14, '64	
Johnson, John	22	Wells	S	Sept. 13, '64	'65: abs. sick; sent to northern hosp.
Kalor, Amos	21	China	S	Dec. 3, '63	'64: died Aug. 18, Barrancas
Katon, William	21	Pittston	S	Dec. 3, '63	'65: died at N. Orleans, Oct. 4, '64
Keef, William* * also listed as "Keefe"	21	Vassalboro	M	Dec. 3, '63	
Keene, Isaac* * also listed as "Keen"	27	Augusta	M	Dec. 3, '63	
Keene, John B.	25	Dresden	M	Mar. 1, '64	'64: died Aug. 2, N. Orleans
Kelly, William	26	Limerick	S	Oct. 15, '64	
Kitchen, Robert J.	21	Vassalboro	S	Dec. 3, '63	'64: died Sept. 30, Barrancas
Knight, Robert E.	19	Jefferson	S	Mar. 4, '64	
Lascon, John	20	Somerset	S	Dec. 3, '63	'64: deserted at Augusta, Feb. 27
Leavitt, Burnett	27	Bradley	S	Sept. 29, '64	'65: disch. by order, Sept. 15
Leonard, Hartly D.	23	Portland	S	Aug. 30, '64	'65: disch. by order, Nov. 17
Libby, Alonzo D.	18	Scarboro	S	Dec. 3, '63	'64: died Aug. 31, Barrancas
Linscott, James A.	18	Jefferson	S	Mar. 1, '64	
Maloney, Edward J.	21	Hallowell	S	Dec. 3, '63	'64: deserted at Portland, Mar. 10
Marr, Erastus	30	Washington	S	Dec. 3, '63	
Marriner, Loring* * also listed as "Mariner"	18	Gardiner	S	Dec. 3, '63	
McGuire, James	22	St. John, NB	S	Dec. 3, '63	
McLaughlin, William H.	24	Hallowell	S	Dec. 3, '63	'64: promoted Cpl.
Meader, Amasa R.	19	Gardiner	S	Dec. 3, '63	'64: trans. to navy, Aug. 1
Merrill, Enoch, Jr.	28	Augusta	M	Dec. 3, '63	
Merrill, John F.	18	Gardiner	S	Dec. 3, '63	'65: died at Barrancas, Nov. 11
Merrill, Leonard H.	18	Augusta	S	Dec. 3, '63	
Merrill, Melville A.	19	Augusta	M	Dec. 3, '63	
Mills, Hiram A.	25	Belgrade	S	Dec. 21, '63	'63: promoted farrier
Morang, James H.	19	Gardiner	S	Dec. 3, '63	

Name	Age	Residence	MS	MD	Remarks
Nash, George M.	28	Cherryfield	M	Dec. 7, '63	'64: trans. from Co. M; died July 20
Noyes, Daniel	21	Jefferson	S	Dec. 7, '63	'65: disch. by order, Nov. 17
Oliver, Luther	22	Gardiner	S	Dec. 7, '63	'64: trans. to navy, Aug. 1
Page, John E.	24	Chelsea	M	Dec. 7, '63	
Peacock, William S.	18	Gardiner	S	Dec. 7, '63	'65: promoted Cpl.
Perry, Joseph J.	22	Gardiner	S	Dec. 7, '63	'63: deserter fr 1st Me Cav
Peterson, Lewis	—	(not given)	—	(not given)	'65: deserted Apr. 8
Pinkham, Joseph	24	Hallowell	S	Dec. 7, '63	'64: died Aug. 21, Barrancas
Pratt, Llewellyn P.	18	N Vineyard	S	Dec. 7, '63	
Priest, Edward A.	19	Vassalboro	S	Dec. 7, '63	'65: died at N. Orleans, Mar. 7
Robinson, Daniel W.	22	Gardiner	S	Dec. 7, '63	'65: disch. for disab'y June 17
Robinson, James W.	18	W Gardiner	S	Dec. 7, '63	
Smith, Charles	18	Addison	S	July 26, '64	'65: died at Barrancas, May 3
Stackpole, William H.	33	Gardiner	M	Dec. 7, '63	'65: disch. for disab'y June 17
Stevens, John	22	Cherryfield	S	Jan. 2, '64	'64: trans. from Co. M; disch. for disab, Aug. 16
Swan, Joseph	22	Georgetown	S	Sept. 9, '64	'65: disch. Sept. 16, term exp.
Tozier, Edward S.	19	Gardiner	S	Dec. 3, '63	
Tozier, Elijah	18	Gardiner	S	Dec. 3, '63	
Trask, Reuel W.	23	Windsor	S	Dec. 3, '63	'64: deserted at Augusta, Feb. 10
Troop, Jesse M.	36	Pittston	M	Dec. 3, '63	
Twiggs, Timothy	34	Limerick	S	Oct. 6, '64	
Ware, Moses A.	23	Pittston	M	Jan. 26, '64	'64: trans. to navy, Aug. 1
Watson, Charles O.	20	Windsor	S	Dec. 3, '63	'63: promoted Cpl.
Wentworth, John Q.	19	Augusta	M	Dec. 3, '63	'64: sick in hosp.; '65: died at Barrancas, Dec. 10, '64
White, Henry W.	18	Vassalboro	S	Dec. 3, '63	
White, Hollis M.	21	Vassalboro	S	Dec. 3, '63	
Whitehouse, Lewis H.	21	Newport	S	Dec. 3, '63	'65: absent; to be mustered for promotion in U.S. Colored Infantry
Williams, George E.	18	Cornville	S	Jan. 14, '64	'64: promoted Sgt.
Woodbury, Arad	18	Chelsea	S	Dec. 3, '63	'64: died May 17, N. Orleans
Worth, Edward E.	18	Litchfield	S	Jan. 2, '64	'64: trans. from Co. M; died Aug. 23
Young, Adam	28	Auburn	S	Dec. 9, '64	

Company D

Name	Age	Residence	MS	MD	Remarks
Commissioned Officers					
Lincoln, John M.	31	Pembroke	M	Dec. 8, '63	
Seavey, George W.	48	Machias	M	Dec. 8, '63	'64: disch. for disab July 27
Gillespie, William	23	Calais	S	Dec. 8, '63	'64: promoted 1st Lt.
First Sergeant					
Lee, Joseph W.	21	Calais	S	Dec. 8, '63	'64: promoted 2nd Lt. 1st DC Cavalry
Q.M. Sergeant					
Jones, Benjamin R.	21	Dennysville	S	Dec. 8, '63	'64: promoted 2nd Lt.

A. Roster

Name	Age	Residence	MS	MD	Remarks
Com'y Sergeant					
Studley, James M.	26	Warren	S	Dec. 8, '63	'64: promoted Q.M. Sgt.
Sergeants					
Pattengill, George M.	27	Pembroke	S	Dec. 8, '63	'64: promoted 1st Sgt.
Norton, Elisha G.	25	Palermo	M	Dec. 8, '63	'64: reduced to ranks
Nash, George M.	28	Cherryfield	M	Dec. 8, '63	'64: reduced to ranks; trans. to Co. M
Thaxter, Marshall	22	Machias	S	Dec. 8, '63	
Downs, Michael	23	Calais	M	Dec. 8, '63	'64: promoted Com'y Sgt.
Corporals					
Nichols, James A.	18	Calais	S	Dec. 8, '63	'64: promoted Sgt.
Butler, Henry	39	Solon	M	Dec. 8, '63	'64: promoted Sgt.
Conolly, Thomas	26	Pembroke	S	Dec. 8, '63	'63: deserted, Dec. 21
Wheaton, Daniel H.*	22	Machias	S	Dec. 8, '63	'64: promoted Sgt.

* Regimental Books, National Archives lists Corporal Wheaton promoted to sergeant "for good conduct in the engagement at Marianna Sept. 27."

Name	Age	Residence	MS	MD	Remarks
Gallagher, James	19	Perry	S	Dec. 8, '63	'63: reduced to ranks (listed as Cpl. in '65)
Gayer, John	42	Calais	S	Dec. 8, '63	'65: disch. by order, Sept. 18
Cambridge, George E.	21	Edmunds	S	Dec. 21, '63	'64: promoted Sgt.
Mullen, George M.	36	Perry	M	Dec. 8, '63	'63: reduced to ranks at own request
Murray, Thomas	21	Liberty	S	Dec. 8, '63	'64: reduced to ranks; promoted Sgt.
Fuller, Edward T.	18	Warren	S	Dec. 8, '63	'64: reduced to ranks
Chisam, John W.	22	China	S	Dec. 8, '63	'64: died of disease, June 7
Buglers					
Reed, Warren	20	Farmington	M	Dec. 8, '63	'64: trans. to Co. F
Wilder, Rufus L.	21	Machias	S	Dec. 8, '63	'63: det. in band; '64: det. to band; promoted chief bugler
Farriers					
Judkins, Lorenzo R.	43	Calais	M	Dec. 8, '63	'65: disch. for dis, May 20
Pottle, James G.	23	Perry	M	Dec. 8, '63	
Saddler					
Caten, Eugene	19	Augusta	S	Dec. 8, '63	'64: died of disease, Oct. 9 at N. Orleans
Wagoner					
Falconer, Hugh	30	Calais	S	Dec. 8, '63	'64: deserted, Mar. 16
Lovering, Frederic	22	Baileyville	S	Dec. 8, '63	'63: reduced to ranks
Privates					
Albee, Josiah T.	18	Wiscasset	S	Feb. 15, '64	
Allen, John H.	18	Saco	S	Oct. 12, '64	'65: disch. Oct. 4; term exp.
Andrews, Atwood A.	18	Biddeford	S	Oct. 12, '64	'65: disch. Oct. 4; term exp.
Andrews, Frank	20	Portland	M	Dec. 9, '63	
Atkinson, Elisha	20	Clifton	S	Dec. 21, '63	'64: died of disease, Sept. 19 at N. Orleans
Bagley, George H.	25	Presque Is.	S	Dec. 22, '63	'64: trans. from Co. A; died Aug. 28, Barrancas

Name	Age	Residence	MS	MD	Remarks
Ball, William H.	18	Dennysville	S	Dec. 8, '63	'64: died Aug. 26, Barrancas
Barker, Daniel W.	18	Portland	S	Dec. 8, '63	'64: died Sept. 20, Barrancas
Blake, Charles H.	18	Pittsfield	S	Dec. 8, '63	
Bowen, John Q. A.	18	Perry	S	Dec. 8, '63	'64: died Oct. 21, Barrancas
Brewster, Joseph, Jr.	40	Belmont	M	Dec. 21, '63	'64: disch. for disab, Sept. 17
Brown, Frederick	18	Perry	S	Dec. 8, '63	'64: sick in hosp.
Brown, Charles	19	Pembroke	S	Dec. 8, '63	
Burns, Charles	22	Portland	S	Dec. 8, '63	'63: abs. w/o leave since Jan. 18; '64: deserted Jan. 21
Butler, Henry	39	Solon	M	Dec. 8, '63	'63: promoted Cpl.
Cambridge, George E.	21	Edmunds	S	Dec. 21, '63	'63: promoted Cpl.
Cambridge, Samuel	18	Edmunds	S	Dec. 8, '63	
Cantlin, Philip	24	Lewiston	S	Aug. 30, '64	'65: disch. Aug. 29; term exp.
Chadwick, Henry F.	21	Vassalboro	S	Dec. 8, '63	'64: promoted trumpeter
Clark, John A.	21	Machias	S	Dec. 8, '63	
Colby, Albion C.	18	Rockland	S	Dec. 8, '63	
Conally, Thomas	26	Pembroke	S	Dec. 8, '63	'64: deserted Dec. 21, '63
Conner, John	18	Millbridge	S	Dec. 8, '63	
Conner, Richard	42	Millbridge	M	Dec. 8, '63	
Conners, Samuel	18	Cherryfield	S	Dec. 8, '63	
Crawford, Robert	25	Belfast	S	Dec. 8, '63	'63: in jail for stealing a horse; '64: deserted, Jan. 21
Crommet, Leander M.	24	Somerville	S	Dec. 8, '63	'64: trans. from Co. E; died June 24, N. Orleans
Crommet, Lewis	21	Somerville	S	Dec. 8, '63	'64: died Aug. 19, N. Orleans
Dean, Jacob M.	19	Perry	S	Dec. 8, '63	'64: died July 2 at Thibodeaux
Dodge, Cassius C.	19	Wiscasset	S	Feb. 15, '64	'64: died at N. Orleans
Donahoe, Peter	22	Portland	S	Dec. 8, '63	
Estabrook, Charles	19	Calais	S	Dec. 8, '63	'65: disch. for dis, Oct. 8, '64
Eldridge, Charles W.	18	Perry	S	Dec. 8, '63	'64: sick in hosp.; '65: disch. for disab., Mar. 8
Falconer, Hugh	30	Calais	S	Dec. 8, '63	'63: appointed wagoner
Fickett, Stillman*	23	Millbridge	M	Dec. 8, '63	'64: promoted Cpl.

* Regimental Books, National Archives has Fickett reduced to ranks from corporal on July 25, 1864, for applying epithets to a private that were "ungentlemanly and not Military."

Name	Age	Residence	MS	MD	Remarks
Fisher, William	32	Charlotte	M	Dec. 8, '63	'64: deserted Mar. 9
Flewelling, Edward	44	Calais	M	Dec. 8, '63	'64: deserted Mar. 16
Fogner, George	27	Calais	M	Dec. 8, '63 "	'63: deserted December 29
Foss, Eugene	18	Concord	S	Dec. 8, '63	'64: died Sept. 18, Alexandria
Freeman, Moses	30	Augusta	M	Dec. 8, '63	'64: promoted wagoner
Fuller, Edward T.	18	Warren	S	Dec. 8, '63	'63: promoted Cpl.
Gallagher, James	19	Perry	S	Dec. 8, '63	'64: promoted Cpl.
Gilbert, Emery	22	Gorham	S	Dec. 8, '63	'64: transferred to Co. I
Goodale, Elbridge	18	Biddeford	S	Sept. 27, '64	'65: disch. by order, Aug. 29
Grant, Andrew D.	19	Palermo	S	Dec. 8, '63	
Grant, Charles A., Jr.	30	No. 14 plnt	M	Dec. 21, '63	'65: disch. by order, Aug. 25
Grant, Elander R.	19	Palermo	S	Dec. 8, '63	
Grant, George W.	18	Dennysville	S	Feb. 28, '64	
Grant, Martin N.	25	Dennysville	M	Dec. 21, '63	
Grant, Samuel N.	19	Dennysville	S	Dec. 21, '63	
Greely, Barzilla B.	32	Palermo	M	Dec. 8, '63	'64: died Dept 12, Barrancas
Green, Albert S.	19	Skowhegan	S	Jan. 14, '64	'64: died Jan. 26 at Augusta
Grinnell, Williston	19	Portland	S	Dec. 8, '63	'65: promoted Cpl.
Hall, Cyrus	42	Concord	M	Dec. 8, '63	'64: deserted Mar. 16

A. Roster

Name	Age	Residence	MS	MD	Remarks
Hall, Lorenzo J.	21	Warren	M	Dec. 8, '63	'64: died Aug. 4, N. Orleans
Hanscom, John W.	20	C Elizabeth	S	Dec. 8, '63	
Harrington, Thomas E.	18	China	S	Dec. 8, '63	'64: trans. from Co. I; '65: trans. to 8th Maine, but not on their rolls
Haskell, Samuel M.	22	Warren	S	Dec. 8, '63	'64: abs. on furlough since Aug. 1; '65: deserted Oct. 21, '64
Holmes, William A.	22	Wilton	S	Feb. 2, '64	'65: disch. by order, May 22
Huson, George J.	20	Machias	S	Jan. 23, '64	
Jeck, James S.	21	Augusta	S	Dec. 8, '63	'63: det. in band; '64: transferred to Co. E
Jewett, Walter S.	18	Solon	S	Dec. 8, '63	'64: sick at Augusta, Me; '65: abs. sick; sent to northern hosp.
Jones, Stephen	19	Dennysville	S	Dec. 8, '63	'64: promoted bugler
Jordan, Lewis M.	24	C Elizabeth	M	Dec. 8, '63	'64: promoted Cpl.
Joy, Stephen D.	31	Cherryfield	M	Dec. 8, '63	'64: transferred to Co. A
Judkins, Thomas S. B.	33	Calais	S	Dec. 8, '63	'64: died Aug. 9, N. Orleans
Kendall, Theodore D.	27	Perry	S	Dec. 8, '63	'64: died July 7, Thibodeaux
Lewis, George	21	Millbridge	S	Dec. 8, '63	'63: in jail for stealing horse
Linton, James	21	Calais	S	Dec. 8, '63	
Lovering, Frederick	22	Baileyville	S	Dec. 8, '63	
Maybury, George	19	Saco	S	Oct. 10, '64	'65: abs. sick, sent to a northern hosp.
Maybury, William R.	19	Windham	S	Sept. 30, '64	'65: disch. by order, Aug. 29
McCarty, Almon	18	Edmunds	S	Dec. 8, '63	
McLeod, Andrew	28	Calais	S	Dec. 8, '63	'64: deserted Mar. 16
McReynolds, John	21	Calais	S	Dec. 8, '63	
Morrison, Ellis	35	Perry	M	Dec. 8, '63	'64: died of disab., N. Orleans
Mullen, George M.	36	Perry	M	Dec. 8, '63	'64: died of disease, Augusta
Murray, Patrick	22	Prescott	S	Dec. 8, '63	'64: died Oct. 20, N. Orleans
Murray, Thomas	21	Liberty	S	Dec. 8, '63	
Mylen, Benjamin	18	Calais	S	Dec. 8, '63	'64: sick in hosp., N. Orleans
Nash, Augustus	20	Calais	S	Dec. 8, '63	'64: died Apr. 3 on passage from Portland to N. Orleans
Norton, Elisha G.	25	Palermo	M	Dec. 8, '63	'65: disch. by order, May 22
O'Neal, Henry	23	Portland	M	Dec. 8, '63	'64: missing since Sept. 28; '65: disch. by order, Sept. 18
Perkins, Herbert D.	18	Calais	S	Dec. 8, '63	
Pettingill, Frederick	18	Pembroke	S	Feb. 26, '64	
Pierce, Charles N.	18	Warren	S	Dec. 8, '63	
Pushor, James A.	31	Pittsfield	M	Dec. 8, '63	
Ray, Benjamin A.	18	Augusta	S	Dec. 8, '63	'64: promoted Cpl.
Reynolds, John F.	19	Dennysville	S	Dec. 8, '63	'64: deserted Jan. 21
Richards, John E.	18	Palermo	S	Dec. 8, '63	'64: died Sept. 3, Barrancas
Ring, Henry C.	33	Lubec	M	Jan. 14, '64	'64: promoted Cpl.
Ross, George H.	19	Calais	S	Dec. 8, '63	
Scott, Henry	44	Calais	M	Dec. 8, '63	
Seavey, Jonas P.	19	Machias	S	Dec. 11, '63	'64: trans. from Co. F; promoted Cpl.
Sherman, Silas A.	28	Washington	M	Dec. 8, '63	'63: abs. w/o leave since Dec. 19; '64: deserted Feb. 28

Name	Age	Residence	MS	MD	Remarks
Shorey, Leonard M.	19	Palermo	S	Dec. 8, '63	
Sinclair, Thomas E.	18	Cherryfield	S	Dec. 8, '63	'64: trans. to invalid corps Aug. 12; '65: trans. to Veteran Reserve Corps
Small, Francis H.	20	Gorham	S	Sept. 30, '64	'65: died at Barrancas, Sept. 5
Temple, Everett	19	Augusta	S	Dec. 8, '63	'64: promoted Cpl.
Temple, Ivory	20	Webster	S	Sept. 7, '64	'65: disch., term expired
Thompson, Actor P.	35	Canton	M	Dec. 8, '63	'64: trans. from field and staff; '65: not accounted for on muster out rolls
Thompson, John C.	18	Pittsfield	S	Dec. 8, '63	'64: died Sept. 1, Barrancas
Thornton, Jerry E.	18	Monmouth	S	Dec. 8, '63	
Varney, Aaron	37	Parsonsfield	S	Oct. 5, '64	'65: disch. Oct. 4, term exp.
Ward, Howard G.	18	China	S	Feb. 4, '64	
Ward, Orrin B.	19	China	S	Feb. 15, '64	'64: died Aug. 10, N. Orleans
Ward, Rishworth A.*	18	Waldo	S	Jan. 14, '64	'64: died Sept. 7, Barrancas

* also listed as "Rishworth C." from China, Maine.

Name	Age	Residence	MS	MD	Remarks
Whitten, Thomas L.	25	Clifton	M	Dec. 21, '63	'64: died of disab., N. Orleans
Wentworth, Edwin E.	27	China*	M	Jan. 22, '64	'65: disch. by order, Aug. 25

* in '63 listed from Waldo

Name	Age	Residence	MS	MD	Remarks
Wilson, John	20	Portland	S	Dec. 8, '63	'63: deserted Dec. 10, '63
Worth, Edward E.	21	Vassalboro	S	Dec. 8, '63	'63: deserted Dec. 10, '63

Company E

Name	Age	Residence	MS	MD	Remarks

Commissioned Officers

Name	Age	Residence	MS	MD	Remarks
Clarke, Samuel W.	25	Newcastle	S	Dec. 10, '63	
Pickard, A.J.	24	Rockland	S	Dec. 10, '63	'64: promoted adjutant
Metcalf, Fred A.	23	Damariscotta	S	Dec. 10, '63	'64: promoted 1st Lt.

First Sergeant

Glidden, Oakman F.	21	Whitefield	S	Dec. 10, '63	'64: promoted 2nd Lt.

Q.M. Sergeant

Clark, Theodore	21	Newcastle	S	Dec. 10, '63	'64: promoted 2nd Lt. 4th U.S. Colored

Com'y Sergeant

Farrar, Edward W.	24	Washington	S	Dec. 10, '63	

Sergeants

Hanaky, Edgar A.	27	Rockland	S	Dec. 10, '63	'64: trans. to navy, Aug. 1
Hoffman, Samuel	39	Damariscotta	S	Dec. 10, '63	'64: trans. to navy, Aug. 1
Haggett, Charles H.*	26	Newcastle	S	Dec. 10, '63	

* Regimental Books, National Archives, lists Sergeant Haggett as reduced to the ranks November 25, 1864.

Name	Age	Residence	MS	MD	Remarks
Stevens, John S.	31	Union	S	Dec. 10, '63	'64: reduced to ranks at own request
Brown, James N.	33	Cushing	M	Dec. 10, '63	'64: promoted Q.M. Sgt. and 1st Sgt. Corporals
Simpson, Edward P.	21	Alna	S	Dec. 10, '63	'64: promoted Sgt.
Leavitt, Adelphus A.	18	Rockland	M	Dec. 10, '63	'64: deserted at Augusta, Mar. 3

Name	Age	Residence	MS	MD	Remarks
Harding, Cyrus	27	Rockland	S	Dec. 10, '63	'64: reduced to ranks at own request
Robbins, James P.	28	Rockland	S	Dec. 10, '63	'64: promoted Sgt.
Hiscock, Gustavus	24	Jefferson	S	Dec. 10, '63	'64: promoted Sgt. and Q.M. Sgt.
Clement, Charles A.	18	Whitefield	S	Dec. 10, '63	'64: reduced to ranks
Newbert, Joseph W.	23	Washington	M	Dec. 10, '63	'64: died Sept. 25, Barrancas
Hall, George	44	Vinalhaven	M	Dec. 10, '63	'64: reduced to ranks; trans. to navy Aug. 1
Dean, John H.	19	Rockland	S	Dec. 10, '63	'65: promoted Sgt.

Buglers

Name	Age	Residence	MS	MD	Remarks
Anderson, William H.	25	Woodstock	M	Dec. 10, '63	'63: deserted Dec. 18, '63
Ripley, Henry	29	Livermore	M	Dec. 10, '63	'64: died July 15, N. Orleans

Farriers

Name	Age	Residence	MS	MD	Remarks
Albee, Leonard J.	26	Whitefield	M	Dec. 10, '63	'65: deserted, August 10
Glidden, Hiram	43	Whitefield	M	Dec. 10, '63	'65: disch. by order, Nov. 22

Saddler

Name	Age	Residence	MS	MD	Remarks
Gardiner, William C.	30	Gardiner	M	Dec. 10, '63	'65: died of disease, Nov. 15, '64

Wagoner

Name	Age	Residence	MS	MD	Remarks
Hyson, David T.	25	Bristol	M	Dec. 10, '63	'64: trans. to navy, Aug. 1

Privates

Name	Age	Residence	MS	MD	Remarks
Anderson, William H.	25	Woods'k NB	M	Dec. 10, '63	'64: deserted Dec. 18, '63
Armbruster, Hubert	28	Hollis	M	Oct. 12, '64	'65: disch. for promotion in colored infantry
Bailey, Ambrose	38	Washington	M	Dec. 10, '63	
Barstow, Joseph H.	18	Damariscotta	S	Dec. 10, '63	
Bartlett, Benjamin	19	Rockland	M	Dec. 10, '63	'65: promoted Cpl.
Blake, Warren	21	Camden	M	Dec. 10, '63	'64: sick at N. Orleans
Brann, Orpheus P.	22	Somerville	S	Dec. 10, '63	'64: promoted Cpl.
Briggs, Gilbert L.	19	Union	S	Dec. 10, '63	'65: died of disease, Jan. 22
Brown, Henry	26	Newcastle	S	Dec. 10, '63	'64: miss'g in action Sept. 27; '65: taken prisoner, Sept. 27, '64, not since reported
Brown, William J.	35	Bremen	M	Dec. 10, '63	'64: trans. to navy, Aug. 1
Burns, James L.	20	Washington	S	Dec. 10, '63	'64: sick in hosp., Augusta
Campbell, Nathaniel	35	Somerville	M	Dec. 10, '63	
Clary, Joseph W.* * also listed as "Clara"	18	Union	S	Dec. 10, '63	'64: sick in hosp., Augusta
Colby, Charles H.	18	Alna	S	Dec. 10, '63	'64: died Mar. 4, Augusta
Collamore, William J.	20	Washington	S	Dec. 10, '63	'64: promoted Cpl.
Crockett, Jonathan	24	Rockland	M	Dec. 10, '63	'65: promoted Cpl.
Crommett, Leander M.	24	Somerville	S	Dec. 10, '63	'64: trans. to Co. D
Day, Augustus D.	21	Jefferson	M	Dec. 10, '63	
Day, John P.	22	Biddeford	S	Oct. 6, '64	'65: disch. Oct. 5; term exp.
Day, Roswell A.	19	Jefferson	S	Dec. 10, '63	'65: died of disease, Jan. 13
Day, Silas	23	Parsonfield	—	Oct. 5, '64	'65: disch. Oct. 5; term exp.
Dean, John H.	19	Rockland	S	Dec. 10, '63	'64: promoted Cpl.
Deans, James	18	Union	M	Dec. 10, '63	
Dill, Ambrose	18	Rockland	S	Dec. 10, '63	'64: died Oct. 10, N. Orleans

Name	Age	Residence	MS	MD	Remarks
Dill, George A.	18	Rockland	S	Mar. 3, '64	'64: trans. to navy, Aug. 1
Dyer, Melzer T.	21	Belfast	M	Dec. 10, '63	'64: trans. to navy, Aug. 1
Eastman, Frank H.	21	Bangor	S	Dec. 11, '63	'64: trans, from Co. G
Elwell, Leander	18	St George	S	Dec. 10, '63	'65: died of disease, Jan. 1
Emery, Harrison	22	S Thomaston	S	Dec. 10, '63	'64: trans. to navy, Aug. 1
Erskine, Mayo	18	Whitefield	S	Dec. 10, '63	'64: died Oct. 9, Barrancas
Fields, Albert L.	18	Rockland	S	Dec. 10, '63	'64: promoted Cpl. and Sgt.
Forbes, Daniel	44	Bangor*	S	Dec. 10, '63	'65: died of disease, Jan. 29
* in '63 listed from Augusta.					
French, Kreutzer C.	22	Norridgewock	M	Dec. 3, '63	'64: trans. from Co. M; '65: disch. for disab., June 22
Gilman, Charles A.	18	Dexter	S	Mar. 1, '64	'65: disch. by order, Sept. 11
Ginn, David R.	21	Vinalhaven	S	Dec. 10, '63	'64: promoted Cpl.; trans. to navy, Aug. 1
Glidden, Nelson C.	32	Nobleboro*	M	Dec. 10, '63	'64: promoted Sgt.
* in '63 listed from Newcastle.					
Gordon, Levy	18	Rome	S	Dec. 10, '63	
Gould, Charles T.	18	Wiscasset	S	Jan. 14, '64	'64: trans. to vet. reserve corps, Aug. 1
Gowen, John W.	18	Union	S	Dec. 10, '63	'65: sick in hosp.
Hagar, George A.	20	Washington	S	Dec. 10, '63	'64: died May 1, N. Orleans
Hall, Timothy	43	Vinalhaven	M	Dec. 10, '63	'64: sick in hosp., Augusta; '65: disch. for disab., Jan. 14
Hall, William C.	18	Jefferson	S	Dec. 10, '63	'64: promoted Cpl.; died Sept. 15, Barrancas
Harding, Cyrus	27	Rockland	S	Dec. 10, '63	'65: died of disease, Feb. 17
Hatch, Alonzo	19	Jefferson	S	Dec. 10, '63	'65: died of disease, Nov. 15, '64
Hewitt, Nathan A.	18	Rockland	S	Dec. 10, '63	'65: promoted Cpl.
Hewitt, Samuel W.	21	Rockland	S	Dec. 10, '63	'64: trans. to navy, Aug. 1
Hodgkins, Samuel R.	21	Jefferson	S	Dec. 10, '63	
Howard, Angelo	18	Washington	S	Dec. 10, '63	
Humes, George W.	22	Washington	S	Dec. 10, '63	'65: died of disease, Mar. 22
Irish, Wilder S.	18	Union	S	Dec. 10, '63	
Jeck, James S.	21	Gardiner	S	Dec. 8, '63	'64: trans. from Co. D
Jones, Wilbert	18	Whitefield	S	Dec. 10, '63	
Kaler, Peter	21	Waldoboro	S	Dec. 10, '63	
Kelleran, William H.	18	Cushing	S	Dec. 10, '63	'64: deserted at Augusta, Feb. 23
Knight, Frank A.	20	Rockland	M	Dec. 10, '63	
Leighton, Charles H.	21	Matinicus	S	Dec. 10, '63	'64: trans. to navy, Aug. 1
Linscott, Abial N.	18	Jefferson	S	Dec. 10, '63	'64: missing in action, Sept. 29; '65: disch. by order, June 20
Maddocks, Alonzo	18	Union	S	Dec. 10, '63	'64: sick in hosp., Augusta
Maddox, Willard	26	Nobleboro	M	Dec. 10, '63	'65: died at home, Sept. 23, '64
Marcou, Levi	30	Skowhegan	S	Dec. 10, '63	'64: deserted at Augusta, Feb. 23
McDaniel, Nelson	20	Somerville	S	Dec. 10, '63	
McNear, Charles H.	18	Newcastle	M	Dec. 10, '63	
McNear, George	18	Newcastle	S	Dec. 10, '63	
Mellus, Francis G.	21	Rockland	S	Dec. 21, '63	
Mills, Isaac	23	Eddington	S	Dec. 11, '63	'64: trans. from Co. G
Moore, Charles A.	21	Richm'nd NB	S	Dec. 10, '63	'63: deserted at Augusta, Dec. 18, '63

Name	Age	Residence	MS	MD	Remarks
Moore, John V.	18	Whitefield	S	Dec. 10, '63	'64: sick in hosp., Augusta
Moore, Waterman S.	18	Whitefield	S	Dec. 10, '63	
Peabody, Josiah	30	Rockland	M	Dec. 10, '63	
Pendleton, Sanford H.	18	Rockland	S	Dec. 10, '63	'64: wounded and left at Marianna, Sept. 27; '65: exchanged prisoner; disch., Sept. 18
Pray, William O.	20	Parsonsfield	S	Oct. 5, '64	'65: disch. Oct. 5, term exp.
Preble, James	24	Whitefield	S	Jan. 14, '64	'64: sick in hosp., Augusta; '65: disch. by order, Oct. 21
Pottle, Thomas C.	22	Alna	S	Dec. 10, '63	'64: died June 19, Thibodeaux
Powers, Thomas	21	Halifax NS	S	Dec. 21, '63	'65: died of disease, Nov. 23
Rhoades, Edward A.	18	Washington	S	Dec. 10, '63	'64: died July 13, Thibodeaux
Rhodes, William A.	18	Whitefield	S	Dec. 10, '63	'65: wounded Mar. 24; abs. on furlough from hosp.
Richardson, Jefferson	20	Dexter	S	Mar. 1, '64	
Riley, George S.	22	Gardiner	S	Dec. 10, '63	'64: deserted at Augusta, Mar. 18
Robbins, Asa	43	Sidney	M	Dec. 10, '63	'64: died Sept. 22, Barrancas
Robbins, David M.	45	Rockland	M	Dec. 10, '63	'64: trans. to navy, Aug. 1
Robbins, Roscoe B.	18	Union	S	Dec. 10, '63	
St. Clair, Ashley	18	Rockland	S	Dec. 10, '63	
Sanders, John E.	18	Rockland	S	Dec. 10, '63	'65: disch. for disab., Jan. 19
Spear, Pearl	19	Rockland	S	Dec. 10, '63	'65: disch. for disab., July 13
Stillings, Joseph B.	18	Whitefield	S	Dec. 10, '63	'65: promoted Cpl.
Thompson, Porter M.	19	Machiasp't	M	Dec. 11, '63	'65: disch. for disab., Apr. 22
Tracey, Michael	28	Rockland	S	Dec. 10, '63	
Turner, Fessenden B.	18	Whitefield	S	Dec. 10, '63	'64: promoted Cpl.
Wasgatt, William	37	Rockland	M	Dec. 10, '63	'64: trans. to navy, Aug. 1; '65: returned from desertion under the P.P.; disch. by order, May 3
Weeks, John G.	21	Jefferson	S	Dec. 10, '63	'64: promoted Cpl.
Wentworth, Charles O.	33	Rockland	M	Dec. 10, '63	'64: trans. to navy, Aug. 1
Wood, Charles P.	19	Rockland	S	Dec. 10, '63	'65: promoted Cpl.
Woodcock, Leander	36	Thomaston	M	Dec. 10, '63	
Worthing, George H.	18	Somerville	S	Dec. 10, '63	'64: deserted at Augusta, Mar. 18
Wyman, Joseph A.	19	Jefferson	S	Mar. 17, '64	

Company F

Name	Age	Residence	MS	MD	Remarks
Commissioned Officers					
Stanley, Gustavus A.	31	Farmington	S	Dec. 11, '63	
Prescott, Evander S.*	27	Wilton	S	Dec. 11, '63	'64: in command of Co. B

  * Regimental Books, National Archives, lists Lt. Prescott as relieved from the command of Co. B. and returned to Co. F. on November 26, 1864.

Parlin, Simon W.*	26	Phillips	S	Dec. 11, '63	'65: disch. by order, May 15

  * also listed as "Simeon"

A. Roster

Name	Age	Residence	MS	MD	Remarks
First Sergeant					
Stoddard, Samuel F., Jr.	19	Farmington	S	Dec. 11, '63	'64: wounded in action at Marianna, Sept. 27; '65: disch. for promotion, Jan. 3
Q.M. Sergeant					
Farrington, John L.B.*	27	Wilton	S	Dec. 11, '63	

* Regimental Books, National Archives lists L.B. Farrington reduced from quartermaster sergeant to sergeant for inefficiency.

Smith, Leroy A.*	25	Phillips	M	Dec. 11, '63	

* listed as Q.M. Sgt. in 1865 report.

Name	Age	Residence	MS	MD	Remarks
Com'y Sergeant					
Hussey, Frederic F.	31	Phillips	S	Dec. 11, '63	'64: died Sept. 18, Barrancas
Williamson, Charles T.*	21	Wiscasset	S	Dec. 11, '63	

* listed as Com'y Sgt. in 1865 report. Regimental Books, National Archives, lists Williamson as promoted to 1st sergeant on January 27, 1865.

Name	Age	Residence	MS	MD	Remarks
Sergeants					
Farrington, John L.B.*	27	Wilton	S	Dec. 11, '63	

* before 1865 report, listed as Q.M. Sgt.

Williamson, Charles T.	21	Wiscasset	S	Dec. 11, '63	
Saunders, Samuel*	21	Falmouth	S	Dec. 11, '63	

* Regimental Books, National Archives, lists Saunders as promoted to com'y sergeant on January 27, 1865.

Tibbetts, Benjamin F.	20	Industry	S	Dec. 11, '63	'64: died Aug. 11, Barrancas
Smith, Leroy A.	25	Phillips	M	Dec. 11, '63	
Huntoon, George D.	31	Rangely	M	Dec. 11, '63	

Name	Age	Residence	MS	MD	Remarks
Corporals					
Bates, John S.	21	Wilton	S	Dec. 11, '63	'63: died Jan. 3, '63
Lovejoy, Rufus N.	21	Chesterville	S	Dec. 11, '63	'65: disch. by order, Oct. 24
Chapman, Asa	28	Madrid	S	Dec. 11, '63	'65: disch. for disab., June 22
Morrison, James,, Jr.	22	Phillips	S	Dec. 11, '63	'65: promoted Sgt.
Whitney, David C.	28	Industry	S	Dec. 11, '63	'64: wounded, taken prisoner, Marianna, Sept. 27; '65: died of wounds, Oct. 24, '64
Sleeper, Charles S.	20	Wilton	S	Dec. 11, '63	'64: det. in hosp.; reduced to ranks (again promoted Cpl. in '65)
Phillips, M. Augustine	20	Weld	S	Dec. 11, '63	'65: promoted Sgt.
Burbank, John	36	Wilton	M	Dec. 11, '63	'64: died Sept. 24, N. Orleans
Baker, George W.*	18	E Machias	S	Dec. 11, '63	'64: wounded in action, Sept.27; promoted Sgt. for bravery

* Regimental Books, National Archives, lists Corporal Baker promoted to sergeant "for conspicuous bravery in engagement with the enemy near Milton, Fla., October 26, 1864."

Brackett, Asa W.*	18	Phillips	S	Dec. 11, '63	

* listed as private before 1865 report. Regimental Books, National Archives lists Private Brackett promoted to corporal November 4, 1864."

Name	Age	Residence	MS	MD	Remarks
Buglers					
Hersey, John E.	18	Canton	S	Dec. 11, '63	'64: reduced to ranks at own request

A. Roster

Name	Age	Residence	MS	MD	Remarks
Pease, George W.*	34	Wilton	M	Dec. 11, '63	
* listed as private before 1865 report.					
Walker, Milton R.	18	Chesterville	S	Dec. 11, '63	'65: disch. for dis, Aug. 22, '64

Farriers

Name	Age	Residence	MS	MD	Remarks
Durgin, William H.	35	Kenn'b'c Fks	M	Dec. 11, '63	
Rollins, Ephraim H.	21	Weld	S	Dec. 11, '63	'64: accidentally killed at Hallowell, Me, Feb. 23

Saddler

Name	Age	Residence	MS	MD	Remarks
Howland, George	23	Phillips	S	Dec. 11, '63	'64: sick in N. Orleans

Wagoner

Name	Age	Residence	MS	MD	Remarks
Young, Orlando	26	Kennebec Forks	M	Dec. 11, '63	'64: died Aug. 15, Barrancas

Privates

Name	Age	Residence	MS	MD	Remarks
Abbott, John A.	20	Rangely	S	Dec. 11, '63	'64: died Sept. 24, Barrancas
Abbott, Moses P.	25	Rangely	M	Dec. 11, '63	
Abbott, Solomon	18	Rangely	S	Dec. 11, '63	'64: died Sept. 12, Barrancas
Bacon, Americus V.	24	Wilton	S	Dec. 11, '63	'65: appointed bugler
Baker, Nathaniel A.*	21	Weld	S	Dec. 21, '63	'65: appointed wagoner
* also listed as "Buker"					
Barter, Frederick	22	Wiscasset	M	Dec. 11, '63	'65: disch. by order, Oct. 30
Bean, Charles T.	—	Warren	M	Jan. 12, '64	'64: det. in hosp., Augusta, trans. from F. and S; '65: disch. for dis, Dec. 4, '64
Bean, Lewis E.	23	Wilton	M	Dec. 11, '63	'64: deserted Jan. 24 ('65 report says July 24, '64)
Berry, Charles C.	18	West Bath	S	Dec. 11, '63	
Blake, Bradbury	19	Wiscasset	M	Dec. 11, '63	
Boodry, John	18	Rangely	S	Dec. 11, '63	'64: died Oct. 19, N. Orleans
Brackett, Ansel	21	Phillips	S	Dec. 11, '63	'64: wounded, taken prisoner Marianna, Sept. 27; '65: died of wounds, Sept. 28, '64
Brackett, Asa W.	18	Phillips	S	Dec. 11, '63	
Brown, Albert	44	Palermo	M	Dec. 11, '63	
Brown, Edward	21	Chelsea	S	Dec. 22, '63	'64: sick in hosp. 65: deserted July 31
Bubier, Alpha	22	Rangely	S	Dec. 11, '63	'65: promoted Cpl.
Bubier, Charles	26	Dallas Plantation	M	Dec. 11, '63	
Campbell, Silas	19	Bath*	S	Dec. 11, '63	'64: killed in action, Marianna, Sept. 27
* in '63 listed from West Bath					
Chapman, Asa	28	Madrid	S	Dec. 11, '63	'63: promoted Cpl.
Chase, Charles I.	18	Weld	S	Dec. 11, '63	
Chase, N. Kimball, Jr.	26	Weld	M	Dec. 11, '63	
Cookson, Alphonzo	21	Pittston	S	Feb. 23, '64	'64: deserted Mar. 17
Corser, Benjamin H.	18	Phillips	S	Dec. 11, '63	
Corson, Van Rensalear	21	Alton	S	Aug. 30, '64	'65: disch. by order, Aug. 29
Crocker, Albert D.	22	Dixmont	S	Sept. 30, '64	'65: disch. Sept. 29; term exp.
Crossman, Benjamin H.	18	Wiscasset	S	Dec. 11, '63	
Cushman, Simeon B.	25	Weld	M	Dec. 21, '63	'64: disch. for disab. Aug. 17
Davis, Frank J.	18	Chesterville	S	Dec. 11, '63	

Name	Age	Residence	MS	MD	Remarks
Dickinson, Levy	23	Wiscasset	S	Dec. 11, '63	'64: deserted Aug. 31 ('65: gives date as Aug. 1)
Dixson, Alpheus C.	19	Wiscasset	M	Feb. 19, '64	'64: wounded July 21, near Berwick, La; '65: died at Augusta, Me, Nov. 17, '64
Dow, James J.	18	Wilton	S	Dec. 11, '63	'65: disch. by order, Nov. 16
Dow, John E.	23	E Machias	S	Dec. 11, '63	'64: trans. to navy, Aug. 1
Dowling, James S.	26	Pittston	S	Feb. 23, '64	'64: deserted Mar. 25
Ellis, Joseph S.	36	Wilton	M	Dec. 11, '63	'64: died Sept. 11, N. Orleans
Farnsworth, Charles L.	23	Jonesport	S	Dec. 11, '63	'64: deserted Feb. 11
Feyler, William H.	32	Thomaston	M	Dec. 11, '63	'63: deserted Dec. 28, '62 [?]; '64: ret. from desertion; sick in hosp.; '65: died in hosp., Dec. 24, '64
Gardner, Joseph A.	18	N Vineyard	M	Dec. 11, '63	'64: died July 16, Thibodeaux
Gardner, Seneca R.	36	N Vineyard	M	Dec. 11, '63	
Godfrey, Marcus M.	18	Temple	S	Dec. 11, '63	'64: died Sept. 10, Barrancas
Hall, Albert R.	19	Saco	S	Oct. 4, '64	'65: died in hosp., Mar. 30
Hamlin, William H.	18	Wiscasset	S	Dec. 11, '63	'64: deserted May 20
Harmon, Alonzo E.	19	E Machias	S	Dec. 11, '63	'64: died July 11, Thibodeaux
Harris, Frank N.	19	New Sharon	S	Dec. 11, '63	
Hawes, Charles E.	20	Weld	S	Dec. 11, '63	'64: died August, N. Orleans
Hoar, Nathaniel B.	22	Rangely	S	Feb. 23, '64	
Holbrook, Samuel G.	18	Wiscasset	S	Dec. 11, '63	'64: deserted Mar. 9; '65: disch. by order, June 26; erroneously listed as deserter in '64 report
Houghton, Edward B.	21	Weld	S	Dec. 11, '63	'65: died while on furlough in Maine, Oct. 22, '64
Humphrey, Charles E.	42	Jay	M	Dec. 11, '63	
Jenkins, Alonzo E.	19	Temple	S	Dec. 11, '63	'65: disch. for dis, July 10
Jenkins, George H.	18	Temple	S	Dec. 11, '63	
Jewett, George F.	20	Sangerville	S	Dec. 22, '63	'65: trans. from Co. I
Johnson, Adriance R.	18	Industry	S	Dec. 11, '63	'65: disch. for dis, Apr. 21
Kelley, Alpheus G.	18	Phillips	S	Dec. 11, '63	'64: promoted Cpl.
Keyes, Abel H.	39	Weld	M	Jan. 7, '64	'64: died May 26, Algiers, La
Keyes, Charles W.	32	Wilton	M	Dec. 11, '63	'64: disch. for promotion, Mar. 2
Kingsbury, Sidney C.	18	Wiscasset	S	Dec. 11, '63	'64: died Sept. 21, Barrancas
Ladd, Samuel	21	Weld	S	Dec. 11, '63	'64: died July at N. Orleans
Langley, William C.	18	Newfield	S	Sept. 28, '64	'65: disch. by order, Aug. 29
Leighton, Cyrus C.	20	Richmond	S	Oct. 10, '62	'65: disch. June 20; term exp. deserted from 24th Reg't Maine Volunteers; arrested and sentenced by military commission to serve 6 months in 2nd ME Cav
Locklin, Martin L.	20	Wilton	S	Dec. 11, '63	
Marr, James B.	21	Saco	S	Oct. 4, '64	'65: disch. by order, Aug. 26
Mason, Thomas	19	Chesterville	S	Dec. 11, '63	
McCrillis, Albert	28	Wilton	M	Dec. 11, '63	'64: deserted Feb. 4
Meader, Clark D.	18	Gardiner	S	Dec. 22, '63	'64: died Oct. 20, N. Orleans
Merchant, Henry*	18	Weld	S	Dec. 11, '63	'65: died on transport, Aug. '64

* also listed as "Marchant"

A. Roster

Name	Age	Residence	MS	MD	Remarks
Merrick, Marcellus H.	23	Wilton	M	Dec. 11, '63	'64: died Sept. 17, Barrancas
Noble, Charles S.	28	Wilton	S	Jan. 24, '64	
Norton, Benjamin W.	18	N Vineyard	S	Dec. 11, '63	'64: died Aug. 27, Barrancas
Nute, George	18	Wiscasset	S	Feb. 18, '64	'64: died July 13, Thibodeaux
Pease, John Q.	21	Salem	S	Dec. 11, '63	'64: died Aug. 7, Warrenton, Fla
Pease, George W.	34	Wilton	M	Dec. 11, '63	
Penney, Charles	25	Alton	S	Aug. 25, '64	'65: disch. by order, Aug. 29
Rackliffe, John	29	Industry	S	Dec. 11, '63	'64: abs. sick; '65: disch. from hosp., May 22
Reed, Ephraim	23	N Vineyard	S	Dec. 11, '63	'64: abs. sick
Reed, Samuel	24	Wilton	S	Dec. 11, '63	
Reed, Warren	27	Chesterville	M	Dec. 8, '63	'64: died Aug. 3, Greenville, La
Roberts, Charles J.	22	Brooks	M	Dec. 11, '63	'64: trans. to navy, Aug. 1
Ross, Reuben W.	21	Rangely	M	Dec. 11, '63	
Rowe, Allen	30	Rangely	S	Mar. 4, '64	'65: died in hosp., July 1, '64
Rowe, Ormandel J.	22	Freeman	S	Dec. 11, '63	'64: died Oct. 16, N. Orleans
Savage, Joshua Y.	40	Wiscasset	M	Dec. 11, '63	
Searles, Oscar	18	Strong	S	Dec. 11, '63	'64: sick in hosp.; '65: died in reg't hosp., Nov. 30, '64
Seavy, Jonas P.	19	E Machias	S	Dec. 11, '63	'64: trans. to Co. D
Sheldon, John	38	Wiscasset	M	Dec. 11, '63	'64: died Mar. 27 on board ship *Westmoreland*
Skeetup, Justus	43	Wilton	S	Dec. 11, '63	'64: abs. sick '65: died in hosp., July 30
Sleeper, Charles S.	20	Wilton	S	Dec. 11, '63	'65: promoted Cpl.; disch. for dis, June 13
Smith, Andrew R. G.	22	—	S	Dec. 11, '63	'63: prom'd hosp. steward
Smith, Charles G.	18	New Sharon	S	Jan. 5, '64	'64: died Sept. 15, Barrancas
Soule, Augustus C.	18	Rangely	S	Dec. 11, '63	'64: died May 19 at Greenville, La
Soule, George	44	Rangely	M	Dec. 11, '63	
Spinney, Andrew J.	19	Industry	S	Dec. 11, '63	'64: sick in hosp.; '65: died in reg't hosp., Nov. 19, '64
Sprague, Theodore S.	18	Chesterville	S	Dec. 11, '63	'64: died Sept. 7, Barrancas
Stain, Albert G.* ** also listed as "Starr"*	28	Wilton	M	Dec. 11, '63	
Stetson, Gilbert	43	Phillips	M	Dec. 11, '63	'64: died Aug. 7, N. Orleans
Stoyell, George W.	21	Farmington	S	Sept. 30, '64	'65: disch. by order, Aug. 29
Sweet, Alanson F.	18	Strong	S	Dec. 11, '63	
Towle, George F.	29	Canton	S	Dec. 11, '63	
True, William	18	Avon	S	Dec. 11, '63	'65: promoted Cpl.
Walker, Ansel	21	Wilton	S	Dec. 11, '63	
Wells, Nathaniel P.	19	Phillips	S	Sept. 29, '64	'65: disch. by order, Aug. 29
Whitehouse, Benj'n F.	28	Newfield	—	Oct. 6, '64	'65: disch. Oct. 5; term exp.
Wilber, Joseph L.	39	Saco	M	Oct. 4, '64	'65: disch. by order, Oct. 3
Wilbur, Harris	19	Phillips	S	Dec. 11, '63	
Wright, David Y.	25	Weld	M	Dec. 11, '63	'64: appointed farrier
Wright, E. Erwin	19	Phillips	S	Dec. 11, '63	'64: died Sept. 3, Barrancas

Company G

Name	Age	Residence	MS	MD	Remarks
Commissioned Officers					
Knowles, Samuel W.	29	Bangor	—	Dec. 11, '63	
Banton, William	41	Lagrange	—	Dec. 11, '63	'64: resig. July 26
Brann, Thomas A.	23	Gardiner	S	Dec. 22, '63	'64: joined as 1st Lt. from 2nd Lt. Co. I
Chandler, Jason C.	21	Corinth	—	Dec. 22, '63	
First Sergeant					
Patten, Alphonzo	22	Bangor	M	Dec. 22, '63	'64: reduced to ranks at own request; det. Hsp. Stew'd 82nd Colored Infantry
Q.M. Sergeant					
Wilson, Charles E.	24	Bradford	S	Dec. 22, '63	'65: promoted Sgt. Maj.
Com'y Sergeant					
Wentworth, John P.	29	Lagrange	M	Dec. 22, '63	'65: promoted Q.M. Sgt.
Sergeants					
Head, Isaac N.	38	Lagrange	M	Dec. 22, '63	'64: promoted 1st Sgt.
Fuller, Fred A.	23	Bangor	S	Dec. 22, '63	'65: disch. for promotion in U.S. Colored Infantry
Gilchrist, Alden*	23	Bradley	M	Dec. 22, '63	'65: dropped from roles as deserter, Aug. 22

* in '63 listed from Bangor; Regimental Books, National Archives, lists Sgt. Gilchrist as reduced to the ranks for absence without leave on May 12, 1865.

Name	Age	Residence	MS	MD	Remarks
Miles, George O.	21	Oldtown	S	Dec. 22, '63	
Jordan, John P.	19	Bangor	S	Dec. 22, '63	'64: died Mar. 6, Augusta
McDuff, Robert J.	31	Lagrange	M	Dec. 22, '63	'65: promoted Com'y Sgt.
Corporals					
Pollard, Luther M.	23	Bradley*	M	Dec. 22, '63	'64: wounded Sept. 27, Marianna, taken prisoner
Brown, Addison J.	21	Bangor	S	Dec. 22, '63	
Mills, Isaac	23	Eddington*	S	Dec. 22, '63	'64: trans. to Co. E

* in '63 listed from Bangor

Name	Age	Residence	MS	MD	Remarks
Herswell, George A.	28	Bangor	M	Dec. 22, '63	'64: promoted Sgt.
Hunt, Thomas A.	18	Oldtown	S	Dec. 22, '63	
Knowles, John S.	24	Bradford*	S	Dec. 22, '63	'65: promoted Sgt.

* in '63 listed from Biddeford

Name	Age	Residence	MS	MD	Remarks
Pierce, Joseph B.	26	Milford	M	Dec. 22, '63	'65: promoted Sgt.

* in '63 listed from Bangor

Name	Age	Residence	MS	MD	Remarks
McDuff, Robert J.	31	Lagrange	M	Dec. 22, '63	'64: promoted Sgt.
Genthner, Isaiah	42	Brewer	M	Dec. 11, '63	'65: disch. by order, Aug. 26
Genthner, Ardel H.	20	Parkman	S	Mar. 10, '64	'65: died at home, June 7
Buglers					
Howland, Osgood M.	18	Presque Isle*	S	Dec. 11, '63	'64: died N. Orleans, date unk.

* in '63 listed from Bangor

Name	Age	Residence	MS	MD	Remarks
Plummer, William M.	21	Augusta	S	Dec. 11, '63	

Name	Age	Residence	MS	MD	Remarks
Farriers					
Luce, Joseph P.	29	Newport*	M	Dec. 21, '63	
* in '63 listed from Bangor					
Moan, Levi W.	23	Oldtown	S	Dec. 11, '63	'64: sick in hosp.
Saddler					
Drummond, John P.	25	Bangor	M	Dec. 11, '63	'65: disch. by order, Aug. 15
Wagoner					
Taylor, Frank	32	Brewer	M	Dec. 11, '63	'65: dropped from roles as deserter, Aug. 22
Privates					
Ambrose, Edwin	18	Orono*	S	Dec. 11, '63	
* in '63 listed from Oldtown					
Austin, William A.	19	Vassalboro	S	Dec. 11, '63	'65: disch. by order, June 23
Bean, William D.	21	Old Town	S	Sept. 8, '64	'65: disch. by order, Aug. 29
Betts, James	18	Hampden*	S	Dec. 11, '63	
* in '63 listed from Bangor					
Blake, George W.	26	Lagrange	S	Dec. 11, '63	'65: promoted Cpl.
Brackett, George	36	Portland	M	Dec. 11, '63	'64: trans. to navy, July14
Bryant, Reuben	20	Lagrange	S	Dec. 11, '63	
Bunker, Burton	26	Bangor	S	Dec. 11, '63	'64: trans. to navy, July 14
Burke, Thomas J.	21	Bangor	S	Dec. 11, '63	
Cary, Rinaldo V.	18	Lagrange	S	Dec. 11, '63	
Clark, Nathan	18	Oldtown	S	Dec. 11, '63	'64: left sick in Augusta; sup. disch.; '65: abs. in Maine since Aug. 7
Cleaves, William	32	Bradford	M	Dec. 11, '63	'65: disch. for disab., May 5
Cronkhite, Jedediah S.	36	Presque Isle	M	Dec. 20, '63	'64: sick in hosp.; '65: disch. by order, Aug. 25
Crowell, Lorenzo C.	18	Vassalboro	S	Jan. 26, '64	
Cunningham, Emery W.	18	Milford*	S	Dec. 11, '63	
* in '63 listed from Lagrange					
Danforth, Newlon H.	18	Lagrange	S	Dec. 11, '63	
Decker, Lorin	18	Lagrange	S	Dec. 11, '63	'65: disch. by order, Dec. 19
Denning, Jerry	22	Bangor	S	Sept. 20, '64	'65: disch. by order, Aug. 29
Dillingham, Edwin	21	Oldtown	S	Dec. 11, '63	'64: died June 5, Augusta
Dodge, John	25	Bradley*	M	Dec. 11, '63	
* in '63 listed from Oldtown					
Dorman, Ephraim D.	19	Bangor	S	Oct. 24, '64	
Dyer, John W.	18	Bradford	S	Dec. 11, '63	
Eastman, Frank H.	21	Bangor	S	Dec. 11, '63	'64: trans. to Co. E
Emery, John G.	22	Lagrange	S	Dec. 11, '63	'65: disch. by order, Sept. 25
Evans, Charles*	18	Bangor	S	Dec. 21, '63	
* also listed as "Evens"					
Fenton, Abram	22	Bangor	S	Sept. 20, '64	'65: disch. by order, Aug. 29
Field, Joseph F.	24	Presque Isle	M	Dec. 21, '63	'64: died Sept. 24, Barrancas
Fogg, Edwin	18	Lowell*	S	Dec. 11, '63	
* in '63 listed from Bangor					
Fogg, John F.	18	Mt. Desert*	S	Dec. 11, '63	'64: trans. to navy, July 14
* in '63 listed from Bangor					
Foster, Charles	18	Orono*	S	Dec. 11, '63	
* in '63 listed from Bangor					

Name	Age	Residence	MS	MD	Remarks
Genthner, Ardel H.	20	Parkman	S	Mar. 10, '64	'64: promoted Cpl.
Genthner, Isaiah	42	Brewer	M	Dec. 11, '64	'64: promoted Cpl.
Giles, David	28	Veazie*	M	Dec. 11, '63	
*in '63 listed from Bangor					
Gonyea, Lewis	18	Old Town	S	Dec. 11, '63	
Haskell, Nathaniel B.	27	Bradley*	M	Dec. 11, '63	
*in '63 listed from Bangor					
Haynes, Richard E.	21	Bangor	S	Dec. 11, '63	'64: trans. to Co. M
Heal, Isaac F.	23	Lagrange	M	Dec. 11, '63	'65: died in hosp. at N. Orleans, Nov. 22, '64
Henries, William	30	Augusta	S	Dec. 11, '63	'63: deserted, Dec. 25, at Augusta
Houston, John	18	Bradford	S	Dec. 11, '63	
Jenks, Edwin S.	21	Atkinson*	S	Dec. 11, '63	'65: promoted Cpl.
*in '63 listed from Bradford					
Johnson, Charles H.	21	Clinton	S	Jan. 25, '64	
Johnson, Edwin S.*	19	Bangor	S	Jan. 25, '64	'64: promoted Cpl.
*Regimental Books, National Archives, lists Corporal Johnson as reduced to the ranks.					
Keith, Eben S.	19	Old Town	S	Jan. 25, '64	'65: died in hosp. at N. Orleans, Nov. 11, '64
Lake, James C.	22	Atkinson*	S	Dec. 21, '63	'65: killed in action, Dec. 18, '64
*in '63 listed from Augusta					
Leighton, Frank G.	27	Bangor	S	Jan. 25, '64	
Libby, Daniel	24	Bradford	M	Dec. 11, '63	'65: killed by rebel torpedo, Apr. 29
Lindsey, Charles A.	18	Medford	S	Dec. 11, '63	'65: appointed musician
Lowell, Philip, L.	21	Bangor	M	Jan. 25, '64	'65: promoted Cpl. and Sgt.
Locke, George B.	21	Bradley*	S	Jan. 25, '64	
*in '63 listed from Bangor					
Lovett, William B.*	18	Bradford	S	Jan. 25, '64	'65: disch. by order, Aug. 25
*also listed as "Lovell"					
Mack, Samuel	19	Milford	S	Dec. 11, '63	'64: sick in hosp., Barrancas; 65: died in hosp., Feb. 27
McAndrew, William M.	18	Bradford	S	Dec. 11, '63	
McLaughlin, William R.	18	Lagrange	S	Dec. 11, '63	
Mills, John	18	Bradford	S	Dec. 11, '63	'65: appointed wagoner
Moore, Henry	19	Bangor	S	Dec. 11, '63	'65: sick in Maine since May
Nason, Marcellus	18	Lagrange	S	Dec. 11, '63	
Page, Eugene	18	Hampden*	S	Dec. 11, '63	
*in '63 listed from Bangor					
Patten, Alphonzo	22	Bangor	M	Dec. 11, '63	'65: disch. for promotion in U.S. Colored Infantry
Perkins, Edward L.	18	Milford	S	Dec. 11, '63	
Perkins, James H. P.	18	Milford	S	Dec. 11, '63	
Pooler, George	18	Newburg*	S	Dec. 11, '63	'64: died Sept. 14, Barrancas
*in '63 listed from Bangor					
Preble, James O.	18	Bangor	S	Dec. 11, '63	
Reed, George	21	Bradley*	M	Dec. 11, '63	
*in '63 listed from Bangor					
Reeves, George M.	21	Gorham	S	Dec. 21, '63	'64: sick at St Louis, Mo; '65: disch. for disab., Jan. 27
Robinson, Benjamin F.	18	Carmel	S	Dec. 11, '63	

Name	Age	Residence	MS	MD	Remarks
Robinson, Benj'n F. (2d)	27	Corinth	M	Dec. 11, '63	'64: sick in N. Orleans; '65: died in hosp. at N. Orleans, Oct. 26, '64
Rogers, Oscar A.	18	Brewer	S	Dec. 11, '63	'64: died Aug. 21, N. Orleans
Sanborn, Rufus A.	20	Lagrange	S	Dec. 11, '63	'65: promoted Cpl.
Sands, William J.	24	Atkinson*	S	Dec. 11, '63	'65: disch. by order, Dec. 5
* in '63 listed from Bangor					
Sherburne, Rolloff N.	18	Atkinson*	S	Dec. 11, '63	'64: died July 12, Thibodeaux
* in '63 listed from Bangor					
Smart, Greenleaf	45	Augusta	M	Dec. 11, '63	'64: died Sept. 24, Barrancas
Smart, James B.*	22	Orono	S	Dec. 11, '63	'64: sick at Barrancas; '65: sick in Me since Mar. 30
* also listed as "Smart, Jonas B." from Bangor					
Smart, Richard N.*	21	Augusta	S	Dec. 11, '63	
* also listed as "Richard M."					
Smith, Frank	19	Brewer	S	Nov. 14, '64	'65: disch. by order, Nov. 17
Smith, George S.	18	Bangor*	S	Dec. 11, '63	
* in '63 listed from Brewer					
Spaulding, Franklin	18	Oldtown	S	Dec. 11, '63	
Spearing, Warren	25	Lagrange	M	Dec. 11, '63	'64: died Aug. 15, N. Orleans
Spencer, Sampson	27	Bradley	M	Oct. 4, '64	'65: disch. Sept. 30; term exp.
Sprague, Edward T.	37	Veazie*	M	Dec. 11, '64	'65: promoted Cpl.
* in '63 listed from Bangor					
Strout, Enoch B.	19	Bradford	S	Dec. 11, '63	
Strout, Major F.	23	Bradford	M	Dec. 11, '63	
Thompson, Porter N.	19	Machias	S	Jan. 7, '64	'64: trans. fr Co. M. to Co. E
Towle, Daniel	29	Lagrange	S	Dec. 11, '63	
Tozier, Charles G.	36	Oldtown	M	Dec. 11, '63	'63: in arrest as deserter from 6th Me Inf.; '64: arrested as deserter from 6th Me Inf.; '65: disch. by order, July 21
Trowbridge, Charles S.	30	Portland	M	Dec. 11, '63	'64: trans. to navy, July 14
Vanwart, James W.	19	St John NB	S	Mar. 14, '64	'64: died Sept. 5
Waltz, Andrew J.	23	Oldtown	M	Mar. 14, '64	
Williams, George S.	38	Lagrange	M	Mar. 14, '64	'64: died of disease, July 12
Wilson, Alexander	19	Presque Isle	S	Dec. 21, '63	'64: deserted at Augusta, Feb. 13
Woodman, Richard M.	18	Oldtown	S	Mar. 14, '64	

Company H

Name	Age	Residence	MS	MD	Remarks
Commissioned Officers					
Mathews, Adolphus B.	29	Belfast	S	Dec. 18, '63	
Simpson, Daniel S.	36	Searsport	M	Dec. 18, '63	'64: acting quartermaster
Vose, Marcus A.	22	Montville	M	Dec. 18, '63	'65: promoted 1st Lt., Co. M
First Sergeant					
Barrows, Ronello A.*	21	Canton Falls	S	Dec. 18, '63	'65: promoted 2nd Lt.
* also listed as "Ronnellow"					
Q.M. Sergeant					
Keene, Thomas S.	38	Freedom	M	Dec. 18, '63	'65: promoted 1st Sgt.

Name	Age	Residence	MS	MD	Remarks
Com'y Sergeant					
Gould, John F.	30	Belfast	M	Dec. 18, '63	'65: promoted Q.M. Sgt.
Sergeants					
Mathews, William R.*	44	Lincolnville	M	Dec. 18, '63	'64: sick in Me; '65: disch. by order, Gen. Dix, July 1
Messer, Willard L.	34	Union	M	Dec. 18, '63	'64: reduced to ranks; det. hosp. nurse
Harris, Isaac B.	33	Appleton	M	Dec. 18, '63	'64: reduced to ranks
Osborne, George T.	26	Belfast	M	Dec. 18, '63	'64: sick in Maine; '65: promoted Com'y Sgt.
Lamson, Frank R.	23	Freedom	S	Dec. 18, '63	'64: died June 9, Thibodeaux

* Regimental Books, National Archives, lists Sergeant Mathews as reduced to the ranks on April 28, 1865.

Name	Age	Residence	MS	MD	Remarks
Corporals					
Hall, William F.	35	Lincolnville	M	Dec. 18, '63	'64: promoted Sgt.
West, George W.	21	Belfast	S	Dec. 18, '63	'64: reduced to ranks
Gilchrist, William	18	Montville	S	Dec. 18, '63	'64: died July 22, Augusta
Carter, Llewellyn	18	Belfast	S	Dec. 18, '63	'64: promoted Sgt.
Warren, Ansel H.	25	Brooks	M	Dec. 18, '63	'64: reduced to ranks
Logan, Thayer	19	Waldo	S	Dec. 18, '63	'65: promoted Sgt.
Ranlett George T.*	19	Unity	S	Dec. 18, '63	'64: trans. to navy, Aug. 1

* also listed as "Ranlet"

Name	Age	Residence	MS	MD	Remarks
Dickey, Reuben H.	32	Lincolnville	M	Dec. 18, '63	
Hussey, George F.	18	Lincolnville	S	Dec. 18, '63	'65: promoted Sgt.
Curtis, Freeman H.	21	Monroe	S	Dec. 18, '63	'65: sick in hosp.
Buglers					
Hovey, Urban H.*	25	Lincolnville	M	Dec. 18, '63	'64: det. as hosp. nurse

* listed as private in 1865.

Name	Age	Residence	MS	MD	Remarks
Rand, Erastus C.	24	Standish	M	Dec. 18, '63	'64: died July 9, Thibodeaux
Farriers					
Cross, David L.	33	Lincolnville	M	Dec. 18, '63	'64: reduced to ranks on account of sickness
Cummings, Otis	44	Northport	M	Dec. 18, '63	'64: sick in Maine; '65: disch. for disab., June 30
Saddler					
Weymouth, Alfred D.	29	Appleton	M	Dec. 18, '63	'65: died Barrancas, Nov. 17, '64
Woods, George G.	24	Freedom	S	Dec. 18, '63	'64: died June 20, Thibodeaux
Wagoner					
Vose, Charles S.	29	Montville	M	Dec. 18, '63	
Privates					
Austin, Reuel	18	Unity	S	Dec. 18, '63	'64: sick at Barrancas; '65: died at Barrancas, Nov. 12, '64
Benner, William O.	19	Northport	S	Dec. 18, '63	'64: died Oct. 8, N. Orleans
Billings, Edward	18	Searsport	S	Dec. 18, '63	'64: trans. to navy, Aug. 1
Black, Henry	23	Dedham	S	Dec. 18, '63	
Burns, Nelson A.	30	Union	M	Dec. 18, '63	

A. Roster

Name	Age	Residence	MS	MD	Remarks
Carr, Alden	18	Searsport*	S	Dec. 18, '63	'64: trans. to navy, Aug. 1
* in '63 listed from Frankfort					
Carter, Dana B.	20	Freedom	S	Dec. 18, '63	'64: died Sept. 26, Barrancas
Caswell, James E.	23	Lewiston	S	Jan. 2, '65	
Chambers, Jesse G.	19	Belfast	S	Dec. 18, '63	'64: sick at Barrancas
Cobb, James M.	18	Durham	S	Sept. 29, '64	'65: disch. Aug. 29, term exp.
Colson, Horace S.	21	Frankfort	S	Dec. 18, '63	'64: promoted Sgt.
Cousens, Nathan H.	30	Monroe	M	Dec. 18, '63	'64: died Aug. 19, Barrancas
Crockett, James S.	18	Winterport	S	Dec. 18, '63	
Cross, David L.	33	Lincolnville	M	Dec. 18, '63	'65: disch. by order, Jan. 19
Cunningham, Ellison	21	Waldo	S	Dec. 18, '63	'65: promoted Cpl.
Currier, Thomas W.	18	Searsport*	S	Dec. 18, '63	
* in '63 listed from Frankfort					
Curry, John	19	St Albans Vt	S	Dec. 10, '64	'65: dishon. disch. Sept. 10 by G.C.M.
Curtis, Freeman H.*	21	Monroe	S	Dec. 18, '63	'64: promoted Cpl.
* also listed as "Fruma"					
Curtis, Lyman	21	Frankfort	M	Dec. 18, '63	'64: promoted Cpl.
Day, Joseph	40	Union	M	Dec. 18, '63	'63: sick in hosp.; '64: died Aug. 18, Barrancas
Dunton, James A.	18	Lincolnville	S	Dec. 18, '63	'65: disch. by order, Sept. 18
Dyer, Alonzo D.*	18	Montville	S	Dec. 18, '63	
* listed as bugler in 1865					
Ellis, Daniel	28	Searsport	M	Dec. 30, '63	'64: missing in action at Marianna, Sept. 27
Elwell, Alonzo P.	18	Waldo	S	Dec. 18, '63	
Emerson, Ephraim L.	31	Searsport	M	Dec. 30, '63	'64: trans. to navy, Aug. 1
Fickett, James H. R.	18	Knox	S	Dec. 18, '63	
Foss, John C.	21	Brooks	S	Dec. 18, '63	
Foster, William G.	21	Freeman	S	Mar. 1, '64	'65: sick in hosp. since Sept. '64
Gibbs, Amos, Jr.	28	Brooks	M	Dec. 18, '63	
Gibbs, Charles	21	Brooks	S	Dec. 18, '63	'64: died July 3, Thibodeaux
Glidden, Samuel	31	Newfield	S	Sept. 15, '64	'65: disch. Aug. 29; term exp.
Gookins, William H.	18	Biddeford	S	Sept. 26, '64	'65: disch. Aug. 29; term exp.
Gowan, William J.	26	Sanford	S	Sept. 29, '64	'65: disch. Aug. 29; term exp.
Gray, Solomon J.	32	Ellsworth	M	Dec. 18, '63	'64: died July 29, N. Orleans
Hale, William A.	43	Lincolnville	M	Dec. 18, '63	'65: promoted Cpl.
Hanscom, Edward P.	33	Freedom	M	Dec. 18, '63	'64: died Aug. 11, N. Orleans
Hart, Byron A.	20	Belfast	S	Dec. 18, '63	'64: trans. to navy, Aug. 1
Haskell, William	22	Alfred	S	July 1, '63*	
* date seems unlikely; more likely July 1, '64					
Heal, Isaac	37	Searsmont	M	Dec. 18, '63	'64: died May 30, Thibodeaux
Howarth, Alexander	19	Harrison	S	Sept. 27, '64	
Hurd, Hartford E.	19	Lincolnville	S	Dec. 18, '63	'65: disch. for disab., May 12
Hussey, Albert O.	19	Lincolnville	S	Dec. 18, '63	
Hussey, George F.	18	Lincolnville	S	Dec. 18, '63	'64: promoted Cpl.
Jackson, Edwin	18	Waldo	S	Dec. 18, '63	
Jones, Oliver	18	Brooks	S	Dec. 18, '63	'64: sick at N. Orleans
Knichler, James	18	China	S	Dec. 18, '63	'64: died Sept. 18, Barrancas
Knowlton, Augustus	19	Swanville	S	Dec. 18, '63	'64: died July at N. Orleans
Ladd, Rufus B.	33	Cranberry Is	M	Mar. 4, '64	'64: died Oct. 8, N. Orleans
Marden, James E.	23	Waldo	S	Dec. 18, '63	

Name	Age	Residence	MS	MD	Remarks
Martin, Francis H.	26	Swanville*	S	Dec. 18, '64	'63: sick at home; (apparently returned to reg't by '64 report)
Martin, Horatio	23	Appleton	S	Dec. 18, '63	'63: sick in hosp.; '64: accid. wounded; absent; '65: disch. June 22 at Augusta, Me
Mathews, Peleg W.*	18	Lincolnville	S	Dec. 30, '63	
*listed as Mathews, Riley in 1865					
McAllister, Judson	18	Lincolnville	M	Dec. 18, '63	
McGrury, Frank	18	Houlton	S	Dec. 18, '63	'64: trans. to Co. A
Messer, Willard L.	34	Union	M	Dec. 18, '63	'65: disch. for dis, Aug. 17
*in '63 listed from Lincolnville					
Moody, Orrin	36	Saco	M	Oct. 4, '64	'65: disch. Oct. 3, term exp.
Moody, Wellington	45	Swanville*	M	Dec. 18, '63	'64: sick at Barrancas; '65: died at Barrancas, Nov. 10, '64
*in '63 listed from Lincolnville					
O'Connell, Henry	24	Harrison	—	Sept. 30, '64	
Orr, Samuel	18	Island Falls	S	Dec. 18, '63	'64: trans. to Co. A
Palmer, James M.	18	Monticello*	S	Dec. 18, '63	'64: sick at N. Orleans; '65: disch. by order, July 17, not accounted for on muster out roles
*in '63 listed from Montville					
Peabody, Sherburne	18	Searsport	S	Dec. 18, '63	
Philbrook, John E.	21	Frankfort	S	Dec. 18, '63	'63: sick at home (apparently returned to reg't by '64 report)
Poland, Alonzo	25	Montville	M	Dec. 18, '63	'64: det. as hosp. nurse
Poland, Sumner	21	Morrill	M	Dec. 18, '63	'65: disch. for disab., June 13
Porter, Charles E.	22	Lincolnville	S	Dec. 18, '63	'64: died Sept. 18, Barrancas
Porter, Marcellus B.	18	Montville	S	Dec. 18, '63	'64: died Oct. 5, N. Orleans
Proctor, Henry A. J.	19	Appleton	S	Dec. 18, '63	'64: died Nov. 5, Barrancas
Putnam, Lauriston	21	Searsport	M	Dec. 30, '63	'64: promoted Cpl.
Rand, Granville H.	19	Steep Falls	S	Dec. 18, '63	'64: died June 25, Thibodeaux
Ray, Benjamin A.	34	Knox	M	Dec. 18, '63	'64: appointed Farrier
Richards, Joel S.	38	Lincolnville	M	Dec. 18, '63	
Richards, Oscar	18	Lincolnville	M	Dec. 18, '63	'64: died Aug. 22, N. Orleans
Ricker, George E.	18	Acton	S	Dec. 15, '64	
Roberts, James E.	18	Waldo	S	Dec. 18, '63	'65: disch. Nov. 17
Roberts, Peter	18	China	S	Dec. 18, '63	'64: deserted Aug. 23 at Barrancas
Seekins, John H.	20	China	S	Dec. 18, '63	'65: disch. by order, Aug. 26
Smith, Charles J.B.	30	Portland	S	Sept. 28, '64	
Smith, Joshua V.	19	Bath	S	Dec. 12, '64	
Smith, Stephen S.	35	Belfast	M	Dec. 18, '63	'64: trans. to navy, Aug. 1
Snow, James O.	27	Lincolnville	M	Dec. 18, '63	'64: died Aug. 29, N. Orleans
Soper, George W.	21	Oldtown	S	Sept. 8, '64	'65: disch. Sept. 29, term exp.
Spinks, Charles	19	Belfast	S	Dec. 18, '63	'65: died at Barrancas, Jan. 21
Stone, George E.	20	Conway NH	S	Sept. 24, '64	
Tewksbury, Timothy	19	Belfast	S	Dec. 18, '63	'64: sick at Washington
Thompson, Charles H.	18	Searsport	S	Dec. 18, '63	'64: died Oct. 22, N. Orleans
Turpin, James	18	Bath	S	Dec. 10, '64	

Name	Age	Residence	MS	MD	Remarks
Vose, Wilbur F.*	24	Monticello	S	Dec. 18, '63	'64: promoted Cpl.
* also listed as "William" from Montville					
Walker, Benjamin R.	21	Searsport	M	Dec. 30, '63	
Walker, John M.	27	Freedom	M	Dec. 18, '63	
Warren, Ansel H.	25	Brooks	M	Dec. 18, '63	'65: disch. by order, July 6
Wentworth, George A.	19	Searsmont	S	Dec. 18, '63	'64: sick at N. Orleans; '65: died in hosp. in New York, Jan. 14, '64
West, Daniel J.	21	Belfast	S	Dec. 18, '63	'64: died Sept. 18, Barrancas
West, George W.	21	Belfast	S	Dec. 18, '63	'65: promoted Cpl.
West, Moses C.	44	Frankfort	M	Dec. 18, '63	'64: accid. wounded; disch. for disab., Aug. 17
Weymouth, Alfred D.	29	Appleton	M	Dec. 18, '63	'64: appointed saddler
Whitcomb, Frank	19	Searsport	S	Dec. 30, '63	
Whitmore, Franklin A.	18	Waldo	S	Dec. 18, '63	
Winship, Frederick	23	Dexter	S	Dec. 15, '64	
Wood, Earnest	28	Biddeford	S	Oct. 10, '64	'65: disch. Oct. 9; term exp.
Woodman, Jonathan	20	Oldtown	S	Aug. 18, '64	'65: disch. Aug. 29; term exp.
Woodman, Warren B.	18	Searsport	S	Dec. 18, '63	'64: promoted Cpl.
Young, Gideon A.	21	Lincolnville	S	Dec. 18, '63	
Young, John	21	Palermo	S	Dec. 18, '63	'64: died July 3, Thibodeaux

Company I

Name	Age	Residence	MS	MD	Remarks
Commissioned Officers					
Haskell, Isaac W.	37	Garland	S	Dec. 22, '63	'65: disch. by order, Feb. 10
Richmond, William L.	25	Winthrop	M	Dec. 22, '63	'65: promoted Capt.
Brann, Thomas A.	23	Gardiner	S	Dec. 22, '63	'64: promoted 1st Lt, Co. G
First Sergeant					
Libby, Nelson F.	24	Corinna	S	Dec. 22, '63	'65: promoted 1st Lt.
Q.M. Sergeant					
Ayer, Ellis W.	23	Gardiner	S	Dec. 22, '63	'64: promoted 2nd Lt; killed Sept. 27, Marianna
Brann, Alfred G.	23	W Gardiner	M	Dec. 22, '63	'65: promoted 2nd Lt.; disch. by order, Dec. 15
Com'y Sergeant					
Millett, John W.	20	Clinton	S	Dec. 22, '63	'65: promoted 1st Sgt.
Sergeants					
Brann, Alfred G.	23	W Gardiner	M	Dec. 22, '63	'64: promoted Q.M. Sgt.
Toothaker, Joel W.	28	Winthrop	M	Dec. 22, '63	'64: reduced to ranks; abs. sick
Bessee, Samuel D.	36	Winthrop	M	Dec. 22, '63	'64: reduced to ranks since died
Moore, Edwin F.	21	Unity	M	Dec. 22, '63	
Blackwell, Henry H.	23	Newport	M	Dec. 22, '63	
Litchfield, Lewis K.	32	Winthrop	M	Dec. 22, '63	'65: promoted Q.M. Sgt.
Knowles, Horatio	25	Corinna	M	Dec. 22, '63	'65: promoted Com'y Sgt.

Name	Age	Residence	MS	MD	Remarks
Corporals					
Quint, Nathan E.	25	Augusta	M	Dec. 22, '63	'64: promoted Sgt.
Jewett, George F.	20	Sangerville	S	Dec. 22, '63	'64: reduced to ranks; sick in Me
Towns, Edwin F.	23	Winthrop	S	Dec. 22, '63	'65: promoted Sgt.
Sabine, George W.*	24	Vassalboro	M	Dec. 22, '63	'64: sick in Me; '65: disch. by order, Aug. 11

*Regimental Books, National Archives, lists Corporal Sabine as "reduced to the ranks for long continued absence from his company" on January 7, 1865.

Houston, Charles F.	22	Richmond	S	Dec. 22, '63	'64: died Sept. 12, Barrancas
Litchfield, Lewis K.	32	Winthrop	M	Dec. 22, '63	'64: promoted Sgt.
Knowles, Horatio	25	Corinna	M	Dec. 22, '63	'64: promoted Sgt.
Dana, Stephen W.	25	Gardiner	M	Dec. 22, '63	'65: promoted Sgt.
Bishop, Riley*	22	Leeds	S	Mar. 25, '64	'65: abs. w/o leave since June 1

* Regimental Books, National Archives, lists Corporal Bishop as reduced to the ranks "for long continued absence without prospect of return."

Owen, Thomas J.*	20	Turner	S	Dec. 22, '63	'65: abs. w/o leave since June 1

* Regimental Books, National Archives, lists Corp Owen as reduced to the ranks "for long continued absence without prospect of return."

Whitney, Chester*	19	Gardiner	S	Dec. 22, '63	'64: promoted Cpl.; missing in action, Sept. 27

* Regimental Books, National Archives, lists Corporal Whitney as reduced to the ranks "for long continued absence without prospect of return."

Name	Age	Residence	MS	MD	Remarks
Buglers					
Atwood, James N.	25	Livermore*	M	Dec. 22, '63	
* in '63 listed from Vassalboro					
Harrington, Thomas E.	18	China	S	Dec. 22, '63	'64: trans. to Co. D
Farriers					
Haskell, Charles	44	Garland	M	Dec. 22, '63	'64: died Sept. 18, Barrancas
Jackman, Justus H.	38	Garland	M	Dec. 22, '63	
Saddler					
Emery, Jacob	32	China	M	Dec. 22, '63	'64: died Aug. 24 on board steamer *Merrimac*
Wagoner					
Haskell, Bennett A.	19	Garland	M	Dec. 22, '63	'64: sick at Barrancas; '65: died at Barrancas, Feb. 10
Privates					
Bartlett, Thomas J.	18	Wayne	S	Dec. 22, '63	'64: abs. sick in Maine
Batchelder, Alonzo F.	21	Garland	S	Dec. 22, '63	
Bessee, Edwin H.	18	Dover	S	Dec. 22, '63	'64: died July 20, N. Orleans
Bishop, Isaiah M.	18	Wayne	S	Dec. 22, '63	'65: died at N. Orleans, Nov. 2, '64
Bishop, Riley	22	Leeds	S	Mar. 25, '64	'64: promoted Cpl.
Bishop, Squire F.	20	Wayne	S	Dec. 22, '63	'65: promoted Cpl.
Bosworth, Daniel A.	23	Garland	S	Dec. 22, '63	
Boynton, Walter L.	23	Waterville	M	Mar. 29, '64	'64: trans. to navy, Aug. 1
Brown, Augustus A.	18	Dover	S	Dec. 22, '63	'64: sick in Maine; '65: died at Barrancas, May 18
Brown, Edward	21	Chelsea	S	Dec. 22, '63	'64: trans. to Co. F

A. Roster

Name	Age	Residence	MS	MD	Remarks
Brown, Gilman N.	18	Dover	S	Dec. 22, '63	'64: died May 29, N. Orleans
Bubier, Sewall M.	33	Dallas Plantation*	M	Dec. 22, '63	
* in '63 listed from Winthrop					
Bush, John O.	18	Foxcroft	S	Dec. 22, '63	'64: abs. without leave; '65: disch. by order, June 26
Cates, Solomon B.	25	Houlton	M	Dec. 22, '63	
Cole, George L.	20	Clinton	S	Dec. 22, '63	'64: disch. for disab. Aug. 11
Coughlin, James	21	Palmyra	S	Oct. 29, '64	
Crosby, Charles O.	20	W Gardiner	S	Dec. 22, '63	'64: died Aug. 12, N. Orleans
Cross, George W.	18	Gardiner	S	Dec. 22, '63	'65: promoted Cpl.
Daniels, Thomas M.	39	Winthrop	M	Dec. 22, '63	'65: disch. by order, Aug. 25
Dearborn, Moses S.	19	Pasonsfield	S	Oct. 13, '64	'65: disch. Oct. 13, term exp.
Dill, James R.	18	Gardiner	S	Dec. 22, '63	
Dill, Joseph C.	42	Gardiner	M	Dec. 22, '63	'64: promoted Cpl.
Dorse, Gowen	18	Anson	S	Mar. 23, '64	
Dudley, Augustus	18	Gardiner	S	Dec. 22, '63	'64: sick in Maine
Freeman, David P.	22	Winthrop	S	Mar. 25, '64	
Gee, James M.	26	Garland	S	Dec. 22, '63	'64: died Aug. 24, Barrancas
Gilbert, Emery	22	Litchfield	M	Dec. 8, '63	'64: trans. from Co. D
Gray, Charles F.	22	Litchfield*	S	Dec. 22, '63	
* in '63 listed from Gardiner					
Hammon, Apollos	25	Winthrop	M	Dec. 22, '63	'64: died Sept. 29, N. Orleans
Hanscomb, Charles O.	18	Biddeford	S	Sept. 29, '64	'65: disch. Sept. 28; term exp.
Hanson, Samuel	22	St Albans	S	Dec. 22, '63	'64: sick at Barrancas; '65: died at Barrancas, Nov. 17, '64
Harlow, Hosea	44	Garland	M	Dec. 22, '63	'64: died Oct. 5, Barrancas
Haskell, Jason F.	19	Garland	S	Dec. 22, '63	'64: abs. sick in Maine; '65: disch. by order, June 1
Holland, Charles	19	Westbrook	S	Oct. 20, '64	'65: deserted Aug. 20
House, William H.	22	Wayne	S	Dec. 22, '63	'64: sick in Maine
James, George W., Jr.	20	Pittston	S	Dec. 22, '63	
Jewett, George F.	20	Sangerville	S	Dec. 22, '63	'65: trans. to Co. F
Johnson, Eliphalet M.	30	Dexter	M	Dec. 22, '63	
Johonet, Fred W.	21	Newport	S	Dec. 22, '63	
Jones, Francis W.	19	Parkman	S	Dec. 22, '63	'64: sick in Maine; '65: abs. w/o leave since Oct. 1, '64
Kendall, Leroy S.	18	Biddeford	S	Oct. 19, '64	'65: disch. by order, Aug. 26
Knapp, Elijah	21	Wayne	S	Dec. 22, '63	'64: sick in Maine
Knight, Charles T.	21	Leeds*	S	Dec. 22, '63	'64: died Sept. 29, Barrancas
* in '63 listed from Gardiner					
Lampher, Orville	19	Dover	S	Dec. 22, '63	'64: promoted Farrier
Lawrence, Charles F.	21	Gardiner	S	Dec. 22, '63	'64: sick in Me; '65: disch. Nov. 10
Lindsay, Roscoe G.	31	Leeds	M	Mar. 25, '64	'64: died Sept. 8, Barrancas
Littlefield, Edwin R.	21	Sangerville	S	Dec. 22, '63	
McPeak, Edward	24	Houlton	S	Dec. 22, '63	'64: deserted on furlough, Mar. 18
Meader, Ansel L.	21	Gardiner	S	Dec. 22, '63	'65: died at Barrancas, Jan. 3
Meader, Clark D.	18	Gardiner	S	Dec. 22, '63	'64: trans. to Co. F
Merrill, Benjamin A.	41	Gardiner	M	Dec. 22, '63	'64: trans. to navy, Aug. 1
Millett, Eugene	18	Glenburn*	S	Dec. 22, '63	'64: died Aug. 24, Barrancas
* '63 lists from Clinton					

Name	Age	Residence	MS	MD	Remarks
Millett, Nelson * '63 lists from Clinton	18	Glenburn*	S	Dec. 22, '63	'64: disch. Sept. 25
Morrill, Matthew	21	Oxford	S	Dec. 22, '63	'65: promoted Cpl.
Murch, George W.	20	Unity	S	Dec. 22, '63	'64: sick in Maine; '65: abs. w/o leave since Dec. 1, '64
Nash, George W. * in '63 listed from Winthrop	19	W. Gardiner*	S	Dec. 22, '63	'64: sick in Maine
Owen, Thomas J.	20	Turner	S	Dec. 22, '63	'64: promoted Cpl.; sick in hosp.
Parris, William W.	20	Pittston	S	Dec. 22, '63	'65: taken prisoner, Dec. 18, '64; never returned to company
Peacock, Edward, Jr.	30	Gardiner	S	Dec. 22, '63	
Perry, Silas	38	Winthrop	M	Dec. 22, '63	'64: died July 24, Thibodeaux
Philbrick, Winfield S.	19	Winthrop	S	Dec. 22, '63	'65: promoted Cpl.; disch. by order, Sept. 18
Piche, Lewis	21	Biddeford	S	Oct. 18, '64	'65: disch. Oct. 17; term exp.
Pickett, Thomas	21	Biddeford	S	Oct. 18, '64	
Plummer, Frank	26	Saco	M	Oct. 18, '64	'65: disch. Nov. 2; term exp.
Reynolds, Joseph E.	19	Unity	S	Dec. 22, '63	'64: sick in Maine; '65: disch. by order, May 20
Reynolds, Lemuel	18	Unity	S	Dec. 22, '63	'64: died Sept. 8, Barrancas
Richardson, Thomas A.	18	Pittston	S	Dec. 22, '63	'64: trans. to Co. M
Rolf, Joseph F.	19	Clinton	S	Dec. 22, '63	'64: sick in Maine; '65: disch. by order, May 20, by order Gen'l Dix
Seavey, Enoch	26	Biddeford	M	Oct. 19, '64	'65: disch. Oct. 13; term exp.
Seavey, Fred H.	18	Unity	S	Dec. 22, '63	'64: died Aug. 31, Barrancas
Seavey, Oren	22	Saco	S	Oct. 4, '64	'65: disch. Oct. 3; term exp.
Siphers, Nathaniel L.	18	New Sharon	S	Dec. 22, '63	'64: died July 9, Thibodeaux
Smith, Benjamin B.	44	Houlton	M	Dec. 22, '63	'64: detailed in hosp.; '65: disch. by order, June 13
Smith, Charles G.	18	New Sharon	S	Dec. 22, '63	'64: trans. to Co. F; '65: disch. by order, July 6
Smith, Cornelius F.	19	New Sharon	S	Dec. 22, '63	'64: detached as orderly at HQ
Smith, Eugene A.	19	Gardiner	S	Dec. 22, '63	'64: died Aug. 22, N. Orleans
Smith, James	27	Corinna	S	Dec. 22, '63	
Smith, John	41	Dexter	M	Dec. 22, '63	'64: died Aug. 8, N. Orleans
Spaulding, Albion	20	Clinton	S	Dec. 22, '63	'64: detailed in pioneer corps
Speed, Horace G.	22	Biddeford	M	Sept. 29, '64	'65: serving sentence of Gen. Ct. Mar.
Spencer, Walter	19	Dover	S	Dec. 22, '63	'64: promoted saddler
Stewart, Samuel	20	Palmyra	S	Dec. 22, '63	'64: promoted Cpl.; died Oct. 15, N. Orleans
Stowell, Charles K.	21	Brownville	S	Dec. 22, '63	'64: died Aug. 18, N. Orleans
Swift, Charles L.	21	Gardiner	S	Dec. 22, '63	'65: promoted Cpl.
Tarbox, Alonzo S.	20	Bath	S	Nov. 12, '64	'65: disch. Nov. 2; term exp.
Tate, Richard	29	Palmyra	S	Oct. 31, '64	'65: disch. Oct. 17; term exp.
Thomas, Frederick P.	21	Garland	S	Oct. 31, '64	'64: sick in Maine
Thurston, Stephen A.	22	Winthrop	S	Oct. 31, '64	'65: promoted Cpl.; disch. by order, Sept. 18

A. Roster

Name	Age	Residence	MS	MD	Remarks
Toothaker, Joel W.	28	Winthrop	M	Oct. 31, '64	'65: disch. by order, May 18; '65: left sick in Maine Feb, '64; never joined company
Towle, Jesse	23	Biddeford	—	Oct. 19, '64	'65: disch. Oct. 13; term exp.
True, Dexter W.	23	Turner	S	Oct. 31, '64	'65: promoted Cpl. and Sgt.
Turner, Emerson, Jr.	25	Gardiner	M	Dec. 22, '63	'64: deserted Mar. 5; retaken and returned to 7th Regiment; '65: arrested and deserted June 16
Wadleigh, Charles R.	18	Saco	S	Oct. 8, '64	'65: disch. Oct. 7; term exp.
Whitmore, James H.	18	Dover	S	Dec. 22, '63	'64: died Sept. 3, Barrancas
Whitney, Chester	19	Gardiner	S	Dec. 22, '63	'64: promoted Cpl.; missing in action, Sept. 27; dropped from rolls
Whitney, Thomas B.	27	Gardiner	M	Dec. 22, '63	'65: abs. sick; sent to northern hosp.
Whitten, William H.	26	Unity	M	Dec. 22, '63	'65: promoted Cpl.
Williams, George W.	22	Winthrop	M	Dec. 22, '63	'64: missing in action Sept. 27; dropped from rolls
Williams, Harry	22	Biddeford	S	Oct. 19, '64	'65: appointed bugler; '65: disch. by order, Sept. 18
Wing, Thomas L.	19	Winthrop	S	Dec. 22, '63	'64: sick in Maine; '65: disch. Mar. 11, by order Gen. Dix
Wing, Hubbard R.	21	Winthrop	S	Dec. 22, '63	'64: died Sept. 1, Winthrop, Me
Wing, Llewellyn T.	20	Wayne	S	Mar. 26, '64	
Young, Amaziah	38	Winthrop	M	Dec. 22, '63	'64: died Aug. 14, Barrancas
Young, Henry	18	Clinton	S	Dec. 22, '63	'63: died in hosp., Jan. 14

Company K

Name	Age	Residence	MS	MD	Remarks
Commissioned Officers					
French, Moses	42	Solon	M	Dec. 24, '63	'63: absent; '64: absent (apparently rejoined reg't in '65)
Holbrook, Samuel	29	St Albans	S	Dec. 24, '63	
Emery, Abner C.	30	Skowhegan	M	Dec. 24, '63	'65: disch. by order July 18
First Sergeant					
Snell, Ora M.	23	St Albans	S	Dec. 24, '63	
Q.M. Sergeant					
Smith, George R.	23	Solon	S	Dec. 24, '63	'65: disch. by order May 22
Com'y Sergeant					
Wyman, John E.	24	Skowhegan	M	Dec. 24, '63	'64: reduced to ranks
Sergeants					
Dunlap, William L.	25	Starks	S	Dec. 24, '63	'65: died Tallahassee, Fla, Oct. 29
Snell, Eben M.	44	St Albans	M	Dec. 24, '63	'64: died Oct. 8
Strout, Albion S.	21	Parkman	S	Dec. 24, '63	

Name	Age	Residence	MS	MD	Remarks
Smart, Edward J.	22	Plymouth	S	Dec. 24, '63	'64: promoted Com'y Sgt.
Taylor, Adoniram J.	28	Nor'idgewok	S	Dec. 24, '63	'64: died Aug. 9
Moore, William J.	19	Steuben	S	Dec. 24, '63	'65: promoted Q.M. Sgt.

Corporals

Name	Age	Residence	MS	MD	Remarks
Maguire, Daniel	40	N Portland	M	Dec. 24, '63	'64: reduced to ranks; died Sept. 19
Quimby, Reuben F.	31	Starks	M	Dec. 24, '63	'64: promoted Sgt.
Chapman, Francis P.*	19	Mercer	S	Dec. 24, '63	'64: promoted Sgt.

  * also listed as "Francis B."

Name	Age	Residence	MS	MD	Remarks
Barbeau, Charles R.	18	Skowhegan	S	Dec. 24, '63	'65: died at home Nov. 25, '64
Moore, William J.	19	Steuben	S	Dec. 24, '63	'64: promoted Sgt.
Fuller, William L.*	19	N Portland	S	Dec. 24, '63	'65: promoted Sgt.

  * Regimental Books, National Archives, lists Corporal Fuller as promoted to sergeant "for uniform good conduct" on July 6, 1865.

Name	Age	Residence	MS	MD	Remarks
Annis, Joseph	26	Hartland	M	Dec. 24, '63	'64: reduced to ranks at his own request
Church, David C.	30	Canaan		Dec. 30, '63	
Quint, Orlando	23	N Portland	M	Dec. 31, '63	'65: disch. by order June 13

Buglers

Name	Age	Residence	MS	MD	Remarks
Priest, Henry W.	21	Skowhegan	S	Dec. 24, '63	'64: died Sept. 22
Varney, George C.	18	Skowhegan	S	Dec. 24, '63	

Farriers

Name	Age	Residence	MS	MD	Remarks
Haines, Charles L.	43	Plymouth	M	Dec. 31, '63	'64: disch. for disab. Oct. 8
Varney, George	44	Skowhegan	M	Dec. 24, '63	

Saddler

Name	Age	Residence	MS	MD	Remarks
Irish, Oliver W.	42	Harmony	M	Dec. 24, '63	

Wagoner

Name	Age	Residence	MS	MD	Remarks
York, Charles E.	28	Skowhegan	M	Dec. 24, '63	

Privates

Name	Age	Residence	MS	MD	Remarks
Annis, Joseph	26	Hartland	M	Dec. 24, '63	'65: disch. by order Dec. 20
Annis, Morrill	28	Hartland	S	Dec. 24, '63	'63: reduced from Cpl. at own request; '65: disch. by order Aug. 25
Athearn, George	18	Starks	S	Dec. 24, '63	'65: disch. by order Sept. 18
Barnes, Charles	18	Canaan	S	Dec. 24, '63	
Barton, Sewell J.*	24	Harmony	M	Dec. 24, '63	

  * in '65 listed as "Baston, Sewell"

Name	Age	Residence	MS	MD	Remarks
Beales, George M.	20	Canaan	S	Dec. 24, '63	'64: trans. to Co. M
Beckwith, Whitefield	18	Starks	S	Dec. 24, '63	'64: died July 13
Booker, Joseph M.	23	Canaan	M	Dec. 24, '63	
Blake, Wilson	19	Brooksville	S	Dec. 24, '63	'64: trans. to navy, July 15
Bragdon, Oliver W.	34	Eastbrook	M	Dec. 24, '63	'65: disch. for disab. June 1
Brawn, John	40	Palermo	M	Dec. 24, '63	'64: died Oct. 23
Brown, Phillips	39	Harmony	M	Dec. 24, '63	
Campbell, Warren W.	19	Anson	S	Dec. 24, '63	'64: deserted at Augusta, Me; '65: deserted Mar. 2, '64
Casey, Joseph L.*	21	Milton Plantation	S	Dec. 24, '63	'64: died Oct. 3

  * also listed as "Joseph K." Regimental Books, National Archives lists Joseph L. Casey as promoted to corporal to date from July 15, 1864.

Name	Age	Residence	MS	MD	Remarks
Child, George B.	22	Sumner	S	Dec. 24, '63	'65: disch. for disab. June 25
Cleaveland, George S. P.	18	Skowhegan	S	Dec. 24, '63	
Clukey, Joseph	18	Skowhegan	S	Dec. 24, '63	
Cone, Isaac	43	Skowhegan	M	Dec. 24, '63	'63: reduced from blacksmith at own request; '64: died June 9
Cookson, John C.	18	Harmony	S	Dec. 24, '63	'64: promoted Cpl.
Cowan, Benjamin	27	N Portland	M	Dec. 24, '63	'63: reduced from Sgt.
Davis, Oliver W.	30	Steuben	M	Dec. 24, '63	'65: disch. by order Aug. 26
Dunn, Daniel D.	21	Livermore	S	Dec. 24, '63	
Farrin, Frank	18	N Portland	S	Dec. 24, '63	'65: disch. by order Nov. 10
Field, William B.	18	St Albans	S	Dec. 24, '63	'64: died July 29
Fish, Reuel W.	18	Skowhegan	S	Dec. 31, '63	'64: died Aug. 31
French, Hovey	21	Canaan	S	Dec. 31, '63	
Gerough, George	23	Skowhegan	M	Dec. 24, '63	
Getchell, Ezra	20	N Portland	S	Dec. 30, '63	
Grant, Charles H.	19	St Albans	M	Dec. 24, '63	'64: promoted Cpl.
Gray, Otis	18	Brooksville	M	Dec. 24, '63	'64: trans. to navy, July 15
Gray, Thomas	18	Brooksville	S	Dec. 24, '63	'64: trans. to navy, July 15
Hackett, Edward	24	Castine	S	Dec. 24, '63	'64: promoted Cpl.; died Sept. 28
Hackett, Joseph	22	Castine	M	Dec. 24, '63	
Hanson, Andrew G.	18	St Albans	S	Dec. 24, '63	'64: died Oct. 9
Hardin, Marcellus A.	22	Unity	S	Dec. 24, '63	'65: disch. by order Sept. 25
Heald, Orrin W.	22	Anson	S	Feb. 22, '64	
Hill, Robert	29	Hodgdon	S	Dec. 24, '63	
Holbrook, Thomas F.	26	Starks	M	Dec. 24, '63	'64: promoted Cpl.
Holmsted, Augustus	24	Skowhegan	—	Oct. 24, '64	
Holt, James H.	18	Canaan	S	Dec. 31, '63	
Huff, Daniel	18	Athens	S	Dec. 24, '63	
Hurd, Harvey R.	18	Harmony	S	Dec. 24, '63	'65: died Chattahoochee, Nov. 7
Hutchins, Orlando G.	19	N Portland	S	Dec. 24, '63	'64: promoted musician
Jewett, Orrin W.	20	Sknowhegan	S	Dec. 24, '63	'63: reduced from Cpl. at own request
Jones, Clarkson	21	Nor'idgew'ck	S	Dec. 24, '63	'64: died Sept. 22
Jones, Eben	30	N Portland	M	Dec. 24, '63	'65: disch. by order Aug. 28
Jones, John O.	18	West Bath	S	Mar. 10	
Jordan, Edwin K.	23	Brighton	S	Dec. 24, '63	'64: died Aug. 18
Judkins, Asa	19	St Albans	S	Dec. 24, '63	
Lane, Alvin D.	19	Anson	S	Dec. 24, '63	'65: disch. by order Sept. 18
Lee, Thomas W.	38	Masardis	M	Dec. 24, '63	'64: died Oct. 28
Leighton, Edward	36	Steuben	S	Dec. 24, '63	'64: trans. to navy, July 15
Luce, Franklin B.	24	Hartland	M	Dec. 24, '63	
Marsh, Henry A.	23	Skowhegan	S	Dec. 24, '63	
Merrill, Hiram G.	19	Milton Plnt'n	S	Dec. 24, '63	
Merrill, John F.	18	Solon	S	Dec. 24, '63	'65: disch. by order Aug. 19
Moore, Alonzo D.*	39	Castine	M	Dec. 24, '63	'64: trans. to navy, July 15
* also listed as "Moores"					
Moore, Henry D.	21	Steuben	S	Dec. 30, '63	'65: promoted Cpl.
Morang, Sanford	28	Steuben	S	Dec. 24, '63	
Page, Edwin V.	18	Sumner	S	Dec. 24, '63	'64: died Oct. 17
Pashor, Albert	23	Hartland	M	Dec. 24, '63	'64: died at N. Orleans
Perkins, Jacob	18	Harmony	S	Dec. 24, '63	'65: disch. by order Oct. 9

Name	Age	Residence	MS	MD	Remarks
Perkins, John H.	18	Harmony	S	Dec. 24, '63	'65: disch. by order Aug. 28
Phelan, Joseph H.	41	Hartland	M	Dec. 24, '63	
Priest, James A.	20	Canaan	M	Dec. 24, '63	'63: deserted, Jan. 23, '64
Quint, Orlando	23	N Portland	M	Dec. 30, '63	'64: promoted Cpl.
Sevano, Frank A., Jr.	18	Skowhegan	S	Dec. 24, '63	
Savage, Norris*	36	N Portland	M	Dec. 24, '63	'64: appointed farrier
*also listed as "Morris"					
Smart, William H.	18	St Albans	S	Dec. 24, '63	'64: died Sept. 22
Snell, Franklin A.	18	St Albans	S	Dec. 24, '63	'64: promoted Cpl.
Snell, Samuel S.	19	St Albans	S	Dec. 24, '63	'64: died Sept. 29
Soule, Abram L.*	40	Hartland	M	Dec. 24, '63	'65: disch. for disab. May 20
*also listed as "Soul"					
Spofford, Edson G.	19	Milton Plantation	S	Feb. 13, '64	'65: promoted Cpl.
Stevens, Everett	18	Steuben	S	Dec. 24, '63	
Stevens, Thomas W.*	18	Steuben	S	Dec. 24, '63	
*in '65 listed as "Stevans, Thomas"					
Warren, John W.	38	Cornville	M	Jan. 2, '64	'64: trans. from Co. M; '65: died at Barrancas, Fla., Dec. 5, '64
Waterman, Franklin	18	Anson	S	Dec. 24, '63	'65: sick in hosp., Augusta, Me
Wescott, Daniel M.	32	Windham	M	Sept. 30, '64	'65: disch. by order Sept. 15
White, John	19	St Albans	S	Dec. 24, '63	'65: disch. by order Aug. 28
Wilber, James F.	20	N Portland	M	Dec. 24, '63	
Williams, Allen	24	Harmony	M	Dec. 24, '63	'65: promoted Cpl.
Williamson, Mason	32	Starks	S	Dec. 24, '63	'65: disch. by order July 17
Wilson, John L.	18	Solon	S	Dec. 24, '63	
Winslow, Ezra, Jr.	26	N Portland	S	Dec. 24, '63	'64: sick in Me; '65: disch. for disab. Mar. 1
Wyman, John E.	23	Skowhegan	M	Dec. 24, '63	'65: disch. for disab. Aug. 21, not accounted for on muster out rolls
Young, Edwin F.	20	Palermo	S	Dec. 24, '63	'64: died July 11

Company L

Name	Age	Residence	MS	MD	Remarks
Commissioned Officers					
Libby, Samuel H.	23	Limerick	S	Dec. 24, '63	
Woodman, Andrew J.	34	Saco	M	Dec. 24, '63	
Moody, William H.	27	Kennebunk	M	Dec. 24, '63	'64: wounded at Marianna, Sept. 27
First Sergeant					
Daggett, Charles B.	21	Farmington	S	Dec. 24, '63	'64: deserted at Greenville, La, May 25
Clark, Elisha E.	19	Limerick	S	Dec. 24, '63	'65: paroled prisoner; disch. by order, July 31
Q.M. Sergeant					
Daggett, Samuel	18	New Sharon	S	Dec. 24, '63	'64: reduced to Com'y Sgt.

Name	Age	Residence	MS	MD	Remarks
Com'y Sergeant					
Staples, William M.	28	Lyman	M	Dec. 24, '63	'64: promoted Q.M. Sgt.; '65: promoted 1st Sgt.
Sergeants					
Clark, Elisha E.	19	Limerick	S	Dec. 24, '63	'64: promoted 1st Sgt.; wounded Sept. 27 and prisoner
Moody, James E.*	24	Kennebunk	S	Dec. 24, '63	

* Regimental Books National Archives list Moody as "reduced to ranks," July 1864.

Sampson, Moses T.	28	Biddeford	M	Dec. 24, '63	'65: disch. by order Aug. 28
Hammatt, Abram	19	Howland	S	Dec. 24, '63	'65: promoted Q.M. Sgt.
Field, George E.	22	Lee	S	Dec. 24, '63	'65: disch. by order Aug. 26
Ham, Orrin F.	35	Saco	M	Dec. 24, '63	'65: died in hosp. Aug. 25, '64
Corporals					
McKenney, Charles F.	21	Limington	S	Dec. 24, '63	
Oakes, George W.	20	Kennebunk	S	Dec. 24, '63	
Holt, Frank H.	18	New Sharon	S	Dec. 24, '63	'64: abs. sick; '65: disch. by order Sept. 25
McCullock, Adam*	33	Kennebunk	S	Dec. 24, '63	'64: trans. to navy, Aug. 1

* also listed as "McCulluck" and in Regimental Books is listed as reduced to ranks in February 1864 for drunkenness on duty.

Wakefield, George W.	28	Kennebunk	M	Dec. 24, '63	'64: promoted Sgt.
Ham, Orrin F.	35	Saco	M	Dec. 24, '63	'64: promoted Sgt.
Davis, Thomas A.	21	Whitefield	S	Dec. 24, '63	'64: killed in battle at Marianna, Sept. 27
Manson, Edwin R.	18	Limerick	S	Dec. 24, '63	
Buglers					
Leavitt, James M.	41	Shapleigh	M	Dec. 24' 63	'64: died in hosp. Nov. 5
York, Charles E.	20	Biddeford	S	Jan. 4, '64	'64: trans. to band
Farriers					
Ames, Enoch J.	42	Exeter	M	Dec. 24, '63	
Joy, Hosea J.	27	Ellsworth	M	Dec. 24, '63	
Saddler					
Baston, Nathan P.	22	Bridgton	S	Dec. 24, '63	'63: reduced from Cpl.; '65: disch. Aug. 7, Augusta, Me
Wagoner					
Garland, Elbra	24	Kennebunk	M	Dec. 24, '63	
Privates					
Allen, Joseph C.	20	N Vineyard	S	Dec. 24, '63	'65: died in hosp., June 18
Allen, Thomas R.*	26	N Vineyard	M	Dec. 24, '63	

* also listed as "Thomas K"

Ames, Fred N.	19	Bangor	S	Mar. 25, '64	
Babb, Samuel C.	28	Buxton	S	Jan. 7, '64	
Bailey, Solomon H. C.	36	Windham	M	Dec. 24, '63	
Blanchard, Alonzo	38	Houlton	M	Dec. 24, '63	'65: disch. by order Dec. 20
Bolton, James K.	19	Portland	S	Dec. 24, '63	'64: died in hosp., Sept. 25
Bond, Lusius H.	22	Monhegan	S	Dec. 24, '63	

Name	Age	Residence	MS	MD	Remarks
Brown, James H.	18	Alfred	S	Dec. 30, '63	'64: trans. to navy, Aug. 1
Cahoon, Lawrence	35	Buxton	S	Dec. 24, '63	
Caulfield, Joseph H.	34	Houlton	S	Dec. 24, '63	
Chute, George C.	18	Jay	S	Dec. 24, '63	
Cleaves, William	35	Kennebunk	M	Dec. 24, '63	
Clement, John H.	22	Berwick	S	Dec. 24, '63	
Clough, Charles H. (1st)	23	Parsonsfield	M	Dec. 24, '63	'65: died in hosp., June 21
Clough, Charles H. (2d)	21	Biddeford	S	Jan. 14, '64	'64: wounded at battle of Marianna, Sept. 27 and prisoner '65: abs. with leave since Sept. 27
Clough, William A.	21	Parsonsfield	S	Dec. 24, '63	
Cobb, Charles	26	Limerick	S	Jan. 7, '64	'65: abs. on furlough since Oct. 1
Cobb, Freeman A.	19	Kennebunk	S	Dec. 24, '63	'64: abs. sick
Conner, John	20	Limerick	S	Jan. 7, '64	
Cook, George O.	18	Kennebunk	S	Dec. 24, '63	
Cook, Joseph	28	Shapleigh	M	Dec. 24, '63	'64: sick in Augusta; not joined Company; '65: never left state; disch. May 11, by order Gen. Dix
Cookson, Charles F.	27	New Sharon	M	Dec. 24, '63	'65: abs. on furlough since Oct. 1
Cromwell, Thomas W.	44	Wiscasset	M	Dec. 24, '63	'64: trans. to navy, Aug. 1
Crowley, Thomas H.	18	Wiscasset	S	Dec. 24, '63	'64: abs. sick; '65: died in hosp., N. Orleans, Feb.
Daggett, Charles B.	21	Farmington	S	Dec. 24, '63	'65: deserted May 25, '64; dishon. disch. May 13; returned from desertion under president's proclamation
Davis, Edgar B.	26	Belfast	S	Jan. 7, '64	'65: disch. by order Aug. 14
Dewitt, Jerome S.	18	Windham	S	Dec. 24, '63	'64: abs. sick; '65: disch. by order June 13
Donley, Daniel	18	Bath	S	Dec. 24, '63	'64: trans. to navy, Aug. 1
Durgin, Almon C.	28	Biddeford	M	Dec. 30, '63	'64: promoted Cpl.
Emerson, John H.	33	Howland	S	Dec. 24, '63	
Evans, Joseph	33	Lyman	M	Dec. 24, '63	'65: disch. by order Sept. 18
Evans, Orrin R.	21	Lyman	M	Dec. 24, '63	'64: wounded at Marianna Sept. 27, taken prisoner; '65: paroled prisoner; disch. July 17
Flint, George H.	18	New Sharon	S	Dec. 24, '63	'64: abs. sick; '65: disch. by order July 7; not accounted for in muster out rolls
Gibbs, Charles H.	19	Berwick	S	Dec. 31, '63	'65: disch. by order June 3
Gould, Noah E.	20	N Vineyard	S	Dec. 24, '63	
Greenlief, John E.	19	N Vineyard	S	Dec. 24, '63	
Hammatt, Walter P.	22	Howland	S	Dec. 24, '63	'64: promoted Cpl.
Hanscomb, John W.	33	Kennebunk	M	Dec. 24, '63	'64: trans. to navy, Aug. 1
Haynes, Samuel T.	24	Howland	S	Dec. 24, '63	'65: died N. Orleans, May 17
Herrin, Stephen R.	21	Biddeford	M	Jan. 7, '64	'64: promoted Cpl.
Hills, Benjamin B.	42	Warren	M	Dec. 24, '63	

Name	Age	Residence	MS	MD	Remarks
Hunt, Christopher C.	26	Windham	M	Oct. 17, '64	'64: disch. Oct. 16, term exp.
Jewell, Benjamin F.	30	Baldwin	M	Dec. 24, '63	'64: deserted at Augusta, Apr. 8
Jordan, Michael	35	Bath	M	Dec. 24, '63	'64: trans. to Co. B
Kimball, Joseph	29	Kennebunk	M	Dec. 24, '63	
Kingsbury, John H.	28	Wiscasset	S	Dec. 24, '63	'64: died in hosp., Oct. 27
Knowles, Thomas H.	23	Biddeford*	S	Jan. 7, '64	'64: appointed bugler
* in '63 listed from Effingham, NH					
Ladd, John D.	26	Saco	S	Oct. 1, '64	'65: disch. Sept. 30, term exp.
Leeman, Charles W.	21	New Sharon	M	Dec. 31, '63	
Lewis, Woodward	18	N Vineyard	S	Dec. 24, '63	'64: abs. sick
Libby, Lorenzo D.	33	New Sharon	M	Dec. 24, '63	'64: trans. to Co. A
Lord, Edward	23	Parsonsfield	S	Dec. 24, '63	
Lowell, William H.	23	Burlington	S	Dec. 24, '63	'65: disch. for disab. Nov. 28
Lunt, Frederick D.	19	Biddeford	M	Sept. 26, '64	'65: disch. Sept. 25, term exp.
McCauslend, Moses B.	26	Farmingdale	M	Dec. 24, '63	
Mears, John	34	Chesterville	M	Dec. 24, '63	'64: left sick in Augusta; not joined company
Moulton, Alonzo P.	21	Parsonsfield	S	Oct. 5, '64	'65: disch. Oct. 4, term exp.
Murphy, John	21	Kittery*	S	Jan. 7, '64	
* in '63 listed from Washington					
Newbit, Andrew	35	Belfast*	M	Dec. 24, '63	'65: died in hosp. Nov. 15, '64
* in '63 listed from Belmont					
Nutt, James W.	35	Dexter	M	Dec. 24, '63	
Palmer, James W.	20	Hollis	S	Dec. 24, '63	
Peavey, Chandler	26	Lyman	M	Dec. 24, '63	'64: trans. to navy, Aug. 1
Pinkham, Charles E.	18	Washington	S	Dec. 24, '63	'63: deserted Jan. 5 (apparently rejoined reg't —mistake?); '65: sick in hosp.
Pratt, John	20	N Vineyard	S	Dec. 24, '63	'64: promoted Cpl.
Redman, Justus F.	18	Biddeford	S	Sept. 26, '64	'65: disch. Sept. 26, term exp.
Rhines, John E.	19	Washington	S	Dec. 24, '63	'65: disch. by order Sept. 18
Robinson, John	31	Appleton	M	Dec. 24, '63	'64: died in hosp., Sept. 25
Sanborn, Andrew F.	18	Standish*	S	Dec. 30, '63	'64: trans. to band
* in '63 listed from Steep Falls					
Seekins, David E.	20	Swanville	M	Dec. 24, '63	'64: abs. sick
Seekins, Nathan T.	18	Swanville	M	Dec. 24, '63	'65: died in hosp. Mar. 8
Smith, James C.	18	Limerick	S	Jan. 4, '64	'64: abs. sick; '65: disch. by order July 15 by order Gen. Canby
Southard, Cyrus	41	Waterville	M	Jan. 7, '64	'65: trans. to navy
Stetson, Alfred	35	Houlton	M	Dec. 24, '63	'64: deserted at Augusta, Mar. 18
Stone, Lewis G.	25	Parsonsfield	S	Dec. 24, '63	
Stuart, Andrew	30	Kittery*	S	Dec. 30, '63	'65: disch. by order Dec. 22
* in '63 listed from Lowell, Mass					
Sukeforth, Charles A.	19	Appleton	S	Dec. 24, '63	'64: abs. sick; '65: died in hosp. July 25, '64
Swazey, William E.	22	Biddeford	S	Jan. 7, '64	
Swett, David N.	22	Montville	S	Sept. 27, '64	'65: disch. Sept. 26, term exp.
Taylor, Horace	21	Kennebunk	S	Dec. 24, '63	
Teague, John M.	18	New Sharon	S	Dec. 24, '63	'64: left sick in Augusta, not joined company

Name	Age	Residence	MS	MD	Remarks
Thomas, Silas C.	31	Camden	M	Jan. 7, '64	'64: trans. from Co. M; '65: disch. by order Aug. 26
Watson, Lorenzo D.	18	Limerick	S	Dec. 24, '63	'64: disch. by order June 13
Wentworth, Israel S.	18	Waterboro	S	Dec. 24, '63	'64: abs. sick; '65: lost from transport *North America* in Feb.
Wentworth, William H.	22	Berwick	S	Dec. 24, '63	'64: trans. to navy, Aug. 6
Wescott, Charles E.	19	Brooksville	S	Dec. 24, '63	
Whiting, Frederick D.	18	Whitefield	S	Dec. 24, '63	
Willey, Daniel E.	26	Lebanon*	M	Dec. 24, '63	
*in '63 listed from Conway, NH					
York, Charles E.	20	Biddeford	S	Jan. 4, '64	'65: had been listed as bugler

Company M

Name	Age	Residence	MS	MD	Remarks
Commissioned Officers					
Roberts, John H.	32	Alfred	M	Jan. 2, '64	'63: trans. from 8th Me; '65: resig. and disch.
Allen, Ivory R.	24	Waterboro	S	Jan. 23, '64	'63 promoted from 1st Me Cav.; '64: A.A.A. Gen. 4th Cav. Brig.; '65: promoted Capt.
Adams, Isaac R.	34	Wilton	M	Jan. 23, '64	'63: promoted from 1st Sgt.; '64: wounded at Marianna and prisoner; '65: died of wounds, Oct. 13, '64
Small, Emilus N. D.	22	Farmingdale	—	—	'65: joined as 2nd Lt. from N.C. 8 (had been RSM)
Vose, Marcus A.	22	Montville	M	Dec. 18, '63	'65: joined as 1st Lt. from Co. H
First Sergeant					
Moors, Albert, Jr.	23	Linneus	S	Jan. 2, '64	'64: died of sun stroke Sept. 2 at Barrancas
Q.M. Sergeant					
O'Brien, Owen St. C.	30	Houlton	S	Jan. 2, '64	'64: promoted Hosp. Stew'd
Waid, William J.	22	Houlton	S	Jan. 2, '64	'65: died in hosp., Nov. 6, '64
Com'y Sergeant					
William J. Waid	22	Houlton	S	Jan. 2, '64	'64: promoted Q.M. Sgt.
Sergeants					
Starbird, Frederick W.	21	Portland	M	Jan. 2, '64	'64: died Sept. 28, Barrancas
Bradbury, Benjamin M.	22	Auburn	S	Jan. 2, '64	'64: reduced to ranks; died Oct. 25, Barrancas
Chapman, Charles D.	33	Passadumkeag	M	Jan. 2, '64	'64: promoted Com'y Sgt.
Smith, Henry H.	25	Freeman	S	Jan. 2, '64	'65: promoted Q.M. Sgt.
Cushman, Edward A.	21	Sumner	M	Jan. 2, '64	'65: disch. for disab. July 25
Adams, Joshua R.	29	Wilton	M	Jan. 5, '64	'65: sick in hosp. since June 1
Phinney, John C.	25	Stockton	S	Mar. 4, '64	'65: disch. for disab. July 1
Crowell, Charles S.	20	Vassalboro	S	Jan. 5, '64	'64: reduced to ranks

Name	Age	Residence	MS	MD	Remarks
Corporals					
Withey, Arthur I.*	26	Eustis Plnt.	M	Jan. 2, '64	'64: promoted Sgt.; reduced to ranks; abs. sick

* Regimental Books, National Archives, list Arthur Withey as promoted back to sergeant on August 5, 1865, but on August 30 was facing a court martial, and on September 2 was reduced to corporal "in accordance with a sentence of Field Officers Court." However, "suspended" is written over the order for his reduction to corporal.

Name	Age	Residence	MS	MD	Remarks
Doble, Samuel W.	18	Dixfield	S	Jan. 2, '64	
Pettingill, Benjamin F.	18	Augusta	S	Jan. 2, '64	'65: promoted Sgt.
Ingersoll, Arthur S.	20	Houlton	S	Jan. 2, '64	'64: abs. sick
Nickerson, Henry O.	21	Linneus	S	Jan. 2, '64	
Phinney, Thomas F.	31	Stockton	M	Jan. 2, '64	'64: promoted Sgt.
Smith, Henry H.	25	Freeman*	S	Jan. 2, '64	'64: promoted Sgt.

* in '63 listed from New Portland

Name	Age	Residence	MS	MD	Remarks
Farwell, William S.	18	Rockland	S	Jan. 2, '64	'64: promoted 2nd Lt., DC Cavalry
Harmon, Shirley, Jr.	18	Gorham	S	Jan. 2, '64	'65: died at home Oct. 28, '64
Cushman, Edward A.*	21	Sumner	M	Jan. 2, '64	'64: promoted Sgt. for bravery; wounded

* Regimental Books, National Archives, lists Corporal Cushman promoted to sergeant "for meritorious conduct at Marianna, Fla., on the 27th [Sept]."

Buglers

Name	Age	Residence	MS	MD	Remarks
Bean, Daniel B.	18	Passadumkeag	S	Jan. 2, '64	'64: reduced to ranks; died Aug. 14, N. Orleans
Cogswell, Thomas C.	39	Dixfield	M	Jan. 2, '64	

Farriers

Name	Age	Residence	MS	MD	Remarks
Palmer, William H.	26	Freeman*	M	Jan. 2, '64	'64: abs. sick; '65: died at Alexandria, Va, Oct. 24, '64

* in '63 listed from Freedom

Name	Age	Residence	MS	MD	Remarks
Pillsbury, George W.	27	Winslow	M	Jan. 7, '64	'64: reduced to ranks; trans. to navy, July 18
Swift, Franklin B.	22	Belmont	S	Feb. 8, '64	'65: disch. for disab. Mar. 4

Saddler

Name	Age	Residence	MS	MD	Remarks
Moore, George W.	19	Canton	M	Jan. 2, '64	

Wagoner

Name	Age	Residence	MS	MD	Remarks
Pickens, Bradford	24	Wilton	M	Jan. 2, '64	'64: died Sept. 17, Barrancas

Privates

Name	Age	Residence	MS	MD	Remarks
Adams, Joshua R.	29	Wilton	M	Jan. 5, '64	'64: promoted Cpl. and Sgt.; wounded Sept. 27
Barker, Hiram E.	22	Corinth	S	Jan. 2, '65	
Barney, Thomas	26	Rockland	S	Jan. 2, '64	'64: deserted Feb. 28
Barrows, Benjamin R.	19	Augusta	S	Jan. 2, '64	'64: det. in reg't band; '64: detailed in regt. band
Batchelder, Charles H.	18	Passad'mk'g	S	Jan. 2, '64	'64: died Sept. 21, Barrancas
Beals, George M.	20	Canaan	S	Dec. 24, '63	'64: abs. sick; trans. from Co. K; '65: sick in hosp. since Oct. 26, '64
Bean, Roscoe G.	18	Wilton	S	Jan. 2, '64	'64: promoted Cpl.
Bell, Joseph	21	Saco	S	Oct. 4, '64	'65: disch. Oct. 10, term exp.

Name	Age	Residence	MS	MD	Remarks
Birlem, Charles H.	19	Dover	S	Jan. 2, '64	'64: abs. sick; '65: died in hosp., N. Orleans, Nov. 19, '64
Boothby, Albert	33	Saco	M	Oct. 4, '64	'65: disch. Oct. 10, term exp.
Bradgon, Benjamin A.	44	Houlton	M	Jan. 2, '64	'64: deserted Feb. 5
Brann, Emery M.	20	W Gardiner	S	Jan. 2, '64	'65: trans. from Veteran Reserve Corps
Butler, George H.	18	Pembroke	S	Mar. 24, '64	'64: died Sept. 22, Barrancas
Byron, Isaiah B.*	20	Linneus	S	Jan. 2, '64	'64: abs. sick in Me; '65: disch. for disab. July 6

  * listed as "Josiah" in 1865

Name	Age	Residence	MS	MD	Remarks
Byron, Jacob T.	22	Linneus	M	Jan. 2, '64	'64: died Sept. 14, Barrancas
Calden, Fred	18	Wilton	S	Mar. 18, '64	'64: abs. sick; '65: disch. by order, May 22
Chandler, Charles H.	18	Winthrop	S	Jan. 2, '64	'63: deserted Jan. 11 (apparently an error?); '64: abs. sick in Maine; '65: disch. by order, May 18
Chase, Sylvester	30	Concord	M	Jan. 2, '64	'63: abs. w/o leave; '64: trans. to Co. C
Chick, Frank M.	18	Shapleigh	S	Oct. 6, '64	'65: disch. Oct. 10, term exp.
Cookson, Eli N.	22	Linneus	S	Jan. 2, '64	
Cookson, Isaiah N.	21	Linneus	S	Jan. 2, '64	'64: abs. sick in Maine
Cox, Charles	44	Perry	M	Jan. 2, '64	'63: abs. w/o leave; '64: deserted Jan. 21 '65: in arrest by sentence of general court martial since Dec. 20, '64
Cushman, Edward A.	21	Sumner	M	Jan. 2, '64	'64: promoted Cpl. and Sgt. for bravery; wounded
Davis, Asa	23	Newfield	—	Sept. 28, '64	'65: disch. by order. August
Delano, Theodore V.	21	Augusta	M	Jan. 7, '64	'64: deserted May 24
Dickey, Adelbert H.	26	Stockton	M	Jan. 2, '64	
Doherty, John	35	Forks Plnt.	M	Jan. 2, '64	'64: trans. to navy, July 18
Dow, Enos	34	Palermo	M	Jan. 2, '64	'64: died Sept. 24, Barrancas
Dyer, John	43	Linneus	M	Jan. 2, '64	'64: mail carrier
Ellis, Cutts D.	18	Biddeford	S	Sept. 26, '64	'65; disch. by order Sept. 29 term exp.
Emery, James	39	N Portland	M	Jan. 2, '64	'64: died Aug. 16, N. Orleans
Estes, Orrin C.	21	Lee	S	Jan. 2, '64	'64: abs. sick; '65: died at home, Jan. 7
Ferren, Lysander	18	Levant	S	Jan. 2, '65	
French, Kruetzer	22	Nor'idgew'k	M	Jan. 2, '64	'64: trans. fr Co. C. to Co. E
Garland, Eli	42	Ellsworth	M	Jan. 2, '64	'64: died Sept. 2, Barrancas
Garvin, Charles O.	18	Shapleigh	S	Oct. 6, '64	'65: disch. Oct. 10, term exp.
Godwin, Richard W.	18	Newfield	S	Oct. 6, '64	'65: disch. Oct. 10, term exp.
Gott, Charles S.	29	Wayne	M	Feb. 23, '64	
Gough, Isaac	24	Pembroke	S	Mar. 24, '64	'64: sick in reg't hosp.; '65: promoted Cpl.
Gould, Bethuel P.	28	Linneus	S	Jan. 2, '64	
Hall, Ivory*	20	Shapleigh	S	Oct. 7, '64	'65: disch. Oct. 10, term exp.

  * Regimental Books, National Archives, lists Private Hall detailed as cook for Regimental Band on June 27.

Name	Age	Residence	MS	MD	Remarks
Hall, Jewett A.	18	Palermo*	S	Jan. 2, '64	'64: died Sept. 15

  * in '63 listed from Palmyra

Name	Age	Residence	MS	MD	Remarks
Hanning, Stephen	44	Monticello	M	Jan. 2, '64	'64: abs. sick; '65: disch. for disab. July 6
Harmon, Shirley, Jr.	18	Gorham	S	Jan. 2, '64	'64: promoted Cpl.; abs. sick
Harriman, Lysander W.	31	Dedham	M	Jan. 2, '64	'65: promoted Cpl.
Hart, Joshua	21	Whitefield	M	Jan. 2, '64	'64: deserted Feb. 18; '65: deserted Feb. 1, '64; disch.
Haskell, Fred B.	21	Auburn	S	Jan. 3, '65	
Haskell, Reuel	22	Auburn	S	Jan. 3, '65	
Hason, George I.*	20	Machias	S	Jan. 7, '64	'64: trans. to Co. D

* also listed as "Huson"

Name	Age	Residence	MS	MD	Remarks
Hathaway, Edgar	18	Passadumkeag	S	Jan. 2, '64	'64: died July 24, Thibodeaux
Haynes, Richard E.	21	Passadumkeag	S	Dec. 11, '63	
Higgins, George D.	32	Thorndike	M	Jan. 2, '64	'63: on detached service; '64: sick in quarters; '65: died in hosp., Dec. 1, '64
Hoyt, Daniel	19	Biddeford	S	Sept. 26, '64	'65: disch. by order Aug. 28
Hunton, Franklin B.	18	N Portland	S	Jan. 2, '64	'64: died Aug. 22, Barrancas
Johnson, James	27	Pembroke	S	Mar. 24, '64	'64: sick in quarters; '65: disch. by order, June 13
Johnson, William L.	18	Litchfield	S	Jan. 2, '64	'64: deserted Feb. 9
Jones, John A.	18	Houlton	S	Jan. 2, '64	'64: died Aug. 24, Barrancas
Jones, Madison T.	18	Washington	S	Jan. 14, '64	'64: sick in reg't hosp.; '65: disch. by order, Oct. 10
Kellran, Charles	18	Windsor	S	Jan. 2, '64	'64: deserted Feb. 28
Kendrick, Seth M.	35	Saco	S	Oct. 4, '64	'65: disch. Oct. 10, term exp.
Kennedy, James D.	34	Weld	M	Jan. 2, '64	'64: died July 4, Thibodeaux
King, Milton J.	25	Saco	S	Oct. 4, '64	'65: disch. Oct. 10, term exp.
Knight, Harrison	40	Dixfield	M	Jan. 2, '64	
Lane, Alfred E.	21	Yarmoutha*	S	Jan. 2, '64	'64: sick in quarters; '65: died en route for home Apr. 10

* in '63 listed from Augusta

Name	Age	Residence	MS	MD	Remarks
Littlefield, Ephraim M.	33	Saco	S	Oct. 4, '64	'65: disch. Oct. 10, term exp.
Longpee, William	23	Machias	M	Jan. 2, '64	'64: trans. to navy, July 18
Lovejoy, Melvin E.	18	N Portland	S	Jan. 7, '64	'65: promoted Cpl.
Lowell, William H.	29	Augusta	S	Jan. 2, '64	'63: detached in reg't band; '64: trans. to Co. A
Lynch, James	24	Biddeford	—	Oct. 15, '64	
Madden, Thomas C.	35	Belfast AcGt*	M	Feb. 11, '64	

*Hometown is Belfast Academy Grant

Name	Age	Residence	MS	MD	Remarks
Mahoney, Philip M.	40	Belfast	M	Jan. 2, '64	'64: abs. sick; '65: disch. by order, May 22
Marr, William W.	23	Saco	S	Oct. 4, '64	'65: disch. Oct. 10, term exp.
Marston, John A.	21	Farmington	S	Jan. 19, '64	'64: abs. sick; '65: deserted from hosp. Oct. 18, '64
Marston, Lendell C.	19	Wilton	S	Jan. 2, '64	'65: promoted Cpl.
Martin, Nelson H.	18	Linneus	S	Jan. 2, '64	'64: abs. sick; '65: disch. by order, June 13
McGrath, James	18	Augusta	S	Jan. 2, '64	'63: deserted Jan. 6; '65: deserted Jan. 3, '64
McMitchell, Wilder	28	China*	M	Jan. 2, '64	

* in '63 listed from Augusta

Name	Age	Residence	MS	MD	Remarks
Millett, Frank W.	18	Levant	S	Jan. 2, '65	
Mitchell, Albert A.	33	Canton	M	Jan. 2, '64	'63: promoted saddler; '64: promoted saddler Sgt.

Name	Age	Residence	MS	MD	Remarks
Mitchell, Henry M.	18	Dover	S	Dec. 15, '64	'65: disch. by order, June 13
Molloy, John	19	Milford Mass	S	June 9, '64	'64: sick in reg't hosp.; '65: died in hosp., Nov, 19, '64
Nash, George M.	28	Cherryfield	M	Dec. 7, '63	'64: trans. fr Co. D. to Co. C
O'Conner, John	18	Moose River	S	Jan. 2, '64	'64: died June 22, Brashear City, La
Palmer, Charles W.	20	Wilton	S	'65: sick in	'64: died Aug. 20, N. Orleans
Palmer, Joseph B.	20	Palermo*	S	Jan. 2, '64	'64: abs. sick; '65: sick in hosp., Augusta, since Nov. 29, '64

* in '63 listed from Palmyra

Name	Age	Residence	MS	MD	Remarks
Patch, John, Jr.	31	Shapleigh	M	Oct. 12, '64	'65: died in hosp., July 9
Perkins, Andrew P.	23	Linneus	M	'65: sick in	'64: abs. sick; '65: disch. for disab. Apr. 18
Phinney, John C.	25	Stockton	S	Mar. 4, '64	'64: promoted Sgt.; abs. sick
Pillsbury, Henry M.	26	Shapleigh	M	Oct. 6, '64	'65: disch. Oct. 10, term exp.
Pooler, James	21	Concord	S	Jan. 2, '64	'64: deserted Apr. 8
Powers, Benjamin C.	26	Linneus	M	'65: sick in	'65: promoted Cpl. and Sgt.
Purington, William B.	22	Canton	S	Mar. 1, '64	'64: sick in reg't hosp.; '65: sick in hosp., Augusta, Me
Rand, Charles E.	25	Standish	M	'65: sick in	'63: det. in reg't band; '64: died Aug. 3, N. Orleans
Ranger, Hannibal R.*	18	Wilton	S	Jan. 2, '64	'64: abs. sick

* listed as bugler in 1865 AG Report.

Name	Age	Residence	MS	MD	Remarks
Rankins, George F.	23	Houlton	S	'65: sick in	'64: died Oct. 1
Ray, Daniel	18	Waterford	S	'65: sick in	'64: died Sept. 18, Barrancas
Richardson, Thomas A.	18	Pittston	S	Dec. 22, '63	'64: trans. fr Co. I to navy, July 18
Robbins, William	20	Wilton	S	Jan. 5, '64	'64: died July 14, Thibodeaux
Roberts, Byron	28	Alfred	M	Mar. 24, '64	'64: promoted Com'y Sgt. and 1st Sgt.
Ryan, Thomas	26	Harrison	S	Sept. 27, '64	
Sabine, Oscar M.	20	Palermo	S	Jan. 2, '64	'64: died July 21
Savage, Charles H.	18	Augusta	S	Oct. 10, '64	'65: disch. Oct. 10, term exp.
Savage, Daniel B.	20	Augusta	S	Aug. 6, '64	'65: disch. Sept. 29, term exp.
Savage, Robert, Jr.	31	Anson*	M		'65: sick

* in '63 listed from New Sharon.

Name	Age	Residence	MS	MD	Remarks
Scates, George	44	Augusta	M	Jan. 2, '64	'65: disch. by order June 13
Seavey, Lafayette	21	Waterford	S	'65: sick in	'64: sick in qrtrs.; '65: promoted Cpl.
Secco, Orrin L.	20	China	S	'65: sick in	'64: died Oct. 11, Barrancas
Sims, Moses	38	Canton	M	Mar. 1, '64	'64: missing since battle of Marianna, Sept. 27; '65: died in hosp., Mar. 7
Spurr, John	27	Kittery	S	Jan. 2, '64	'64: died Aug. 1, N. Orleans
Steadman, Henry P.	18	Milo	S	'65: sick in	'64: abs. sick; '65: disch. by order, Sept. 18
Stetson, Joseph B.	21	Houlton	S	'65: sick in	'65: disch. by order, June 13
Stevens, John	22	Waterford	S	'65: sick in	'64: trans. to Co. C
Swift, Franklin B.	22	Belmont	S	Feb. 8, '64	'64: appointed farrier; abs. sick
Taylor, William	43	Ellsworth	M	Jan. 2, '64	'64: died Aug. 19, Barrancas
Thomas, Silas C.	31	Camden	M	Jan. 7, '64	'63: det. in Q.M. dept; '64: deserted Feb. 6; arrested and trans. to Co. L

Thompson, George F.	31	Shapleigh	S	Oct. 6, '64	'65: disch. Oct. 10, term exp.	
Thompson, Porter	19	Machias	S	Jan. 7, '64	'64: trans. to Co. G	
Trask, David E.*	26	Leeds	M	Jan. 7, '64	'64: died July 12, Thibodeaux	
*also listed as "Daniel" from Gardiner						
Walker, Ruvillo R.	18	Wilton	S	Feb. 4, '64	'64: abs. sick; '65: died in hosp., Jan. 5	
Warren, John W.	38	Cornville	M	Jan. 2, '64	'63: det. in reg't band; '64: trans. to Co. K	
Whittier, True	45	Augusta	M	Jan. 2, '64	'64: promoted Vet'y Sur.	
Wing, Charles E.	18	Wayne	S	Mar. 4, '64		
Withee, Richard W.	26	Forestville	S	Jan. 2, '64		
Withee, William A.R.*	21	Lyndon	S	Nov. 24, '63	'64: died July 19, Thibodeaux	
*not listed in '63 AG roster.						
Withey, Arthur I.	26	Eustis Plnt.	M	Jan. 2, '64	'65: promoted Cpl. and Sgt.	
Works, Charles C.	18	New Sharon	S	Jan. 19, '64	'64: died Sept. 16, Alexandria	
Worth, Edward E.	18	Vasselboro	S	Jan. 2, '64	'64: trans. to Co. C	
Wright, James	23	Lincolnville	M	Jan. 2, '64	'64: disch. for disab., Apr. 10	
Yeaton, Benjamin A.	20	Augusta	M	Jan. 7, '64	'64: deserted May 24	
Young, Stephen O.	21	Rockland	S	Jan. 2, '64		

B. Causes of Death in the Different Theaters of the War

It is often stated that many more men died in the Civil War from disease than from combat-related causes. While that is true, the ratio of deaths from disease vs. battle varied considerably from one geographic locale to another.

For cavalry units from Maine, the difference is quite obvious. The First Maine Cavalry was stationed in Virginia and fought in major battles in Virginia, Maryland, West Virginia, and Pennsylvania. These "major battles" indicate an obvious difference in the nature of the combat seen by the 1st and 2nd Maine Cavalry. The 1st Maine, for example, began fighting the Confederates at Middleton and Winchester in May 1862 and saw action at such battles as Brandy Station, Rappahannock Station, Thoroughfare Gap, 2nd Bull Run, Antietam, Fredericksburg, Middleburg and Upperville, Gettysburg, Shepardstown, many of the engagements of the Overland Campaign, and ending with battles at Petersburg, and finally at Appomattox Court House. Their time of active service was also longer than the 2nd Maine's. However, when looking at the deaths due to disease, we see the clear difference that geographic location makes.

1st Maine Cavalry: 154 men killed or died of wounds, 165 died in Confederate prisons, and 171 died of disease.

2nd Maine Cavalry: 10 men killed or died of wounds, 1 died at Andersonville Prison, and 334 died from disease.

It is fairly easy to compare figures for Maine's 9 month regiments, since they tended to spend their entire term of service in one area. Here we can see the number of deaths due to disease for regiments that were sent to the Gulf and for those kept nearer Washington.

Department of the Gulf

(In each case, the number "killed in battle" includes those who died of wounds.)

22nd Maine: (Gulf—Irish Bend, Port Hudson) 160 from disease; 9 killed in battle

21st Maine (Gulf—Port Hudson): 145 from disease; 27 killed in battle
24th Maine (Gulf—Port Hudson): 190 from disease; 1 killed in battle
26th Maine (Gulf—Irish Bend, Port Hudson): 131 from disease; 23 killed in battle
28th Maine (Gulf—Port Hudson, Donaldsonville): 143 from disease; 11 killed in battle

Defense of Washington

(duty at various forts and installations guarding the capital)

23rd Maine: 56 from disease
25th Maine: 20 from disease
27th Maine: 22 from disease

For Maine's 3 year regiments, the comparisons are a bit more difficult, since some moved from one theater of the war to another. But, here is a comparison of two regiments that spent their time in one area.

15th Maine (Gulf and Texas): 343 from disease; 5 killed in battle
20th Maine (Virginia, Pennsylvania): 146 from disease; 147 killed in battle

Other 3 year Maine regiments:

12th Maine (Gulf '62 and '63 and later Virginia): 239 from disease; 52 killed in battle
13th Maine (Gulf and Texas): 181 from disease; 14 killed in battle
14th Maine (Gulf '62 and '63 and later Virginia): 332 from disease; 86 killed in battle
17th Maine (Virginia): 163 from disease; 207 killed in battle
19th Maine (Virginia): 184 from disease; 192 killed in battle

C. General Courts-Martial for Members of the 2nd Maine Cavalry

The below are summarized from the Court-Martial Files, National Archives, unless otherwise indicated. (There were other courts-martial, "Regimental Courts Martial," which were held within the regiment, but no record was found of those trials.)

Barker, Silas C.   2nd Lieutenant, Company A

General Orders No. 22   Jan. 31, 1865

Charge: Violation of 36th Article of War

Specification 1st: sold to infantry soldiers 4 regulation hats, property of U.S. government for his own private profit; hats for which Capt. Twitchell was responsible and which Twitchell sent to Barker at Houma, La. to be issued to troops in Company A. On or about June 20, '64.

Specification 2nd: Lieut. Barker, Company A, sold and applied to his private use thirty-three dollars worth of grain or forage, property of U.S. government for which Capt. Twitchell was responsible which had been sent to Barker at Houma, La. for public animals under Barker's charge. On or about July 2, '64.

Lt. Barker pleaded not guilty.

Testimony addressed whether the hats were sold to other soldiers or were surplus to the needs of the 2nd Maine Cavalry and were therefore given to members of another regiment. No testimony was given that Lt. Barker had sold the hats. The forage was apparently in a barn and no testimony was given that Lt. Barker had sold it.

Found "not guilty" on both specifications and on the charge and acquitted. The court did state that the accused did not take proper care of government property trusted to his care; that carrying excess personal baggage had taken too much room that should have been given to government property.

Capt. S. W. Knowles appeared as counsel for the accused Barker.

Witnesses:

Capt. Twitchell for the prosecution, and Sgt. David Small, Company A, Corporal Andrew P Webber, Company H.

Lieut. Barker apparently had his wife with him? One of the documents of testimony talks about having his "wife's things" in the wagon on the way to Houma.

Bell, John Private   Company A

(From Regimental and Company Books, National Archives)
Jan. 15, 1865, Barrancas.   General Orders No. 3   Extract

"1st Before a General Court Martial which convened at Barrancas Florida on the 27th day of December 1864, persuant to special Orders No. 306 Dated December 26, 1864, from these Head Quarters, and of which Major CA Miller 2nd Regt. Maine Cavalry is President, was arraigned and tried.

"2nd   Private John Bell Co A 2nd Regt Me Cav."

Charge 1st: Conduct to the prejudice of good order and military discipline.

Specifications: "In this that he, the said John Bell, a private in Co A 2nd Regt Maine Cavalry, did, on or about the 9th day of September 1864 while on Picket duty, leave his guard without permission, and assault a negro Servant in the employ of Capt Heering of the 34th Iowa Vols, and did, without authority and with violence, take away from the said negro, a knife, a pistol, and a pair of shoes, the property of the said negro, also some victuals belonging to the said Capt Heering. This at Mobile Point, Alabama."

Charge 2nd: Quitting his post to plunder and pillage

Specification: "In this, that he, the said John Bell a private in Co A 2nd Regt Maine Cavalry, did on or about the 9th day of September 1864, while on Picket duty, leave his guard without permission, and assault a negro servant in the employ of Capt Heering, of the 34th Iowa Vols, and did, without authority, and with violence, take away from said negro a knife, a pistol, and a pair of shoes, the property of the said negro, also some victuals belonging to the said Capt Heering. This at Mobile Point, Alabama."

Bell pleaded to the specification to 1st charge, guilty, except the words "leave his guard without permission." To the 1st charge, not guilty. To specification to 2nd charge, guilty, except the words "leave his guard without permission" and to the 2nd charge, not guilty."

Bell was found guilty of the first charge and specification, except the words "leave his guard without permission," and likewise for the second charge and specification.

He was sentenced "to be confined at hard labor for the period of one month and forfeit to the Government his monthly pay for the period of two months."

Review and Orders: "Sentence confirmed and will be carried into effect at Fort Pickens under direction of the Commanding officer of that Post. The stoppage of pay will be made by the proper officer and to prevent the effect of any ambiguity in the reading of the sentence, the amount to be stopped is hereby limited to thirteen dollars per month for the time specified."

By Command of
Brig. Gen. McKean
Comdg. Dist. of West Florida

Butler, Frank H.   Corporal, Company B

Tallahassee, Nov. 21, 1865

Charge: Assault and Battery with the intent to Kill
Specification: "did attempt to shoot and kill with a spencer carbine, his superior Officer Capt B G Merry, Comp B 2d Maine Cavalry, firing at him ... seven shots, some of which passed through the tent of the said Officer, one shot lodging at his feet, while other shots passed over the said Officer's tent and entering the Barracks occupied by the men of Company E 2nd Maine Cavalry, thereby endangering the lives of many men of Company E." At Barrancas, 9 November 1865 between 9 and 10 p.m.

Plea: "Not Guilty"

The first witness was Capt. Merry, who testified regarding being fired at, calling out the guard, and finding Butler in his tent, fully clothed and perspiring. He had gone to Butler's tent because "I recognized him, or thought I did, from the flash of the carbine." The carbine found was identified as Butler's Spencer carbine, one of only 3 in that company. He could not see clearly the two men running from the scene of the firing.

Butler was found not guilty of the specification and charge.

Breen, Peter R.   Private, Company B

Tallahassee, Nov. 21, 1865

Charge: Assault and Battery with the intent to Kill
Plea "not guilty"
Captain Merry stated he saw Frank H. Butler fire the carbine with Breen fairly close by. Chased to Butler's tent with a member of the guard. Another witness, 1st Lt. William Gillespie of Company D, stated he heard Breen say to somebody, "For god's sake hide the cartridges or you will be found out." Breen appeared very much intoxicated.

Unfortunately, we don't have any record of the court's deliberations. There was no apparent evidence that either Butler or Breen fired at Capt. Merry intentionally. Did the court believe that they were simply being irresponsible and not making an attack specifically against Capt. Merry? And there was no evidence that Breen had fired any shots.

Breen was found not guilty.

Both Breen and Butler apparently had somewhat checkered careers. Butler was promoted from private to corporal on August 16, 1864, and to sergeant on August 18, 1864.

He was reduced to the rank of corporal on April 15, 1865, and then reduced to the rank of private for "refusing to do duty as a Corporal." Private Breen was promoted to corporal on August 12, 1864, but the order was revoked on August 16.

Cain, Michael   Pvt. Company A

Tallahassee. Florida, Nov. 1, 1865

Charge: Violation of the ninth article of war

Specification: "In this that Michael Cain, Private, Company A, 2nd Maine Cavalry did strike his superior officer, Captain James Csermlyi, 82nd U.S. Col'd infty, and did in a [illegible] and most disrespectful manner, in other and various ways, offer violence to the said Captain Csermlyi ... his superior officer." At Barrancas, Fla., on or about 25 September 1865.

Pleaded as follows: Cain pleaded not guilty to the specification and charge.

The first witness, Sgt. David Carpenter, Company A, 2nd Maine Cavalry, stated he was with Cain and did not see Cain strike the captain. There was a large crowd there, and the captain "acknowledged on the following morning that the prisoner [Pvt. Cain] was not the man who struck him." There had been trouble between Cain and the captain that night. Carpenter and Cain and others had been in swimming and when they walked by the captain, who was talking to "these fellows" the captain was struck. The prisoner was standing with Carpenter at the time. "I did not see him [the Captain] struck." Cain said nothing to the captain and the captain said nothing to Cain.

Witness Sgt. J.E. Blackwell, Company A, 2nd Maine Cavalry, said he heard Cain the next morning "say that he struck a Dutch Captain." Was not sure of the date and was not present at the time the alleged offense took place.

Private Cain was found not guilty and was acquitted.

This letter found in the Regimental and Company Books, National Archives, shows why Private Cain was tried for the offense above:

Oct. 28th 1865,Barrancas
Lieut AC Putz [?] AAA Genl

Lieut.

I have the honor to submit the following statement and accompanying affidavits and papers having reference to the case of Sergt Augustus Thomas Co A 2nd Maine Cavalry now in confinement at Fort Pickens.

Charges were preferred against Sergt Thomas by Capt Csermlyi 82nd U.S.C. Inftry [James Csermelyi, Captain, Company I, 82nd U.S. Colored Infantry] for an attack made upon him by a party of soldiers on the evening of the 25th of Sept. (as explained in the copy of Capt Csermlyi's statement). The only ground which Capt Csermlyi had for preferring charges was upon the affidavit of Michael Cain Privat Co A of this Regiment. The Captain never confronted the accused, never recognized him, neither did he ever call on the commanding officer of the 2nd Maine Cavalry for permission or assistance to do so.

The charges are based solely upon the statement of Cain, a man of disreputable character, a disorderly and quarrelsome soldier and an enemy of Thomas. There is abundance of evidence that Cain made this statement (false as it is proved to be) to clear himself, that he in fact wearing a Sergeant's jacket and disguised as a sergeant was the man who committed the assault upon Capt Csermlyi.

I have known Sert Thomas as a reliable soldier, and have often marked his prompt and faithful attention to duty. During the whole time this regiment has been in existence, I know of no instance wherein for improper conduct he deserved a reprimand. An examination of the evidence set forth in the accompanying papers, I am led to belive, will not fail to convince any one of the innocence of Thomas and the great injustice that would be done should he be detained in Fort Pickens upon charges of so serious a character without trial after the regiment shall have been mustered out of service and disbanded.

I respectfully and earnestly request that this case may receive that careful investigation which I am thoroughly convinced it should have and that Sergt Thomas may be released from the charges preferred against him, or if that should be found impracticable that a court may be convened at as early a day as possible in order that he may receive the benefit of a speedy trial. I trust that the Comd'g General will appreciate the motive that prompts me in my effort for the relief of a conscientious and worthy Soldier of my regiment, who I well know does not deserve the fate which grave and serious charges, preferred without any real foundation may bring upon him.

I am Lieutenant, Very Respectfully Your Obt Servt
Eben Hutchinson Maj Comd' Regt

Dodge, Randolph   2nd lieutenant, Company C
Thibodaux, La., July 6, 1864

Charge I: Absence without Leave

Specification: Got permission from Major A.B. Spurling to visit New Orleans, if he first got permission from his company commander. Did not get that permission and left camp to go to New Orleans. At Greenville, La., on or about May 25, '64.

Charge II: Conduct Unbecoming an Officer and a Gentleman

Specification: Prepared a pass for himself and presented it to Acting Adjutant Lt. I.R. Allen saying that Major Spurling "says you will approve this by his orders; or words to that effect, which statement was false." At Greenville, La, on or about May 25, '64.

Specification 2nd: When he brought the unsigned pass to Lt. Allen and was asked why it was not signed by his company commander, he replied, "Capt. Johnson says it is all right; or words to that effect, which statement was false." At Greenville, La., on or about May 25, '64.

Charge III: Violation of the 6th Article of War

Specification: "did, in conversation with Capt. E.D. Johnson, Co C use contemptuous and disrespectful language when speaking of ... Maj Spurling, saying he is a liar, if he prefers charges againt me, I will be even with him before I leave the show; or words to that effect." At Greenville, La., on or about May 25, '64.

Lt. Dodge pleaded not guilty to all charges and specifications

Dodge offered a written statement saying that the evidence does not sustain the first charge and specification: he had proper authority to leave the camp.

2nd Charge & specification: court only has Spurling's word for what he (Spurling) said, and Dodge denies it. Dodge said he understood Spurling to mean that Dodge had to have the consent of his company commander, not his actual signature. Either Spurling "may be mistaken in the words used," or the accused misunderstood the meaning. An officer being granted a leave for a few hours was a "common and frequent" occurrence. Dodge states that Spurling had admitted he would not have preferred charges had he not heard that Dodge had used contemptuous language against him. In leaving the camp, the accused confessed to having "acted thoughtlessly, but with no intention of doing wrong or thought that he was acting inappropriately."

3rd Charge & specification: "there was considerable discrepency among the witnesses as to the language used." "The Court will also bear in mind that Lt Dodge was speaking under the pain of a recent arrest, that he was excited and that he was speaking to a man who was hostile to him and who he believed caused his arrest, and may have used the language he did without meaning any disrespect to Major Spurling." Dodge spoke "rather in justification of himself than with the thought of abusing Major Spurling." And, "this conversation was in the privacy of his own tent and not expected to go beyond it."

On the first charge and specification, the court found Dodge not guilty. On the second charge and specification, not guilty. On the third charge and specification, guilty.

Sentence: "to be reprimanded by the Commanding Officer of his Regiment, in the presence of the officers of his Regiment."

Gonyea, Lewis   Private, Company G
November 17, 1864

Charge I: Theft
Specification: "did take, without proper authority, from the enclosure near District Headquarters, one sorrel Mare Mule, the property of the United States Government."

At Barrancas. On or about Aug. 30, 1864.

Charge II: Trafficking in Government Property
Specification: "did, without proper authority, sell or exchange one sorrel Mare Mule, the property of the United States Government, to or with a certain Thomas Chambers, for one grey Horse, and did sell the said Horse to one Buck Houston, for the sum of fifty dollars, and did afterwards take the said sorrel Mare Mule from Thomas Chambers without remunerating him for it." At Warrington, Florida, on or about Sept. 1, 1864.

To the first charge and specification Gonyea pleaded not guilty.

To the second charge and specification he pleaded not guilty.

Capt. J.H. Roberts of 2nd Maine Cavalry detailed as a member of the court, but was absent for Gonyea's trial.

No counsel was appointed for the accused.

Witnesses: Capt. Geo Maynard (district provost marshal), Thomas Chambers, "colored," and Buck Houston, "colored."

Maynard testified as to the mule going missing and Maynard's assistant "ascertained it had been exchanged by Gonyea for a horse which was there" in the 2nd Maine Cavalry's camp. Chambers and Houston testified that Gonyea had traded the mule for the horse and then the mule was taken away by "a file of soldiers." "I don't know the accused was with them." Houston testified that he had bought the horse from Gonyea.

To the first charge and specification, Gonyea was found not guilty. To the second charge and specification, guilty "except so much as charges him with taking the mule away from Thomas Chambers, without remunerating him for it."

He was sentenced to hard labor for the period of three months, and to forfeit his monthly pay for two months.

Sentence to be carried out at Fort Pickens.

Haynes, Albert A.   2nd Maine Cavalry (no company given)
[Pvt. Albert A. "Haines," Company C?]
Jan. 27, 1865, Alexandria, Va.

Charge: Desertion
Specification: "having been duly enlisted in the military service of the United States,

did, without proper authority absent himself from the Company and Regiment and so remain until apprehended at or near Harrisburg Pa on or about the 21st day of November 1864."

Haynes pleaded guilty to the specification but not guilty to the charge.

He was found guilty of the specification, not guilty of the charge, but guilty of absence without leave.

Statement of Albert Haynes:

I enlisted at Rockland, Me, on some time in June 1861 for 3 years. I joined and served with my regt until Feb. 14, 1863, when I was discharged by reason of surgical certificate of disablilty at Alexandria, Va. I again enlisted at Bangor, Me, on 25th of Sept. 1864 for one year. I received $475 bounty, was sent to Camp Berry, Portland, from there to Gallop Island, Boston Harbor, remained there until the 1st of Nov. 1864, when I was sent together with a number of other recruits to join our regt. I left the Squad I belonged to at Harrisburg, Pa, on or about the 20th of Nov, 1864 with a verbal permission to go & get some breakfast. During my absence the squad had left in the cars for Camp Chase, Ohio, and I was arrested the following morning 21st of Novbr. 1864, taken before the Pro. Mar. [provost marshal] at Harrisburg and by him confined as a deserter and sent to this prison.

Sentence: "to be returned to his Regiment under guard for duty, and to forfeit ten (10) dollars per month of his monthly pay for the period of two months."

(It is assumed that the Albert "Haynes" referred to is Albert A "Haines," muster dated Sept. 29, '64 and assigned to Company C, 2nd Maine Cavalry; discharged by order Sept. 15, '65. There is an Albert A "Haynes," in Company A, 4th Maine, but there is no indication that he is the man who was on trial.)

Holland, Charles   Private, Company I

July 26, 1865, at Montgomery, Ala.

Charge 1st: Violation of the 46th Article of War
Specification: "having been regularly detailed upon guard did without the consent or knowledge of his commanding Officer leave his post while on duty and remain absent between the hours of 11 o'clock A.M. and 8 o'clock P.M. This at camp of Detachment 2nd Maine Cav. at Montgomery Ala on or about the 15th day of June 1865."

Charge 2nd: Violation of the 38th Article of War
Specification: "having been regularly detailed upon guard did abandon his post, without being regularly relieved and taking his carbine and equipments did leave camp and getting grossly intoxicated broke and spoiled his carbine. This at or near camp, Detachment 2nd Regt Maine Cav. at Montogomery Ala on or about June 15, 1865."

Charge 3rd: Violation of the 21st Article of War
Specification: "did on the 5th of June inst. and on divers of the days since said 5th of June, without leave from his commanding Officer absent himself from his detachment remaining absent from four to eight hours each day. This at or near Camp Detachment 2nd Regt Maine Cav. at Montgomery Ala."

Holland pleaded not guilty to the 1st and 2nd charges and specifications, but guilty to the 3rd.

Pvt. Holland admitted to being drunk before he was called to go on guard duty on June 15, but did not break his carbine. It was broken before he went on guard duty and he used another man's carbine. Evidence from another member of the guard (Sgt. William Dunlap of Company K) was that Holland had been absent from duty without permission.

Holland's verdict was guilty of charges 1 and 3 but not guilty of charge 2.

He was sentenced "to forfeit to the United States, six months pay and allowances."

Johnson, Henry   Private, Company G

(Was this Charles H. Johnson, Private, Company G?
There is no "Henry" listed in the regiment.)
Barrancas, May 13, '65

Charge: Conduct prejudicial to good order and military discipline
Charge and Specifications preferred by Capt H.K. Southwick, provost marshal, Dist. West Fla.

Specification 1st: "did enter the forage house belonging to the Chief Quartermaster District of West Florida and did conspire with one Jack Walsh or Waltz and when said Walsh had extinguished the light belonging to the guard there stationed over certain seized liquors and other goods, did steal and take away a quantity of liquor, to wit, two demyjohns of Whiskey or other liquor kind unknown, and did appropriate the same to his own use." At the Wharf at Barrancas, Fla., at or about 12 o'clock on the night of March 20, 1865.

Specification 2nd: "being drunk, did insult and abuse the sergeant of his guard calling him a 'damned son of a bitch' and threateneing to kill his said Sergeant."

Witnesses: Sgt. S.K. Litchfield, Company I, Corp. Alpheus G Kelly, Company F, Pvt. Ansel Walker, Company F, and Pvt. Van Rensalear Corson, Company F, all of the 2nd Maine Cavalry.

No testimony from the witnesses is recorded in the material at the National Archives.
Plea: Not Guilty

The court found Private Henry Johnson not guilty of the 1st specification, but guilty on the 2nd specification and charge.

Sentence: "To be confined at hard labor at Fort Pickens, Fla., for four months, and to forfeit to the United States $8 per month of his monthy pay for the same period."

Knowles, Samuel W.   Captain, Company G

General Orders No. 36, Headquarters District of
West Florida, Barrancas, Sept. 1, 1864

Charge I: Neglect of duty
Specification: abandoned a box of ammunition, "leaving it by the road side, without taking measures to turn it over, or secure its transportation, and without reporting it to his Commanding Officer." At Napoleonville, La. On or about 15 June 1864.

Charge II: Conduct to the prejudice of good order and military discipline
Specification: abandoned his command "when formed for the march, and remained absent therefrom without leave for about three hours, during which time his squadron marched from Thibodeaux to Terrebonne, Louisianana." Thibodeaux, La, on or about 26 June 1864.

Charge III: Violation of the 43rd Article of War
Specification: "was drunk when in command of his squadron and on duty moving from Terrebonne to Algiers, Louisiana." Terrebonne, La, on or about 26 July 1864.

Charge IV: Disobedience of Orders

Specification 1st: violated General Orders No. 8—failed "to be present at stable call, without having been excused by the Commanding Officer or by the Regimental Surgeon." Barrancas, on or about 26 August 1864.

Specification 2nd: also Gen Orders No. 8, failed "to be present at stable call" as above except date is 27 August 1864.

Capt. Knowles pleaded not guilty to all charges and specifications.

Captain Stanley was appointed as his counsel.

Witnesses for prosecution:

Capt. Moses French: found ammo box by road and sent it to Colonel "thought it was Capt Knowles'" no marks on it.

Col. Woodman: was sent ammo boxes; asked Knowles about it, who said he had lost an ammo box and thought it sank in the bayou. Regarding the absence from stable call, Woodman stated that the 2nd lieutenant was left in command and Knowles had no authority to be absent.

In Capt. Knowles' written statement, however, he stated that Col. Woodman had given him permission to act as counsel for Captain Stanley, who was facing a court-martial charge. Capt. Knowles said he was absent from stable call for that reason.

As to the charge of being drunk, various testimony was given. Lt. Col. Spurling and Lt. Chandler believed Knowles was drunk. Major Hutchinson stated that Knowles had been drinking, but was not drunk. Lt. Gillespie and Capt. Kerswell said that if Knowles had been drinking, he was not impaired and was able to do his duty.

Findings: not guilty of all except Charge II and specification was changed from 3 hours to 2 hours. Found "guilty" of specification as altered, but "not guilty" of charge and acquitted.

Libby, Samuel H.   Captain, Company L

Charge: Violation of the 44th Article of War

Specification: failed "to appear at the time fixed to the place of regimental parade appointed by his commanding officer." At the camp of the 2nd Maine Cavalry, Barrancas on or about 16 August 1864.

Capt. Libby pleaded not guilty

Capt. John H. Roberts assigned as his counsel

Charge made by Col. Woodman

Witness: Adjutant Pickard was asked about making a report of those absent from parade: "Capt Libby with several other Officers were reported absent." The other officers were Captains Lincoln, Clark and Haskell. Capt. Lincoln was put in arrest with Libby; Capt. Clark was examined by the surgeon and excused from duty. "Capt Haskell was not noticed. I think he was overlooked or forgotten."

Witness: Lt. Andrew Woodman, from the same company as the accused and was in command of the company at that parade at Capt. Libby's request, said, "If there are any inquiries made for me, say I am sick."

Cross examined: when asked if Libby was sick, he answered, "He had been unwell for some time, complaining of being troubled with the Diarhrea."

Called Surgeon George Martin: testified he saw Libby in his tent in the evening of Aug. 16 at the request of the colonel and he "appeared to be well." On the morning before,

Libby had been seen by the assistant surgeon and said to be unfit for duty. Problem was diarrhea. The surgeon also examined Lincoln and Clark.

Defense called 1st Sgt. Elisha Clark, Co L: stated that Libby had complained of being unwell and had sent Sgt. Ham to the surgeon for medicine on the day previous to the parade.

Written statement by Libby: There had never been a regimental order "requiring all commissioned Officers to be present at Parade, and at previous parades all officers have not been required to attend, and no notice has heretofore been taken of absentees." At the time of Libby's arrest, Captain Lincoln was also "placed in arrest and subsequently released, and another [who was absent] (Captain Haskell) of whose absence no notice whatever was taken." "While I do not wish to accuse my Commanding Officer of persecution, I can see no just reason by I should be singled out of four to be made an example of and hope the court will duly consider this point in their deliberation." It was the first time he had ever requested a subordinate to take parade duty. He was angry about being examined by the surgeon.

Found "guilty" of the specification, but "not guilty" of the charge, Captain Libby was acquitted and returned to duty.

O'Connell, Henry (found in roster in Company H)
Alexandria, Va., Jan. 13, 1865

Charge: Desertion
Specification: "having been duly enlisted in the military Service of the United States did without proper authority absent himself from his Camp and so remain until apprehended at or near Washington, D.C. on or about the 8th day of November 1864 in Citizens Clothing. This at or near Camp Distribution Va on or about the 8th day of November 1864."

O'Connell pleaded guilty to the specification and not guilty to the charge.

He submitted a written statement (apparently dictated): "I enlisted at Portland, Me, on or about the 18th of Sept. 1864 for 3 yrs. I received $500 bounty and was sent to Camp Berry near Portland, Me. From there I was sent to City Point Va. I remained there until the 8th of November 1864, when I left Camp without permission and remained absent until I was arrested by a detective at Washington, D.C., the same day, (Nov 8th 1864) in a citizen coat, was taken before the Provost Marshal and by him confined as a deserter in Forrest Hall Prison, Georgetown, D.C. and from there I was sent to Washington St Mil Prison in Alexandria Va."

A second statement is apparently in his own handwriting: "When I enlisted I was to receive 900 dollars bounty. They took me to the Provost Marshal and swore me in. they would not give me the money but put it in an envelope and sent it out to Camp Barry with me. From Camp Berry we was forwarded to City Point Va by Transports, on which we received our money. My envelope only contained 500 dollars instead of 900. I was sent from City Point to Camp Distribution. I left there to go to Washington for the purpose of seeing the State [agent?] in regards to the bounty. While there I was arrested. I have a Wife two Children and a Mother to support. I was desirous of obtaining the money for their benefit."

Of the specification, O'Connor was found guilty. Of the charge he was not guilty, but guilty of absence without leave. He was sentenced "to be returned under guard to his regiment for duty and to forfeit ten dollars per month of his monthly pay for the period of six months."

Reed, William   Private, Company A

Barrancas, Feb. 23, '65

Charge 1st: Conduct to the prejudice of good order and military discipline
Specification: "did on or about the 9th day of September 1864 while on Picket, leave his guard and arrest a Negro servant, in the employ of Capt Heering of the 34th Regt Iowa Vols and did without authority and with violence take away from the said Negro a Knife, a Pistol, and a pair of shoes, the property of the said Negro, also some rations belonging to Capt Heering. This at Mobile Point, Alabama"

Charge 2nd: Quitting his post to plunder and pillage
Specification: "did on or about the 9th day of September 1864 while on picket, leave his guard without permission, and arrest a Negro servant in the employ of capt Heering of the 34th Iowa Vols, and did without authority, and with violence, take away from the said Negro a knife, a pistol, and a pair of shoes, the property of said Negro, also some victuals belonging to the said Capt Heering."

Reed pleaded not guilty to all.

Witnesses: Sgt. Edward Jones and, Thomas B. Moore, both of the 2nd Maine Cavalry.

Sgt. Jones testified he did see a Negro with something wrapped in paper saying he was to bring breakfast to a Captain who was on picket duty. Jones says there was no captain there and would not let the Negro go further. The man then went to the reserve where Reed was and was again turned back. Jones did not see Reed molest the Negro. Reed did not have in his possession any of the property of the Negro or of Capt. Herring. Reed did not leave his post without permission.

Thomas B. Moore, wagoner of Company A, said he saw the Negro and saw "the boys" talking and laughing with him. He did not see Reed molest the Negro or take anything from him or leave his post.

The court found Reed not guilty. "He will be released from confinement and returned to duty with his company."

Capt. Knowles of 2nd Maine Cavalry was appointed judge advocate of the general court-martial convened.

An obvious question: Why was Reed tried in February of '65, when Pvt. John Bell had been found guilty of the same charges back in late December?

Smith, Walter S.   Unassigned, 2nd Maine Cavalry

Alexandria, Va., Feb. 3, 1865

Charge: Desertion
Specification: "having been duly enlisted in the miltary service of the United States did without proper authority absent himself from his Company and Regiment and so remain until apprehended at or near Brooklyn N.Y. on or about the 27th day of December 1864 in Citizens clothes. This at or near Portland Maine on or about the 27th day of October 1864."

To the charge and specification, Smith pleaded guilty.

He offered a written statement: "I enlisted Oct. 19, 1864, at Portland Maine for 3 years. I received $150 bounty. I was sent to Camp Berry near Portland Maine which place I left without permission on or about the 27th Oct 1864. I was absent until on or about the 27th Dec 1864, when I was arrested at Brooklyn N.Y. by detective, when I was taken to the Prv

Mar [provost marshal] at Brooklyn who committed me to Prison. I was in Liquor at the time of enlistment and was dissatisfied with the bounty which I had received. I was dressed in Citizens Clothing when arrested."

Smith was found guilty and sentenced "to be assigned and sent under guard for duty to such regiment as the General Commanding shall direct to make good all time lost by absence, to forfeit all pay and allowances due and the sum of ten U.S. dollars per month of his monthy pay for the period of twelve (12) months." General Orders No. 150 directed that he "be delivered to the Provost Marshal General, Army of the Potomac for assignment to duty with such regiment as he may designate."

Speed, Horace G.   Private, Company I

Montgomery, Ala., May 26, 1865

Charge 1st: Stealing
Specification: "did on or about the 24th day of May 1865 in company and assisted by certain others steal and carry away from the posession of one G.M. Ormand citizen of the town of Greenville state of Alabama one silver Hunting case watch valued at about ($16) Sixteen Dollars, the property of him the said Ormand and contrary to the laws of the Unites States of America and existing military orders. This at or near the town of Greenville, state of Alabama, at the time above specified."

Charge 2nd: Robbery
Specification: "did on or about the 24th day of May 1865 in company and assisted by certain other parties at or near the residence of one 'Simon' a colored man at or near the town of Greenville state of Alabama and did then and there feloniously and violently and against the will of him the said Simon, and by putting him the said Simon in bodily fear and danger of his life by threats and actually placing a rope around the neck of said Simon did then and there take rob and carry away from the possession of him the said Simon the sum of ($1) one dollar in silver coin the property of said Simon contrary to the laws of the United States of America and existing military orders. This at or near Greenville state of Alabama at the time above specified."

Speed pleaded not guilty to both charges and specifications.

The first witness, Dr. G.M. Ormand, testified that Speed and four other men "dressed as soldiers in federal uniforms and armed" came into his house. Took the watch and a trunk. The watch was later returned to him by Sergeant Barr on the same day it was taken. First Sgt. Harvey D. Barr of Company B, 32nd Iowa Infantry, testified that he had arrested Pvt. Speed in a private house and found the watch in that house, which the inhabitants of the house said was not theirs, and which Dr. Ormand identified as his. Thomas J. Mings, private, Company A, 19th Kansas Volunteers, testified that he saw the watch in the private house mentioned by Sgt. Harvey and in the hands "of a fellow by the name of Hardy." Simon testified that he could not be sure of identifying Speed as the one who took his money and did not think that Speed was one of the men who robbed him.

On specification and charge 1 he was found guilty. On specification and charge 2, not guilty. Speed was sentenced "to forfeit to the United States all pay and allowances for one year and to be confined at hard labor for the same period." (At the time of the 2nd Maine Cavalry's muster out, the adjutant general's report lists Private Speed as "serving sentence of Gen. Ct. Mar.")

Stanley, G. A.   Captain, Company F

Barrancas, Sept. 1, '64.

Charge I: Violation of the 6th Article of War.

Specification: "on being reproved by his Commanding Officer for allowing one enlisted man to leave the ranks on the march, and then asking permission as though he had not done so, did reply saying: 'there is no need of putting on so much style about it, I can order him back,' or words to that effect, and when his commanding Officer said 'I don't want the man in the ranks, if it is necessary that he should fall out, but I won't allow you to answer me in that manner,' did reply, saying: 'I don't care, I don't like that style and you may do what you like about it,' or words to that effect. This on the march from New Orleans to Greenville, Louisiana, on or about the 2nd day of August 1864."

Charge II: Conduct to the prejudice of good order and military discipline.

Specification 1st: "did, when his superior and inspecting officer called his attention to a rusty carbine in the hands of a private of his squadron, saying in reply to the Captain's excuse, that the man was company cook, 'If the cook has no time to clean his arms, you should have your light duty men do it,' reply: 'there is enough for the light duty men to do, beside looking after the company cook's arms,' or words to that effect. This at Algiers, La., on or about the 1st day of August 1864."

Specification 2nd: "did, give the first lieutenant of his squadron 'leave of absence' from his troop without consulting or referring him to the commanding officer of the datament, of which his command formed a part. This on the march from New Orleans to Greenville, La., on or about the 2nd day of August 1864."

Charge III: Breach of Arrest

Specification: "having been placed in arrest by his commanding officer, did go on duty and appear on inspection in command of his squadron, wearing his sabre without having been released from arrest or ordered on duty yet saying to the inspecting officer, 'The colonel has ordered me to come on inspection in command of my squadron,' or words to that effect. This at Greenville, La., on or about the 3rd day of August 1864."

Stanley pleaded not guilty.

All charges brought by Major Cutler.

Capt. Knowles was counsel for the accused.

Colonel Woodman, called as witness for prosecution in regards to the event on the march to Greenville, said that Major Cutler was in command and he (Woodman) had remained in Algiers. Stanley was placed in arrest by Major Cutler. When Capt. Stanley "had appeared on inspection wearing his sabre and in command of his Company, I ordered the Adjutant to go to the Captain, take his sabre and inform him that he was still under arrest. I wished that there should be no mistake about it. I had been informed that Capt Stanley was under the impression he had been released by my order."

When Woodman was asked in cross examination if he called all company commanders to his office when he arrived at Greenville, he answered yes. Apparently Capt. Stanley was among those present. "Might have given them some order, don't recollect of it. I didn't intend to do anything that could cause Capt Stanley to consider himself released from arrest." But, asked if he (Woodman) had made any distinction between him (Stanley) and others, Woodman answered, "No sir. Not as far as anything that occurred." Woodman also testified that he was not feeling well that day. "If I had known he was present I would have spoken to him and have told him it was an improper place for him to be. If I spoke to him at all, I didn't think of his being under arrest. There was a large assembly, officers from twelve Companies being around the tent." Woodman said Stanley had served under him for 22 months [assumed to include Stanley's time under Woodman in the 28th Maine]. "I never had any cause of complaint of Capt Stanley when under my immediate command. He has always served me faithfully and to my satisfaction, always been respectful and obedient."

Major Cutler testified about the man absent on march that Stanley had given permission for a man to fall out who was reported by the 1st sergeant as having diarrhea and then asked permission from Cutler to do so. Upon the reply stated above, Cutler said he "placed him [Stanley] under arrest and as there were no Lieutenants present with his Company, I put the 1st Sergeant in command of it." He said Stanley had also apparently given his 1st lieutenant permission to absent himself from the march for some reason.

Regarding the charge of breach of arrest, Major Cutler felt that Capt. Stanley may have believed, mistakenly, that when Col. Woodmen sent for him and other company commanders, that he (Stanley) was released from arrest. Major Cutler said he filed the charge of breach of arrest because he was ordered to do so by Col. Woodman. If he had not been ordered to file the charges, he would not have done so and would have expected that Stanley would have been given a reprimand by the colonel.

1st Lt. Evander Prescott testified he had been absent briefly while going with the 2nd lieutenant to look at a horse that the 2nd lieutenant was afraid they might lose while being transported on a ferry.

2nd Lt. Simon Parlin, Company F, reported overhearing a conversation between Stanley and Capt. Lincoln in which Lincoln said that Stanley's having been sent for by Col. Woodman as the company commander would indicate that Stanley had been released from arrest. He also said that men who needed to fall out while on the march were typically allowed to do.

Captain Lincoln, Company D, was called and agreed that Stanley was at the meeting and had been given orders regarding ammunition for an upcoming march. He stated that Major Cutler sometimes "exhibited an air of pomposity." Lincoln himself had apparently been under attest at one time and had been sent for by Col. Woodman, who gave him back his sword and told him to return to duty. No direct comment was made to Capt. Stanley during the meeting in Woodman's tent. Lincoln stated that when Stanley was sent for by the colonel, "I thought if he was sent for to go on duty he was released from arrest." But he stated that no other officers had been released from arrest in that way. He said, "The Colonel and Major and Capt Stanley had been like three brothers and it wouldn't look reasonable that they would wish to punish him if they could get out of it."

Captain Samuel Clarke, Company E, was called to testify: "It has always been the custom for Commanding Officers of squadrons to allow their men to fall out when necessary." Same thing applied to officers; "I have always allowed my Lieutenants to be absent temporarily for a few moments and nothing has been said about it."

After two days of testimony, on the third day the court accepted a written statement from Capt. Knowles, and the court was cleared for deliberation.

Stanley was found guilty of the first charge and specification. On both specifications to the second charge, he was found guilty, but found not guilty of second charge. On the specification to the third charge, he was found guilty, but found not guilty of third charge.

Sentence: "To be reprimanded in General Orders by the Commanding General." Captain Stanley "is hereby reprimanded for disrespectful conduct to his Superior Officers. He will be released from arrest and returned to duty."

Waltz, Andrew J.   Private, Company G

Barrancas, May 2, 1865

Charge: Conduct prejudicial to good order and military discipline

Specification: "did enter the Forage house of the Chief Quartermaster Dist of West Florida at the wharf at Barrancas Fla and did blow out the light belonging to the Provost Guard statioined over some liquors and other goods and did in the darkness steal and take away a quantity of liquor, to wit: two demyjohns of Whiskey or other liquor unknown." On or about the night of March 20, 1865.

Plea: Not guilty

Witnesses for prosecution: Sgt. L.K. Litchfield, Company I, Corp. Alpheus G. Kelly, Company F, Pvt. Ansel Walker, Company F, and Pvt. Van Rensalear Corson, Company F, all of the 2nd Maine Cavalry.

Witness for defense: Pvt. Edwin S. Jenks, Company G, 2nd Maine Cavalry.

No testimony from witnesses was found in the records at the National Archives. Three officers from the 2nd Maine Cavalry were among those detailed for the court: Capt. Merry, Capt. Knowles and Lt. Holbrook.

On the specification Waltz was found guilty, except the words "and did blow out the light belonging to the Provost Guard, stationed over some liquors and other goods."

Sentence: "To be confined at hard labor at Fort Pickens Fla., for four months and forfeit to the United States $8 per month of his monthly pay for the same period."

* * *

The following list is taken from Regimental Books, National Archives, but no record of the charges or details was found:

The "Field Officers Courts" held in the 2nd Maine Cavalry included trials for:

Cunningham, Pvt. Ellison, Company H, March 28, 1864
Davis, Corporal Thomas, Company L, August 25, 1864
Downs, Sgt. Michael, Company D, January 13, 1864
Fogg, Pvt. John, Company G, March 23, 1864
Gilchrist, Sgt. Alden, Company G, June 21, 1864
Grant, Corporal Mark, Company B, March 1864
Hanake, Sgt. Edgar, Company E, July 14
Hewitt, Pvt. Samual, Company E, April 1864
Patten, 1st Sgt. Alphonzo, Company G, January 28, 1864
Robbins, Corporal James, Company E, April 1864
Rogers, Pvt. Oscar, Company G, March 23, 1864
Thomas, Pvt. Silas, Company L, July 21
Withey, Sgt. A.J. April 1865 (perhaps another trial for Withey in early September 1865)

D. Men of the 2nd Maine Cavalry Held at Andersonville Prison

Information is taken from http://www.itd.nps.gov/cwss/andSearchp.cfm and the *Maine Adjutant General's Reports* (AG). Below each man's name is the information from the Andersonville web site, and then any further information from the *Maine Adjutant General's Reports*.

2nd Maine Cavalry

Brown, Henry, pvt., Company E, captured Sept. 27, '64, at Marianna, held at Andersonville and survived. AG '64: age 26, single, from Newcastle, Maine, missing in action, Sept. 27. AG '65: taken prisoner Sept. 27, 1864; not since reported.

Clark, Elisha E., sgt., Company L, captured Sept. 27, '64, at Marianna, held at Andersonville and survived. AG '64: age 19, single, from Limerick, Maine, promoted to 1st sgt. AG '65: paroled prisoner; discharged by order July 31, wounded Sept. 27 and taken prisoner.

Clough, Charles H., pvt., Company L, captured Sept. 27, '64, at Marianna, held at Andersonville and survived. AG '64: age 21, single, from Biddeford, Maine, wounded, Battle of Marianna, Sept. 27, and taken prisoner. AG '65: absent with leave since Sept. 27.

Cutler, Nathaniel, major, wounded and taken prisoner September 27, at Marianna, held at Andersonville and survived in command of the last group of prisoners released on April 29, 1865

Ellis, Daniel, pvt., Company H, captured Sept. 27, '64, at Marianna, died at Andersonville and buried in National Cemetery. AG '64: age 28, married, from Searsport, missing in action at Marianna, Sept. 27. AG '65: taken prisoner Sept. 27.

Evans, Orrin R., pvt., Company L, captured Sept. 27, '64, at Marianna, held at Andersonville and survived. AG '64: age 21, married, from Lyman, Maine, wounded at Marianna, Sept. 27 and taken prisoner. AG '65: paroled prisoner discharged July 17, 1865.

O'Neal, H., pvt., listed as Company B (actually Company D), capture date unknown, capture site unknown, held at Andersonville and survived, exchanged April 1, 1865. AG '64: O'Neal, Henry pvt., Company D, age 23, married, from Portland, Maine, missing since Sept. 28. AG '65: discharged by order Sept. 18, '65.

Pendleton, S. H., pvt., Company E, capture date unknown, capture site unknown, held at Andersonville and survived, exchanged April 1, 1865. AG '64: Pendleton, Sanford H.; 18 years old, single, from Rockland, Maine, wounded and left at Marianna, Sept. 27. AG '65: exchanged prisoner; discharged Sept. 18.

Pollard, Luther M., corp., Company G, captured Sept. 27, '64, at Marianna, held at Andersonville and survived. AG '64: age 23, married, from Bradley, Maine, wounded Sept. 27 at Marianna, taken prisoner. AG '65: wounded and prisoner Sept. 27, 1864.

Sims, Moses, pvt., Company M, captured Sept. 27, '64, at Marianna, held at Andersonville and survived. AG '64: age 38, married, from Canton, Maine, missing since battle of Marianna, Sept. 27. AG '65: died in hospital, March 7, '65.

Whitney, Chester, pvt., Company I, captured Sept. 27, '64, at Marianna, held at Andersonville and survived. AG '64: age 19, single, from Gardiner, Maine, missing in action Sept. 27, dropped from rolls. AG '65: taken prisoner Sept. 27; not returned to company.

Whitney, David C., corp., Company F, captured Sept. 27, '64, at Marianna, held at Andersonville and survived. AG '64: age 28, single, from Industry, Maine, wounded and taken prisoner, Marianna, Sept. 27. AG '65: died of wounds, Oct. 24, '64 (survived, according to Andersonville site).

Williams, George W., pvt., Company I, capture date unknown capture site unknown, held at Andersonville and survived, exchanged April 1, 1865. AG '64: Williams, George W. age 22, married, from Winthrop, missing in action Sept. 27, dropped from rolls. AG '65: discharged by order Sept. 18.

Others Listed on Andersonville Website

Shuman, G., pvt., Company G, 2nd Maine?, capture date unknown, capture site unknown, held at Andersonville and survived, recorded on Andersonville website, but there is no G. Shuman listed as a member of the 2nd Maine Cavalry or the 2nd Maine Infantry.

Zerner, Nicholas, pvt., Company E, 2nd Maine?, capture date unknown, capture site unknown, held at Andersonville and survived. Sent to Millen, Nov. 11, 1864; no such name found in AG's index of men serving from Maine.

E. Officers Mustered Out in Florida

The following officers chose to be discharged in Florida and took a cash payment in lieu of transportation back to Maine.

Colonel E.W. Woodman
Lt. Col. Andrew Spurling
Major Charles Miller
Surgeon George Martin
1st Lt. and Adjutant A.J. Pickard
Captains: B. G. Merry, E.D. Johnson, John Lincoln, Samuel Clarke, Gustavus Stanley, Samuel Knowles, Samuel Libby, Ivory Allen
1st Lieutenants: Warren Mansur, Warren Pierce, Fred Metcalf, Evander Prescott, Daniel Simpson, Samuel Holbrook, Marcus Vose
2nd Lieutenants: Silas Barker, Benjamin Jones, Oakman Glidden, William Moody

Chapter Notes

Chapter One

1. Quoted in Allan Nevins, *The Fruits of Manifest Destiny*, pp. 240–241.
2. The CSA Constitution. Retrieved July 15, 2011. http://www.law.ou.edu/ushistory/csaconstitution/.
3. Augusta, Georgia, *Daily Constitutionalist*. March 30, 1861.
4. "Declaration of the Immediate Causes Which Induce and Justify the Secession of South Carolina from the Federal Union." Retrieved December 18, 2010. http://teachingamericanhistory.org/library/document/south-carolina-declaration-of-causes-of-secession/.
5. Quoted in James McPherson, *Battle Cry of Freedom*, p. 106.
6. Brig *Kentucky*. Penobscot Marine Museum. Retrieved May 12, 2012; http://www.penobscotmarinemuseum.org/pbho-1/collection/brig-kentucky University of Kentucky Libraries; Retrieved May 12, 2012; http://nkaa.uky.edu/record.php?note_id=1617.
7. *Nightingale. Dictionary of American Naval Fighting Ships*. U.S. Navy Historical Center. Retrieved September 19, 2012. http://www.history.navy.mil/danfs/n5/nightingale-i.htm.
8. *Harper's Weekly*, March 8, 1862. "Abolition of the Atlantic Slave Trade in the United States." Retrieved February 4, 2005. http://www1.american.edu/TED/slave.htm.
9. Email communication. Anthony Douin, Maine State Archives. September 15, 2013. "St. Marks River, the Early Years. Retrieved July 6, 2012. http://www.littletownmart.com/fdh/st-marks-river.htm North. *History of Augusta, Maine*.
10. *New York Times*. May 15, 1861.
11. "The Abolition of The Slave Trade: Revivial of the Slave Trade." Retrieved April 6, 2012. http://abolition.nypl.org/print/revival_of_slave_trade/.
12. Diane Monroe Smith, *Fanny and Joshua*, pp. 108–109.
13. Smith, *Fanny and Joshua*, pp. 108–109.
14. Mark Hatfield, "Vice Presidents of the United States—Hannibal Hamlin (1861–1865)" Retrieved January 12, 2008. www.senate.gov/artandhistory/history/resources/pdf/hannibal_hamlin.pdf+Hannibal+Hamlin&hl=en&gl=us.
15. Surdam, "Traders or Traitors."
16. Personal communication. Sylvia Sherman, Maine State Archives. April 20, 2010.

Chapter Two

1. Peters, *The Forida Wars*, pp. 149–152, 177–205.
2. Wynne, *Florida in the Civil War*, p. 10.
3. Wynne, *Florida in the Civil War*, p. 21.
4. Parker, "John Milton, Governor of Florida." *The Florida Historical Quarterly*. Vol. 20, number 4. April 1942. "Florida Governor John Milton." Retrieved June 6, 2013. http://www.nga.org/cms/home/governors/past-governors-bios/page_florida/col2-content/main-content-list/title_milton_john.html Pearce. *Pensacola During the Civil War*, p. 4.
5. Pearce, *Pensacola During the Civil War*, p. 9, p. 14.
6. Pearce, *Pensacola During the Civil War*, pp. 8, 11–12, 14, 114–117.
7. Pearce, *Pensacola During the Civil War*, pp. 12, 24, 42–44.
8. Pearce, *Pensacola During the Civil War;*, pp. 15–30. Callum. *Biographical Reigister West Point* (1868), p. 155. National Park Service. "Fort Pickens." Retrieved October 8, 2011. http://www.nps.gov/guis/planyourvisit/fort-pickens.htm. National Park Serivice. "Fort Barrancas." Retrieved October 8, 2011. http://www.nps.gov/guis/planyourvisit/fort-barrancas.htm.
9. Stahr, *Seward, Lincoln's Indispensable Man*, p. 266–269.
10. Wynne, *Florida in the Civil War*, pp. 78–82.
11. Wynne, *Florida in the Civil War*, pp. 80–81.
12. "A Guide to Civil War Records. Florida Unionists." Retrieved April 14, 2013. http://www.floridamemory.com/collections/civilwarguide/history.php. Williams, George W. *A History of the Negro Troops in the War of the Rebellion*, p. 140.
13. Burllingame, *At Lincoln's Side*, pp. 75–79.
14. Lincoln Papers, Library of Congress.
15. Lincoln Papers, Library of Congress.
16. Davis, *The Civil War and Reconstruction in Florida*, p. 415.
17. Davis, *The Civil War and Reconstruction in Florida*, pp. 218–241.
18. Davis, *The Civil War and Reconstruction in Florida*, p. 226.

19. Davis, *The Civil War and Reconstruction in Florida*, p. 227.

Chapter Three

1. *General Orders affecting the Volunteer Force*, pp. 134–137.
2. *General Orders affecting the Volunteer Force*, pp. 134–137.
3. Letter from Col. Woodman to General Thomas McKean. January 19, 1865. Maine State Archives Correspondence files.
4. *General Orders affecting the Volunteer Force*.
5. Letter from J.S. Chadwick to Maine Adj. Gen. John Hodsdon. September 1863. Maine State Archives Correspondence files.
6. Letter from Lt. Samuel Knowles to Adj. Gen. Hodsdon. Maine State Archives Correspondence files.
7. Letter from Isaac B. Harris to Maine Governor Abner Coburn. September 1863. Maine State Archives Correspondence files.
8. Letter from George W. Martin to Governor Coburn. September 1863. Maine State Archives Correspondence files.
9. Letter from Assessors of Haynesville, Maine to Adj. Gen. Hodsdon. December 4, 1863. Maine State Archives Correspondence files.
10. In 2000, Haynesville remained a very small town, with a population of 122 and a median household income of $23,542. "Haynesville, Maine." Retrieved June 3, 2013. http://www.city-data.com/city/Haynesville-Maine.html.
11. Letter from Captain Twitchell to Mr. Leland. November 26, 1863. Maine State Archives Correspondence files.
12. *Maine Adjutant General's Report, 1864–65*.
13. Letter from Jacob Frye to Adj. Gen. Hodsdon. December 8, 1863. Maine State Archives Correspondence files. (John George, age 32, single from Patten, Pvt., Co. A; discharged for disability, June 27, '65).
14. Letter from B.F. Minor (Chairman of Selectmen, Pembroke, Maine) to Adj. Gen. Hodsdon. December 14, 1863. Maine State Archives Correspondence files.
15. Letter from George Field to Adj. Gen. Hodsdon. December 1863. Maine State Archives Correspondence files.
16. Letter from James M. Deering to Maine Governor Abner Coburn. December 1863. Maine State Archives Correspondence files. (Andrew J Woodman, age 34, married, from Saco, Maine, 1st Lt. Company L was wounded at Marianna, Sept, 1864).
17. Letter from Owen O'Brien to Maine Governor Samuel Cony. December 23, 1863. Maine State Archives Correspondence files.
18. Letter from Arthur Ingersoll et al. to Governor Cony. January 4, 1864. Maine State Archives Correspondence files.
19. Letter from Colonel Ephraim Woodman to Adj. Gen. Hodsdon. July 28, 1864. Maine State Archives Correspondence files.
20. *Maine in the War for the Union*, p. 563.
21. *Maine Adjutant General's Report, 1863*; *1864–65*. *Maine in the War for the Union*, pp. 442–443.
22. Sawyer, *Civil War Letters of John Franklin Godfrey*, pp. 14–16.
23. Boatner, *Civil War Dictionary*, p. 81, 861. *Maine Adjutant General's Reports*. 1861–1863. Pension file, Andrew B. Spurling. National Archives. "Gen. Andrew Barclay Spurling." Retrieved May 3, 2011. http://www.cranberryisles.com/photos/andrew_spurling.html.
24. Butler, *History of Farmington, Maine*, p. 453.
25. John Pullen, *The Twentieth Maine*.
26. Email communication from Anthony Douin, Maine State Archives. October 15, 2013. (In 1860, Mr. French is listed in the census records as a farmer, living with his wife Sarah, 4 children, and Sarah's mother.).
27. Personal communication from Anthony Douin, Maine State Archives. May 8, 2012.
28. Shaw, *The First Maine Heavy Artillery*, p. 210 and company rosters.

Chapter Four

1. Regimental and Company Books, Second Maine Cavalry. National Archives.
2. Regimental and Company Books, Second Maine Cavalry. National Archives.
3. Regimental and Company Books, Second Maine Cavalry. National Archives.
4. Regimental and Company Books, Second Maine Cavalry. National Archives.
5. Regimental and Company Books, Second Maine Cavalry. National Archives.
6. Regimental and Company Books, Second Maine Cavalry. National Archives.
7. Regimental and Company Books, Second Maine Cavalry. National Archives.
8. Stewart Sifakis, *Who Was Who in the Union*, p. 57. Boatner, *Civil War Dictionary*, p. 107. "Burnside Carbine." Smithsonian. Retrieved June 10, 2013. http://www.civilwar.si.edu/weapons_burnside.html.
9. Kerry Barlow, "Handguns of the Civil War." Retrieved July 10, 2013. http://civilwarhandgun.com/remington.htm.
10. *Maine Adjutant General's Report, 1864–65*. Regimental and Company Books, Second Maine Cavalry. National Archives.
11. *Maine Adjutant General's Report, 1864–65*.
12. *Supplement to the Official Records*, March and April 1864. *New York Times*, March 20, 1864. *New York Times*, April 1, 1864. Letter from Col. Woodman to Adj. Gen. Hodsdon. April 23, 1864. Maine State Archives Correspondence Files. *Maine Adjutant General's Report, 1864–65*.
13. Boatner, *Civil War Dictionary*, pp. 476–477. Warner, *Generals in Gray*, pp. 181–182.
14. *Official Record*, Vol. 6, p. 881. Warner, *Generals in Gray*, pp. 194–195.
15. *Official Record*, Vol. 6, p. 882.
16. *Official Record*, Vol. 6, p. 882.
17. *Official Record*, Vol. 6, pp. 884–885.
18. *Official Record*, Vol. 6, p. 884.

19. *Official Record*, Vol. 34, Pt. 3, p. 25.
20. *Maine Adjutant General's Report, 1864.* Letter from Col. Woodman to Adj. Gen. Hodsdon. April 23, 1864. Maine State Archives Correspondence files.
21. Joiner, *One Damn Blunder*, pp. 15–18. Johnson, *Red River Campaign*, p. 13, pp. 67–78.
22. Sifakis, *Who Was Who*, p. 172. Boatner, *Civil War Dictionary*, p. 685. Johnson, *Red River Campaign*, p. 36, pp. 78–80. For more about Henry Halleck, his rise to power in the Lincoln administration, and his method of issuing orders, see Diane Monroe Smith's *Command Conflicts*.
23. Johnson, *Red River Campaign*, p. 71–72, p. 36.
24. Warner, *Generals in Gray*, pp. 299–300.
25. Johnson, *Red River Campaign*, p. 81, pp. 101–104.
26. Johnson, *Red River Campaign*, pp. 97–98, pp. 146–147. Joiner, *One Damn Blunder*, pp. 115–116.
27. Johnson, *Red River Campaign*, pp. 207–214.
28. Smith, *Command Conflicts*, p. 68.
29. Johnson, *Red River Campaign*, pp. 237–240.
30. *Official Record*, Vol. 34, Pt. 1, p. 583.
31. Johnson, *Red River Campaign*, pp. 249–251. Boatner. *Civil War Dictionary*, p. 38.
32. Letter from Sgt. F.W. Pearce to his brother. April 21, 1864. Quoted in Joiner, *Little to Eat and Thin Mud to Drink*. (Sgt. Frank W Peace was in Company A, 2nd Maine Cavalry, not in Company H, as stated in the book. Company H was not one of the companies that went to the Red River. In the letter, Pearce mentions Capt. Twitchell, who was Company A's commander.).
33. *Official Record*, Vol. 34, Pt. 1, p. 461–462. *Official Record*, Vol. 34, Pt. 4, p. 29. "John Montgomery Crebs" Biographical Directory of the United States Congress. Retrieved September 4, 2013. http://bioguide.congress.gov/scripts/biodisplay.pl?index=C000900. Lt. Col. Crebs, previous to the Civil War, had been a practicing lawyer in Illinois. He resumed his practice after the war and, from 1869 to 1873, served as a member of Congress from Illinois.
34. Johnson, *Red River Campaign*, pp. 262–266. Joiner, *One Damn Blunder*. Chapters 9 and 11. *Official Record*, Vol. 34, Pt. 3, pp. 517–518.
35. Burlingame, *Inside Lincoln's White House*, p. 250.
36. *Official Record*, Vol. 34, Pt. 1, p. 591. *Official Record*, Vol. 34, Pt. 3, p. 518.
37. *Maine Adjutant General's Report, 1864–65*, p. 219.
38. Johnson, *Red River Campaign*, pp. 182–183. *Official Record*, Vol. 34, Pt. 1, p. 581. *Official Record*, Vol. 34, Pt. 3, p. 518.
39. *Official Record*, Vol. 34, Pt. 1, pp. 586–588.
40. *Official Record*, Vol. 34, Pt. 1, p. 592.
41. Johnson, *Red River Campaign*, p. 272.
42. *Official Record*, Vol. 34, Pt. 1, pp. 590–591.
43. *Official Record*, Vol. 34, Pt. 1, p. 589.
44. *Official Record*, Vol. 34, Pt. 1, pp. 590–591.
45. *Official Record*, Vol. 34, Pt. 1, p. 447.
46. *Official Record*, Vol. 34, Pt. 1, pp. 592–593.
47. Joiner, *One Damn Blunder*, p. 170. Johnson, *Red River Campaign*, p. 273. *Official Record*, Vol. 34, Pt. 1, p. 593.
48. *Maine Adjutant General's Report, 1864–65*. Johnson, *Red River Campaign*, p. 275. Joiner, *One Damn Blunder*, p. 171. *Official Record*, Vol. 34, Pt. 1, pp. 593–594.
49. *Official Record*, Vol. 34, Pt. 1, p. 593–594.
50. *Official Record*, Vol. 34, Pt. 1, p. 594.
51. *Maine in the War for the Union*, p. 565.
52. Johnson, *Red River Campaign*, pp. 147–149, pp. 283–284.
53. Boatner, *Civil War Dictionary*, p. 118.
54. Boatner, *Civil War Dictionary*, p. 827.
55. Letter from Col. Woodman to Adj. Gen. Hodsdon. April 23, 1864. Maine State Archives Correspondence files.
56. *Maine Adjutant General's Report, 1864–65*. Roberts, *A Story of General Andrew Spurling*, pp. 10–11.
57. Roberts, *A Story of General Andrew Spurling*, p. 11.
58. Dale Cox, *The Battle of Marianna*, pp. 27–28.
59. *Official Record*, Vol. 34, Pt. 4, p. 29. *Maine Adjutant General's Report, 1864–65*.

Chapter Five

1. *Official Record*, Vol. 34, Pt. 4, p. 427.
2. *Official Record*, Vol. 34, Pt. 4, p. 614—617.
3. Letter from Col. Woodman to Adj. Gen. Hodsdon. July 6, 1864. Maine State Archives Correspondence files.
4. *Official Record*, Vol. 41, Pt. 2, p. 95; p. 260.
5. Letter from Col. Woodman to Governor Cony. April 23, 1864. Maine State Archives Correspondence files.
6. Letter from Major Miller to Adj. Gen. Hodsdon. July 12, 1864. Maine State Archives Correspondence files.
7. Letter from Captain Twitchell to Adj. Gen. Hodsdon. July 24, 1864. Maine State Archives Correspondence files.
8. Roberts, *A Story of General Andrew Spurling*, p. 7, p. 14. (It always makes me nervous to rely on a single source for information that is not found in other sources. In this case, however, the fact that this book was presented at a regimental reunion would, I feel, assure at least substantial accuracy, given that the men to whom it was presented were those who had taken part in the actions described.).
9. Letter from Col. Woodman to Governor Cony. August 8, 1864. Maine State Archives Correspondence files. (The Colonel Rust mentioned is most likely Col. Henry Rust, who commanded the 13th Maine Infantry, Colonel Beal most likely Col. George Beal of the 29th Maine Infantry, and General Nickerson was Grig. Gen. Franklin Nickerson who had been a major in the 4th Maine Infantry, colonel of the 14th Maine Infantry, and at the time of this letter, commanded the 1st Brigade, 2nd Division, 19th Army Corps.) .
10. Johnson, *Red River Campaign*, p. 101. Personal communication, Anthony Douin, Maine State Archives. August 2013. *Official Record*, Vol. 10, Pt. 2, pp. 26–27.

11. Letter from Col. Woodman to Governor Cony. August 8, 1864. Maine State Archives Correspondence files. *Maine Adjutant General's Report, 1864–65.*
12. Court Martial Proceedings. National Archives. ARC Identifier 1831798 / Local Identifier LL-2675 / MLR Number PC29 15A.
13. Letter from Col. Woodman to Governor Cony. August 8, 1864. Maine State Archives Correspondence files.
14. Letter from RQM John Milliken to Governor Cony. August 27, 1864. Maine State Archives Correspondence files.
15. Pearce, *Pensacola During the Civil War*, p. 215.
16. Boatner, *Civil War Dictionary*, pp. 27–27. Sifakis, *Who Was Who in the Union*, p. 11. (Asboth began his service in July 1861 as chief of staff for Union General John C. Fremont and rose to the rank of brigadier general in March 1862. He fought in the Arkansas Campaign, was seriously wounded at the Battle of Pea Ridge, and participated in the Siege of Corinth as a brigade commander. Before his assignment to command the District of West Florida, was commanding garrisons in Kentucky and Ohio.).
17. Pearce, *Pensacola During the Civil War*, p. 193, p. 207.
18. Pearce, *Pensacola During the Civil War*, p. 76.
19. Warner, *Generals in Gray*, p. 165–166.
20. *Official Record*, Vol. 6, p. 881–882, p. 884.
21. Pearce, *Pensacola During the Civil War*, pp. 143–147, pp. 158–159. "Civil War, Pensacola." University of Southern Florida. Retrieved July 18, 2011. http://fcit.usf.edu/florida/docs/c/civatpen.htm.
22. *Official Record*, Vol. 35, Pt. 2, pp. 149–150.
23. Pearce, *Pensacola During the Civil War*, pp. 186–192; "Fort Pickens." Retrieved November 6, 2010. http://www.nps.gov/nr/twhp/wwwlps/lessons/38pickens/38facts1.htm.
24. John B. Wilson, Capt. Co. H, 15th Me. Quoted in Haines, *Letters from Pensacola*, p. 83. Pearce. *Pensacola During the Civil War*, pp. 188–195.
25. Pearce, *Pensacola During the Civil War*, p. 197. *Official Record*, Vol. 26, Pt. 1, p. 817–818.
26. Pearce, *Pensacola During the Civil War*, pp. 208–209.
27. Pearce, *Pensacola During the Civil War*, p. 206–207. *Official Record*, Vol. 35, Pt. 1, p. 385. "14th New York Cavalry." Retrieved October 14, 2011. http://dmna.ny.gov/historic/reghist/civil/cavalry/14thCav/14thCavMain.htm.
28. "The Kossuth Nephews in America." Retrieved August 16, 2012. http://www.skszeged.hu/statikus_html/vasvary/newsletter/11dec/kossuth.html *Official Record*, Vol. 35, Pt. 2, p. 160, pp. 165–166.
29. *Official Record*, Vol. 35, Pt. 2, pp. 165–166. *Official Record*, Vol. 35, Pt. 1, pp. 424–425. *Official Record*, Vol. 35, Pt. 2, p. 181.
30. *Official Record*, Vol. 35, Pt. 2, pp. 223–224.
31. *Official Record*, Vol. 35, part 2, p. 228.
32. Regimental and Company Books. National Archives.
33. General Order No. 8. August 16, 1864. Regimental and Company Books. National Archives.
34. General Order No. 11. SePt. 3, 1864. Regimental and Company Books. National Archives.
35. Regimental and Company Books. National Archives.
36. Regimental and Company Books. National Archives.
37. *Supplement to the Official Records,* August 1864.
38. Surgeon's Papers, 2nd Maine Cavalry. Maine State Archives. (Dr. Julius Augustus Skilton had graduated from Rensselaer Polytechnic Institute in 1849 with a Bachelors of Natural Science. He went on to get an A.M. from Wesleyan University and an M.D. from Albany Medical College. He enlisted in the Union Army as an assistant surgeon at the outbreak of the Civil War and rose through the ranks to become Surgeon in Chief of Cavalry, Dept. of the Gulf.).
39. Haines, *Letters from Pensacola*, pp. 87–88.
40. Haines, *Letters from Pensacola*, p. 89.
41. *Official Record*, Vol. 35, Pt. 2, pp. 232–233.
42. *Supplement to the Official Records*, August 1864.
43. *Official Record*, Vol. 35, Pt. 1, p. 426.
44. Bearss, "Asboth's Expedition." pp. 165–166.
45. *Official Record*, Vol. 35, Pt. 2, p. 231.
46. Bearss, "Asboth's Expedition." pp. 162–166.
47. *Supplement to the Official Records,* August 1864.
48. *Official Record*, Vol. 35, Pt. 2, pp. 253–254, p. 257.
49. *Supplement to the Official Records,* August 1864.
50. "Milton, Florida." Retrieved June 16, 2012. http://www.ci.milton.fl.us/living/history.htm Pearce. *Pensacola During the Civil War*, p. 195–196.
51. *Official Record*, Vol. 35, Pt. 1, p. 442.
52. *Official Record*, Vol. 35, Pt. 1, pp. 442–443.
53. "Barbiers Cavalry Battalion." Retrieved August 16, 2013. http://www.algw.org/bullock/barbieres_cavalry_battalion.htm.
54. Pearce, *Pensacola During the Civil War*, p. 217. *Official Record*, Vol. 16, Pt. 1, p. 805. *Official Record*, Vol. 15, Pt. 1, pp. 137–138. *Official Record*, Vol. 49, Pt. 2, p. 253. *Official Record*, Vol. 14, p. 24.
55. "Chart: Distribution of Arms." LSU Libraries, Special Collections. Bilby, Joe, "The Lorenz." Retrieved August 16, 2004. www.washingtonbluerifles.com/bilbylorenz.htm.
56. Letter from Samuel Sprague to Adj. Gen. Hodsdon. August 29, 1864. Maine State Archives Correspondence files.
57. Letter from Adj. Gen. Hodson to Lt. Col. Spurling. September 3, 1864. Maine State Archives Correspondence files. Letter from Frank Howes (N.E. Soldiers Relief Association) to Adj. Gen. Hodsdon. September 6, 1864. Maine State Archives Correspondence files. Letter from Alfred Marshall to Adj. Gen. Hodsdon. September 25, 1865. Maine State Archives Correspondence files. Letter from Alfred Marshall to Adj. Gen. Hodsdon. October 30, 1865. Maine State Archives Correspondence files.
58. Haines, *Letters from Pensacola*, p. 92.
59. General Order No. 10. August 25, 1864. Regimental and Company Books. National Archives.

Chapter Six

1. Pearce, *Pensacola During the Civil War*, p. 218.
2. Haines, *Letters from Pensacola*, p. 91.
3. Haines, *Letters from Pensacola*, p. 89.
4. *Official Record*, Vol. 35, Pt. 1, p. 37.
5. "Florida Union Cavalry." Retrieved June 18, 2012. eHistory Archive: Ohio State University. http://ehistory.osu.edu/uscw/features/regimental/florida/union/cavalry/fl/0001.cfm "Florida in the Civil War; Unionism in Florida." Florida Dept. of State, Division of Historical Resources. Retrieved June 18, 2012. http://www.flheritage.com/facts/reports/civilwar/08.cfm "United States Colored Troops Infantry," The Civil War Archives, Union Regimental Histories. Retrieved June 18, 2012. http://www.civilwararchive.com/Unreghst/uncolinf1.htm.
6. *Official Record*, Vol. 35, Pt. 1, pp. 443–445.
7. Bangor, Maine, *Whig & Courier*. Letter dated October 8, 1864. Quoted in Roberts, *A Story of General Andrew Spurling*, pp. 19–20. Cox, *The Battle of Marianna, Florida* Boyd. *Battle of Marianna*, p. 228.
8. Weston, *Nothern Monthly*. Vol. 1, p. 638.
9. "September 23, 1864—New Account of the Skirmish at Eucheeana." Retrieved July 18, 2013. http://civilwarflorida.blogspot.com/2010_09_01_archive.html.
10. Boyd, *Battle of Marianna*, p. 229.
11. "Eucheeanna Community." Walton County Florida. History. Retrieved April 6, 2013. http://www.co.walton.fl.us/index.aspx?NID=316 .
12. McKinnon, *History of Walton County*, pp. 327, 330.
13. McKinnon, *History of Walton County*, pp. 164–176, pp. 340–347.
14. *Official Record*, Vol. 35, Pt. 1, p. 443–445.
15. Letter from Pvt. Edgar Davis to Adj. Gen. Hodsdon. October 2, 1864. Maine State Archives Correspondence files. *Maine in War for the Union*, p. 565. Roberts, *A Story of General Andrew Spurling*, p. 20.
16. Roberts, *A Story of General Andrew Spurling*, pp. 20–22.
17. Cox, *The Battle of Marianna, Florida*, p. 86.
18. Bangor, Maine, *Whig & Courier*. Letter dated October 8, 1864. Quoted in Cox. *The Battle of Marianna, Florida*, p. 86.
19. Roberts, *A Story of General Andrew Spurling*, p. 21.
20. *Official Record*, Vol. 35, Pt. 1, p. 443–445. Cox. *The Battle of Marianna, Florida*, pp. 45–46.
21. "Alexander B. Montgomery." The Battle of Marianna. Retrieved July 14, 2012. http://www.floridalcv.org/prelim3.htm.
22. Cox, *The Battle of Marianna, Florida*, pp. 46–47.
23. Cox, *The Battle of Marianna, Florida*, p. 1.
24. Cox, *The Battle of Marianna, Florida*, p. 46.
25. Letter from Fanny Bryan Chapman to "Dear Niece." September 1908. Quoted in Cox. *The Battle of Marianna, Florida*, p. 50.
26. Boyd, "The Battle of Marianna." p. 231.
27. Cox, *The Battle of Marianna, Florida*, pp. 50–51. Boyd. "The Battle of Marianna." p. 232.
28. Cox, *The Battle of Marianna, Florida*, p. 52.
29. Cox, *The Battle of Marianna, Florida*, p. 53.
30. Cox, *The Battle of Marianna, Florida*, p. 54.
31. Cox, *The Battle of Marianna, Florida*, pp. 55–56.
32. Letter from Pvt. Edgar Davis to Adj. Gen. Hodsdon. October 2, 1864. Maine State Archives Correspondence files.
33. *Official Record*, Vol. 35, Pt. 1, pp. 443–445.
34. Beyer and Keydel, *Deeds of Valor*. Vol. 1, p. 415.
35. Boyd, "The Battle of Marianna." p. 233, 234. Brevard. *A History of Florida*, p. 171.
36. Muster Rolls, 82nd U.S. Colored Infantry. National Archives.
37. Quoted in Cox, *The Battle of Marianna, Florida*, pp. 64–65.
38. Quoted in Cox, *The Battle of Marianna, Florida*, pp. 65. (Charles Wilson was the Quartermaster Sgt. of Company G, 2nd Maine Cavalry, and the letter that is quoted appeared in the Bangor, Maine, *Whig & Courier*, December 22nd, 1864).
39. Cox, *The Battle of Marianna, Florida*, p. 64.
40. Cox, *The Battle of Marianna, Florida*, p. 65.
41. Cox, *The Battle of Marianna, Florida*, p. 66. Norris, quoted in Trudeau, *Like Men of War*, p. 268–269.
42. Cox, *The Battle of Marianna, Florida*, p. 66. Boyd, "The Battle of Marianna," p. 235.
43. Smith, *The 22nd Maine*, pp. 255–157. "The Battle of Olustee." Retrieved October 16, 2012. http://battleofolustee.org/battle.html *Official Record*, Vol. 32, Pt. 1, pp. 519–540, pp. 554–555.
44. Cox, *The Battle of Marianna, Florida*, pp. 113–114, p. 117.
45. Boyd, "The Battle of Marianna." pp. 235–236. Cox, *The Battle of Marianna, Florida*, p. 118. *Maine Adjutant General's Report, 1864 & 1865*. "Search for Prisoners: Andersonville." Retrieved June 20, 2012. http://www.nps.gov/civilwar/search-prisoners.htm.
46. "Statement of Dr. George Martin." Pension file of Nathan Cutler, 2nd Maine Cavalry. National Archives.
47. Cox, *The Battle of Marianna, Florida*, p. 67.
48. *Official Record*, Vol. 35, Pt. 1, p. 443–445. Cox, *The Battle of Marianna, Florida*, pp. 89–90.
49. *Official Record*, Vol. 35, Pt. 1, pp. 443–445.
50. Cullum, *Biographical Register of the Officers and Graduates of the United States Military Academy*. Vol. 1. #785, p. 586. "Alexander B. Montgomery." The Battle of Marriana. Retrieved September 5, 2012. http://www.floridalcv.org/prelim3.htm.
51. *Official Record*, Vol. 35, Pt. 1, pp. 444–445.
52. Roberts, *A Story of General Andrew Spurling*, p. 21–22. Letter from Pvt. Edgar Davis to Adj. Gen. Hodsdon. October 2, 1864. Maine State Archives Correspondence. *Maine in War for Union*, p. 566.
53. Roberts, *A Story of General Andrew Spurling*, pp. 21–22. Cox, *The Battle of Marianna, Florida*, pp. 85–86.
54. *Official Record*, Vol. 35, Pt. 1, p. 444–445.
55. *Maine Adjutant General's Report, 1864–65.*.

Chapter Seven

1. Letter from Capt. Twitchell to Governor Cony. October 9, 1864. Maine State Archives Correspondence files.
2. *Official Record*, Vol. 35, Pt. 1, p. 38.
3. *Official Record*, Vol. 35, Pt. 1, p. 446.
4. *Official Record*, Vol. 35, Pt. 1, pp. 445–446.
5. *Official Record*, Vol. 35, Pt. 1, p. 38. *Official Record*, Vol. 35, Pt. 1, p446.
6. *Official Record*, Vol. 35, Pt. 1, pp. 447–448.
7. *Official Record*, Vol. 35, Pt. 1, pp. 448–450.
8. *Official Record*, Vol. 35, Pt. 1, pp. 450.
9. *Official Record*, Vol. 41, Pt. 4, p. 365. "The Kossuth Nephews in America." Retrieved August 12, 2012. http://www.sk-szeged.hu/statikus_html/vasvary/newsletter/11dec/kossuth.html.
10. *Supplement to the Official Records*, November 1864.
11. *Supplement to the Official Records*, November 1864. *Official Record*, Vol. 44, pp. 418–419.
12. *Official Record*, Vol. 44, pp. 418–419.
13. Letter from Major Miller to Adj. Gen. Hodsdaon. December 4, 1864. Maine State Archives Correspondence files.
14. Letter from Major Miller to Adj. Gen. Hodsdaon. December 4, 1864. Maine State Archives Correspondence files. Comments on the Miller letter. Maine State Archives web site. Retrieved April 6, 2012. http://www.maine.gov/tools/whatsnew/index.php?topic=arcsesq&id=163714&v=article.
15. Col. George Robinson, "Official Report of an Expedition to Pollard, Ala." December 21, 1864. Quoted in Roberts *A Story of General Andrew Spurling*, pp. 27–34. *Maine in the War for the Union*, p. 567.
16. *Maine in the War for the Union*, p. 567. *Supplement to the Official Records*, December 1864.
17. *Maine in War for the Union*, p. 567.
18. Pension File. Spurling, Andrew. National Archives.
19. *Supplement to the Official Records*, December 1864. *Maine in the War for the Union*, p. 567–568.
20. *Supplement to the Official Records*, December 1864. *Maine in the War for the Union*, p. 567–568.
21. *Maine in the War for the Union*, p. 567–568.
22. *Supplement to the Official Records*, December 1864.
23. *Maine in the War for the Union*, p. 567–568.
24. *Official Record*, Vol. 44, p. 449.
25. Col. George Robinson, "Official Report of an Expedition to Pollard, Ala." December 21, 1864. Quoted in Roberts. *A Story of General Andrew Spurling*, p. 33.
26. *Official Record*, Vol. 44, p. 449.
27. Warner, *Generals in Gray*, pp. 187–188.
28. Dunbar, *Military History of Mississippi*.
29. *Official Record*, Vol. 44, p. 449.
30. Chris Lyons, "Battle at Pine Barren Creek, Florida." Retrieved April 4, 2012. http://www.16thconfederatecavalry.com/timelinebattles/pinebarren.html Lyons, Chris. "Sixteenth Confederate Cavalry." Retrieved April 4, 2012. http://www.16thconfederatecavalry.com/home.html.
31. *Supplement to the Official Records*, December 1864.
32. *Maine Adjutant General's Report, 1864–65*.
33. Roberts, *A Story of General Andrew Spurling*, p. 43.
34. Roberts, *A Story of General Andrew Spurling*, p. 43. *Official Record*, Vol. 41, Pt. 4, p. 932.
35. *Official Record*, Vol. 41, Pt. 4, p. 977.
36. Generals Schofield and Thomas are notable, not only for their military activities, but for the former's constant self promotion and the latter's lack of same. Thomas was very a very successful general, winning decisive and important victories, and yet ran afoul of U.S. Grant and "Grant's Men." For further reading see Diane Monroe Smith, *Command Conflicts*.

Chapter Eight

1. *Supplement to the Official Records*, January 1865. *Maine Adjutant General's Report, 1864–1865*, p. 220.
2. Roberts. *A Story of General Andrew Spurling*, p. 50–51.
3. Roberts. *A Story of General Andrew Spurling*, pp. 44–49.
4. Roberts. *A Story of General Andrew Spurling*, pp. 44–45.
5. Roberts. *A Story of General Andrew Spurling*, pp. 49–50.
6. Roberts. *A Story of General Andrew Spurling*, p. 51.
7. *Official Record*, Vol. 49, Pt. 1, p. 904.
8. *Maine Adjutant General's Report, 1864–65*.
9. Letter from Col. Woodman to Commanding Officer, District of West Florida. January 19, 1865. Maine State Archives Correspondence files.
10. Letter from George Martin to Col. Woodman. March 6, 1865. Maine State Archives Correspondence Files.
11. Regimental and Company Books. National Archives.
12. Letter from Col. Woodman to Adj. Gen. Hodsdon. January 1865. Maine State Archives Correspondence files.
13. Special Orders #12. Regimental and Company Books. National Archives.
14. Letter from Col. Woodman to Adj. Gen. Hodsdon. January 1865. Maine State Archives Correspondence Files.
15. Sifakis, *Who Was Who in the Union*, pp. 117–118.
16. Letter from Col. Woodman to Adj. Gen. Hodsdon. January 1865. Maine State Archives Correspondence Files.
17. *Supplement to the Official Records*, January 1865.
18. *Official Record*, Vol. 49, Pt. 1, pp. 577–578.
19. *Supplement to the Official Records*, February 1865.
20. Letter from Col. Woodman to Adj. Gen. Hodsdon. February 1865. Maine State Archives Correspondence Files.
21. Wynne and Taylor, *Florida in the Civil War*, pp. 80–88, p. 104.

22. Letter from Col. Woodman to Governor Cony. February 8, 1865. Maine State Archives Correspondence Files.
23. Letter from Col. Woodman to Governor Cony. February 8, 1865. Maine State Archives Correspondence Files.
24. Letter from Captain Roberts to Governor Cony. February 11, 1865. Maine State Archives Correspondence Files.
25. Letter from Major Miller to Governor Cony. February 12, 1865. Maine State Archives Correspondence Files. Letter from Major Hutchinson to Governor Cony. February 12, 1865. Maine State Archives Correspondence Files.
26. Letter from Captain Roberts to Governor Cony. February 12, 1865. Maine State Archives Correspondence Files.
27. Letter from Col. Woodman to Governor Cony. February 12, 1865. Maine State Archives Correspondence Files.
28. Letter from Major Miller to Adj. Gen. Hodsdon. February 13, 1865. Maine State Archives Correspondence Files.
29. Letter from Col. Woodman to Adj. Gen. Hodsdon. February 13, 1865. Maine State Archives Correspondence Files.
30. *Official Record*, Vol. 49, Pt. 1, pp. 49–50.
31. *Official Record*, Vol. 49, Pt. 1, p. 72.
32. Letter from Col. Woodman to Governor Cony. February 27, 1865. Maine State Archives Correspondence Files.
33. *Official Record*, Vol. 49, Pt. 1, p. 749.
34. Letter from Lt. Col. Spurling to Governor Cony. January 26, 1865. Regimental and Company Books. National Archives.
35. *Maine Adjutant General's Report, 1865*. Regimental and Company Books. National Archives.
36. *Official Record*, Vol. 49, Pt. 1, p. 843.
37. *Official Record*, Vol. 49, Pt. 1, p. 866.
38. *Supplement to the Official Records,* March 1865.
39. *Supplement to the Official Records,* March 1865.
40. *Official Record*, Vol. 49, Pt. 1, p. 1043.
41. *Official Record*, Vol. 49, Pt. 1, page 1042.
42. Letter from Col. Woodman to Adj. Gen. Hodsdon. March 2, 1865. Maine State Archives Correspondence Files.
43. Letter from Lt. Col. Spurling to Governor Cony. March 2, 1865. Maine State Archives Correspondence Files.
44. Letter from Major Miller to Adj. Gen. Hodsdon. March 7, 1865. Maine State Archives Correspondence Files. Letter from Col. Woodman to Governor Cony. March 7, 1865. Maine State Archives Correspondence Files.
45. John Eaton, Surgeon's Papers, 2nd Maine Cavalry. Maine State Archives Correspondence Files.
46. John Eaton, Surgeon's Papers, 2nd Maine Cavalry. Maine State Archives Correspondence Files.
47. John Eaton, Surgeon's Papers, 2nd Maine Cavalry. Maine State Archives Correspondence Files.
48. General Orders No. 226. July 8, 1864. Regimental and Company Books. National Archives.
49. Letter from Lt. Col. Spurling. March 12, 1865. Regimental and Company Books. National Archives.

Chapter Nine

1. Letter from General C.C. Andrews to President Lincoln. March 8, 1865. Lincoln Papers. Library of Congress.
2. *Official Record*, Vol. 49, Pt. 1, p. 1043.
3. *Maine Adjutant General's Report, 1865*. *Official Record*, Vol. 49, Pt. 2, p. 23–34.
4. *Official Record*, Vol. 49, Pt. 1, p. 790.
5. *Official Record*, Vol. 49, Pt. 2, p. 26.
6. *Supplement to the Official Records,* March 1865. *Official Record*, Vol. 49, part 1, pp. 108–109.
7. *Official Record*, Vol. 49, Pt. 1, p. 897.
8. *Official Record*, Vol. 49, part 1, pp. 309–310.
9. Roberts, *A Story of General Andrew Spurling*, p. 70. *Official Record*, Vol. 49, Pt. 1, p. 281. "Gen. Andrew Barclay Spurling." Retrieved May 3, 2011. http://www.cranberryisles.com/photos/andrew_spurling2.html.
10. *Official Record*, Vol. 49, Pt. 1, p. 312–313. *Official Record*, Vol. 49, Pt. 1, pp. 309–310.
11. *Official Record*, Vol. 49, Pt. 1, pp. 309–310.
12. *Official Record*, Vol. 49, Pt. 2, p. 1149.
13. *Official Record*, Vol. 49, Pt. 2, p. 1154, p. 1156.
14. *Official Record*, Vol. 49, Pt. 2, p. 1154.
15. *Official Record*, Vol. 49, part 1, pp. 309–310.
16. *Official Record*, Vol. 49, Pt. 1, pp. 280–281.
17. *Official Record*, Vol. 49, Pt. 2, pp. 80–81.
18. Pearce, *Pensacola During the Civil War*, p. 229.
19. *Official Record*, Vol. 49, Pt. 2, p. 1156, 1158, 1161.
20. *Official Record*, Vol. 49, Pt. 2, p. 133.
21. *Maine Adjutant General's Report, 1864–65*.
22. Boatner, *Civil War Dictionary*, p. 298, pp. 558–559. "The Campaign to take Mobile." Retrieved June 16, 2013. http://www.esploresouthernhistory.com/mobilecampaign.html.
23. *Official Record*, Vol. 49, Pt. 1, p. 311. Boatner, *Civil War Dictionary*, pp. 780–781.
24. *Official Record*, Vol. 49, Pt. 2, p. 269.
25. *Official Record*, Vol. 49, Pt. 1, pp. 311–312.
26. *Official Record*, Vol. 49, Pt. 2, p. 268.
27. *Official Record*, Vol. 49, Pt. 2, p. 288.
28. *Official Record*, Vol. 49, Pt. 2, p. 1168.
29. *Official Record*, Vol. 49, Pt. 2, p. 1176.
30. *Official Record*, Vol. 49, Pt. 2, pp. 1176–1177.
31. *Official Record*, Vol. 49, Pt. 2, p. 1180.
32. *Official Record*, Vol. 49, Pt. 2, pp. 1200–1201.
33. *Official Record*, Vol. 49, Pt. 2, p. 1199.
34. *Official Record*, Vol. 49, Pt. 2, p. 1219.
35. *Official Record*, Vol. 49, Pt. 2, p. 305. Boatner, *Civil War Dictionary*, p. 780–781. Pearce, *Pensacola During the Civil War*, p. 230. Boatner, *Civil War Dictionary*, p. 68.
36. Boatner, *Civil War Dictionary*, p. 559. "The Campaign to Take Mobile." Retrieved June 14, 2012. http://www.exploresouthernhistory.com/mobilecampaign.html.
37. *Official Record*, Vol. 49, Pt. 2, p. 351.
38. Maury, *Recollections of a Virginian*, p. 225–226.

Chapter Ten

1. *Maine Adjutant General's Report, 1864–65.*
2. *Official Record*, Vol. 49, Pt. 2, p. 358.
3. Roberts, *A Story of General Andrew Spurling*, p. 77.
4. William Watson Davis, *The Civil War and Reconstruction in Florida*, p72. Trudeau, *Like Men of War*, pp. 172–187. Wilson, *Under the Old Flag*, pp. 232–233.
5. Roberts, *A Story of General Andrew Spurling*, p. 76.
6. Quoted in Roberts, *A Story of General Andrew Spurling*, pp. 77–78.
7. Quoted in Roberts, *A Story of General Andrew Spurling*, p. 78.
8. *Official Record*, Vol. 49, Pt. 2, pp. 1263–1264.
9. *Official Record*, Vol. 49, Pt. 2, p. 1268.
10. Diane Monroe Smith, *Command Conflicts*, p. 220. Anders, *Henry Halleck's War*, pp. 590–692. Johnston. *Narrative of Military Operations*, p. 403.
11. *Official Record*, Vol. 49, Pt. 2, p. 1270.
12. "Surrender Negotiations." Bennett Place State Historic Site. Retrieved May 5, 2012. http://www.bennettplacehistoricsite.com/history/surrender-negotiations/ "The Surrender of the Confederate Armies." Retrieved May 5, 2012. http://www.civilwarhome.com/confederatesurrender.htm.
13. Boatner, *Civil War Dictionary*, p. 225–226. Wilson, *Under the Old Flag*, p. 329. Smith, *Command Conflicts*, p. 223. "Conclusion of the Civil War." Retrieved February 8, 2013. http://en.wikipedia.org/wiki/Conclusion_of_the_American_Civil_War.
14. *Official Record*, Vol. 49, Pt. 2, pp. 1289–1290.
15. *Official Record*, Vol. 49, Pt. 2, pp. 612–613.
16. *Official Record*, Vol. 49, Pt. 2, pp. 797–798. *Official Record*, Vol. 49, Pt. 2, p. 577.
17. *Official Record*, Vol. 49, Pt. 2, p. 865. *Official Record*, Vol. 49, Pt. 2, p. 913. *Official Record*, Vol. 49, Pt. 2t, p. 927.
18. Letter from Col. Woodman to Gen. Christensen. May 22, 1865. Regimental and Company Books. National Archives.
19. *Maine Adjutant General's Report, 1865. Official Record*, Vol. 49, Pt. 2, pp. 1044–1045.
20. *Official Record*, Vol. 49, Pt. 2, p. 1045.
21. *Official Record*, Vol. 49, Pt. 2, p. 571.
22. Personal Communication, Anthony Douin, Maine State Archives. June 25, 2012.
23. Letter from father of Edward Cushman to Adj. Gen. Hodsdon. May 22, 1865. Maine State Archives Correspondence Files.
24. Letter from Arnold Wentworth to Adj. Gen. Hodsdon. August 16, 1865. Maine State Archives Correspondence Files.
25. Letter from Matilda Whitney to Governor Cony. September 11, 1865. Maine State Archives Correspondence Files.
26. *Maine Adjutant General's Report, 1864–65.* U.S. Census for 1880, Aroostook County, Maine.
27. *Maine Adjutant General's Report, 1864–65.*
28. *Maine Adjutant General's Report, 1864–65.*
29. *Maine Adjutant General's Report, 1864–65.*
30. *Maine Adjutant General's Report, 1864–65.*
31. *Maine Adjutant General's Report, 1864–65.* Email Communication, Anthony Douin, Maine State Archives. September 12, 2013.
32. *Maine Adjutant General's Report, 1864–65.*
33. Personal Communication, Anthony Douin, Maine State Archives. September 12, 2013. Boyd. "The Battle of Marianna." p. 239.
34. Letter from Col. Woodman to Governor Cony. September 13, 1865. Maine State Archives Correspondence Files.
35. *Official Record*, Vol. 49, Pt. 1, pp. 569–570.
36. Letter from Matilda Whitney to Governor Cony. October 20, 1865. Maine State Archives Correspondence Files.
37. Letter from Honora Turpin to Adj. Gen. Hodsdon. December 13, 1865. Maine State Archives Correspondence Files.
38. *Maine Adjutant General's Report, 1864–65.*
39. Regimental and Company Books. October 28, 1865. National Archives.
40. *Maine Adjutant General's Report, 1864–65.* Court Martial Record, Cain, Michael, Private Co. A, 2nd Maine Cavalry. National Archives.
41. Court Martial Record, Butler, Frank, Corporal, Co. B, 2nd Maine Cavalry. National Archives. Court Martial Record, Breen, Peter, Private Co. B, 2nd Maine Cavalry. National Archives.
42. Regimental and Company Books. National Archives.
43. Letter from J. Dewey to Adj. Gen. Hodsdon. October 21, 1865. Maine State Archives Correspondence Files.
44. Regimental and Company Books. National Archives.
45. Surgeon's Papers, 2nd Maine Cavalry. Maine State Archives Correspondence Files.
46. Surgeon's Papers, 2nd Maine Cavalry. Maine State Archives Correspondence Files.
47. *Maine Adjutant General's Report, 1864–65.*
48. *Maine Adjutant General's Report, 1864–65.*
49. Email communication, Anthony Douin, Me State Archives. October 20, 2013.
50. "General Andrew Barclay Spurling." Retrieved May 3, 2011. http://www.cranberryisles.com/photos/andrew_spurling2.html http://www.cranberryisles.com/photos/andrew_spurling.html.

Bibliography

Anders, Curt. *Henry Halleck's War*. Carmel: Guild Press of Indiana, 1999.

Bearss, Edwin C. "Asboth's Expedition up the Alabama and Florida Railroad," *Florida Historical Quarterly* Vol. 39, No. 2 (October 1960), pp. 159–66.

Bearss, Edwin C. "Civil War Operations in and Around Pensacola," *Florida Historical Quarterly* Vol. 36, No. 1 (July 1957–April 1958) pp. 125–165.

Bearss, Edwin C. "Civil War Operations in and Around Pensacola Part II," *Florida Historical Quarterly* Vol. 39, No. 3 (January 1961).

Bearss, Edwin C. "Civil War Operations in and Around Pensacola Part III," *Florida Historical Quarterly* Vol. 39, No. 4 (April 1961).

Beyer, W.F., and O.F. Keydel, eds. *Deeds of Valor: How American Heroes Won the Medal of Honor*. Detroit: Perrien-Keydel, 1906.

Boatner, Mark M. *The Civil War Dictionary*. New York: Vintage Books, 1991.

Boyd, Mark F. "The Battle of Marianna," *Florida Historical Quarterly* Vol. 29, No. 4 (April 1951).

Brevard, Caroline Mays. *A History of Florida*. New York, Cincinnati, Chicago: American Book, 1919.

Burlingame, Michael, ed. *At Lincoln's Side: John Hay's Civil War Correspondence and Selected Writings*. Southern Illinois University Press, 1997.

Burlingame, Michael, and John R. Turner (eds.). *Inside Lincoln's White House: The Complete Civil War Diary of John Hay*. Southern Illinois University Press, 1999.

Butler, Francis Gould. *A History of Farmington, Franklin County, Maine, from the Earliest Explorations to the Present Time, 1776–1885*. Farmington, Maine: Knowlton, McLeary, 1885.

Cox, Dale. *The Battle of Marianna, Florida*. Fort Smith, Arkansas: Dale Cox, 2007.

Cullum, George W. *Biographical Register of the Officers and Graduates of the United States Military Academy*. Vol. 1. New York: D. Van Nostrand, 1868.

Cullum, George W. *Biographical Register of the Officers and Graduates of the United States Military Academy*. Vol. 1; Third Edition. Boston and New York: Houghton Mifflin, 1891.

David, John, ed. *Black Soldiers in Blue: African American Troops in the Civil War Era*. University of North Carolina Press, 2003.

Davis, William Watson. *The Civil War and Reconstruction in Florida*. New York: Columbia University Press, 1913.

Douglas, Marjory Stoneman. *Florida: The Long Frontier*. New York: Harper and Row, 1967.

Dunbar, Rowland. *Military History of Mississippi, 1803–1898: Taken from the Official and Statistical Register of the State of Mississippi*. Jackson: Mississippi Secretary of State, 1908.

Estes, Claud. *List of Field Officers, Regiment and Battalions in the Confederate Army 1861–1865*. Macon, Georgia: Burke, 1912.

Ford, Lacy K. *Deliver Us from Evil: The Slavery Question in the Old South*. Oxford University Press, 2009.

Haines, Norman W. *Letters from Pensacola: The Civil War Years*. Pensacola, Florida. Civil War Soldiers Museum, 1993.

Johnson, Ludwell H. *The Red River Campaign: Politics and Cotton in the Civil War*. Kent, Ohio: Kent State University, 1993.

Johnston, Joseph E. *Narrative of Military Operations, Directed During the Late War Between the States*. New York: D. Appleton, 1874.

Joiner, Gary D., ed. *Little to Eat and Thin Mud to Drink*. Knoxville: University of Tennessee Press, 2007.

Joiner, Gary Dillard. *One Damn Blunder from Beginning to End: The Red River Campaign of 1864*. Wilmington, Delaware: Scholarly Resources, 2003.

Maury, Dabney H. *Recollections of a Virginian in the Mexican, Indian, and Civil Wars*. New York: Scribner's, 1894.

McKinnon, John L. *History of Walton County*. Atlanta, Georgia: Byrd Printing, 1911.

Nevins, Allan. *Ordeal of the Union Vol. 1: Fruits of Manifest Destiny*. New York: Scribner's, 1971.

North, James W. *The History of Augusta, Maine*.

Somersworth, New Hampshire: New England History Press, 1981 (a copy of the original 1870 edition).

Parker, Daisy. "John Milton, Governor of Florida." *The Florida Historical Quarterly* Vol. 20, No. 4 (April 1942).

Pearce, George F. *Pensacola During the Civil War: A Thorn in the Side of the Confederacy*. Gainesville: University Press of Florida, 2000.

Peters, Virginia Bergman. *The Florida Wars*. Archon Books, 1979.

Pullen, John. *The Twentieth Maine*. Dayton, Ohio: Morningside Press, 1984.

Roberts, Cassius C. *A Story of General Andrew Spurling and the 2nd Maine Cavalry*. 1904 (no publisher listed).

Sawyer, Candance, and Laura Orcutt, eds. *The Civil War Letters of John Franklin Godfrey*. Sawyer and Orcutt, 1993.

Shaw, Horace H. *The First Maine Heavy Artillery*. Portland, Maine, 1903.

Sifakis, Stewart. *Who Was Who in the Union*. New York: Facts on File, 1988.

Smith, Diane Monroe. *Command Conflicts in Grant's Overland Campaign*. McFarland, 2012.

Smith, Diane Monroe. *Fanny and Joshua: The Enigmatic Lives of Francis Caroline Adams and Joshua Lawrence Chamberlain*. Gettysburg, Pennsylvania: Thomas, 1999.

Smith, Ned. *The 22nd Maine Volunteer Infantry in the Civil War*. McFarland, 2010.

Stahr, Walter. *Seward, Lincoln's Indispensable Man*. New York: Simon & Schuster, 2012.

Surdam, David. "Traders or Traitors: Northern Cotton Trading During the Civil War," *Business and Economic History* Vol. 28, No. 2 (Winter 1999).

Trudeau, Noah Andre. *Like Men of War: Black Troops in the Civil War*. Boston, New York: Little, Brown, 1998.

Warner, Ezra J. *Generals in Gray*. Baton Rouge: Louisiana State University Press, 1959.

Watson, William W. *The Civil War and Reconstruction in Florida*. New York: Columbia University Press, 1913.

Weston, Edward P., ed. *The Northern Monthly: A Magazine of Original Literature and Military Affairs*. Vol. 2. Portland: Bailey and Noyes, 1864.

Whitman, William E.S., and Charles H. True. *Maine in the War for the Union: A History of the Part Borne by Maine Troops*. Lewiston, Maine: Nelson Dingley, Jr., 1865.

Williams, George W. *A History of the Negro Troops in the War of the Rebellion*. New York: Harper and Brothers, 1888.

Wilson, James H. *Under the Old Flag*. Vol. II. New York and London: D. Appleton, 1912.

Winters, John D. *The Civil War in Louisiana*. Baton Rouge: Louisiana State University Press, 1991.

Wynne, Lewis N., and Robert A. Taylor, *Florida in the Civil War*. Charleston: Arcadia, 2001.

Official Reports and Documents

Adjutant General's Office. *General Orders Affecting the Volunteer Force*. Washington, D.C.: Government Printing Office, 1864.

Maine Adjutant General's Report, 1862. Augusta, Maine, 1863.

Maine Adjutant General's Report, 1863. Augusta, Maine, 1864.

Maine Adjutant General's Report, 1864–65. Augusta, Maine, 1865.

The Official Military Atlas of the Civil War. Avenel, New Jersey: Gramercy Books, 1983 (a reprint of the original title: *Atlas to Accompany the Official Record of the Union and Confederate Armies*, 1891–95. Washington, D.C.: Government Printing Office).

Regimental and Company Books of the Second Maine Cavalry Regiment. National Archives, Washington, D.C. ARC identifier: 6340703 MLR #: MLR Number PI-17 112, PI-17 112A.

Supplement to the Official Records of the Union and Confederate Armies. Part II, Record of Events and Itineraries. Vol. 25 and 26, Serial No. 37, Maine Troops. Wilmington, North Carolina: Broadfoot, 1996.

United States War Department. *The War of the Rebellion: A Compilation of the Official Records of the Union and Confederate Armies* [*The Official Record*]. Washington, D.C.: Government Printing Office, 1880–1901.

Index

Adams, Gen. Daniel W. 126, 128
Adams, Lt. Isaac 28, 79, 85, 108, 111, 112
African American soldiers in white regiments 35, 36
Alabama and Florida Railroad 16, 64, 66, 125, 126
Alabama military units: 1st Alabama Artillery 69; 7th Alabama Cavalry 69, 73, 74; Capt. Thomas Goldsby's Alabama Cavalry 74, 75
Alabama River 130
Alexandria, Virginia 205, 210
Algiers, Louisiana 207, 212
Allen, Com'y. Sgt. George 119
Allen, Lt. Ivory 108, 117, 143, 216
Andalusia, Alabama 124, 125
Anderson, General Patton 22
Anderson, Gen. William 91
Andersonville Prison 90, 109, 143, 199, 214–216
Andrews, Gen. Christopher C. 122, 124, 127, 139, 140
Andrews, Leonard 106
Appomattox, Virginia 137
Armistead, Col. Charles G. 102, 104, 130
Armistead's Cavalry 104
Armstrong, Commodore James 16
Asboth, Gen. Alexander 63, 66, 67, 69, 71–75, 96, 127, 140, 141, 144, 220; raid on Marianna, Florida 78–92
Atlanta, Georgia 105
Austin, Pvt. Alvarez 88
Austin, Pvt. William A. 88
Ayer, Lt. Ellis W. 28, 79, 85

Bagdad, Florida 74, 95, 104, 114
Bailey, Gen. Joseph 94, 96
Bailey, Lt. Col. Joseph 47–48, 50
Baker, Sgt. George W. 98
Banks, E.H. 106

Banks, Gen. Nathaniel 42, 43–53, 67
Banton, Lt. William 59
Barbiere, Maj. Joseph 75
Barker, Lt. Silas 48, 200, 201, 216
Barr, Sgt. Harvey D. 211
Barrancas, Florida see Fort Barrancas
Barrows, Sgt./Lt. Ronello A. 117
Baton Rouge, Louisiana 98
Battle of Five Forks 133
Bayou Cheramie, Louisiana 57
Bayou Grande, Florida 66, 72
Bayou Mulatte, Florida 74, 75
Beal, Col. George 60, 219
Beauregard, Gen. Pierre G.T. 65, 102, 116, 117
Bell, John 12
Bell, Pvt. John 201, 202
Benning, Henry L. 3
Berryman, Lt. Otway 14
Bigger, Pvt. Alexander 142, 143
Bigger, Pvt. Archibald 142, 143
Bigger, Pvt. Ebenezer 142, 143
Black Bayou, Florida 74
Black soldiers in white regiments 35, 36
Blackwater Bay 93, 94, 104
Blackwater River 124
Blackwell, Sgt. Joshua, E. 203
Blakely, Alabama see Fort Blakely
Bluff Springs, Florida 100, 102
Boutte Station, Louisiana 58
Bragg, Gen. Braxton 64
Brann, Lt. Thomas 61
Brashear City, Louisiana 53, 54, 58
Breckinridge, John 10
Breen, Pvt. Peter 147, 202, 203
Brewton Station, Alabama 126
Brooklyn, Alabama 126
Brooklyn, New York 210, 211
Brooks, Pvt. Darius 142
Brooks, Pvt. Joseph 142
Brown, Albert Gallatin 4

Brown, Pvt. Henry 215
Buchanan, James 9, 10
Burleigh, Parker 106
Burnside, Gen. Ambrose 40
Burnside carbine 40
Butler, Gen. Benjamin 42
Butler, Cpl./Sgt. Frank 81, 98, 147, 202

Cain, Pvt. Michael 146, 147, 203, 204
Calhoun, John 8, 9
Camp Berry, Portland, Maine 206, 209, 210
Camp Chase, Ohio
Camp Coburn, Augusta, Maine 37, 38, 39, 40, 99
Camp Distribution, Virginia 209
Campbellton, Florida 82
Canby, Gen. Edward 53, 73, 108, 128–131, 137–139
Canoe Station, Alabama 128
Carpenter, Sgt. David 147, 203
Cawthorn, William 80
Cerro Gordo, Florida 82
Chacahoula, Louisiana 58
Chamberlain, John Calhoun 7, 8
Chamberlain, Joshua, family 7, 8
Chambers, Thomas 205
Champion No. 3 (transport) 47
Chandler, Lt. Jason 61, 208
Charlotte, North Carolina 117
Chase, Salmon 20
Chase, William 16, 17
Chattanooga, Tennessee 66
Chicago Rawhide Manufacturing Company 150
China, Maine 35, 36
Chipola River 84, 87
Choctawhatchee Bay 81, 90–92
Choctawhatchee River 80, 82, 85, 130
Christensen, Ass't. Adj. Gen. 73, 133, 140
City Point, Virginia 209
Civil Rights Act of 1866 145

227

Index

Clanton, Gen. James A. 66, 116, 125, 126, 132
Clark, Sgt. Elisha 70, 78, 85, 90, 209, 215
Clarke, Capt. Samuel 34, 41, 76, 77, 78, 208, 209, 213, 216
Clay, Cassius M 20
Cleaveland, Lt. James 70
Clinton (steamer) 74, 75
Clough, Pvt. Charles H. 215
Cobb, Howell 3, 22
Coburn, Abner 26, 28, 60
Cockrell, Gen. Frances 132
Compromise of 1850 8
Confederate military units: 15th Confederate Cavalry 67, 73, 74, 80, 81, 98, 99
Connecticut military units: 28th Connecticut Infantry 63
Continental (transport) 41
Cony, Samuel 60, 62, 93, 111, 112, 115, 117, 142, 145
Cook, Pvt. George 1, 149, 150
"Copperheads" 10, 26
Corps de Afrique 20, 67, 79
Corson, Pvt. Van Rensalear 207, 214
Courts-Martial, General 200–214
Craven, Cmdr. Tunis 128, 129
Crebs, Lt. Col. John 48, 219
Creigler's Mills 124, 125
Crommet, Pvt. Leander 142
Crommet, Pvt. Lewis 142
Csermelyi, Capt. James 146, 147, 203
Cunningham, Pvt. Ellison 214
Cushman, Cpl./Sgt. Edward A. 92, 141
Cutler, Adj't./Maj. Nathan 28, 31, 32, 55, 58, 59, 79, 85, 90, 91, 109, 111, 143, 149, 212, 213, 215

Daily Mail, Montgomery, Alabama 136
Davis, Pvt. Edgar (report on Marianna raid) 84, 85, 87
Davis, Jefferson 42, 44, 115, 133, 138, 139; Proclamation for Day of Fasting, Humiliation, and Prayer 120, 121
Davis, Mrs. Jefferson 139
Davis, Cpl. Thomas 85, 214
DeBeque, Sgt. Wallace 52
Declaration of Independence 7
Dewey, J. 148
Dinwiddie Court House 133
Dodge, Lt. Randolph 204, 205
Douglas, Stephen 8, 10
Douglas Ferry 80
Dow, Gen. Neal 110
Downs, Sgt. Michael 214
Duncan, Gen. Johnson K. 42
Dunlap, Sgt. William 207

Eastport (gunboat) 46, 47
Eaton, Ass't. Surgeon John 118, 119, 148, 149
Elba, Alabama 140
Ellis, Pvt. Daniel 90, 215
Emancipation Proclamation 37
Emerson, Maine State Representative A.P. 107
Emery, Saddler Jacob 76
Erie (ship) 5
Escambia Bay 74, 93, 94
Escambia River 67, 100, 101, 124, 128
Eucheeanna, Florida 80–82
Evans, Pvt. Orrin R. 215
Evening Star, Washington, D.C. 132, 133, 138
Evergreen, Alabama 122–126, 128, 132

Farragut, Capt./Adm. David 41, 42, 63, 66, 128
Federalist Party 6, 7
Field, Sgt. George 27
Fifteen Mile Station 67, 74
Fillmore, Millard 9, 10
Filibusters 4
Florida: food source for Confederacy 19, 20; plan to rejoin the Union 21; political influence of slave owners 12; refuge for Confederate deserters 20, 67; refuge for escaped slaves 11; slaves impressed to serve Confederate military 22; statehood 11; treatment of slaves 21, 81
Florida Historical Quaterly 80
Florida military units, Confederate: 1st Regiment Florida Infantry Reserves 6; Capt. Henry Robinson's cavalry 84; Jackson County Home Guards 83
Florida military units, Union: 1st Florida Battery 74, 93; 1st Florida Cavalry 20, 67, 79, 81, 94, 96–98, 100, 102, 104, 110, 124, 125, 128, 130, 134, 139, 140; 2nd Florida Cavalry 20, 130; Florida Cavalry 69; Florida Rangers 111
Fogg, Pvt. John 214
Forest, Gen. Nathan Bedford 75, 137–139
Forrest Hall Prison, Georgetown, Virginia 209
Fort Blakely 116, 127–132
Fort Barrancas 13–16, 18, 19, 63–76, 78, 79, 91–95, 97, 98, 102, 104, 115, 116, 119, 124, 127, 128, 137, 139, 141, 143, 149, 201, 205, 207, 208, 210, 214
Fort Gaines 129
Fort Jackson 41, 42
Fort McCree 14, 15, 18, 64–66
Fort Morgan 73, 128, 129
Fort Pickens 14–17, 63, 65, 66, 91, 92, 146, 205, 207
Fort Pillow 54, 55, 75, 89
Fort Powell 128, 129
Fort St. Philip 41, 42
Fort Stedman 133
Fort Sumter 13, 17
Franklin, Benjamin 7
Franklin, Tennessee 104, 105
Frémont, Gen. John C. 9, 10, 12, 63, 220
French, Capt Moses 34, 35, 208, 218
Fugitive Slave Act 4, 8
Fuller, Sgt. Fred 141

Gallop Island, Boston, Massachusetts 206
Garibaldi, Giuseppe 67
General Barnes, (steamer)
Geneva, Alabama 81
George, Pvt. John 27
Gibson, Gen. Randall L. 130, 131
Gilchrist, Sgt. Alden 214
Gillespie, Lt. William 61, 147, 148, 202, 208
Gilman, Lt. Jeremiah 13
Glidden, Lt. Oakman 216
Godfrey, Lt. Col. John 28, 29–30, 55, 58
Godwin, Capt. Alexander 82, 84
Goldsby, Capt. Thomas 74, 75
Gonyea, Pvt. Lewis 205
Gonzales, Florida 67, 74
Gordon, Lt. Francis 80
Gordon, Gen. John B. 133
Gordon, Nathaniel 5
Grand Lagoon, Florida 72
Granger, Gen. Gordon 78, 79, 106, 110, 115, 128, 129
Grant, Cpl. Mark 214
Grant, Gen. U.S. 44, 56, 77, 105, 132, 137, 222
Greenville, Alabama 132, 136, 211, 212
Greenville, Louisiana 56, 58, 204
Greenwood, Florida 84
Gregg, Gen. David 31

Haines (Haynes), Pvt. Albert A. 205, 206
Halleck, Gen. Henry 44, 60, 108, 138, 219
Ham, Sgt. Orrin F. 209
Hamlin, George 6
Hamlin, Hannibal 6, 9, 10, 107

Hamlin, John 6
Hamlin, Nathanial 6
Hamlin, Weld 6
Hanake, Sgt. Edgar 214
Harris, Sgt. Isaac B. 26
Harrisburg, Pennsylvania 206
Hart, Allen 80
Hartford Convention 6, 7
Haskell, Capt. Isaac W. 34, 208, 209
Hay, John 20, 48
Haynesville, Maine 26, 27, 218
Heering, Capt. 201, 210
Herald, New York 136
Hewitt, Pvt. Samuel 214
Hodsdon, Adj't. Gen. John 26, 53, 59, 98, 99, 107, 111, 142, 148, 149
Hodsdon, Lizzie 99
Hodsdon, Mrs. 99
Holbrook, Lt. Samuel 214, 216
Holland, Pvt. Charles 206, 207
Holt, Cpl. Frank 35
Hood, Gen. John Bell 98, 99, 104
Hooker, Gen. Joseph 20
Hopkins, Edward 13
Houma, Louisiana 200, 201
Houston, Buck 205
Hutchinson, Pvt. Daniel 142
Hutchinson, Maj. Eben 28, 29, 30, 31, 60, 61, 85, 91, 96, 98, 109, 112, 143, 146, 149, 204, 208
Hutchinson, Pvt. John 142

Illinois military units: 2nd Illinois Cavalry 124–126, 128, 129; 87th Illinois Mounted Infantry 48
Indiana military units: 11th Indiana Infantry 57; 26th Indiana Infantry 57
Iowa military units: 19th Iowa Infantry 74, 93, 94; 32nd Iowa Infantry 211; 34th Iowa Volunteers 201, 210
Irwin, Ass't. Adj. Gen. Richard 43

Jackson, Gen. William H. 137
Jefferson, Thomas: Declaration of Independence 7; Embargo Act of 1807 6; Louisiana Purchase 6; Nonintercourse Act of 1809 6
Jenkins, Cpl. Otis 108
Jenks, Pvt. Edwin S. 214
Johnson, Andrew 139, 144, 145
Johnson, Capt. Elijah D 32, 96, 106, 109, 116, 125, 140, 204, 216
Johnson, Pvt. Henry (Charles H.) 207

Johnston, Gen. Joseph E. 66, 67, 77, 137–139
Jones, Lt. Benjamin 81, 216
Jones, Gen. Samuel 42, 64, 65
Jones, Capt. William 90
Jordan, Sgt. John P. 40

Kansas military units: 19th Kansas Volunteers 211
Kansas-Nebraska Act 9
Kelly, Cpl. Alpheus G. 207, 214
Kentucky (brig) 5
Kerswell, Capt. George 61, 208
Keyser, Capt. 113
Kielmansegge, Lt. Col. Eugene Von 104
Kilpatrick, Gen. Hugh Judson 99
"Know-Nothing" Party 9
Knowles, Capt. Samuel 26, 34, 43, 61, 62, 110, 148, 201, 207, 208, 210, 212–214, 216
Kossuth, Lajos 63, 96

LaGrange, Florida 81
Lake, Pvt. James 104
Latham, Milton 60
Lee, Gen. Albert Lindley 98, 99
Lee, Gen. Robert E. 41, 42, 56, 65, 77, 105, 110, 115, 117, 128, 130, 133, 137–139
Lee, Gen. W.H.F. "Rooney" 110, 133
Leed (Leigh), Capt. 98
Libby, Capt Samuel H 35, 208, 209, 216
Liberia 5
Liddell, Gen. St. John Richardson 102, 116, 122, 131, 132
"Lt. Clark" 81
Lincoln, Abraham 5, 12, 17, 20, 44, 106, 108, 122, 137, 138, 144
Lincoln, Capt. John 27, 32, 34, 43, 95, 208, 209, 213, 216
Lincoln-Douglas debates 8
Litchfield, Sgt. Lewis K. 207, 214
Little Escambia River 100, 102
Lizzie Davis (steamer) 69, 80, 81, 91, 94, 95
Longfellow, Stephen 6
Lorenz Austrian rifled musket 75, 76
Louisiana, military units: 1st Louisiana Cavalry (Union) 30, 48
Lovell, Gen. Mansfield 42
Lowell, Pvt. Byron 141
Lucas, Gen. Thomas 124
Lyons, Capt. Francis 100, 130

Madison, James 6
Magnolia, Florida 5, 6

Maine: connection with slave trade 4–6; statehood 8
"Maine Law" (Temperance) 110
Maine regiments: 1st Maine Cavalry 31, 199; 1st Maine Heavy Artillery 36, 60; 1st Maine Infantry 32; 1st Maine Mounted Artillery 29; 4th Maine Infantry 206; 6th Maine Infantry 32; 7th Maine Infantry 32; 8th Maine Infantry 29, 32, 35, 59, 62, 112; 10th Maine Infantry 60; 12th Maine Infantry 200; 13th Maine Infantry 200; 14th Maine Infantry 200; 15th Maine Infantry 63, 66, 200; 16th Maine Infantry 113; 17th Maine Infantry 200; 19th Maine Infantry 200; 20th Maine Infantry 34, 200; 21st Maine Infantry 31, 32, 34, 200; 22nd Maine Infantry 34, 199; 23rd Maine Infantry 200; 24th Maine Infantry 30, 200; 25th Maine Infantry 200; 26th Maine Infantry 34, 200; 27th Maine Infantry 35, 200; 28th Maine Infantry 29, 30, 32, 34, 112, 200
Manson, Cpl. Edward 88
Mansur, Lt. Warren 48, 109, 110, 143, 144, 216
Marianna, Florida 67, 109, 111, 141, 143; Gen. Asboth's Raid 78–92
Marson, Pvt. Edward 88
Martin, Surgeon George 26, 70, 90, 106, 108, 125, 149, 208, 216
Matamoras (steamer) 75, 104, 110, 114–116, 124, 128
Mathews, Capt. Adolphus B. 34, 58, 116, 117
Maury, Col./Gen. Henry 67, 73, 74, 98, 122, 130–133, 138
Maynard, Cpt. George 88, 205
McKean, Gen. T.J. 102, 108, 202
Meade, Gen. George 145
Meridian, Mississippi 133, 139
Merrimac (steam transport) 76
Merry, Capt. Benjamin 32, 57, 106, 109, 114, 143, 147, 202, 214, 216
Metcalf, Lt. Fred 216
Mexico, War with 8
Military Road, Florida 80
Miller, Maj. Charles A. 28, 29, 30, 43, 52, 53, 58–60, 62, 81, 93, 98–100, 107, 109, 112, 113, 118, 125, 143, 149, 201, 216
Millett, Pvt. Eugene 143
Millett, Sgt. John 143
Millett, Pvt. Nelson 143

Index

Milliken, Reg't Quartermaster John F. 40, 62, 63
Milton, John 12, 83
Milton, Florida 67, 74, 93–95, 104, 106, 113–116, 124, 125, 139
Mings, Pvt. Thomas J. 211
Mississippi (steam transport) 69
Mississippi military units: 8th Mississippi Cavalry 95; 46th Mississippi Infantry 129
Missouri Compromise 8
Mitchell's Creek, Florida 102, 104
Mobile, Alabama 42, 64–66, 74, 102, 110–112, 114, 116, 118, 122, 126, 127, 129, 137, 139
Mobile and Great Northern Railroad 66, 100
Mobile and Montgomery Railroad 124, 128
Mobile Bay, Alabama 63, 106, 117, 124, 127, 128, 130, 133
Mobile Campaign 128–132
Mobile Point, Alabama 201, 210
Mobile River 133
Mohican (U.S. Navy ship) 5
Montgomery, Col. Alexander B. 79, 83, 84, 87, 91
Montgomery, Alabama 64, 65, 118, 122, 125, 126, 130, 133, 134, 140, 141, 143, 206
Montgomery Hill Landing 133
Moody, Lt. William H. 40, 85, 86, 216
Moore, Maj. Franklin 125, 126
Moore, Pvt./Saddler George 34
Mower, Gen. Joseph 46, 52
Muddy Creek 126
Mudgett, Col. 94
Murder Creek 124

Napoleonville, Louisiana 58, 207
Nash, Pvt. Augustus 41
Nashville, Tennessee 105
Nason, Chaplain Charles 99, 106, 107, 108
Native American Indian troops 2, 142, 143
New Orleans, Louisiana 41, 42, 48, 65, 76, 98, 139, 204, 212
New York City 149
New York military units: 14th New York Cavalry 67, 100, 103
Nickerson, Gen. Franklin 60, 219
Nightingale (clipper) 5
Northern Monthly 80
Norwood, Capt. Jesse 83

O'Brian, Sgt./Hospital Steward Owen 28, 148
Observer, Greenville, Alabama 134

O'Connell, Pvt. Henry 209
Olustee, Battle of 2, 20, 89, 90
O'Neal, Pvt. Henry 215
Ormand, G.M. 211
Ostend Manifesto 4

Parlin, Lt. Simon 213
Pascagoula, Mississippi 106
Patten, Sgt. Alphonzo 61, 214
Patten, Maine 27
Pearce, Sgt. Frank W. 48, 219
Pembroke, Maine 27
Pendleton, Pvt. Sanford H. 215
Pennsylvania Society for the Aboliton of Slavery 7
Pensacola, Florida 42, 64, 65, 73, 106, 124, 130, 137, 140, 149
Pensacola Bay 75
Pensacola Navy Yard 14–17, 64, 65, 74
Perdido Creek 106
Perdido River 69, 71, 75
Perry, Madison 13
Petersburg, Virginia 105, 133
Pickard, Adj't Adoniram 149, 216
Pickett, Gen. George 133
Pierce, Lt. Warren 216
Pierce's Mill 94, 95
Pine Barren bridge 69, 74, 96–98
Pine Barren Creek, Florida 96–98, 101, 102, 104
Planter (steamer) 74, 75, 93–95
Pollard, Alabama 66, 67, 74, 75, 95, 96–104, 113, 114, 122–128, 132
Pollard, Cpl. Luther M. 215
Pomeroy, Samuel 20, 21
Pope, Gen. John 145
Popular Sovereignty 8
Port Hudson, Louisiana 29, 30, 32, 34, 37, 43, 90, 98, 112
Porter, Adm. David 44–48
Portland, Maine 209, 210
Prescott, Lt. Evander 213, 216
Putz (?), Acting Ass't Adj't Gen'l A.C. 203

Quincy, Florida 83

"Radical Republicans" 145
Rand, Pvt. Charles 72
Rand, Pvt. Erastus 72
rations: for hospital 119; for regular regimental use 119
Reconstruction 144–146; orders issued during 144, 145; 13th and 14th Amendments 145
Red River Campaign 43–53, 58, 59
Reed, Pvt. William 210
Remington revolver 40, 41
Republican Party 9

Reynolds, Gen. Joseph 43
Richmond, Virginia 133
Richmond Daily Dispatch 120, 121
Richmond Whig 116–117
Robbins, Cpl. James 214
Roberts, Sgt. Byron 111–113
Roberts, Cassius C. 60
Roberts, Capt. John H. 35, 40, 94, 108, 109, 111–113, 117, 118, 205, 208
Robinson, Col. George 99, 100–102
Robinson, Capt. Henry 84
Rogers, Pvt. Oscar 214
Rogers, Pvt. William 99
Rust, Col. Henry 60, 219
Ruttkay, Maj. Albert 96, 97, 98

St. Luke's Church, Marianna, Florida 88, 90
Sanders, Lt. 97, 98
Santa Rosa Island, Florida 91, 92
Saratoga, USS 5
Savannah, Georgia 105
Schofield, Gen. John 99, 104, 222
Schryver, Lt. F.M. 149
Scott, Gen. Winfield 17
Seavey, Lt. George 59
secession 4, 6, 7
Seco, Pvt. Orrin 35, 96
Selma, Alabama 118, 126, 128, 133, 136, 140
Seminole Wars 11, 12
Seward, William 17
Sheldon, Pvt. John 41
Sherman, Gen. William T. 44–46, 77, 98, 99, 105, 137, 138
Ship Island, Louisiana 99
Shoal River 80
Shuman, Pvt. G. 216
Simon, "a colored man" 211
Simpson, Lt. Daniel 216
Sims, Pvt. Moses 215
Skilton, Dr. Julius A. 70, 220
slaves/slavery: cause of the Civil War 3, 4; Maine's connection with the slave trade 4–6; paternalistic attitude toward 81; planned expansion 4; proposal to arm as Confederate soldiers 21, 22; proposed reintroduction of slave trade 8
Slemmer, Lt. Adam 13–17, 64
Slough, Maj. R.H. 132
Small, Maj. Abner 113
Small, Sgt. David 201
Small, Sgt. Maj./Lt. Emilius N.D. 111–114
Small, Sgt./Lt. Sylvanus 148
Smart, Pvt. Greenleaf 142

Index

Smart, Pvt. Richard 142
Smith, Gen. Andrew J. 45, 59, 128, 134, 136, 137, 140
Smith, Gen. Kirby 50, 51
Smith, Pvt. Walter 210, 211
Soldier's Home, New York City 142
Soule, Pvt. Augustus 142
Soule, Pvt. George 142
Southwick, Capt. H.K. 207
Spanish Fort 128–132
Speed, Pvt. Horace G. 211
Sprague, Samuel 76
Sprague, Pvt. Theodore S. 76
Spurling, Maj./Lt. Col. Andrew 28, 31, 40, 53–55, 58–61, 78, 80, 92, 109, 111, 112, 128, 132–134, 140, 143, 149, 150, 204, 205, 208, 216; April 1865 in Montgomery, Alabama 136, 137; April 1865 scouting toward Stockton 130; behind Confederate lines during Marianna expedition 81, 82, 91, 92; December 1864 raid on Milton, Florida 104; December 1864 raid on Pollard, Alabama 99–104; February 1865 raid on Milton, Florida 113–115; January 1864 disguised as Confederate officer 116; January 1864 raid on Milton, Florida 110; March 1865 raid on Greenville & Pollard 122–127; Medal of Honor 125; November 1864 raid on Pine Barren Creek 96–98; raids to collect logs, bricks, etc; Escambia Bay, Blackwater Bay 93–96; recommended for promotion to Brig. Gen. 106–108; requesting alternate rations 120, 121; requesting recruits for regiment 116; service prior to 2nd Maine Cavalry 31
Spurling Block, Elgin, Illinois 150
Stanley, Capt. Gustavus 34, 62, 70, 208, 212, 213, 216
Stearns, Capt. 94, 95
Steele, Gen. Frederick 45, 114, 115, 118, 122, 124, 127, 128, 130, 131
Stephens, Alexander 4
Stewart, Pvt. Michael 41
Stickney, Lyman 20
Stockton, Alabama 127–130
Stuart, Gen. J.E.B. 56
Supply (ship) 16

Tallahassee, Florida 83, 202, 203
Tamerlane (ship) 41
Taylor, Gen. Richard 43, 44–47, 50–53, 116, 126, 128, 137–139
Taylor, Sarah Knox 44
Taylor, Ass't. Adj. Gen. W.H. 42
Taylor, Zachary 44
Tecumseh (ironclad monitor) 128, 129
Tennessee (ironclad) 128, 129
Tennessee military units: Capt. Thomas Tobin's Tennessee Battery 73; Tennessee Artillery 69
Tensaw River 74
Terrance, Col. W.H. 80
Terrebonne, Louisiana 207
Texas, admission to Union 8
Thayer, Eli 20
Thibodeaux, Louisiana 57, 58, 62, 204, 207
Thomas, Sgt. Augustus 146, 147, 203
Thomas, Gen. Bryan 132
Thomas, Gen. George 99, 104, 105, 220
Thomas, Pvt. Silas 214
Tigerville, Louisiana 57
Tobin, Capt. Thomas 73
"torpedoes" 128
Townsend, Ass't Adj. Gen. E.D. 119
Tucker, William 27
Turpin, Pvt. John 146
Twitchell, Capt. Joseph F. 27, 32, 43, 48, 59, 62, 93, 109, 111, 143, 144, 200, 201

U.S. Colored Troops: 25th U.S. Colored Infantry 67, 94, 110, 124; 82nd U.S. Colored Infantry 67, 79, 87–89, 94, 96, 100, 102, 104, 110, 124, 203; 86th U.S. Colored Infantry 67, 79, 94, 100, 102, 104, 110, 124; 97th U.S. Colored Infantry 99, 100, 102, 103, 110; U.S. Colored Infantry 2
U.S. Military Asylum (hospital), Togus, Maine 149

Van Doren, Gen. Earl 42
Vermont military units: 7th Vermont Infantry 67, 79
Vernon, Florida 90
Vicksburg, Mississippi 43, 45, 46, 98
Vose, Lt. Marcus 96, 97, 106, 117, 126, 216

Walker, Pvt. Ansel 207, 214
Walker, Gen. John George 51
"Walker's Greyhounds" (Walker's division) 51
Waltz, Andrew J. ("Jack?") 207, 214
Warrington, Florida 205
Washington, D.C. 209
Washington Point (Choctawhatchee Bay) 90–92
Washington St. Military Prison, Alexandria, Virginia 209
Watts, Lt. John W. 125, 126
Watts, Thomas 125, 126, 128
Webber, Cpl. Andrew W. 201
Wentworth, Arnold 142
Wentworth, Pvt. George 142
West Florida News 88
Wharton, Gen. John 52
Wheaton, Cpl./Sgt. Daniel H. 92
Whig and Courier, Bangor, Maine 80, 82
White, Thomas 84, 90
Whitehouse, Pvt. Lewis 141
Whitney, Pvt. Charles W. 142
Whitney, Pvt. Chester 215
Whitney, Cpl. David C. 215
Whitney, Pvt. John C. 142, 145, 146
Whitney, Matilda 142, 145, 146
Wilder, Pvt. Rufus 33
Williams, Pvt. George W. 215
Wilson, Pvt. Charles 88
Wilson, Gen. James 133, 136, 137, 139
Wilson, Capt. John 66
Winder, Major John 13
Wisconsin military units: 11th Wisconsin Infantry 56, 57
Withey, Sgt. Arthur J. 214
Woodman, Lt. Andrew 28, 69
Woodman, Col. Ephraim W. 28, 29, 32, 34, 39, 41, 43, 53, 55, 58–62, 77, 78, 93, 96, 98, 99, 104–113, 115, 117, 118, 139, 140, 143, 144, 149, 208, 209, 212, 213, 216
Wyandotte, USS 14–16

Young, Capt. 79

Zerner, Pvt. Nicholas 216
Zulavsky, Col. Ladislas 67, 88, 91, 96

www.ingramcontent.com/pod-product-compliance
Lightning Source LLC
Chambersburg PA
CBHW081552300426
44116CB00015B/2856